2 21

The Art of Rulership

A STUDY IN ANCIENT CHINESE POLITICAL THOUGHT

ROGER T. AMES

University of Hawaii Press / Honolulu

Library of Congress Cataloging in Publication Data

Ames, Roger T., 1947–
  The art of rulership.

  Includes English translation of: Huai-nan tzu. 9.
Chu shu hsün / Huai-nan tzu.
  Bibliography: p.
  Includes index.
  1.   Huai-nan tzu, d. 122 B.C. Huai-nan tzu. 9. Chu
shu hsün.   2.   Political science—China—History.
I.   Huai-nan tzu, d. 122 B.C. Huai-nan tzu. 9. Chu shu
hsün. English. 1983.   II.   Title.
BL1900.H825A43   1983   320'.01   82-25917
ISBN 0-8248-0825-8

For D. C. Lau

Contents

Preface

AN IMPORTANT COMPENDIUM of knowledge and philosophical speculation was presented to the Chinese court of Wu Ti during the first century of the Former Han (206 B.C.–A.D. 8). This text, the *Huai Nan Tzu,* takes its name from the prince of Huai Nan, Liu An, who gathered scholars and adepts from all over the empire at his court. This assembly of learned men conferred, researched, debated as house guests of the prince, and contributed their efforts to his anthology.

This Han dynasty anthology discusses many of the basic ideas and beliefs that had evolved during the period of the "Hundred Schools," the formative years of the Chinese religio-philosophical traditions. There is also much generally unrecognized originality in the work—an early Han integration of concepts that had occasioned fierce intellectual exchange in late Chou China. The refinement of these ideas has occupied the finest Chinese minds up to the present day and has determined, moreover, the course and configuration of China's religious and philosophical growth. On the Taoist side this text represents one of our most valuable and revealing documents, linking the philosophical Taoist tradition and the emergence of religious Taoism as an institution during the Eastern Han. On the Confucian side, it is a sourcebook for the fundamental precepts of Confucianism and their Han interpretation at a time when Confucian theory was beginning to shape the intellectual and political life of China. From the perspective of the Legalist school and its political theory, the *Huai Nan Tzu* demonstrates the extent to which Han philosophy was impressed by the efficacy of Legalist institutions and attitudes.

Despite the importance of this text, to date there has been little done to introduce it to the English reader. Several developments during the past decade, however, have brought such a project into the realm of possibility. First, although there is still no modern Chinese translation, Yü Ta-ch'eng, professor in the Chinese literature department of Chung-yang University in Taiwan, has spent much of his career collating a great deal of earlier textual work as a basis for resolving textual problems and has then gone on to offer suggestions for reconstructing many problematic portions of the text. Second, Japanese scholars such as Kanaya Osamu, Togawa Yoshio, and Kusuyama Haruki have written insightful commentary on the text and have prepared well-researched and generally accurate modern Japanese translations. Third, in recent years another contemporary Chinese scholar, Hsü Fu-kuan, has brought a lifetime of study to bear on the intellectual history of the Han dynasty and has contributed much to our understanding of philosophical developments during this period. Of chastening significance is the extent to which my attempt at critical analysis in this book simply documents Hsü Fu-kuan's insights into a very difficult text. Finally, the recent archaeological excavations of Han tombs have uncovered a wealth of previously unknown material which not only facilitates textual reconstruction but sheds new light on dark corners of the text. The *Sun Pin Art of Warfare (Sun Pin ping-fa)* uncovered in the Yin-ch'üeh-shan dig, for example, is of considerable value in dealing with concepts developed by the Militarist school theorists generally and in understanding the *Huai Nan Tzu*'s Book Fifteen specifically, a treatise devoted wholly to military strategy.

Given these recent advances in the study of the *Huai Nan Tzu,* the time seems right to undertake the long-term project of producing for publication an annotated translation and critique of at least the principal doctrinal treatises of this text. This book is one step in this direction. My studies of the *Huai Nan Tzu* have been guided and encouraged by D. C. Lau (Liu Tien-chüeh), formerly professor of Chinese at the School of Oriental and African Studies (University of London) and presently professor of Chinese language and literature at the Chinese University of Hong Kong. Professor Lau has been pursuing his own examination of the text for many years, and in the process of directing my research he has been very generous in sharing his knowledge and insights. In return for the inspiration and encouragement I have received from this consummate scholar, I can only offer the poor payment of my gratitude and respect, and the dedication of this book.

I would like to acknowledge my appreciation to the Canada Council, which supported my research in London, and to the American Council of Learned Societies and the National Endowment for the Humanities, which have supported my efforts to present this research in its present form. I would like to thank the editors of *Philosophy East and West* and the *Journal of Chinese Philosophy* for permission to incorporate portions of papers that have appeared previously in their journals.

David L. Hall of the University of Texas, El Paso, is a speculative philosopher whose work is a rich source of inspiration for comparative philosophy. Having read my work in manuscript, he has been generous with important and positive criticisms, and I am indebted to him. I would also like to thank Eliot Deutsch and Cheng Chung-ying, colleagues in the philosophy department of the University of Hawaii who have provided stimulation and support in the process of bringing this work to completion. For help in preparing the manuscript, I would like to thank David Barnett, Dawn Fujii, and Dolores Springer. Finally, I want to express a profound debt to my wife, Bonnie, whose patience and quiet encouragement have sustained this work from its inception.

Introduction

THIS BOOK is basically an exercise in conceptual reconstruction. After tracing the historical origins and evolution of certain crucial concepts in the growth of early Chinese political philosophy, I want to analyze these concepts as they are developed in *The Art of Rulership,* an early Han dynasty treatise on political philosophy included in the *Huai Nan Tzu* anthology.

I hope in writing this book to contribute to the understanding of Chinese philosophy in several ways. First, because of the obvious dangers of cultural reductionism, it is essential that Western scholars develop a conceptual vocabulary to inform and structure their understanding of Chinese political thought. The vocabulary presented in this book is important to all students of Chinese culture irrespective of discipline: it is important to the general researcher in the humanities and social sciences as a guide to the process of early Chinese cultural development, to the historian of ideas as a means of separating the Confucian, Taoist, and Legalist strands in the general fabric of Chinese thought, and to the political scientist as a structure illuminating historical and contemporary political attitudes and issues.

In clarifying the distinctions among these philosophical concepts and pursuing coherence in the systems which they support, I have frequently found it necessary to penetrate to their metaphysical foundation and make these presuppositions explicit. The "organismic" metaphysics which explicates the relationship between part and whole and constitutes the common ground on which the Confucian and Taoist traditions have been erected, when fully appreciated, can be extended to virtually all areas of Chinese culture and used as a basis for understanding why the Chinese have traditionally chosen to construe human experience in the way that they do. Moreover, a cultivated grasp of these underlying presuppositions can help to clarify cultural components that go far beyond the concerns of this investigation.

Further, and ultimately explicable in terms of the underlying meta-physics, important insights regarding the evolution of Chinese thought can be derived from the manner in which the political concepts dealt with here have been couched in the philosophical literature. A sharp distinction must be made between locution and concept. A peculiarity of Chinese philosophical development immediately apparent from my analysis is that rival schools in the tradition have a shared vocabulary in advancing their different ideas. Under the five locutions which constitute my chapter headings, I discuss some twenty distinct concepts. Obviously this common language hides significant conceptual disparity. An important question thus arises: Why would these early thinkers choose to redefine popular terminology rather than generate a new vocabulary to express their novel reflections? This question is closely related to their reasons for choosing to associate these ideas with, if not attribute them to, some prominent historical figure rather than establishing their own claims of originality. Answers to these questions can perhaps be derived by drawing a distinction between history and tradition.

In the development of Western thought, based on a strongly "atomistic" and "essentialistic" commitment traceable to the early Greeks, the prominence of a historical figure is usually a function of the degree to which that figure reflects *discontinuity* with what has gone before. A Descartes, Kepler, or Einstein is most visible because of the extent to which he challenges the status quo and stands sharply in relief to it. Such figures are perceived by history as being responsible for setting their respective disciplines on a new track. This historical paradigm is reflective of the act/agent distinction usually presupposed in the Western interpretation of human experience and is, moreover, consistent with a perception of historical research as being primarily concerned with identifying agency and imputing responsibility for past events.

By contrast, the Chinese intellectual tradition is generally characterized by a commitment to *continuity*. The development of Confucianism is a good example. That is, before Confucianism emerged from the Chou dynasty it had been extended to accommodate thinkers as radically different as Mencius and Hsün Tzu. Eclectic Han Confucians such as Chia I and Tung Chung-shu and the Buddhist-influenced neo-Confucians with their elaborate metaphysics are all constituent to the organismic growth of the continuous Confucian tradition. Even today, scholars such as T'ang Chün-i and Fung Yu-lan could be described as "neo-neo-Confucian." In this traditional paradigm, a figure achieves prominence not from standing out in contrast to his historical inheritance but rather from the degree to which he embodies, expresses, and amplifies his tradition. It is for this reason that from earliest times there has been such an extraordinary emphasis on historical records in China. These records represent a repository of the past cultural tradition out of which the new can emerge. This is again what one would expect in view of the metaphysical presuppositions that form the basis of this culture.

Given the commitment to continuity characteristic of the Chinese tradition, it would be much easier for a philosopher to gain a hearing and win support for a new concept by reinterpreting the existing and popularly accepted vocabulary than it would for him to advance his own original set of categories. This same commitment to continuity meant that the authority one's ideas might gain by operating within the bounds of an existing tradition would far outweigh concerns for pride in authorship. It is for this reason that much in the evolution of philosophical ideas tends to be expressed not through a dialectical process of thesis and antithesis but rather in a process of organic growth. A set of explanatory categories, rather than being openly challenged and overturned in the act of establishing a new and more adequate set, is absorbed and then elaborated in new and different directions.

Another characteristic feature of Chinese philosophical literature is that, rather than seeking to persuade readers with a series of sequential arguments, it attempts as a heuristic device to engage them in their own philosophizing. I have tried in this book to present the results of my own reflections while at the same time providing readers with sufficient text to pursue the analysis on their own. That is, in exploring these ancient Chinese political concepts I offer quotations from the classical sources in sufficient quantity to give the reader more than simple support for the conclusions of my own research. It is hoped that these quotations and the manner of their presentation will suggest to the nonspecialist reader the kind of textual analysis essential to the understanding of Chinese philosophical activity. At the same time, I have included enough of the original texts to enable thoughtful readers to go beyond my speculations in their own philosophizing.

Finally, I have tried to contribute to our growing understanding of Chinese philosophy by making available to the reader the previously untranslated political treatise *The Art of Rulership*. It is an unfortunate feature of our knowledge of Chinese thought that, beyond the obvious classics, we tend to invest with disproportionate importance those texts which have been selected in a rather random process and made available to us in English. Given our high esteem for discontinuity, we have a predilection to be most impressed by what is immediately novel and original and to show little interest in anything less. Since novelty in the development of Chinese thought is often expressed within the tradition as opposed to against it, this predisposition can cause us to overlook much that is valuable.

The *Huai Nan Tzu* is a case in point. But the importance of the *Huai*

Nan Tzu has not only gone generally unnoticed in Western scholarship; it has also to a degree been neglected in the Chinese commentarial tradition itself. There are several reasons for this neglect. The fact that the rival schools from whom the philosophical vocabulary was inherited would present their doctrines in overlapping locutions has always posed formidable difficulties for the commentator. Add to this general linguistic ambiguity the fact that this text was written during the first century of the Han dynasty, a period in which philosophical literature is characterized by a ready eclecticism. The difficult language typical of early Han works and an abundance of textual problems in the *Huai Nan Tzu* itself are further obstacles that have dissuaded scholars from giving this text more attention. Finally, the "Miscellaneous Schools" *(tsa chia)* classification of the *Huai Nan Tzu* has not only reinforced the impression that it lacks originality but has even occasioned serious doubts about the coherence of the text. Only in this century have Chinese and foreign scholars alike begun to appreciate the real importance and originality of this text.

Because the *Huai Nan Tzu* still remains virtually unquarried for the majority of Western sinologues,[1] something must be said by way of introduction. *The Art of Rulership,* the focus of this study, is Book Nine of the *Huai Nan Tzu,* an anthology of diverse and far-ranging contents compiled under the patronage of Liu An and possibly submitted to the Han court of Wu Ti as early as 140 B.C.[2] While the preface prepared by Kao Yu (d. circa A.D. 220) does list a number of guests who might well have participated in its authorship, very little is known about these persons.[3] In the biographical material which still exists concerning the patron, Liu An, he is credited with having been a person of immense literary talents. In both the *Historical Records (Shih-chi)* 118 and *History of the Han (Han-shu)* 44 biographies, this point is made emphatically and at some length. Moreover, the sheer volume of material listed in the "Record of Literary Works" *(Yi-wen chih)* of the *History of the Han (Han-shu)* which claims his name as title is a fair indication of his literary involvement in the first century of the Western Han. That he himself had some hand in the writing and editing of the *Huai Nan Tzu* is well within the realm of possibility.

The contents of the *Huai Nan Tzu*'s twenty books and postface are broad and varied, probably following the *Lü-shih ch'un-ch'iu* in attempting to provide a compendium of existing knowledge. It is a syncretic text which borrows widely and heavily from pre-Ch'in sources and adapts earlier contributions to its own ends. In fact, the composite nature of the *Huai Nan Tzu* has led some scholars to dismiss it as "unoriginal."[4] On the contrary, as is borne out by this analysis of Book Nine, *The Art of Rulership,* the originality and depth of the *Huai Nan Tzu* lie in its capacity for reconciling selected elements of conflicting ideologies and, out of this activity, constructing new philosophical theory. While the individual treatises certainly vary a great deal in orientation, there is a general spirit of eclecticism which pervades the text and gives it its unmistakable Han signature. In this book, by tracing the sources and identifying the orientation of *The Art of Rulership*'s political philosophy, I hope to demonstrate the degree to which a creative syncretism must be reckoned with in gaining a full appreciation of the *Huai Nan Tzu*'s place in early Chinese philosophical literature.

The Art of Rulership has long been characterized as basically a Legalist document.[5] This attribution is in large part due to the frequent use of Legalist terminology, analogies, metaphors, and allusions. While first impressions do suggest a Legalist-oriented political philosophy, a more careful examination of the chapter takes us behind the facade of isolated concepts and certain locutions into a highly original and profound system of government. It should be stressed that while this treatise does make free and uninhibited use of ideas drawn from the whole spectrum of pre-Han political philosophy, it selects, adapts, and further integrates these originally Confucian, Taoist, and Legalist concepts to the extent that the ultimate disposition of its scheme of government is both internally consistent and original. This then becomes the first objective of this work: to demonstrate that the political theory contained in *The Art of Rulership,* although constructed with an obvious Legalist facing, shares an underlying sympathy with precepts of Taoist and Confucian origin and, taken in total, contains a systematic political philosophy that is not only unique but compelling.

The author of *The Art of Rulership* couches his political philosophy in a series of loosely connected yet consistent discussions devoted to predominantly Legalist concepts. However, there is a definite distance between Legalist doctrine in its traditional presentation and *The Art of Rulership*'s interpretation of these same concepts. The nature of this divergence can be demonstrated by a careful comparison between the concepts outlined in Legalist literature and their representation in *The Art of Rulership*.

Historical context is of considerable importance in understanding the structure and content of *The Art of Rulership*'s political philosophy. Given the available historical information, it is possible to formulate an interpretation consistent with and sympathetic to this text. At the founding of the Han dynasty, political expedience demanded that Liu Pang parcel out his newly acquired empire to those who had contributed to his success in becoming the first emperor of the Han. For the following century, it became one of the main tasks of the central Han court to disenfranchise these vassals and consolidate its own power at their expense. It was thus that Liu An, patron of the *Huai Nan Tzu,* ruled his territory with the specter of ultimate annexation hanging over his court. It was under this weight of imminent destruction that Liu An sought a theoretical resolution to his problem. The central Han court until the reign of Wu Ti, while structured around Legalist institutions inherited from the Ch'in, had evidenced strong Taoist sympathies. Under such circumstances, Liu An set about the task of combining the practical vocabulary of Legalist theory with basic Taoist and Confucian principles in order to convince the Han court that there is a workable alternative to totalitarian control. This alternative, while maintaining the security of the Legalist institutions, would adapt them in a manner that expressed the Taoist conviction in the primacy of natural realization and the Confucian commitment to the primacy of the people's welfare. Further, this alternative would underwrite the principle of universal self-determination on the basis that the realization of the part is coextensive with the realization of the whole—that individual fulfillment leads directly and inevitably to social harmony and political stability. The historical fact that the Han court did not adopt the *Huai Nan Tzu* alternative and that Liu An, one of the leading literary figures of the age, did fall victim to the expanding centralism simply underscores the attractiveness of the political alternative he had advocated.

This interpretation of the political philosophy of *The Art of Rulership* suggests, then, that the treatise was compiled with the intention of providing a political structure conducive to the development of precepts derived from the Taoist and Confucian traditions at a practical political and social level. While sharply aware of the pragmatic inadequacy of earlier Taoist political theory and the historical fact that the Confucian alternative of government by moral suasion had lost out to Legalism's system of political control, the author of this chapter proposes a theory of government which will accept a certain amount of political structure as a necessary condition for maximizing the principles of free expression and personal achievement at the heart of Taoist and Confucian philosophy. Surely it would have been politically expedient for the author of this document to retain at the least the outward semblance of the existing political structure. The extent to which he advocated a modification of the institutions making up this political structure, however, represents the spirit and purposes of his new political theory.

The preparation of this book has fallen into several stages: abstracting the central concepts in *The Art of Rulership*'s political philosophy; tracing the evolution of these concepts through pre-Han philosophical texts in order to understand their historical development and their significance for the early Han author; analyzing *The Art of Rulership*'s interpretation of these concepts; and comparing the traditional significance of these concepts and their representation in *The Art of Rulership* in order to delineate this treatise's political philosophy.

While I leave the detailed results of my strategy for the body of this work, there are two general observations which can be made here. First, although *The Art of Rulership* shapes its theory out of the entire corpus of pre-Han literature, there is a consistency in its proposed method of government. Where this consistency breaks down, as in the final portion of the treatise, the fault would appear to be textual corruption rather than structural weakness. That is to say, a strong argument can be mounted that the final section of this work (9/20b: "The capacity of Confucius was such that . . .") is a later accretion. Second, there have been many attempts at political theory which, while brilliantly devised and appealing to man's higher nature, are simply unworkable. The anarchism proffered by the early philosophical Taoists is perhaps one of these systems. This treatise presents a political theory which attempts to temper lofty ideals with a functional practicability. While the spirit of the work is strongly Taoist and Confucian, this spirit is provided with a political framework in which it can be implemented, nurtured, and cultivated.

In citing references, I have attempted to assist the reader by considering both facility and reliability. As a general principle, my first choice has been to cite the *Harvard-Yenching Institute Sinological Index Series* and the *Research Aids Series* of Chinese Materials Center, Inc., in recognition of their important place in the sinologist's reference library and their convenience for the reader. Where a text has not yet been included in these research aids, my second choice has been to refer to the *Ssu-pu ts'ung-k'an* (2100 *ts'e*) compiled by Commercial Press in a photolithographic edition during 1920-1922. If the cited work is not included in the *Ssu-pu ts'ung-k'an,* the *Ssu-pu pei-yao* (1372 *ts'e*) compiled and published by Chung-hua in 1927-1935 is consulted. Where the work is not included in any of these sources, I refer to a popularly accessible but reliable text. The Bibliography indicates which text has been cited. The following abbreviations have been used throughout:

BMFEA: Bulletin of the Museum of Far Eastern Antiquities
BSOAS: Bulletin of the School of Oriental and African Studies
LWT: Liu Wen-tien (see Bibliography)
SPPY: Ssu-pu pei-yao
SPTK: Ssu-pu ts'ung-k'an
TPYL: T'ai-p'ing yü-lan

1

Philosophy of History

THIS ANALYSIS of the political philosophy propounded in *The Art of Rulership* begins by examining the way in which its author chooses to construe his historical tradition. By focusing on the manner in which a philosopher construes history, it is possible to identify the aspects of human experience he invests with the greatest importance. History, far from being an objective account of incontrovertible fact, is a highly interpretative undertaking. The way in which philosophers interpret it often reveals their most fundamental presuppositions and the project that their philosophical speculations are meant to serve. Marx's economic interpretation of history in terms of dialectical materialism, for example, reveals both his fundamental philosophical categories and his ultimate concern: the realization of the classless society. Bertrand Russell's idiosyncratic interpretation of the development of Western philosophy is perhaps most informative of his own philosophical presuppositions and commitments—at least those of the 1946 Russell. Similarly, we can expect that the important disparities distinguishing the Confucian, Taoist, and Legalist attitudes toward their historical tradition will point to conspicuous differences in their respective philosophies that can serve us in determining the orientation of *The Art of Rulership*'s political theory. The project here, then, is to determine how representative figures in each of the three main pre-Ch'in philosophical traditions construed historical change. Did they believe that human society had developed and progressed with the passage of time? Did they believe that it had certainly changed but had neither improved nor regressed? Or did they believe that it had degenerated from some earlier ideal?

CONFUCIUS AND THE CONFUCIAN CONCEPTION
OF HISTORY

Confucius believes that a person's potential for achieving moral rightness *(yi)* in various situations is a vital component of his or her natural endowment. It is the cultivation of rightness through the dynamics of interpersonal conduct and its realization in the social and political orders which enables people to integrate themselves into the cosmic order and to participate in an essentially moral universe—this then is the "Way" of human beings. The process of attaining and consummating this Way in government and society must begin at the top with the ruler's commitment to self-realization. That is, Confucius advances a notion of education through emulation which is tied closely to his belief in the efficacy of the ruler's "moral potency" *(te)*. It is because of the ruler's essential position in the chain of influence that Confucius as a trustee of the Way directs his efforts at winning over the ruler to the notion of administration by moral edification and transformation. Because the powers-that-be were recalcitrant and the times were set against realization of the Way, however, Confucius and small pockets of like-minded individuals, denied the arena of government service, took it as their life's work to cultivate themselves and transmit their moral insights to later generations. While succeeding generations may have found the times more or less conducive to the achievement of moral rightness in the various aspects of human life, and while the amount of energy invested in the coextensive projects of personal, social, and political realization would surely vary, the pursuit of personal realization through assiduous moral and intellectual effort is in itself unchanging.

Confucius believed, moreover, that all people are by nature similar,[1] and that their disparity is a matter of instruction and discipline—in other words, they vary in the degree to which learning and authentication in action have resulted in moral growth. Since the natural endowment of each person is reasonably consistent, it follows that at least in terms of individual capacity people have the same possibility of realizing the Way in their social relationships and government from one generation to the next. And yet in the *Analects* it is apparent that some historical periods are accredited with having attained the Way[2] while the age in which Confucius himself lived, for example, is viewed as falling far short of this ideal. The *Analects* conveys the general impression of an upward trend in the development of human society from ancient times until the early Chou peak, when it enters a period of steady decline. If the natural capacity of people to realize the Way has been constant and the possibility for them to achieve an integrating rightness in their actions has remained unchanged, what then has determined their degree of success in past ages? For Confucius, one of the most significant variables is "cultural tradition"—the institutionalized moral insights of past generations which can not only nurture but elevate the human experience.[3] Ultimately it is the quality of the tradition and the effort the present heir is willing to make in embodying, modifying, and superseding it that determines the degree to which a society supports or retards the project of becoming human. It is significant that this project is open-ended and encourages perpetual self-transcendence (*Analects* 32/15/29): "It is the human being that can extend the Way, not the Way that extends the human being." The Way as the method for realization remains the same, but the human ideal is a distant, indistinct fiction that is constantly pursued but never reached.

Yao and Shun, the sage rulers of high antiquity, accorded with the Way in their governments, as did the early Chou rulers, and yet Confucius looks to the latter as his primary exemplars. The potential for pursuing the realization of the human moral nature has been a constant factor in the course of history—it was there in high antiquity and is still here in the present day. Why then does Confucius favor the Chou rulers over Yao and Shun? The answer again lies with the cultural tradition.

Because Confucius is convinced that the sage-rulers cultivated the Way in their personal conduct and in their stewardship of the empire, and had captured and articulated the Way in their teachings and cultural contributions, he treats their words as scripture[4] and their culture as a sacred trust.[5] It is in this respect that he asserts his love for the past[6] and denies any personal contribution to the cultural tradition he is transmitting.[7] He sees ancient culture as a creative construction and institutionalization of past moral realizations which has always provided a formal guide for personal development and socialization (*Analects* 14/8/8): "The Master said: 'Man is inspired by poetry, takes his stand on social norms, and is rounded out by music.' "

It is for this reason that there is a recurring emphasis on learning in the Confucian texts—an emulation of the ancients' exemplary model. But learning is not simply being programmed by the acceptance of some external set of criteria for human behavior and blind conformity to these criteria in one's conduct. Rather, it refers to the process of first ingesting social norms through enacting them. This is *formal* learning. The practical function of these formalized moral insights in the process of learning is obvious. Next, through conscious reflection and introspection one strives to understand the moral content embedded in the form. This entire process is referred to as transformation through education. It is only when a prescribed social action is informed by an intuited grasp of the moral content of the action that a person is truly living in accordance with the Way. And as one's perception of the moral content of social norms clarifies and one's capacity to act authentically human grows through the process of disciplined living, one "learns" to be moral in all one does. The passage describing Confucius himself in this process of learning immediately comes to mind (*Analects* 2/2/4): "The Master said: 'At fifteen I was committed to learning, at thirty I took my position, at

forty I was of one mind, at fifty I understood the unfolding of nature, at
sixty I followed my instincts, and at seventy I could follow my heart's
desire without going astray.' "

Given the important practical function of the formal aspects of Confucian learning, there is a profound respect for reputation and achievement
in the tradition.[8] At the same time, however, Confucius was by no means
suggesting that his contemporaries should attempt to reconstitute the
ancient way of life in modern times. In fact, he specifically rejects this
attitude in *Hitting the Mark in the Everyday (Chung-yung)* 28: "The
Master said: 'To be stupid yet fond of relying on oneself, to be in a low
position yet fond of exercising authority, to be born into the modern era
yet attempt to return to ancient ways—a person like this will suffer disaster in his own lifetime.' "

Rather, Confucius sees civilization as cultural growth, born in the past
and groomed through time to the present day. Although Yao and Shun
can be extolled for having followed the Way, the scant remnants of their
culture are by and large insufficient to serve as guides to present experience. However, where aspects of this culture have been preserved—the
Shao dances of Shun, for example—Confucius is certainly not averse to
taking full advantage of them.[9] Even the more recent Hsia and Shang
cultures cannot be utilized directly in the absence of information concerning the customs.[10] The Chou culture, on the other hand, is not only
preserved in Confucius' own state of Lu,[11] but further, coming after the
Hsia and Shang, has had the benefit of absorbing what was of abiding
value from these two earlier traditions (*Analects* 5/3/14): "The Master
said: 'The Chou surveys the two preceding dynasties. How resplendent is
the culture! My choice is with the Chou.' "

Perhaps the first priority that we find in this Confucian philosophy of
education is the notion of education by example: both the inherited cultural tradition and those who best reflect an understanding of it have a
paradigmatic function. In Confucius' efforts to propound a viable social
and political system which will not only lift society out of its present difficulties but will create an environment congenial to human moral development, he takes as a practical beginning the inheritance of a formal
model to which modern society can look for direction. It is not altogether
surprising that he chooses the unambiguous Chou model over the faintly
defined and insubstantial antique alternatives.

Although Confucius idealizes the early Chou period as a golden age in
the development of Chinese civilization,[12] his ideal state is by no means a
simple revival of early Chou institutions and culture. Rather, it is a coming together and blending of many diverse elements (*Analects* 31/15/11):
"Yen Yüan [Yen Hui] asked how to administer a state. Confucius
replied: 'Use the calendar of Hsia,[13] ride about in the state carriage of

Yin,[14] wear the ceremonial cap of Chou, and as for music there are the Shao dances [of Shun]. Ban the sounds of Cheng music and keep sycophants at arm's length because the sounds of Cheng are wanton and sycophants are dangerous.' "

Though Confucius professes sincere interest in the formal and ceremonial aspects of culture, what he really strives to understand and transmit to later ages are the moral insights embodied in the earlier institutions and human examples (*Analects* 40/19/22):

> Kung-sun Ch'ao of Wei asked Tzu-kung: "What has Confucius learned from?" Tzu-kung replied: "The Way of Kings Wen and Wu has not yet fallen into oblivion. Because those of superior character record the significant elements while those without such qualities work on the minor aspects, everyone embodies in some respect the Way of Wen and Wu. What is there that the Master has not learned from? Further, what fixed teacher can there be for this?"

While repeatedly asserting that the ways of the ancients must be preserved,[15] Confucius tempers this respect for antiquity with the practical consideration that this inherited knowledge must be made relevant to prevailing circumstances (*Analects* 3/2/11): "The Master said: 'He who in reviewing the old can come to know the new has the makings of a teacher.' "[16] A person must labor assiduously to acquire the knowledge transmitted from ancient times, but even more crucial, one must be able to take it one step further in applying it to present conditions (*Analects* 25/13/4): "The Master said: 'If a man can recite three hundred of the *Odes* and yet when given a government post cannot fulfill it, or when sent out to distant quarters cannot speak for the government without waiting for instructions, then although he knows a lot, what good is it to him?' " This notion of "practical application" is at the heart of the distinction Confucius draws between "learning" *(hsüeh)* and "thinking" *(ssu)* (*Analects* 3/2/15): "The Master said: 'He who learns but does not think remains in the dark; he who thinks but does not learn will strain himself.' "

In short, Confucius believes that culture—the social refinements developed primarily to encourage and articulate proper moral feelings—is cumulative and generally progressive.[17] Whereas people living in high antiquity had the capacity for developing their moral nature, they were lacking in the cultural institutions and formal guidance necessary to maximize this capacity. That Yao and Shun were able to nurture this moral nature in their conduct and administration and, in doing so, were able to make a signal and lasting contribution to China's emerging civilization, was due more to their own personal excellence than to the congeniality of their environment. By the early Chou period, however, the development of Chinese culture had culminated in a sophisticated pattern for social intercourse—fertile ground indeed in which to encourage human kind's moral nature. The cultural institutions and conventions established by the earlier sages who themselves had "lived" the Way were adapted to structure society and guide contemporaries toward a comparable level of humanity. For Confucius, the early Western Chou period marks a high point in the evolution of Chinese society. Unfortunately, however, this high point was short-lived. Having achieved the golden age of early Chou, people were gradually deflected from the Way by growing political strife. By the end of Western Chou, the political institutions had been drained of substance and the Chou kings had become puppets manipulated by ambitious feudal lords. In the process of degeneration, the glory that had been the early Chou culture was divested of its underlying moral content; only the name and the ceremonial shell remained intact. In response to this process of spiraling decline, Confucius advocated a return to the Way of Chou and a revival of the fertile and substantial culture which had fostered this golden age.

While Confucius' emulation of the past is much noticed, little has been said about his belief in the future. Given his faith in the potential of human nature to progress and his devotion to education as the foremost means of encouraging natural fulfillment, it can be inferred that Confucius would at least accept the possibility of social progress. Again, as we have seen, there are passages in the *Analects* which describe a notion of progressive and cumulative culture. Confucius harks back to the early Chou as the high water mark in the course of history— not a high water mark that has come and gone but a height which can again be attained and even surpassed.[18]

LAO TZU AND THE TAOIST CONCEPTION OF HISTORY

As in the Confucian tradition, the criterion applied by the Taoists to evaluate historical change is the degree to which an era was conducive to the development of human kind's original nature. Again the *Lao Tzu* literature of the Taoist school,[19] similar to the Confucian *Analects*, suggests that there was a time in the past which provided an environment more congenial to the realization of human nature than that of the present day. As is readily apparent from the following description of the Taoist utopia, several features distinguish this idealization of the past from the golden age of the Confucian tradition (*Lao Tzu* 80):

Make your state small, make your people few.
Even though you have military equipment,

Have no recourse to use it.
Cause the people to regard dying [in their native place] as no light matter
And thus make them loath to move far away.
Although you have boats and chariots,
You should have no reason to mobilize them;
Although you have armor and weapons,
You should have no reason to parade them.
Cause the people to restore the practice of knotting ropes
And to implement this system.
They can take relish in their foodstuffs,
Beautify their clothing,
Find contentment in their dwellings,
And take pleasure in their customs.
Although neighboring states be within seeing distance of each other,
And the sounds of their chickens and dogs can be heard from one to the
    other,
The people of one state will reach old age and pass away
Without ever having had contact with the people of another.

In the *Lao Tzu*'s description of the ideal state, certain features are notable. First, the ideal Taoist state is small both in size and population. In this respect it is diametrically opposite to the Confucian ideal of empire: an idyllic representation of agrarian China in ancient times.[20] The agrarian society of ancient China was composed of innumerable self-governing and self-administering villages, each constituting a self-sufficient economic, social, and political unit. The relative weakness and vulnerability of the ideal Taoist state can be construed as a theoretical challenge to the concepts of strength, size, power, and expansion that dominated the political thinking of Eastern Chou China.

Second, it is often assumed that the Taoist ideal is a raw primitivism wholly devoid of the conveniences of civilized society. This tribal style of life gives rise to practical doubts regarding health, sanitation, and life expectancy. But in the society depicted here, it is not that the people do not have modern conveniences—surely "boats and chariots" and "armor and weapons" are symbols of what is conventionally considered civilized society. Rather, their natural and unembellished style of living and, in particular, their uncontaminated system of values make labor-efficient devices and the notion of protection wholly unapplicable.

Finally, this ideal society is anarchic. Although it has a "government" which follows a policy of *wu-wei* (noncoercive activity) and broods over the people, treating "them all as infants,"[21] this government is a natural condition and is nonauthoritarian.

We arrive, then, at a singularly important question in traditional commentary: is the political state recommended in the *Lao Tzu* characterized by a popular and widespread realization of the *tao* by all the people, or is this Taoist enlightenment a characteristic of the ruler alone? Is the *Lao Tzu* a handbook on how to stupefy the people and achieve political control, or is the objective of the Taoist sage-ruler, like that of his Confucian counterpart, to lead his people toward their own fulfillment?

The ambiguity of the *Lao Tzu* is such that it can quite comfortably accommodate both interpretations. While the notion that the political philosophy of Lao Tzu is "purposive" has a wide following,[22] the alternative interpretation—that the sage-ruler in his relationship to the people is analogous to the *tao* in its relationship to the myriad things—has the positive feature of establishing consistency between the metaphysics and the political philosophy of the text. In chapters 10 and 51 a similarly worded passage is used to describe the sage and the *tao* respectively. Neither the *tao* nor the sage-ruler is interested in control, possession, or the realization of some selfish end. Rather, their "purpose" is to provide the myriad things and the people with an environment and circumstances congenial to self-realization.[23]

The *Lao Tzu* frequently uses metaphor in describing a human being's uncontaminated nature, variously likening it to the "uncarved block,"[24] the innocence of a spewing infant,[25] and the seeming distance of a moron.[26] The original nature is a constant. Although its pristine simplicity has been smothered by layer upon layer of the "knowledge" and "desire" generated in a contrived and unnatural society, this encrustation of social norms, values, and conventional erudition can be pared away through a cultivation of the Taoist Way and a return to the beginning (*Lao Tzu* 48):

> In pursuit of learning,
> One daily expands his sphere of activity,
> But in the pursuit of the *tao*
> One must daily reduce it—
> Reduce it and reduce it again
> Until one attains a state of "nonactivity."

We are all capable, then, of repudiating the distorting influences of civilization and recovering our original nature. While the simplicity and purity of human nature are constant inasmuch as they still exist and can be restored, it is the cultural tradition which stands between the potential of the ideal person and his actualization. Contrary to the *Analects,* the *Lao Tzu* literature idealizes antiquity not *because* of its culture but rather the lack of it. For Confucius, the transmission of the ancient culture which embodies and expresses human moral achievement is at the root of his pedagogic emphasis.

By contrast, the disdain which the *Lao Tzu* directs at this same culture leads to its insistence that one must unlearn conventional knowledge and reject all artificially established values before one can return to a natural and uncontaminated state. The cultural snowball which over the centuries has gathered around and given expression to the moral possibilities inherent in human nature is, to the Confucians, a source of intense pleasure and pride. For the *Lao Tzu* theorists, this cultural accumulation around one's original nature—this unnatural carving of the "uncarved block"—represents a real deterioration of the human condition. In Confucius' interpretation of history, culture is both beneficially cumulative and progressive; for the Taoists, it is harmfully cumulative and retrogressive. Again, where the Confucian tradition credits history with a positive element of cultural evolution, the *Lao Tzu* tradition sees only a devolutionary slippage from a past utopian lifestyle.[27]

Although this discussion has been based on the antique utopia depicted in the *Lao Tzu* 80, the notion of historical decline is one of the most popular and consistent themes in this kind of early Taoist literature. There are elaborations on this same *Lao Tzu* description in the "Primitivist" portion of the *Chuang Tzu*.[28] In chapters 28 and 29 of the "Individualist" section of the *Chuang Tzu* text, there are also lengthy utopian passages. Again, beyond the Primitivist and Individualist areas of the *Chuang Tzu* the entire "Restoring the Original Nature" *(Shanhsing)* chapter, as the title implies, is devoted to a description of the corruption and fall of "natural" man.

SHANG YANG AND THE LEGALIST CONCEPTION OF HISTORY

From the preceding discussion of the Confucian and Taoist conceptions of history it is clear that both traditions look to an antique model as an example to which the modern person can in some sense aspire. The idealized representation of a golden age serves these schools both as a device for communicating their philosophical systems—an "educational aid," as it were—and as a historical sanction to lend authority to their ideas. In the Legalist texts,[29] this notion of renaissance based on a past model is repudiated and an entirely new attitude toward the unfolding pattern of history is expounded.

Certainly the iconoclastic and antitraditional attitude of Legalist thought precludes any notion of reviving a past ideal. Historically speaking, the doctrines of this school contain a strong revolutionary element inasmuch as they construe the established order as the foremost obstacle to the successful implementation of the Legalist political program. The

Legalist principle of a universally applicable system of laws, for example, was a direct challenge to the hereditary privilege of the powerful families who had hitherto considered law as a personal device for controlling underlings and who saw themselves as being immune from such regulation. Moreover, the concept of "political purchase" *(shih)* and the various policies subsumed under the rubric "techniques of rulership" *(shu),* all of which were directed at checking the power vested in any one minister, were an affront to the ambitions of men who preferred to leave their political prospects open-ended. The policy of suppressing intellectuals and their rival doctrines raised the ire of the intelligentsia. The principle of limiting "merit" and its commensurate rewards and honors to agrarian and military accomplishments could only arouse resentment among the mercantile rich. In fact, that virtually all the vested interest groups stood to lose ground in the successful implementation of a Legalist regime is evidenced in the rise and sudden end of this school's earliest powerful proponent, Shang Yang.[30]

In Shang Yang's ascent to power under the patronage of Duke Hsiao of Ch'in, he systematically siphoned the previously diffused powers of the old order into the central court, making Ch'in strong by consolidating its strength under one man. That Shang Yang had succeeded in offending every pocket of power in Ch'in is the essential message of his would-be mentor, Chao Liang: "Once the King of Ch'in, taking leave of his guests, no longer attends the court [that is, when he dies], the reasons for the state wanting to get hold of you are ample indeed! You will be dead in the bat of an eye!"[31] In devising and effecting the Legalist system of government, Shang Yang created such powerful opposition that when Duke Hsiao, his single support, died, the taut spring of resentment snapped back on him like a mousetrap. Although Shang Yang himself fell victim in his campaign against the established order, his attitudes toward tradition, culture, and power-sharing were retained as an essential element in the doctrine which eventually led to the unification of China under Legalist rule.

Inasmuch as Legalist policies were new and revolutionary, they could not count on the authority and sanction of history. On the contrary, the traditional attitudes and the political precepts and values of the old order represented alternatives to their concept of "one standard" and unified rule—alternatives which could not be safely entertained. In the construction and operation of their political machine, the interference of traditional standards was intolerable and had to be eradicated. In disposing of these traditional attitudes, the Legalist theorists, rather than arguing against their intrinsic validity, quite cleverly devised a rational and very persuasive argument (*The Book of Lord Shang* 2/10b, p. 32):

The sage neither imitates antiquity nor follows[32] the status quo. To imitate antiquity is to be behind the times; to follow the status quo is to be bogged down in the face of changing circumstances. The Chou did not imitate the Shang and the Hsia did not imitate the ways of Yü. These three ages were characterized by different circumstances and yet they were all able to rule the world.

The *Han Fei Tzu* 341:3 makes a similar point:

Therefore the sage deliberates on the size and shape of things, discusses them, and then administers his government accordingly. Thus where penalties are light it is not because of compassion and where punishments are severe it is not because of perversity. He simply carries them out as dictated by the demands of custom. Circumstances are determined by the age, therefore, and measures for dealing with things correspond to the circumstances.

The assertion that the intelligent ruler must make his political measures appropriate to the changing times is really the essence of the Legalist's conception of history. Different periods have different problems, and different problems require new and innovative solutions. Old principles of government, even when proved effective in their own historical context, are more than likely obsolete. And the primary concern of the ruler when carrying new political measures into effect has to be their successful implementation and efficacy (*Han Fei Tzu* 87:6): "Those who know nothing of proper government are certain to say: 'Don't change old ways! Don't alter regular practices!' As for changing or not changing, the sage is not interested. His only concern is proper government. This being so, whether or not he changes old ways or alters conventions depends on whether they will meet the present contingency."

Antiquity stretches across a long period of time, of course, and many different sage-rulers have used many different methods to maintain peace and stability in their respective times (*The Book of Lord Shang* 1/ 2a–b, pp. 3–4): "Kung-sun Yang said: 'Since previous ages have not shared the same doctrines, which 'ancients' do we imitate? Since these emperors and kings did not repeat those gone before, which social norms do we follow? . . . Therefore, I say, there is no one way to rule the world, and so long as something is expedient to the state, it need not be an imitation of antiquity.' "

In addition to the primary principle that political solutions must answer the times, the Legalist texts advance a secondary although less convincing argument against the use of an antique model. In the preceding discussion of Confucius' conception of history, one of his reasons for giving preference to the Chou model is because it remains clear and intact while the others have gradually eroded with the passage of time. Han Fei

Tzu goes one step further, suggesting that not only is the "orthodox"
interpretation of these past models themselves the subject of constant
wrangling, but even the "correct" understanding of their place in the
teachings of Confucius himself has given rise to altercation among his
followers (*Han Fei Tzu* 351:8):

> Although Confucius and Mo Tzu both take their "Way" from Yao and
> Shun, what they take and what they discard is not the same, and yet both
> claim to represent the authentic Yao and Shun. Since Yao and Shun cannot
> be brought back from the dead, who is going to decide which of the Confu-
> cians and Mohists is right? From Yin and early Chou times it has been over
> seven hundred years, and the Shun era and Hsia dynasty go back more than
> two millennia. If we cannot determine who is right between Confucians and
> Mohists, how can we hope to be clear about the Way of Yao and Shun some
> three thousand years earlier!

Thus the Legalist thinkers insist that since historical models are open to
subjective interpretation by their advocates, there is no objective standard on which to base acceptance or rejection of proposed policies. The
models, or at least the modern versions of the models, are simply unreli-
able.

In the teachings of Confucius, we have seen that culture is regarded as
cumulative and generally progressive, and inasmuch as it reflects past
moral development, it is considered highly conducive to the continued
growth of human kind's moral nature. In the *Lao Tzu* tradition, this
same culture is rejected as an unnatural interference in the growth and
maturation of a person's original nature. While the Legalists follow the
Taoist school in rejecting culture, their motivation is to keep the people
in a state of ignorance in order to impose their own exclusive and absolute standard of conduct. Unlike Confucius and the *Lao Tzu,* their purposes have nothing to do with cultivation of personal life or its societal
implications. Rather, their concern is effective political control, and culture is rejected as inimical to this end.

Several recent Chinese scholars,[33] perhaps influenced by Ch'en Ch'i-
t'ien's analysis of Han Fei's political doctrine,[34] suggest that in contrast
to the Confucian devolutionary conception of history, the Legalists posit
an evolutionary interpretation. Ch'en Ch'i-t'ien states:

> Philosophy of history is a kind of attitude toward history. From the time
> when Huang Ti established the state down to the Warring States period,
> China already had more than two millennia of history. Each of the pre-
> Ch'in schools was dissatisfied with the conditions of the Ch'un-ch'iu and
> Warring States period. Because the viewpoints of their philosophies of his-
> tory differed, however, there developed two main streams on how to reform

the conditions. The first stream considered that history is "devolving" and that to reform conditions we must simply imitate the ancients *(fa ku)*. This stream is represented by the Confucian school. Their banner of "imitating the ancients" is "inherit and transmit the teachings of Yao and Shun, emulate and glorify those of Wen and Wu." [From *Hitting the Mark in the Everyday (Chung-yung)* 30]

The other main stream considered that history is "evolving" and that to reform conditions we simply innovate. This stream is represented by the Legalist school. Their banner of "innovating" is "deliberate on the affairs of the age and make the necessary arrangements." [From *Han Fei Tzu* 339:10]

This interpretation of the early Chinese philosophies of history is simplistic and, at best, misleading. While there is considerable support for the "imitating the ancients" *(fa ku)* principle as one aspect of Confucius' interpretation of history, this assertion without substantial qualification does a great injustice to the progressive element in the Confucian position. In fact, the Confucian position properly understood is more evolutionary than devolutionary.

The Legalist theorists go to great lengths to insist that political measures have had to change as new problems have arisen. What is appropriate and successful under one set of circumstances is in all probability inappropriate to another. The Legalist attitude toward particular historical periods tends to be generally descriptive rather than critical and evaluating.[35] In any case, they refuse to attach value judgments to specific political solutions, always returning to the notion that a political solution is only as good as it is appropriate to its historical context. The policies of Yao and Shun, if applied today, would lead to certain disaster. Because the value of political measures can only be ascertained relative to the times, there can be no absolute good and the concept of evolution cannot be applied. In the Legalist conception of history, there is only change— change *without* progress or evolution.

THE *HUAI NAN TZU'S* CONCEPTION OF HISTORY

Before turning to *The Art of Rulership*'s interpretation of history and attempting to place it in relation to these earlier traditions, it will be instructive to take a brief look at several of the other philosophies of history represented in the *Huai Nan Tzu* text as a whole. This excursion will provide additional examples of the essential differences underlying the Confucian, Taoist, and Legalist positions and demonstrate further the extent to which a creative syncretism is a characteristic to be reckoned with not only in *The Art of Rulership* but throughout the text.

The first two treatises of the *Huai Nan Tzu* are based on the *Lao Tzu* and the *Chuang Tzu* respectively.[36] It is therefore not unexpected that they both contain a fundamentally Taoist attitude toward historical change. There is, for example, a lengthy chronological account of deteriorating conditions in the world, from an ideal "age of superlative virtue" down to the decline of Chou, brought about by a gradual and increasing neglect of the original nature and the Way—deterioration from unity and oneness to plurality and distinction (2/8b–9b):

In the age of superlative virtue, man dozed contentedly in a realm of boundless vacuity and roamed about in a world of vast expanse; he dealt with the cosmos and abandoned the myriad things. With the Hung Meng plain as his sundial, he rambled freely on the border of the perimeterless. Thus the sage breathed the vapors of the *yin* and *yang,* and all the multifarious living things, reverently esteeming his virtue, were harmonious and compliant. At this time, with nothing superintending things, they all mysteriously unfolded and matured of their own accord. Chaotic and surging, the pure stuff of their natures had not yet separated. Coalescing as one organism, the myriad things abounded. Thus even if one had had the acumen of an Yi there would have been nowhere to apply it.[37]
. . . By the time the House of Chou had fallen into decline, they had diluted their original stuff and squandered their natural substance. As they became estranged from the Way in their actions and put on the appearance of virtue in their conduct, the buds of cleverness and erudition began to sprout. When the House of Chou had declined and the Way of the True King had fallen into disuse, the Confucians and Mohists then began to formulate their Ways and debate over them, dividing up into factions and quarreling among themselves. Thereupon, studying a broad range of things, they mimicked the sages and used this tinsel and pretense to browbeat the people. Strumming, singing, drumming and dancing, and lacing their rhetoric with the *Book of Odes* and *Book of History,* they purchased a reputation from the world. They amplified the social graces obtaining among superiors and subordinates to the extent that an assemblage of the entire populace would still be unable to perform them in all their permutations and embellished ceremonial robes and caps to the extent that an accumulation of their wealth would be insufficient to defray the expenses. Thereupon people generally began to forget the proper path and lose their way, each wanting to apply his knowledge and craft to make his way in the world and stake out his reputation and fortune. Thus the people spilling everywhere like unchecked floodwaters lost their grip on the root of the Great Ancestor.

Book Eight, *The Fundamental Constancy (Pen-ching),* is from beginning to end wholly given over to this Taoist notion of decline from a natural utopia. Like Book One, *Tracing the Tao (Yüan-tao),* there is much here to compare with the *Lao Tzu.*[38] The departure from human kind's original nature gave rise to erudition, morality, artificial contrivances, and all such components of modern civilization. As people became more and more estranged from their natural course of development, their society became correspondingly complex and artificially contrived. This spiral of human decline has led to the degradation of the present day. Of particular note in this treatise is its overt criticism of the current government. Not only does the author condemn this government for oppressive economic policies and its general abuse of the people but, further, he goes so far as to suggest that in ancient times, given a similar situation, the people would have moved against such tyranny (8/10b–11a):

> In antiquity, the emperor had a territory one thousand *li* square and the various nobles had one hundred *li* square. Each maintained his allotment without encroaching on that of the others. When there was one among them who did not practice the Way of the True King, who on top of tyrannizing the people, contending over and seizing upon the territory of others, and setting the administration in chaos, would not come when summoned, would not carry out what was dictated, would not cease doing what was prohibited, and would not change his ways when instructed, they would mobilize their troops and punish him. They would execute the ruler, eradicate his faction, build tombs for his victims, sacrifice at the national shrine, and select a person from among his heirs to replace him.

A lengthy section of Book Six, *Perceiving the Imperceptible (Lan-ming),* gives a chronological account, mainly descriptive, of the society with and without the Way (6/6a–9b). Nü Wa brought the Way to a land of fire, water, and predatory animals and transformed it by repairing the physical world and bringing peace and contentment to the inhabitants. The state of the people under the capable rule of Nü Wa is very Taoistic in tone (6/7a):

> At this time the people lay down blankly and awoke in a daze. One moment they thought they were a horse and the next an ox. They tottered along and looked about bemused. With perfect genuineness they all attained a state of contentment, but none knew from whence it came. Drifting and wandering they had no idea what they were looking for; shrouded in shadows they did not know their destination.

From this antique highpoint of fulfillment and general contentment, conditions gradually worsened. Chieh of the Hsia having lost the Way caused havoc in the spheres of both man and nature. More recently, the age of the Seven States, similarly without the Way, is described as a period of war, human carnage, and degradation. All through the Three Dynasties (Hsia, Shang, and Chou) the people have suffered because of war and divisiveness. But with the present emperor (Wu Ti) on the throne, the whole world comes together to form one, and the Way of the Five Emperors of antiquity has been restored.

While the interpretation of history in *Perceiving the Imperceptible (Lan-ming)* generally conforms to the Taoist pattern of decline, it differs from *The Fundamental Constancy (Pen-ching)* account in two significant respects. First, while describing the contented people of high antiquity in unambiguously Taoist terms, *Perceiving the Imperceptible* does not share the enthusiasm of *The Fundamental Constancy* for repudiating Confucian virtues and values. It simply says nothing. Second, *The Fundamental Constancy* condemns the current government with considerable candor. In *Perceiving the Imperceptible,* this criticism is replaced with perhaps less honest but certainly more prudent adulation for Wu Ti and his restoration of the Way.

Book Eleven, *Equalizing Customs (Ch'i-su),* describes the decline from a state of pristine ignorance and spontaneous relationships—a decline characterized by the proliferation of Confucian virtues. These virtues are symptomatic of an age having lost the Way and the people having abandoned their infant bliss (11/1a–b):

Conducting oneself by following one's original nature is called the Way; acquiring one's heavenly endowment is called virtue. When one's original nature has been lost, he then esteems benevolence; when the Way has been lost, he then esteems rightness. For this reason, when benevolence and rightness are established, the Way and virtue have been supplanted; when social norms and music are set on display, the pure and the simple has dissipated; when right and wrong appear, the people are in a state of befuddlement; when pearls and jade are prized, the world is torn by contention. Generally, these four are innovations and instruments of a period in decline. Now, social norms are a means of differentiating the venerable from the lowly and the honorable from the base. Rightness is a means of harmonizing the relationships between sovereign and minister, father and son, elder and younger brother, husband and wife, and friend and friend. Since those who practice social norms in the present age boast reverence and respect while being injurious to others, and those who practice rightness boast generosity while placing others under obligation, the sovereign and ministers come to censure each other and those of the same flesh and blood harbor resentments about each other. These then are persons who have lost sight of the roots of social norms and rightness. Hence they are frequently condemned as dissemblers. Now, just as when water collects it gives rise to fishes which eat each other, and when earth is accumulated it gives rise to animals which dig themselves into it, when social norms and rightness are established, they give rise to hypocritical and deceitful persons. Now to blow on ashes and yet hope to avoid getting them in the eyes, or to wade across a river and yet hope to avoid getting wet—these are impossible expectations.

In antiquity the people were as ignorant as infant children. Their appearance did not go beyond their feelings; their words did not overstep their actions. Their clothing was only for the sake of warmth and was without adornment; their weapons were dull and blunt and without a sharp edge; their songs were simply for the sake of pleasure and were free of complication; their crying was inspired by grief alone and was free of any contrived wailing. Digging out wells they drank from them; ploughing their fields they ate. Without any means of making their merits known, they did not seek after anything. Among family members there was no praise or blame; among friends there were no favors or resentment.

With the rise of social norms and rightness and the value which came to be placed on material wealth, deceit and hypocrisy sprouted and flourished, praise and condemnation became muddled, and resentment and the bestowal of favors became rife. Whereas this certainly gave rise to the merits of Tseng Ts'an and Hsiao Chi, it also spawned the wickedness of Tao Chih and Chuang Ch'iao.

Hence if there is the imperial carriage, the dragon banners, the feathered canopy, the dangling tassels of the headpiece, the team of four steeds, and the mounted escort, there will certainly be the wickedness of tunneling thieves, lockbreakers, grave robbers, and burglars. If there is fine brocade, embroidery, glossed silk, and sheer silk, there will certainly be thatch sandals, irregular footwear, and rough, tatty, and coarse garments. The fact that "high and low lean upon each other, short and long form each other" is very clear indeed.

Equalizing Customs follows the Taoist tradition in laying the blame for the fall on the gradual encrustation of culture which has coated and smothered man's original nature (11/4a–b):

If we examine man's original nature, that it is overgrown and polluted and does not achieve its clarity and brilliance is probably due to some external thing defiling it. When the babies of the Ch'iang, Ti, Po, and Ti are first born they all make the same sound. On their reaching maturity, we cannot communicate with them even given a team of interpreters because their education and customs are different. Now, if a three-month-old baby has been born in our country but then is moved to another, he will be unable to know his native customs. Viewing it from this perspective, clothing, social norms, and customs are not the original nature of man but are received from without. Now, the original nature of bamboo is that it floats; but if one splits it up into writing slips, bundles them up, and tosses them into the river, they will sink. This is because the bamboo has lost its original physical form. The original nature of man is free from depravity, but if he is steeped in customs over a long period of time, this will be changed. Changing and forgetting his origins, he is compromised by other natures. Thus, although the sun and moon want to shine brightly, the floating clouds obscure them; although the waters of the Yellow River want to be clear, silt and rocks pollute them; although human nature wants to be calm, passions and desires injure it. Only the sage is able to divorce himself from external things and return to himself.

Now, a person who loses his way on board a ship does not know which direction is which, but on seeing the pole star his confusion is dispelled. The original nature, then, is the pole star of a human being. If one has a clear perception of his own self, he will not lose sight of the true nature of external things. If, however, he does not have this perception of himself, moving along with things he will become confused and disconcerted. This is just like swimming to the west of Lung Mountain—the more one kicks the faster he sinks.

Equalizing Customs states quite clearly that to realize the self is to realize the Way (11/7b):

> To be enlightened does not mean seeing other things, but simply seeing oneself; to be discerning does not mean hearing other things, but simply hearing oneself; to be penetrating does not mean knowing other things, but simply knowing oneself. Therefore one's own person is that on which the Way depends. If one's own person is realized, then the Way is realized. If one realizes the Way, when he looks he is perspicacious, when he hears he is discerning, when he speaks he is heard everywhere, and when he acts he is followed.

The culture which obscures the true and original self has been developed by taking natural human sentiments and embellishing them with artificial customs and ceremonies. These customs and ceremonies become so elaborate that the link is lost between the natural emotion which originally gave rise to them and the customs themselves (11/6b):

> In ancient times it was not that they did not know how to proliferate the ceremonies of the court or how to arrange themselves for the *ts'ai-ch'i* and the *ssu-hsia* music, but rather that they considered these to be a waste of time and a vexation to the people without being of any practical use. Thus they inaugurated ceremonies which were simply adequate to support the realities of the situation and express their basic meaning. In ancient times it was not that they were unable to set out the bells and drums in rows, to make an extensive display of flutes and pipes, to brandish shields and battle axes, and to wave streamers and banners, but rather that they considered these to waste resources and disrupt the political administration. Thus they composed music which was simply adequate to share their pleasure and make known their intentions. In ancient times[39] it was not that in funeral ceremonies they were unable to exhaust the nation, crush the people, empty their treasuries, and deplete their resources, placing pearls in the mouths of the dead, dressing them in garments of jade mail, and binding them with silk and braided ropes, but rather that they considered these to exhaust the people and interrupt the business of life without being of any particular benefit to the bleached bones and rotting flesh of the dead. Hence their burials were simply adequate to gather up and inter their dead.

Standing in stark contrast to the treatises that view history as a process of human decline are the Confucian-oriented sections of the text. These treatises describe the historical development from primitive society to civilization with pride and an undisguised sense of achievement. Book Nineteen, *Striving with Effort (Hsiu-wu),* describes this evolution in the following terms (19/1a–2a):

In antiquity, people fed on grass and drank water, gathered the fruits of trees and bushes, and ate the meat of wasps and clams. At this time there were frequent cases of illness and poisoning. Thereupon Shen Nung came and taught the people to sow the five grains and examine the congeniality of the ground—its irrigation, fertility, and contours. He tasted the flavors of the myriad plants and the sweetness of the spring water, enabling the people to know which to use and which to avoid. At this time, in a day Shen Nung would encounter seventy noxious plants.

Yao established the principles of filial piety, compassion, benevolence, and love and treated the people like his own sons and younger brothers. In the west he instructed the Yao people and in the east the Black Teeth people. To the north he gave a helping hand to the Yu-tu people; to the south he guided the people of the Chiao-chih. He exiled Huan Tou to Ch'ung-shan, banished the San-miao to San-wei, transported the minister of waterways to Yu-chou, and executed Kun at Yü-shan.

Shun built houses, erected walls, thatched roofs, cleared the land, and planted grains. He persuaded the people to abandon their cave dwellings and to have family houses. While marching a punitive expedition to the south against the San-miao, he died at Tsang-wu.

Yü, with the rain drenching him and the gales combing his hair, diverted the course of the Yangtze, led the flow of the Yellow River, dug out Lung Pass, and opened a passage through Yi-ch'üeh Mountain. He built dikes on the P'eng-li marshlands, made use of four kinds of vehicles, and, cutting back mountain forests, he brought the water and the land under control and stability to the eighteen hundred states.

T'ang arose early and retired late into the night to contribute his full powers to the tasks at hand, lightened the taxes and exactions to make the lives of the people more congenial, spread his virtue and magnanimity widely to relieve the poor and distressed, mourned the dead and asked about the sick in order to look after the orphaned and widowed. The people came to love him, and his policies and commands prevailed everywhere. Then marshaling his troops at Ming-t'iao and pursuing Chieh of Hsia to Nan-ch'ao, he called him to account for his crimes and banished him to Li-shan.

The single most significant factor in the transition from primitive squalor to sophisticated and comfortable civilization has been the careful accumulation and dispensation of knowledge through education (19/8a):[40]

In ancient times Tsang Chieh devised the written word, Jung Ch'eng contrived the calendar, Hu Ts'ao developed clothing, Hou Chi originated domestic farming, Yi Ti created wine, and Hsi Chung invented the carriage.
. . . Since the establishment of the House of Chou, there have been none

who could match the abilities of these six men, and yet all have continued to refine their contributions. How is it that these later people, not having the talents of even one of the six, have been able to understand the ways of these six outstanding men? It is because the teachings of the six have been continuously passed on and their knowledge and ability have been transmitted down to succeeding generations. If we look at it from this perspective, it is clear that learning cannot be dispensed with.[41]

Corollary to the importance of education is unrelenting effort in the pursuit of knowledge (19/9a):

> Those who have not been able to reach this level live in quiet retreat, meditate, strum the zither, and read the ancients. They look back and examine antiquity; they study and debate with men of superior character and station, enjoying themselves day after day. They gather in the affairs of the world and differentiate white from black, beneficial from harmful. Weighing its feasibility, they determine whether or not a project is propitious. Setting up standards and rules, they can devise laws and regulations, investigate all aspects of the Way, and make an exhaustive study of the basic nature of affairs. They establish what is right, repudiate what is wrong, and then make it clear for posterity. On dying they pass on their work, and even while alive they have glory and reputation. This, then, is what man's ability is capable of attaining. That none are able to achieve this, however, is because, being indolent and idle, they are too much at leisure.[42]

It is the combination of education and sustained effort which has been responsible for the ascent of mankind and progress in human society (19/9a–b): "Viewing it from this perspective, the moron who is fond of learning is better than an intelligent man who does not exert himself. There has never been a person from the ruler and ministers of state down to the ordinary people who has been successful without diligence. . . . Reputation can be made by hard work; achievement can be gained through diligence."

Perhaps the dominant theme of Book Thirteen, *Perennial Discussions (Fan-lun),* is that the attitudes and methods of government must change in response to the times (13/11b):

> Therefore the sage, in contemplating the course of an affair, gears his response to the changes in external circumstances without applying any fixed standard. At times advancing and at times retreating, he is soft and pliant like a reed and yet it is not from fear or faintheartedness; he is firm, strong, and formidable and his determination reaches the skies, and yet it is not boastfulness or vanity. In all cases he takes the tide and responds to change.[43]

While both Legalist and Confucian conceptions of history accept this principle that customs and culture must change to meet new circumstances, the amoralistic Legalist doctrine is profoundly uninterested in the Confucian conviction that the ultimate meaning of human existence lies in creative moral achievement. *Perennial Discussions* gives clear voice to this Confucian commitment (13/4a–b):

> Thus the path which the sage follows is called "the Way"; what he does is called his "affairs." The Way is like the percussion instruments—once tuned they do not change. Affairs are like the zither and lute—each time you string them, they need tuning. Therefore laws and social norms are the tools of government, but they are not that on which government is based. Thus it is that benevolence and rightness constitute the framework. These have been unchanging for all time.

Again, it is the welfare of the people rather than a mechanical devotion to convention which is the foremost concern of good government (13/3a):

> If the regulations of the former kings are not suitable, put them aside. If something of recent times works out well, make use of it. It is for this reason that there has never been anything constant in social norms and music. Thus the sage controls social norms and music rather than being controlled by them. There is something constant in the governing of a state, the basis of which is benefiting the people; there is a regular pattern in political instruction and education, the most important element of which is the carrying of orders into practice. If something is beneficial to the people, it need not be in imitation of the ancients; if something always works out well, it need not be consistent with established practices.

Although the conception of history expounded in *Perennial Discussions* shares the Legalist principle of changing the methodology of government to accommodate the times and contains many allusions to Legalist texts,[44] in its essential concern for the welfare of the people it is unquestionably closer to the Confucian position. True to the spirit of Han eclecticism, even the Taoist philosophy of history does not go unrepresented in this one treatise (13/3a–b):

> The various streams while having different sources all pour into the sea; the various philosophies while pursuing different aims all address themselves to proper order. When the Way of the True King was wanting, the *Odes* arose; when the House of Chou was in decline and social norms were degenerate, the *Spring and Autumn Annals (Ch'un-ch'iu)* arose. While the *Odes* and the *Spring and Autumn Annals* are masterpieces of literature, they are both the compilations of degenerate ages. The Confucians on the basis of these works instruct and guide in the world, and yet how can they compare with the

heights of the Three Dynasties! If, taking the *Odes* and *Spring and Autumn Annals* as the Way of the ancients, we are to esteem them, what about the time prior to their compilation! It is better to take the Way when it was whole rather than when it was incomplete. Hearing the actual words of the former kings is better than reciting their odes and writings. And realizing what is behind the words is better than hearing their words. What is behind the words, however, cannot be articulated. Thus "the Way which can be spoken of is not the constant Way."

This survey of the several interpretations of historical change to be found in the *Huai Nan Tzu* underscores the composite nature of the text and illustrates the degree to which traditionally disparate doctrines have been brought together and reworked. As a result the text is at the same time syncretic and original. The spirit of bringing together the old to fashion the new, perhaps the most striking feature of *The Art of Rulership*'s entire political philosophy, can be seen in these interpretations of historical change.

THE ART OF RULERSHIP'S CONCEPTION OF HISTORY

There are treatises in the *Huai Nan Tzu* anthology—*The Fundamental Constancy (Pen-ching),* for example—that are devoted almost entirely to an exposition on historical change. *The Art of Rulership* is not one of these. It is devoted to a statement of political theory and in fact concerns itself with history only to the extent that historical examples can be used to illustrate general principles of government. It would be a distortion to say that the philosophy of history which *The Art of Rulership* expounds in the course of outlining its political theory is one of its more conspicuous features. Even so, a careful examination of relevant passages can provide important insights into the author's attitude toward historical change, insights that help to reveal the sources and orientation of his political philosophy.

In discussing the process of historical change and comparing the past with the present, *The Art of Rulership* combines elements that we have found characteristic of the Taoist and Confucian philosophies of history. The outstanding feature of the Taoist interpretation of history—the notion of decline from an ancient and primitive ideal—is present in the chapter from the outset. In the following passage a contrast is drawn between the idyllic rule of Shen Nung and the degenerate government of recent times—a contrast that is reminiscent of the strongly Taoistic portions of the *Huai Nan Tzu* text, notably the *Tracing the Tao (Yüan-tao), The Beginning Reality (Ch'u-chen),* and *The Fundamental Constancy (Pen-ching)* treatises (9/1b–2a):

In ancient times when Shen Nung governed the world, his spirit did not gallop out from his breast, his wisdom did not extend beyond the four directions, and he cherished the benevolent and sincere mind. The sweet rains fell at the proper time and the five grains flourished. In spring they would sprout forth, in summer they would grow, in autumn they would be harvested, in winter they would be stored up. With monthly examinations and seasonal evaluations, at the year's end the record of accomplishments would be offered up, and tasting the grain at the proper season, sacrifice would be made in the Ming T'ang. . . .

His intimidating presence was awesome yet not put to the test, punishments were there yet he did not have to invoke them, and his laws were few in number and not overwhelming. Hence his transformation of the people was godlike. In his territory stretching from Chiao-chih in the south to Yu-tu in the north, T'ang-ku in the east and San-wei in the west, there was no one who would not submit to his rule. At this time the laws were liberal, the punishments were tolerant, and the prisons were empty. The world was one in custom and none were of a wicked mind.

The government in a declining age is a different matter: those above are fond of taking without any conception of proper limit while subordinates are self-assertive and wholly given over to avarice. The people, impoverished and distressed, contend angrily, and working themselves to the bone, never achieve anything. Cleverness and deception sprout forth, bandits and thieves are increasingly evident, ill-will appears between superiors and subordinates, and edicts and orders are not implemented.

The authorities do not devote their efforts to returning to the right path. Going against the roots, they cultivate the nonessentials; cutting back on their bounty, they increase their punishments. And yet by doing such things they are trying to establish proper order! This is no different from holding a catapult and hoping to attract a bird, or wielding a cane to tame a dog. It will just make matters worse.

Yao too represents an ideal government of antiquity. The description of an orderly world under a sage-king is contrasted with the decline of more recent times (9/10b–11a):

In accepting the empire it was not as if Yao coveted the wealth of the myriad peoples or the ease of being ruler. Seeing that the common people struggled among themselves, the strong dominating the weak and the many oppressing the few, Yao then personally comported himself in accordance with moderation and frugality, and elucidating the virtue of mutual love he brought the people together in harmony. Thus it was that his roofing thatch was not trimmed, his rafters were not cut and finished, his royal carriage was not ornamented, his mats were not hemmed, his pottage was not seasoned, and his grain was not polished. Going on his royal progress and spreading his guidance, he labored assiduously in the empire and traveled to each of the five sacred peaks. Surely it was not that the lifestyle of the emperor would be anything but enjoyable but that he took the whole empire for the sake of the empire and not because he derived any personal benefit from it. When he became old and weary and abdicated in favor of Shun, it was just like stepping back and kicking off his sandals.

When the age is in decline, however, it is a different matter. The ruler, having once gained the wealth of possessing the empire and having occupied the purchase attendant upon his position, will then exhaust the energies of the common people in catering to his own desires. His mind is wholly preoccupied with buildings, pavilions, ponds, gardens, ferocious animals, precious stones, and exotic objects. Consequently, the poor people do not even have husks and chaff to eat and yet the tigers, wolves, and bear fill themselves on fine meats; the common people are sparsely clothed in coarse rags and yet palaces and halls are draped with silk and embroidery. The ruler gives priority to those undertakings which serve no useful purpose, and the people of the empire become haggard and gaunt. Thus it is that he causes the people of the empire to become discontented with their lot in life.

In *The Art of Rulership,* one repeatedly encounters two features: a contrast drawn between the ideal ruler and his decadent counterpart[45] and adulation for the contributions and competent administration of former kings.[46] The early period in which the ancients ruled the world is generally depicted with admiration as an age of enlightened government (9/20a):

Of old, when the emperor would hold court, the high ministers would proffer honest admonition, the learned scholars would chant the odes, the music masters would sing their criticisms, the common people would communicate their opinions, the court historians would chronicle errors in judgment, and the court chefs would reduce the number of dishes at meals, but still this was not considered enough. Thus Yao set up a drum for those offering bold admonition, Shun established a notice board for criticisms, T'ang instituted an independent judicial authority, and King Wu provided a small drum to forewarn him against rashness. Before an error could show itself there was already a safeguard against it.

Although *The Art of Rulership* expounds a devolutionary theory of history consistent with the Taoist tradition, this doctrine of decline has been so modified by the introduction of Confucian attitudes that its interpretation can only be described as syncretic. In discussing the early Taoist and Confucian conceptions of history we have seen that their conflicting attitudes toward culture mark a sharp divergence between the two schools of thought. While the Taoists pointed to the accumulation of culture and the development of civilization as the essential cause of social decline, the Confucians regarded this same culture as the expression of moral achievements and its transmission as the essential impetus behind social progress. *The Art of Rulership,* far from rejecting cultural heritage, singles out rulers of antiquity and praises them for their ability to influence both their own times and the subsequent course of history through their efforts in personal cultivation. These rulers, for example, developed music and ceremony in order to represent their innermost feelings (9/17b):

> The ruler of antiquity was concerned about the hardships of his subjects to the extent that if there were people starving in his state, at each meal he would have only one single dish, and if there were people freezing in winter he would not attire himself in fur garments. Only when the harvest was good and the people had plenty would he then set up the bells and drums and display the shields and axes, and with ruler and subject, superior and subordinate, all enjoying these together, there was no sorrowful person left in the whole state.
>
> The use of metal, stone, pipes, and strings by the ancients was to express their joy. Weapons, armor, battleaxes, and broadaxes were to give a more polished expression to their anger. The ceremonies of libations and offerings were to represent their gladness. Funeral garments and sedge footwear, beating of the breast, and weeping were to demonstrate their grief. These are all instances of the general truth that what fills one inside will be given formal expression outside.

The substance of their personal cultivation was formalized as social norms and music, and these have been transmitted as a cultural legacy from ancient times (9/4a):

> With the sage-kings of antiquity, when the most essential vapors were embodied within, likes and dislikes did not lie on the outside. Their words were spoken to express what was truly on their minds and they issued commands to show their purposes. Setting these out in social norms and music and recounting them in song and verse, their deeds have been known to each succeeding generation and have spread to every corner of the world. They could even shape and transform birds, beasts, and insects. How much more so could they administer the law and implement edicts.[47]

It is this cultural heritage which is most efficacious in transforming the people and achieving enlightened government. While *The Art of Rulership*'s devolutionary theory of history might be associated with the Taoist writings, the respect for traditional culture as a formal representation of ancient moral values is an ingredient which can only be traced to the Confucian camp. In this treatise, the ancients are exalted not for maintaining a village utopia but for their innovative contributions to human civilization.

In *The Art of Rulership*—a treatise which superficially appears to describé a Legalist system of political control—the Legalist interpretation of historical change is not represented. There is no portion of the text which conveys the Legalist rejection of historical examples as irrelevant or its insistence that new problems require new solutions. Rather, the conception of history is basically a Taoist devolutionary theory modified by a thoroughgoing respect for the cultural contributions of past eras. These two seemingly conflicting positions are reconciled in the suggestion that the deterioration of the human condition is the result of a failure to appreciate the substance and spirit behind the institutions which fortify human society. Above all it has been the failure of the ruler, the hinge between political order and chaos, to master the art of rulership and thereby realize the Way of the True King that has led to this unfortunate result.

At the outset of this chapter, I suggested that by examining the way in which representative philosophers of the Confucian, Taoist, and Legalist schools construe historical tradition it would be possible to discover their fundamental philosophical concerns. From the attitudes of Confucius, Lao Tzu, and Shang Yang, therefore, certain characterizations may be drawn.

Confucius, for example, begins from a positive conception of human nature and takes as his major concern a method for pursuing universal self-realization. The metaphysical ground which can be reconstructed from the *Analects* and which informs the organismic structure of Confucius' philosophical system serves one primary project: the personal, social, and political attainment of the *tao*. Importance is invested in the creative moral achievement of personhood by first disciplining oneself in the formal structures of the cultural tradition and then seeking rightness in the uniqueness of one's own situation. It is significant that for Confucius natural action is fundamentally moral and, moreover, that the achievement of this rightness integrates human being in a harmonious universe.

Lao Tzu similarly begins from a positive conception of human nature and takes as his major concern a method for pursuing universal self-realization. The conceptual structure that can be generated from the *Lao Tzu* serves the ideal of universal self-realization: the personal, social, and political attainment of the *tao*. Importance for Lao Tzu is invested in the creative achievement of personhood by first disciplining oneself in the natural functions of the cosmos and then expressing just-so-ness in the uniqueness of one's own situation. For Lao Tzu, the inherited cultural tradition is an artificial encumbrance that distracts people and distorts their natural expression. Natural human action, on the other hand, is coextensive with the natural operations of the cosmos.

Shang Yang and the Legalists generally have little interest in fundamental philosophical concerns such as human nature and its potential for self-realization beyond those insights that can be turned to account in pursuing the ruler's purposes of political control. The cultural tradition is similarly interpreted only to the extent that it can serve this political end. Importance for the Legalists is invested entirely in the construction of a political apparatus that will enable the ruler to effect and sustain his totalitarian control.

Thus *The Art of Rulership*'s interpretation of history is basically a synthesis grounded in the Confucian-Taoist concern for universal self-realization. History, then, is evaluated by determining the extent to which it has been conducive to this end. In the chapters that follow, I explore the fundamental ideas that structure *The Art of Rulership*'s political philosophy. From the analyses of these concepts, and from the integrated picture that emerges out of their juxtaposition, it will become clear that the fundamental concern sustaining this political treatise is universal self-realization based on a positive conception of human nature. If this conclusion is in fact correct, it means that although there are certainly Legalistic characteristics in the presentation of this political philosophy, at a fundamental level it shares a common ground with the Confucian and Taoist traditions.

2
WU-WEI
(Nonaction/Doing Nothing/Acting Naturally)

WU-WEI IN PRE-CH'IN CONFUCIAN TEXTS

ALTHOUGH *wu-wei* is generally regarded as a decidedly Taoist concept,[1] it does play an important role in Confucian political theory. This discussion of a Confucian interpretation of *wu-wei* should perhaps begin with what is certainly one of the earliest examples of this expression in our extant sources (*Analects* 31/15/5): "The Master said: 'If anyone could be said to have effected proper order while remaining inactive *(wu-wei),* it was Shun. What was there for him to do? He simply made himself respectful and took up his position facing due south.' "

This passage is not an odd, unrepresentative excerpt from the *Analects*. On the contrary, it can be regarded as a succinct characterization of the Confucian attitude toward government. In the ideal Confucian administration, the ruler does not personally attend to matters of government, but by setting a positive example and through the charismatic influence of his "virtue" *(te)* the people are led into a manner of conduct in which they seek moral achievement (*Analects* 2/2/1): "The Master said: 'A ruler who governs by virtue can be compared to the pole star which merely lodges in its place while the other stars pay it homage.' "[2]

The ruler, then, cultivating and giving expression to his fundamental moral endowment, serves as an example for others to emulate in the development of their own natures (*Analects* 24/12/17): "Chi K'ang Tzu asked Confucius about government, and Confucius replied: 'Government *(cheng)* is rectification *(cheng)*. If you lead with rectitude, who would dare be otherwise?' "[3] That the expression of all natures results in a harmonious social order is guaranteed by the possibility of achieving "rightness" *(yi)* in each unique situation—the moral objective of human existence.

The Confucian ruler, regulating his conduct so that his activities reflect a commitment to the expression of his moral nature, is able to influence his subordinates and transform his people. This is the political principle of the guidance and transformation of the people through moral example. The ruler "does nothing" inasmuch as his personal cultivation, possible only through interaction with his people, does not require the projection of arbitrary demands on his subordinates. His relationship with these subordinates is characterized by a total absence of compulsion. That the particular realization of these subordinates happens to be congruent with that of the ruler is due to their common participation in a creative moral order. It should be noted that there is a fundamental difference between the Taoist notion of *wu-wei* and its Confucian counterpart: Taoism is unwilling to interpret cosmic activity in terms of human moral categories; Confucianism insists on the coincidence of human moral achievement and cosmic harmony. For the early Confucians, *yi* is a possibility for moral achievement which ties the natural endowment of individuals to their natural and social environments. As Duyvendak observes: "Moral endeavor is . . . the principal concern of Confucianists. They take pains, however, to demonstrate that the moral is equivalent to the natural."[4] Since in Confucian ethical theory morality is entirely natural and intrinsic, it is not necessary for the ruler actively to augment the character of his subordinates in order to achieve social and political order. Rather, it is a matter of his participating with them in the realization of the incipient virtue which is already theirs by nature. Both the ruler and the subordinate pursue the consummation of their natural possibilities in this dialogue. The subordinate looks to the ruler as an actualizing model of human potential— a model of what he himself can achieve. While this model evokes emulation, it must be stressed that the locus of the potential for cultivation and signification is the individual. In the ideal relationship between individual and ruler, neither imposes on the other or elicits from him anything which is inconsistent with his own natural development.

Although there is only one explicit example of the term *wu-wei* in the *Analects,* from an analysis of the political theory propounded in this text it can be argued that *wu-wei* is an appropriate description of the ideal Confucian ruler: one who reigns but does not rule. A second instance of *wu-wei* in the Confucian tradition appears in the *Hitting the Mark in the Everyday (Chung-yung)* book of the *Record of Rites (Li-chi).* This passage characterizes "the highest sincerity" in the following terms (*Record of Rites* 31/23): "A thing of this description is brilliant without making a display, changes without moving, and completes without acting *(wu-wei).*" This is an extension of a preceding passage from the same book which states (*Record of Rites* 31/20): "Only the most sincere in the world is able to realize his nature fully. To be able to realize his nature fully is to be able to realize the natures of others fully, and this in turn is to be able to realize the natures of other things fully." Cheng Hsüan suggests that "the most sincere in the world" in this passage refers to the ruler,[5] while Chu Hsi interprets it as a reference to the sage.[6] In either case, we once again encounter the Confucian ideal of the consummate person adopting a policy of *wu-wei* in the pursuit of personal, social, and political realization. In doing so, he is able "to complete without acting."

In the *Record of Rites* there is yet another passage which uses the expression *wu-wei* (27/6):

> The Duke said: "May I ask what is meant by 'completing one's character'?" Confucius replied: "In conducting oneself by not interfering with things— this is the meaning of 'completing one's character'. Not interfering with things is the Way of heaven." The Duke said: "May I ask what the superior man values in the Way of heaven?" Confucius replied: ". . . Things are completed while it remains inactive *(wu-wei)*—this is the Way of heaven."[7]

In this passage we are first told that the "completion of one's character" is the Way of heaven. Next, the Way of heaven is explained as things achieving realization without active interference from an external source. Extended to the political sphere, this is the proposition that the ruler in achieving his own realization contributes to the realization of his subjects.

Before examining the two examples of *wu-wei* to be found in the *Hsün Tzu,* we should first note the *Hsün Tzu*'s divergence from the Confucian orthodoxy of the day. While Hsün Tzu is generally categorized as a Confucian, he revises the Confucian concept of humanity and its place in the cosmos. He begins with an amoral heaven. Out of this amoral heaven— perhaps "nature" is more appropriate—is spawned a basically amoral man who becomes immoral only after he himself develops a system of morality. This system of morality is the product of the moral "mind"—a wholly human innovation developed and transmitted by the early sages to resolve the horror of the human condition. The moral mind is humanity's promise and its salvation. Through education and the cultivation of this moral mind, all people are capable of achieving sagehood—the highest level of human existence.

Given Hsün Tzu's restructuring of the Confucian ideal, it follows that his conception of *wu-wei* too is somewhat different from that expressed in the *Analects* and *Record of Rites*. While early Confucianism could be said to regard *wu-wei* as a means to realize humanity's morally endowed nature, for Hsün Tzu *wu-wei* is the method to actualize the moral mind and cultivate its ethical principles. The significant difference is that for Hsün Tzu *wu-wei* refers to the cultivation of an *artificial* ethical system which has the potential to lift the individual out of a morass of social conflict and transform him into a socialized person.

While this kind of gap can be sketched between the *Analects'* conception of humanity and its *Hsün Tzu* counterpart, ultimately, as D. C. Lau points out, an obvious question arises: "Why does Hsün Tzu exclude the heart (or mind) from human nature and so look upon morality as contrary to nature?"[8] As Lau goes on to suggest, the difference lies primarily in the disparate definitions of human nature.

In the *Hsün Tzu,* there are two instances of the term *wu-wei.* The first is a passage which in purport is reminiscent of the *Analects* 2/2/4: "At seventy I could follow my heart's desire without going too far." The *Hsün Tzu* 81/21/66 states: "Thus the person of benevolence in carrying the Way into practice is without activity; the sage in carrying the Way into practice is without constraint. The thoughts of the person of benevolence are respectful; the thoughts of the sage are happy. This is the Way of the properly ordered mind." Although this passage is not specifically political in content, it is clear that the fulfillment of the morally superior person lies in nurturing the dictates of ethical values inculcated in him through the development of his moral mind. Given Hsün Tzu's interpretation of human nature,[9] we cannot say that *wu-wei* is following the course of one's original nature. Rather, we might say that it is a matter of expressing one's natural capacity for goodness. Under the discipline of his moral mind, it is the human being realizing what it is possible for him to become. As a political principle, *wu-wei* would be the morally superior person encouraging his subordinates through his own example to express their potential for morally superior conduct. It should be remembered that while Hsün Tzu lacks faith in the basic human instincts and impulses, he is utterly persuaded as to human potential (89/23/72): "The man on the street can become a Yü [has the capacity to become a sage]— this is certainly true. But that the man on the street is really able to become a Yü [is really able to realize this potential]—this is not necessarily so."

The second instance of *wu-wei* in the *Hsün Tzu* is a passage relating an anecdote about Confucius. In this passage, as in the political theory of the *Analects,* we have the association of *wu-wei,* virtue *(te),* and rightness *(yi)* (103/28/27):

When Confucius was gazing on the eastward flow of water, Tzu Kung asked him: "Why is it that the superior man, on seeing a large body of water, would necessarily stand gazing on it?" Confucius replied: "Inasmuch as it spreads everywhere to nurture the myriad things yet does nothing *(wu wei)*, it resembles virtue *(te)*. Inasmuch as its flow in twisting its way downhill must always follow the contours of the terrain, it resembles rightness *(yi)*. Inasmuch as, glittering and sparkling, it is inexhaustible, it resembles the *tao*.''

At first glance this passage seems rather Taoistic in tenor,[10] but on closer examination it will be seen that this kind of Confucian statement illuminates a fundamental difference between the Confucian and Taoist interpretations of the cosmos. In both the Confucian and Taoist traditions there is a strong association between the emanation of *te* and the concept of *wu-wei*. In other words, in order to be successful in *wu-wei* there must be *te*. The significant difference lies in the fact that the Confucians believe that *te* must be expressed in such a manner as to achieve rightness *(yi)* in each human situation. The Taoists, on the other hand, interpreting *yi* as a normative standard, reject such moral principles as both artificial and arbitrary.

With respect to this Confucian belief in the integration of human moral achievement and cosmic harmony, Duyvendak observes that even in the highly stylized ritual of Confucian government, the ruler models his ritual expression on the operations of the cosmos.[11] The principles behind the early Confucian interpretation of cosmic activity have correlative principles in their program for the proper administration of the state. The ruler, adhering to the principle of *wu-wei,* emanates morally potent *te* which influences his people and encourages them in the cultivation of their own moral natures. Thus, while seemingly ''doing nothing,'' he is able to bring about social harmony.

While Confucius as depicted in the *Analects* clearly advocates the principle of government by moral suasion and dynamic example as the core of his political philosophy, this commitment to an ideal does not preclude the preeminently practical Confucius from giving imposed social organization and positive law a place in his political thought as an unfortunate but decidedly necessary backstop for moral education. In Confucius there seems to be a constant tension working between the ideal to which man can aspire, on the one hand, and a realistic appraisal of the human condition and its possibilities, on the other. It is the practical Confucius, aware of the enormity of his project, who comments (*Analects* 25/13/11): ''The Master said: 'True indeed is the saying: Only after the state has been manned by good people for a hundred years can we overcome oppression and do away with killing.' '' And again (*Analects* 25/13/12): ''The Master said: 'Even where there is a True King it will still be a full generation before he can cause benevolence to prevail in the state.' ''

Confucius states categorically that all persons are basically equal (*Analects* 35/17/2): "People are similar to each other in terms of nature, but differ greatly as a result of practice." Nevertheless he clearly reflects the tension which operates between his ideal and his resignation to existing conditions (*Analects* 14/8/9): "The Master said, 'The common people can be made to comply, but they cannot be made to understand why.' " A clear distinction between the Confucian and Taoist interpretations of *wu-wei* follows from the fact that Confucius insists on tempering the pursuit of an ideal with realistic expectations.

Returning to Hsün Tzu's concept of *wu-wei,* it is best understood as a variation on a Confucian theme in which human participation in the natural cosmic harmony is made possible by a discipline of moral cultivation conceived by the early sages and transmitted to later ages. For Hsün Tzu, then, *wu-wei* as a political principle would be the ruler's expression of his *te* which in turn originates in the cultivation and realization of his moral mind.

WU-WEI IN PRE-CH'IN TAOIST TEXTS

This exploration of the Taoist conception of *wu-wei* is based on the two most representative Taoist texts, the *Lao Tzu* and *Chuang Tzu.*[12] The expression *wu-wei* occurs twelve times in the *Lao Tzu* and is one of the central concepts of the work.[13] Moreover, related terms such as "nonintervention" *(wu-shih)* and "nondeployment" *(wu-hsing)* occur with some frequency.[14]

Before analyzing the concept of *wu-wei,* it is helpful if not essential to have a sense of the metaphysical ground underlying the Taoist system as a whole. As William James remarked, all great philosophers have their vision—a way of making sense out of the "buzzing, blooming confusion" we call reality. When one has grasped the vision of a philosopher, the system in its many parts is readily understood. At the center of *Lao Tzu*'s vision is the notion of *tao,* and any discussion of the *Tao Te Ching* must begin from an explication of this concept.

A very real obstacle in attempting to give a coherent account of Taoist philosophy is its ambiguous use of language. Its advocates are inclined to use the same locution to connote very different concepts. The central locutions—"knowledge" *(chih),* "sagely person" *(sheng jen),* "heart/mind" *(hsin),* and "virtue *(te)*—can be used on different levels with diametrically opposite meanings. The concepts "true knowledge" and "obstructive erudition," for example, are discussed using one and the same locution, "knowledge" *(chih),*[15] and readers are left to context and their own devices to determine which is meant. Chapter 18 of the *Lao Tzu* states:

> The six relationships among family members must be disharmonious
> Before there can be filial piety *(hsiao)* and parental compassion *(tz'u)*.

This is followed immediately by chapter 19:

> Spurn benevolence and repudiate righteousness
> And the people will return to filial piety *(hsiao)*
> and parental compassion *(tz'u)*.

Although the same expressions are used, *hsiao* and *tz'u* in chapter 18 refer to contrived and ossified social conventions whereas in chapter 19 they denote the natural and spontaneous expressions of the child-parent relationship. This kind of ambiguity becomes especially apparent when it comes to the notion of *tao*. Although scholars have identified many levels of this term in analyzing its place in the *Lao Tzu,* I shall limit myself to a discussion of only three: the constant *tao,* the natural *tao,* and the *tao* of the consummate person.

The constant *tao* is the Taoist epithet for the sum total of reality. It can be described as the ultimate metaphysical reality, the absolute, the unconditioned, the undifferentiated and holistic, the uncreated, the all-pervading, the ineffable. It is the process of becoming. It is the "source" of the phenomenal world in an immanent rather than transcendent sense and in an ontological rather than chronological sense. The *tao* is transcendent in that it "goes beyond" any particular; yet it is not transcendent in that it is not a separate reality. It is changing in that it is the locus of all phenomenal change; yet it is unchanging in the sense that it suffers neither increase nor diminution. There are two polar aspects of the constant *tao:* the metaphenomenal and the phenomenal. The metaphenomenal *tao* is the *tao* apprehended in its indeterminate and undifferentiated totality as existence. It is described variously in the text as vacuous, empty, formless, the nameless, the constant, and so on as a means of underscoring its organismic pervasiveness.[16] There is nothing which is not *tao*. Its phenomenal aspect is the *tao* apprehended as the phenomenal world in its particularity, plurality, diversity, and facticity or "thingness." It is described variously as *te,* fullness, the myriad things, form, the named, the changing, and so on as a means of emphasizing the reality of the phenomenal world. In order to apprehend the *tao* as phenomena it is necessary to differentiate the particular from the whole and yet fully understand the same particular with reference to the whole—hence the generative idea of "origin," of "returning," of "mother," the notion of the "uncarved block" and "the dispensation of names." These two polar aspects of the constant *tao,* the metaphenomenal and the phenomenal, are the basis on which all dichotomous predications used to describe it can be reconciled (constant/changing, big/small, formless/formal, absolute/relative, and so on).

There are two presuppositions underlying this notion of *tao* which are not always taken into consideration. The first is an organismic and holistic conception of reality which forms the basis for Taoist relativism and explains the relationship between the phenomenal and metaphenomenal aspects of the *tao*. This doctrine of organism denies the essentialistic finality of distinctions, insisting that a thing is a *focus* of relationships determined by its context in the whole. The thing is particular and relative in the sense that it can be differentiated from the whole, but it is "identical"[17] with every other thing and absolute in the sense that the full consequence or definition of any conditioned particular (that is, the full set of its conditions) *is* the unconditioned whole. This doctrine of organism affirms the ontological reality of both the particular and the whole, the phenomenal and the metaphenomenal, but denies any notion of final autonomy, discreteness, or discontinuity in reality. It insists that particulars are mutually determining, mutually defining, and mutually conditioned—and, as such, each particular is a window on the whole. To understand any particular in its fullness is to understand the whole.

The second presupposition operative in the *Lao Tzu* and in fact characteristic of much of the pre-Ch'in philosophical tradition is a conceptual distinction between human being and nature, expressed variously as the "three powers or spheres" *(san ts'ai),* as human being *(jen)* and heaven *(t'ien),* and as human being *(jen)* and heaven-earth *(t'ien-ti).* This distinction, which can be seen throughout the corpus of early Chinese philosophical literature, makes the human being in some sense an exception to nature, something other than nature.[18] Whereas the sphere of nature is characterized by the spontaneous development of each constituent particular, the sphere of the human being has not only the possibility of spontaneous development in harmony with nature but also the possibility of distorted development caused by one's unexplained proclivity to misinterpret his reality in dichotomous terms by perceiving himself as separate and distinct from what he mistakenly construes as an external world. This restricted understanding of self as occupying a fixed perspective is the source of relative value judgments, desires, attachments, and concepts such as life and death. In both Confucianism and Taoism, to achieve consummation one must understand one's particularity relative to the whole and then restructure one's values accordingly. In both traditions, ego-self is the source of human "dis-integration" with nature. In the teachings of Confucius, people are encouraged to cultivate themselves through a self-conscious performance of social norms which reflect past achievements of rightness. For people informed by their cultural tradition to pursue rightness in the uniqueness of their own situation is for them to do what is distinctively and naturally human. This natural action integrates people with both their human and their natural environments. The alternative, to pursue "personal profit" *(li),* can be inconsistent with rightness and hence unnatural.

This integrating ground between human being and nature is also evident in Taoism, where people are enjoined to use the sphere of nature as a model for "natural" conduct (*wu-wei*) and as a cathartic device for eliminating "unnatural" behavior. This emulation of the natural does not mean that the creative process of becoming a human being is the same as that of a tree, but rather that people in understanding the process of spontaneous development and the ecological dependency obtaining between such natural phenomena as trees and their environment can come to understand the true nature of reality and their ultimate identity with all things. By living out this understanding in action, people can realize themselves as human beings. The consummate person in the Taoist tradition, through achieving integration with nature, contributes to cosmic harmony:

> To know the operations of nature *(t'ien)* and to know the operations of human being *(jen)* is the highest level of knowledge. To know the operations of nature is innate. To know the operations of human being is to use those elements of knowledge which one knows to nurture those which one does not. And to exhaust one's natural span of years without expiring prematurely—this is the fullness of knowledge.[19]

As we can see, the *Chuang Tzu* frequently uses the terms "human being" *(jen)* and "nature" *(t'ien)* to establish a conceptual distinction.[20] While the *Lao Tzu* sometimes uses the same terminology to make this distinction, it generates considerable confusion at times by using the expression *tao* in place of nature. This use of *tao* as nature, then, is its second level of meaning.

In the *Lao Tzu,* the expressions *t'ien,* literally "heaven," and *t'ien-ti,* literally "heaven and earth," are frequently used to represent nature:

> Understanding constancy, one is magnanimous;
> Being magnanimous, he is then catholic;
> Being catholic, he is then complete;
> Being complete, he is in accord with nature *(t'ien);*
> Being in accord with nature, he is then in accord with the *tao.* [16]

> I do not know its name;
> Constrained, I would give it the rubric *"tao,"*
> And if forced to assign it a name,
> I would call it "great." . . .

> Thus the *tao* is great;
> Heaven *(t'ien)* is great;
> Earth *(ti)* is great;
> And man too is great.
> In this cosmos, there are four "greats,"
> And the human being is one of them.[25]

And the way in which nature unfolds is frequently referred to as "the natural (literally, 'heavenly') *tao (t'ien chih tao)*" or simply "the *tao*":

> The natural *tao* diminishes that which has superfluity
> And subsidizes that which has deficiency,
> But the *tao* of the human being is certainly not the same—
> It diminishes the stores of those who suffer insufficiency
> In order to present them to those who have superfluity.
> Who is really able to offer his superfluity to the world?
> Only those who have the *tao*.[77]

This natural *tao* reflects what the *Lao Tzu* perceives to be the order and regularity of natural change: the reversion principle, natural equilibrium, implicit opposites, impartiality, and so on. Now, this regularity is also characteristic of the constant *tao* inasmuch as the natural *tao* is an aspect of it, but it is not characteristic of it inasmuch as the constant *tao* must also account for the human maverick who is very capable of living at variance with the natural *tao*. That is to say, the "constant *tao*" and "natural *tao*" distinction is necessary in order to accommodate human conduct which is inconsistent with the natural *tao* but does not go beyond the parameters of the constant *tao*.

The Taoist takes as his project the emulation of the natural *tao* as a vehicle for achieving identity with the constant *tao:*

> The human being emulates earth;
> Earth emulates heaven;
> Heaven emulates the *tao;*
> And the *tao* emulates that which is natural to it.[25]

Although it is beyond our concerns here to speculate on what it might mean to achieve identity with the constant *tao,* passages in the *Lao Tzu* and *Chuang Tzu* suggest that this involves an awareness of the unity of all existence in which the self/other dichotomy is reconciled. That both texts do describe human consummation as consisting in identity with the constant *tao* is clear:

> Therefore the sage embraces the One to become the model of the world.
> [*Lao Tzu* 22]

Do you think blindness and deafness are limited to just the physical body? One's understanding can also suffer from them. . . . This person and this kind of inner potency will extend things in all directions to make one. [*Chuang Tzu* 2/1/32]

Because of this, while we distinguish between a stalk and a bean, a leper and the classic beauty Hsi Shih, the *tao* unifies every weird and wonderful, strange and extraordinary thing as one. The discrimination of a thing is its actualization, and its actualization is its destruction. Where things are free of actualization and destruction, they are reunified as one. Only the enlightened person understands this principle of unifying as one. [*Chuang Tzu* 4/2/35]

This leads us to the third level of *tao*. As an exception to nature one can either strive to be in accord with the environment, achieving realization in a way consonant with the underlying principles of nature, or one can pursue life in a way inconsistent with the natural condition.[21] These are the two possibilities. The *tao* of the consummate human being is a mode of living patterned on and in concert with the natural *tao*. This is the *tao* referred to in the following passage:

Therefore when we neglect the *tao*,
Then *te* arises;
When we neglect *te*,
Then benevolence arises;
When we neglect benevolence,
Then rightness arises;
When we neglect rightness,
Then social norms and rites arise. [38]

Only when the *natural* expression of interpersonal relationships breaks down and unnatural activity becomes commonplace is it necessary to articulate standards for human conduct. In Taoist philosophy, it would appear that the *tao* of the consummating person is an analog to the natural *tao* and the consummating person is an analog to the constant *tao*. In order to put flesh on these abstractions and relate them to the texts, we now return briefly to the *Lao Tzu* and *Chuang Tzu*.

The *Lao Tzu* is primarily a political treatise directed at the ruler already in power. Although it contains wisdom literature of much earlier vintage, it probably congealed and was edited into its present form sometime between 250 and 150 B.C., a century of fierce upheaval. The pressing problem of the age was social and political order, and it is to this problem that the *Lao Tzu* addresses itself.[22]

It is important at this stage to note that the *Lao Tzu* shares with the *Chuang Tzu* the technique of recommending an ineffable alternative to the prevailing situation by discrediting current beliefs. For example, although the *Chuang Tzu* does not attempt to articulate a conception of "true knowledge" *(chen chih)* or "unconditioned freedom" *(hsiao-yao-yu)*, it does hammer away at what is conventionally regarded as knowledge and freedom to discredit popular misconceptions and suggest that alternatives might be considered. Similarly, the *Lao Tzu* does not articulate its conception of "government by nongovernment" in any clear and concise way, but rather seeks to undermine the prevailing authoritarian alternative by demonstrating its own internal contradictions. At this level the *Lao Tzu* is interested in convincing the ruler in power that policies which are aggressive, authoritarian, rigid, and violent will not succeed in achieving the goal they have set for themselves—namely, political control. Hence the *Lao Tzu* takes as its tasks first to convince the ruler that the present form of government is inadequate to effect political control and then, second, to suggest an alternative to political control—namely, natural order. And to achieve a state of natural order the ruler is to emulate the natural *tao*.

The project of human consummation as conceived by the Taoists is for people to emulate the natural *tao* as a means of achieving integration and ultimate identity with the constant *tao*. This characterization is borne out in the language of the *Lao Tzu*, which draws a correlation between the natural *tao* and the *tao* of the consummate person (that is, the means) and between the constant *tao* and the ruler as consummate person (that is, the achievement). The following characteristics are shared analogously by both the natural *tao* and the *tao* of the ruler and by both the constant *tao* and the ruler as a consummate person:

1. "Nonaction" *(wu-wei)*
    Tao: The *tao* is constantly nonactive
        And yet there is nothing it does not do. [37]

    Ruler: In acting according to "nonaction,"
        There is nothing which is not properly administered. [3]

        He attains a state of "nonactivity,"
        And yet there is nothing he does not do. [48]

2.   "Seldom issuing commands" *(hsi-yen)*
    Tao: Seldom issuing commands is in accordance with the natural.
        Hence a whirlwind does not last for the duration of a morning.
        And torrential rains do not persist for the duration of a day.

. . . If heaven and earth are unable to express themselves
for long periods of time,
How much less is the human being able! [23]

Ruler: The most excellent ruler—the people do not know that he
exists; . . .
Relaxed, he prizes his words. [17]

3.   "A state of vacuity and tranquillity" *(ch'ung/hsü-ching)*
Tao: How is the sphere of heaven and earth unlike a bellows?
It is empty but inexaustible;
Once aroused more and more is emitted.
It is better to preserve vacuity
Than talk a lot and accelerate the end. [5]

Ruler: Attain the highest level of vacuity
And preserve the profoundest depths of tranquillity. [16]

4.   "Soft and weak" *(jou-jo)*
Tao: Reversal is the movement of the *tao;*
Weakness is the function of the *tao.* [40]

Ruler: The weak vanquishes the strong
And the soft vanquishes the hard—
There is no one in the world who does not understand this
principle
And yet none are able to put it into practice. [78]

5.   "Not contending" *(pu-cheng)*
Tao: The *tao* of heaven:
It does not contend, yet it is adept at vanquishing. [40]

Ruler: Those adept at vanquishing their opponents
Do not join the fray; . . .
This is called the potency of not contending; [68]

6.   "Dwelling below/last" *(ch'u-hsia/hou)*
Tao: The highest adeptness is like water, . . .
It dwells in places which all men disdain,
And because of this, it is closest to the *tao.* [8]

Ruler: Therefore the sage places himself last and yet he is made
first. [7]

7.   "natural genuineness"
Tao: The *tao* is a constant nameless genuineness *(p'u).* [32]

Ruler: As the valley of the world,
        His constant *te* is sufficient
        And he returns to a state of genuineness like unworked
        wood. [28]

8. "Not appropriating" *(pu-yu)*
    Tao: Therefore the *tao* engenders them. . . .
          It engenders things, but does not appropriate them;
          It does things to assist them, but does not claim that they
          depend on it;
          It nourishes things, but does not attempt to control them.
          [51]

Ruler: The sage permits the myriad things to arise of themselves,
        But does not attempt to be their master;
        He assists the growth of things,
        But does not appropriate them;
        He does things to assist them,
        But does not claim that they depend on him. [2]

The analogy between the natural *tao* and the *tao* of the ruler as consummate human being is reinforced even further by direct parallels in the
text:

Heaven and earth are amoral;
They consider the myriad things to be straw dogs.
The sage is amoral;
He considers the common people to be straw dogs. [5]

The natural *tao* benefits without injuring;
The *tao* of the sage does without contending. [81]

These characteristics which are attributed to both the natural *tao* in its
relationship to the phenomenal world and the sage-ruler in his relationship to the people are, for the most part, corollary to the notion of *wu-
wei*—that is, they are alternative ways of saying "pursue only natural
activity." Just as the natural *tao* does not impose constraints on the myriad phenomena, the sage too refrains from inhibiting the natural development of his people by subjecting them to imposed social and political
regulation. *Wu-wei* is the main precept behind the *Lao Tzu*'s conception
of government as a peculiarly Taoistic anarchism: the minimum amount
of external interference projected onto the individual from those in power combined with an environment most conducive to the individual's
quest for personal fulfillment. As in Confucian political theory, the ruler
and his position in society are taken as natural conditions. While he func-

tions to facilitate the orderly operation necessary to sustain social living, he is authoritative rather than authoritarian in his relationship to the people. His position in the state is best seen as an analog to the role of the father in the family. In realizing himself in his natural role as ruler he creates a situation fertile for the realization of his subordinates. The circumstances and shape of this Taoist ideal are delineated in *Lao Tzu* 3, perhaps the most misunderstood chapter in the text:

> By not exalting the superior man
> One can prevent the people from contending one with another;
> By not considering precious those things difficult to come by
> One can prevent the people from becoming thieves;
> By not displaying that which can be coveted
> One can prevent the peoples' hearts from becoming agitated.
> Therefore, under the proper administration of the sage:
> He empties their minds and fills their bellies,
> He weakens their sense of purpose and strengthens their bones;
> He constantly ensures that the people are without knowledge and without
>   desires,
> And prevents the clever from daring to initiate activity.
> In acting according to "nonaction,"
> There is nothing which is not properly administered.

Some scholars have used this chapter to project an almost Legalist mentality onto the Taoist ruler and to read a strong sense of purpose into Taoist political theory.[23] It can perhaps be better understood as a parody on autocratic rule. Under the administration of the Taoist sage-ruler, by rejecting unnatural *yu-wei* activity (that is, by not subscribing to artificially and arbitrarily determined values, not exalting one human quality over another, and not attaching importance to material acquisitions), the sage-ruler ensures the physical well-being of his subjects (strong bones and full stomachs) and further provides an environment in which they can develop naturally without constraint or distraction (he empties the peoples' minds, weakens their sense of purpose, and constantly ensures that they are without knowledge and without desires). In the context of Taoist philosophy, to interpret "emptying the peoples' minds," "weakening their sense of purpose," and "ensuring that the people are without knowledge" as a stupefying policy of political oppression is to ignore the whole thrust of Taoist thought as the emulation of the natural *tao*. It must be remembered that the Taoist ideal is the state of the uncontaminated infant (chap. 55) and the unhewn block of wood (chap. 15, 19, 28, 32, 37, 57). The state of pristine naturalness is regarded as the highest level of potency and the exemplar of virtue *(te)*. The principal idea presented in chapter 3 is that the sage-ruler, by adhering to a policy of *wu-*

wei, creates a situation in which the people are free to express their own untrammeled potentiality and to develop naturally and fully without suffering the contaminations of externally imposed "purposes." Perhaps the clearest statement of the sage-ruler's attitude is in chapter 57:

> I remain nonactive
> And the people are transformed of their own accord;
> I cherish tranquillity
> And the people are rectified of their own accord;
> I have no involvement
> And the people are prosperous of their own accord;
> I am without desires
> And the people return to their natural genuineness of their own accord.[24]

With this sketch of the *Lao Tzu*'s concept of *wu-wei* in hand, we now turn our attention to the *Chuang Tzu.* The difference between the interpretation of *wu-wei* in the *Lao Tzu* and that of the *Chuang Tzu* is one of emphasis rather than substance.[25] As a text the *Chuang Tzu* is for the most part addressed to the project of individual enlightenment rather than the social and political consequences of this higher state of mind. While the *Chuang Tzu* does use *wu-wei* to characterize the *tao,*[26] and further regards it as an apt description of cosmic change,[27] when *wu-wei* is extended to the human condition the *Chuang Tzu* stresses the state of the individual mind rather than the sociopolitical ramifications of adopting a *wu-wei* attitude. The *Chuang Tzu* uses *wu-wei* to characterize the sublime level of mind attained once unnatural obsessions and commitments have been set aside through a process variously referred to as "I have left my ego-self behind" *(wu sang wo)* (3/2/3) and "sitting and forgetting" *(tso wang)* (19/6/92). When one has extricated oneself from the bondage of ego-self and its attendant attachments, one is free to find communion with the cosmic whole: "When these four sets of six distractions are not tossed about in the breast, you will be orderly. To be orderly is to be still; to be still is to be perspicacious; to be perspicacious is to be vacuous. And when one is vacuous, you do nothing and yet all is done."[28]

Wu-wei is frequently associated with the "spiritual rambling" quality of the enlightened person who has overcome the distorting influence of ego-self and is able to experience the totality of things (18/6/70):

> They are going to be friends with the fashioner of things and ramble in the organismic totality of the cosmos. . . . Again, how can such as these pay any mind as to which comes first in the succession of life and death? They lodge in different things yet dwell in the same entity. Forgetting their liver and gall and dismissing their ears and eyes, they continually repeat the cycle of beginning and end so that they do not know where the starting point is.

They soar, unconstrained, beyond the mundane world and wander freely in
the activity of nonaction.[29]

Without going into a lengthy discussion of this enlightened person in
the *Chuang Tzu,* we can list his most salient features. First, his identity
with the constant *tao* enables him to realize the unity of existence and a
state of unconditioned freedom. Second is his reconciliation of opposites: a transcending of the self/other distinction and all of the desires,
attachments, and dichotomous values created by the notion of a discrete
self (this/that, good/bad, right/wrong, life/death, and so on). Third is
his indifference to worldly conditions reflective of an understanding of
the arbitrary nature of value judgments. This characteristic, often misin-
terpreted as quietism or resignation, should perhaps be understood as
tolerance and catholicism that does not preclude "active" (*wei wu-wei*)
participation and interaction in the world. Fourth, the enlightened person is characterized by efficacy-in-action in virtually *any* capacity from
high minister (Sun-shu Ao) to butcher (Cook Ting), from sage-ruler (31/
12/50) to brigand (Robber Chih), from military leader (15/6/11) to muti-
lated criminal. The repeated illustration of this efficacy in menial occupation reflects the absence of conventional value commitments. Fifth,
although incapable of prescribing values for others, he is identified by
others as a leader by virtue of his receptivity and natural ability in whatever he does (as was Ai T'ai-t'o). And sixth, he lives out his natural span
—not because of an attachment to life but because of a *freedom* from
any attachments which are themselves seen as the primary cause of pre-
mature death.

The faintness of this descriptive outline can be attributed to the fact
that the consummate person is really a consummating person engaged in
the process of self-transcendence and as such is defining rather than
defined, determining rather than determined. Even so, the profile which
emerges from this characterization is not inconsistent with that of the
sage-ruler of the *Lao-Tzu*—a consummate person whose catholicism, tolerance, and ability enable him to respond appropriately and efficaciously
to any set of circumstances.

In analyses of *Chuang Tzu,* attention is usually directed to the enlightenment experience in which the consummate person achieves his identity
with all things, and this is not wrong. But this achievement of oneness
with the constant *tao* should not obfuscate the real nature of his particularity and the ontological reality of his unique activity in the phenomenal
world. The *Chuang Tzu* warns against this kind of misplaced emphasis
(31/12/68):

Confucius said: "He is one of those who relies on cultivating the technique
of Mr. Hun-tun. He only knows the one without knowing plurality. He con-

centrates on the proper ordering of his mind without ordering his environment. How startled are you going to be when you encounter someone who is
perspicacious and pure to the point of simplicity, who is inactive and returns
to pristine naturalness, who realizes his original nature and embraces his
spirit, and in attaining this level rambles about in the mundane world. As for
the techniques of Mr. Hun-tun, how are the likes of you and me supposed to
understand them!''

Although the emphasis of the *Chuang Tzu* in discussing *wu-wei* is on
the individual mental and spiritual experience, it also gives this concept a
political dimension. A coextensive relationship between the political application of *wu-wei* which we found typical of *Lao Tzu* and the enlightened psychological condition found in what A. C. Graham isolates as
the Primitivist portions of the *Chuang Tzu*[30] can be clearly demonstrated
in the following passage (25/11/1):

> I have heard of leaving the world free and open, but I have not heard of
> ordering it. He concentrates the attention of the empire because he is afraid
> of polluting its original nature; he restricts the attention because he is afraid
> of it losing its virtue *(te)*. If the world does not pollute its original nature or
> lose its virtue where is there any need for governing it? . . . Thus if the supe-
> rior man has no choice but to manage the world, it is best for him to follow a
> policy of nonaction. Once there is nonaction, nature and destiny will find
> stability. Therefore, where a person values his own person more than gov-
> erning the world, he can be given the world. Thus if the superior person is
> able to avoid injuring his vital organs and does not agitate the sharpness of
> his senses, he can be as still as a corpse while having the presence of a dra-
> gon, he can be deep and silent while having the impact of thunder. His spirit
> moving, it follows the lead of heaven. Unhurried and composed in nonac-
> tion, the myriad things are motes of dust in the sunlight. His reaction will
> be: "Why do I have to *govern* the world?"

Since Taoistic anarchism is the ideal form of government, if the enlightened mind of the consummate person has the weight and responsibility
of political administration thrust upon it, *wu-wei* is the only policy which
will prevent personal distortion while protecting the natural and social
environments. Again, as in the *Lao Tzu,* frequent reference is made to
wu-wei as a correlative principle between the operations of the cosmos
and the proper attitude of mankind. It applies to a particular person (46/
18/11):

> I regard nonaction as real happiness, but ordinary people consider it very
> unpleasant indeed. Thus it is said: The ultimate in happiness is to be without
> happiness; the ultimate in reputation is to be without reputation. In the final
> analysis, what is right and wrong in the world cannot be ascertained. Even
> though this is so, a policy of nonaction can settle the problem of what is
> right and wrong. The ultimate in happiness can sustain one's person, and

only in nonaction does it exist. Suppose we try and discuss this. The heavens must be nonactive in order to be clear; the earth must be nonactive in order to be stable. When these two states of nonaction are complementary, the myriad things are all nurtured. Nebulous and hazy, we do not know from whence they come. Hazy and nebulous, their source has no form. The myriad things in their abundance are all produced from nonaction. Thus it is said: The heavens and earth are nonactive and yet all is accomplished. What man understands the mystery of nonaction?

But *wu-wei* also applies in a sociopolitical context (72/25/62):

The four seasons have different weather, but because heaven shows no preference, the yearly cycle reaches its conclusion. The five offices of the state have different duties, but because the ruler shows no partiality, the country is properly ordered. With respect to civil and military matters, because the man of consequence shows no preference, his virtue is whole. The myriad things have different principles, but because the *tao* shows no partiality, it is without name. Because it is without name, it is nonactive. It is nonactive and yet all is done.

Perhaps the most striking indication of the ground shared between the *Lao Tzu* and *Chuang Tzu* in the basic interpretation of *wu-wei* is the fact that three of the extended passages in the *Chuang Tzu* which discuss *wu-wei* are attributed to Lao Tan (including the "The World" *(T'ien-hsia)* chapter's description of Lao Tzu's ideas)[31] while no less than five others contain either direct parallels with the *Lao Tzu* or allusions to it.[32]

In summarizing the concept of *wu-wei* propounded in the *Lao Tzu* and *Chuang Tzu,* several points should be noted. First, *wu-wei* is the application of "do nothing and everything will be done"—the basic function of the natural *tao*—to the person and society. That is to say, in a political context *wu-wei* does not go beyond total devotion to the natural condition. Second, in the philosophical system described in these two texts the accent is very heavily upon personal growth and natural development. It contains a radical notion of self-cultivation which, when taken to its logical political conclusions, proposes an anarchism, a government by nongovernment. Since the notion of person operative in these texts is fundamentally organismic, the ultimate consequence of personal realization is an empire well ordered of its own accord. For this reason, political administration is very much a secondary consideration.[33] As an anarchistic political theory, the Taoist concept of *wu-wei* cannot be supported by any elaborate apparatus for practical implementation. This means that *wu-wei* as a principle of political action stands the danger of being dismissed as an unrealistic notion of "government by the rejection of government"—at best attractive in theory but unfeasible in application.[34]

WU-WEI IN PRE-CH'IN LEGALIST TEXTS

The chronological and doctrinal relationship between the Taoist and Legalist traditions is a subject which goes beyond the bounds of this study. Even so, an analysis of *wu-wei* in the Legalist texts stimulates a line of reasoning which, when followed to its logical conclusions, permits a certain amount of speculation as to the evolution of this concept within the borders of the Legalist tradition itself.

Wu-wei does not occur in *The Book of Lord Shang* at all.[35] It does occur as a special term some nine times in the *Kuan Tzu*,[36] but of these nine occurrences only the six in the "The Art of the Mind: Part I" *(Hsin-shu shang)* chapter have any relevance to the Legalist interpretation of *wu-wei*. In this chapter of the *Kuan Tzu,* we find a brief statement of the basic principles around which Legalist political doctrine is woven. But because the political implications of these principles are not elaborated upon, their relationship to Legalist political philosophy is not immediately apparent. There is, for example, a seemingly mixed School of Names and Legalist discussion of "name and form" *(hsing-ming)* (2:65-8):

> "A thing has a certain form and a form has a certain name." This means that the name cannot go beyond the reality and vice versa. Suppose we treat a given form as a form, find a name based on this form, inspect language, and regulate names. . . . The way of nonaction is according with what things are. According with what things are prevents any addition or diminution, and it assigns name according to the form. This is the technique of according with what things are.

When this passage is compared with a *Han Fei Tzu* elaboration on the same theme, however, the political application of this "name and form" abstraction as "accountability" becomes very explicit (30:13):

> In the Way of using oneness, the most important thing is name. Where names are correct, things can be pinned down; where they are out of kilter, things are unstable. Therefore the sage finds tranquillity by grasping oneness. He makes the ministers set their own definitions in their claims and fix their own limits in affairs. Because he does not show his colors, his subordinates are simple and forthright. Responding to what they do, he appoints them and causes them to serve him of their own accord. Responding to what they do, he makes dispensations to them and makes them promote themselves. He rectifies laws to deal with them and makes them all define themselves. Those in high offices are promoted on the basis of name; when he is unsure about the name, he returns to check the performance. He matches performance against name and uses the results. When name and performance can really be trusted, subordinates then show their real selves.

Perhaps "The Art of the Mind: Part I" chapter of the *Kuan Tzu* comes closest to drawing the political implications of its theory in the analogy between the human body and the political state (2:63-13):

> The ears and eyes are the organs of sight and hearing. Where the heart has no part in the processes of seeing and hearing, these organs will be able to carry out their rightful duties. When the heart has desires, however, things pass in front of it without being seen and sounds occur without being heard. Thus it is said: "Where superiors depart from the Way, subordinates will not fulfill their affairs." Therefore the working of the heart lies in controlling the sense orifices while remaining nonactive.[37]

In this passage, *hsin* (translated "heart" but embracing the notion of "mind" as well) is analogous to the ruler and the sense organs correspond to ministers with their specific functions. Only the heart is *wu-wei* while the sense organs go about their individual tasks. The idea that *wu-wei* is the appropriate posture for the ruler whereas activity is appropriate to his subordinates—that is, a clear distinction between the "Way of the ruler" *(chu tao)* and the "Way of the minister" *(ch'en tao)*—is very much a characteristic of the Legalist interpretation of *wu-wei*.[38]

While in the *Kuan Tzu* there is only a theoretical suggestion of the Legalist interpretation of *wu-wei,* the *Han Fei Tzu* inflates this theory into a practical principle of political control. This is not to say that the *Han Fei Tzu*'s elaboration on *wu-wei* can be traced to the *Kuan Tzu.* There are several reasons which suggest that in fact the *Han Fei Tzu* owes the initial Legalist interpretation of *wu-wei* to an anterior branch of Legalist theory which developed in the Cheng area and can probably be associated with Shen Pu-hai. Apart from the evidence for such a conclusion put forward by Creel, I would add some observations based on an examination of the *Han Fei Tzu.* First, as Creel notes, there is a passage in the *Han Fei Tzu* (238:10) which attributes a Legalist interpretation of *wu-wei* directly to Shen Pu-hai:[39]

> Shen Tzu said: "Where the perspicacity of the ruler is apparent, people will take precautions against it. Where his lack of it is apparent, people will mislead him. Where his intelligence is apparent, people will mislead him. Where his lack of it is apparent, people will hide things from him. Where his desires are apparent, people will dangle bait in front of him. Where his lack of them is apparent, people will manage him. Therefore it is said: 'I have no basis on which to know them. Only in doing nothing can I keep an eye on them.' "
>
> Another version has it that Shen Tzu said: "Be prudent in what you say because others will know you. Be prudent in what you do because others will follow you. If it is apparent that you are informed, others will hide things from you. If your ignorance is apparent, others will size you up. If you are informed, others will keep things from you, whereas if you are ignorant they

will put things over on you. Therefore it is said: 'Only in doing nothing can I keep an eye on them.' "

There is a significant association between the concepts of *wu-wei* and what might be called "showing nothing" *(wu-hsien)*. Two of the other seven *Han Fei Tzu* passages which contain *wu-wei* occur with this association in quotations attributed to a man known obliquely as "an elder of Cheng" (239:6): "An elder of Cheng has a saying which states: 'Vacuous, still, and nonactive, he shows nothing.' " And elsewhere (257:6): "An elder of Cheng has a saying: 'Embody the *tao*, be nonactive, and show nothing.' " There is one more related passage which is attributed to this "elder of Cheng" (239:1): "An elder of Cheng, on hearing this, said: 'T'ien Tzu-fang was aware that the ruler should make himself a hiding place, but he did not grasp how he should go about making it. Vacuity and not showing anything are his hiding place.' "

In terms of abstracting an interpretation of *wu-wei* from the *Han Fei Tzu*, the two most important chapters are without question "The Way of the Ruler" *(Chu-tao)* and "Wielding Authority" *(Yang-ch'üan)*. In these two chapters the wording of the passages which contain the expression *wu-wei* is so similar to the elder of Cheng's quotations cited here that Liang Ch'i-hsiung considers these portions of the "Way of the Ruler" and "Wielding Authority" chapters to be an explanation of the elder of Cheng's notion of "vacuity and showing nothing."[40] Compare the following excerpts from these two chapters with the elder of Cheng passages cited above:

18:12 (from "The Way of the Ruler"): Being vacuous, still, and free of commitments, from your dark corner observe the faults of others.

30:3 (from "Wielding Authority"): Do not desire to show your power—remain simple and nonactive.

32:10 (from "Wielding Authority"): Vacuity, stillness, and nonaction—this is the disposition of the Way.

Of the nine *Han Fei Tzu* passages which include a Legalist interpretation of *wu-wei*, two are attributed directly to Shen Pu-hai, two are contained in passages attributed directly to the elder of Cheng, and the five remaining occurrences appear in what might be elaborations on the elder of Cheng's initial hypothesis. Thus a question arises—what is the real identity of this man called "the elder of Cheng"? Like Shen Pu-hai, he draws an association between the notions of *wu-wei* and "showing nothing" *(wu-hsien)*. According to Ch'ien Mu's analysis of the existing references to the elder of Cheng, he was not earlier than T'ien Tzu-fang, counselor to Lord Wen of Wei (r. 424–387 B.C.) and was not later than

King Hsüan of Ch'i (r. 319–301 B.C.).[41] The only reference to the elder of Cheng's writings is in the "Record of Literary Works" *(Yi-wen chih)* of the *History of the Han (Han-shu)* under the Taoist classification. If the character *cheng* in the elder of Cheng does in fact refer to the state of Cheng which was annexed by Han in 375 B.C., the elder of Cheng was a native of the same state as Shen Pu-hai, lived at approximately the same time as Shen Pu-hai (d. 337 B.C.), and propounded a doctrine of *wu-wei* which appears to be very similar if not identical with that of Shen Pu-hai.[42] This does not mean that the elder of Cheng is necessarily an alternative designation for Shen Pu-hai,[43] although it is a possibility. And even if the elder of Cheng and Shen Pu-hai are not one and the same person, there would seem to be enough information to trace the Legalist interpretation of *wu-wei* to the Cheng/Han region during the first half of the fourth century B.C.

Having suggested a possible source for this Legalist interpretation of *wu-wei,* I turn now to the actual meaning of this term. Because the concept of *wu-wei* is one thread in the austere fabric of Legalist political theory, we begin with a brief characterization of the Legalist vision of ideal government. Since the *Han Fei Tzu* provides a consistent and relatively comprehensive exposition of Legalist political theory, we shall rely on it as our primary source.

Legalist political philosophy might be described as "government of the ruler, by the ruler, and for the ruler." In other words, the end served by this kind of government is first and foremost the interests of the ruler. These interests involve total control over the lives and actions of his subjects to serve the ends of absolute power, stability, personal safety, military strength, wealth and luxury, and freedom to enjoy the privileges due his position. While such interests may seem rather mundane, one must bear in mind the historical context and the domestic and international strife which gave rise to this form of totalitarianism.

The Legalist theorists conceived of an administration structured on self-regulating "systems" as the most effective means of achieving the purposes of the ruler. The first of these systems is the codification of an objective and universally applicable body of laws. From the ruler's perspective, the elimination of the human element and the reduction of litigation to a machinelike process guarantees order within his borders. Once established and set in motion, the laws arrest social irregularity and function automatically to ensure swift and severe punishment for anyone bold enough to challenge the system.

Another important system is the establishment of a bureaucratic organization kept in check by a political application of the "name and form" theory: "accountability" *(hsing-ming).* The bureaucracy, like the society at large, is regulated by being held constantly and unconditionally responsible for its conduct. The theory behind accountability is straight-forward. The duties and obligations of each office are clearly defined (hence the "name" *ming*). At given intervals, the performance (hence the "form" *hsing*) of officeholders is compared with their prescribed duties. Where performance is congruent with the objective definition of the office, rewards and promotions are both generous and constant; where discrepancies occur, however, the axe falls both swiftly and decisively. The important point is that the officeholder, before embarking on any course of action, is wholly aware of the consequence of that action.

The same notion of accountability is applied in a less formal way to those who approach the throne with sundry propositions. When such men are engaged, a careful record is made of their claims; if a gap is found between claim and services rendered, again the axe falls with speed and decision.

The ruler, having structured the empire's administration on the basis of these systems, controls the state rather than administers it. That is, the ruler whose absolute authority is guaranteed by the very operation of these systems simply reclines in confidence, overseeing the routine and efficient operation of his government machinery. His *shih*—the political advantage due him by virtue of his position—coupled with strict adherence to the *shu*—the prescribed techniques of rulership—are sufficient to ensure his continuing control.

Of these techniques of rulership, perhaps the foremost is *wu-wei* and its corollary implications. In the conception of the state outlined above, the positions and occupations of ruler and minister are clearly defined. The ministers are integral, functioning, and active components in the bureaucratic system; the ruler is not. Rather, he is the human embodiment of the authority of the governmental machinery as a whole. As such, any activity on his part violently disrupts the structure of the individual systems. Any intervention on his part with respect to law, for example, introduces an arbitrary element into an otherwise automatically functioning system, seriously threatening if not undermining public conviction in the absoluteness of law. Any personal intervention with respect to the bureaucracy, moreover, disturbs the faith of officialdom in the certainty of wealth and promotion through fulfillment of responsibility and devotion to duty.

Just as in the Taoist and Confucian interpretations of *wu-wei,* in the *Han Fei Tzu* there is an attempt to correlate the operations of the cosmos and the proper functioning of the political state. Characteristics attributed to the metaphysical *tao* are projected onto the ideal ruler (31:13):

> Therefore it is said: The *tao* is not the same as the myriad things, virtue *(te)* is not the same as the *yin* and *yang,* a pair of scales is not the same as heavi-

ness and lightness, the marking line is not the same as the variations it measures, the *ho* flute [a reed instrument unaffected by humidity] is not the same as wetness and dryness, and a ruler is not the same as his various ministers. All six of these come out of the *tao*, but because the *tao* is not a plurality, it is called the One. Therefore the perspicacious ruler values the disposition of the solitary *tao*. The ruler and his ministers do not have the same *tao*. The subordinates define their proposals and the ruler takes a firm hold on these definitions. The ministers then deliver their performance, and where definition and performance are congruent there is harmony between ruler and subordinate.

By maintaining his attitude of *wu-wei,* the ruler cannot be deceived by clever people who are able to anticipate his reactions. Rather than trying to second-guess the ruler, these people look to the laws and to their responsibilities of office as their standards of conduct. Further, the ruler can avoid censure for any failures while basking in the praise of his subordinates for any successes. He can avoid personal competition with his subjects who, collectively, surpass him in virtually all respects. This means that even a ruler of very common parts—not an altogether uncommon phenomenon—can maintain political control. In the *Han Fei Tzu* passages which discuss the political technique of *wu-wei,* there are a variety of corollary techniques which are really implications of the *wu-wei* attitude. There is, for example, "showing nothing" *(wu-hsien)*—not demonstrating one's likes and dislikes, not proffering an opinion on any given subject, not revealing ambitions or personal desires. In maintaining this posture, the ruler shields the contours of his character and intellect from public sight. There is also personal solitude and secrecy, keeping one's own counsel and the encouragement of a personal mystique by a lack of direct contact. By remaining beyond the range of public scrutiny, the ruler becomes an ideal invested with a superlative degree of all things worthwhile. Because his subordinates have no knowledge of his actual limitations, they attribute powers to him far beyond his real capacities. The *Han Fei Tzu* describes this ruler in the following terms (32:10):

> Now, the Way of listening is to match the performance against the proposal. Therefore examine proposals carefully in fixing offices and clarify duties in making distinctions. The Way of listening is to say to yourself: Assume the characteristics of drunkenness. Lips! Teeth! I am not the first to move! Teeth! Lips! Be ever more inscrutable! I will take advantage of other people exposing themselves to understand them. Different opinions converge on the ruler at the hub, but do not play any part. Vacuity, stillness, and nonaction—this is the shape of affairs. Examine subordinates by comparing what has come to light and scrutinize them by bringing these into the hub. Where

the trunk and roots do not change, things will not go astray. In motion, in stillness, make all changes through nonaction. When you like subordinates, affairs will proliferate; when you dislike them, you will give rise to resentment. Therefore abandon likes and dislikes, and make your heart vacuous in order to become the lodging place of the Way. The ruler does not join together with his subjects in administering affairs, and the people respect him. He does not discuss things with them, and makes them carry them out by themselves. He bolts his chamber door firmly and from his room watches the courtyard. The standards already being set in place, everyone takes up his proper role.

As this passage makes clear, in Legalist political theory *wu-wei* and the related techniques of rulership were intended to prevent any insight into the ruler's personality which might interfere with the operations of the governmental machinery.

WU-WEI IN *THE ART OF RULERSHIP*

The disparate interpretations of *wu-wei* in the Confucian, Taoist, and Legalist traditions have now been outlined. While the same locution is used in each of these traditions to represent an ideal posture for the ruler, the interpretations, seen in the context of their respective systems, are fundamentally at variance. In the Taoist political theory, for example, *wu-wei* is the leading principle in a philosophical anarchism. In Legalist theory, on the other hand, it is taken to the opposite extreme as a technique used to buttress a highly structured totalitarianism.

The concept of *wu-wei* put forward in *The Art of Rulership* is basically an unlikely synthesis of the Confucian, Taoist, and Legalist traditions. It is unlikely because, given the obvious disparity in their interpretations of *wu-wei,* an internally consistent and practicable compromise is really quite hard to envision. And yet in the discussion of *wu-wei* so prominent in this treatise we can see the true shape of Han eclecticism.

Wu-wei is one of the main themes in *The Art of Rulership*—no less than half the text is devoted to it and its ancillary concepts. Because the interpretation of *wu-wei* is constructed upon a basically Legalist framework using Legalist terminology and metaphor, perhaps the most effective method of analyzing this Confucian-Taoist-Legalist synthesis is first to identify the elements in *The Art of Rulership's* representation of *wu-wei* that deviate from Legalist theory. The next step is then to examine these elements one by one to determine their sources and the extent of their influence on the political theory presented in this treatise.

Rejection of the ruler's interests in favor of the general welfare of the people. The first characteristic of Legalist political thought is that the

entire governmental apparatus is constructed to serve the interests of the
ruler—interests regarded as being fundamentally at odds with those of
his ministers (*Han Fei Tzu* 179:12): "Because the interests of the ruler
and those of the minister are different, no minister is loyal, and where
the minister's interests are served, the ruler's are subverted." Thus the
ruler uses rewards and punishments to encourage and coerce his subordinates away from private interests and toward a contribution to the state.
In *The Art of Rulership,* however, this preoccupation with the interests
of the sovereign is superseded by a concern for the general welfare of the
people—a theme which pervades the entire chapter (9/7a): "Putting the
whole world under his bounty instead of bringing his own intelligence
into play, the ruler follows what the people find beneficial. Now by lifting his heel, he is able to benefit the empire. Hence he takes his place
above and yet they do not find him heavy; he dwells in front of them and
yet they do not find him an obstacle; though they raise him up, they do
not feel he is too high; though they support him, they do not grow tired
of it."[44]

The Art of Rulership does not accept the basic antagonism between the
benefit of the people and the interests of the ruler. Rather, consistent
with the notion that personal, social, and political fulfillment are coextensive, it holds that while the people are seeking their own benefit and
the ruler is seeking political stability, the means of achieving these ends
are one and the same. This treatise not only rejects the notion that conflict exists between private and public interests; it insists that in benefiting the people, the ruler benefits himself (9/17a): "If the ruler prevents
that which the people consider injurious while encouraging that which
they consider beneficial, his authority will prevail like the opening of a
dike or the breaking of a dam. Hence if one goes downstream with the
current, he will easily get to his destination; if one gallops along with the
wind at his back, he will easily cover a great distance." This assertion
that the interests of the people and the ruler in fact coincide is also the
basis for the Confucian conviction that ultimately the political stability
of the ruler is dependent upon the continuing goodwill of the people.[45]
Where the ruler chooses to alienate his people, he is in fact undermining
his own political well-being. In *The Art of Rulership,* then, the character-
istically Legalist tension between ruler and minister is supplanted by an
attitude of cooperation and the Legalist interest in exploiting the people
is superseded by the principle of benefiting the people *(li min).*

*Rejection of the will of the ruler as the basis of law in favor of the will
of the people.* According to Legalist political theory, the most efficient
means of serving the interests of the ruler is to construct a government
apparatus operating on the basis of self-regulating systems. The two

most important systems are a code of objective and universally applicable laws and a bureaucratic organization governed by objective standards embodied in the application of accountability *(hsing-ming)*. The political theory advanced in *The Art of Rulership* takes this notion of systems from the Legalists and advocates both a code of universal laws and a bureaucratic administration controlled by this principle of accountability. Given the smooth functioning of the law and the bureaucracy, the ruler simply reclines in a state of *wu-wei* as the human embodiment of the authority in which these systems are grounded. With respect to terminology and presentation, the concept of laws may appear to have been inherited wholesale from the Legalist tradition but, in fact, there are several notable characteristics which clearly distinguish it from its Legalist counterpart. In the first place, the laws originate in what is appropriate and equitable to the people rather than in the arbitrary will of the ruler and, as such, are in general sympathy with the human condition. Moreover, the will of the ruler is itself subject to the universally applicable laws and social norms. Further, the laws are seen as having their basis in the moral achievement of the people. And finally, the guarantee of absolute equality before the law for all people regardless of status is present in the Legalist doctrine but only as an unintentional by-product of absolute control. In *The Art of Rulership*'s interpretation of law, the concept of equality attracts considerably more emphasis.

Replacement of the Legalist dependence upon coercion and constraint with a theory of particular development and collective contribution. In the following passage from *The Art of Rulership* (9/15b–16a), the principle of accountability as a basis for bureaucratic organization is put forward in a manner very reminiscent of the *Han Fei Tzu:*

> The ruler in possession of the Way extinguishes thought and dispenses with intentionality. Waiting in limpidity and vacuity, he uses words that do not boast and takes action that does not rob subordinates of responsibility. He makes demands of fulfillment according to claims made. He lets them get on with their duties without telling them how; he expects them to fulfill their duties without instructing them. He takes "not knowing" as his Way and the question "What am I to do?" as his treasure. Acting in this way, each of the various officials will then have his appointed tasks.[46]

What really distinguishes this passage from the *Han Fei Tzu,* however, is that while in the *Han Fei Tzu* there is a very real preoccupation with ministerial containment and control, here in *The Art of Rulership* the bureaucracy is seen as only one corner of a much larger concept—an acknowledgment of the value of each element in the operation of the organic whole. In Legalist political theory, the raison d'être for a bureaucratic system is efficiency in ruling the state. The ruler, regardless of his personal attributes and quality, is only one man and labors under the obvious restrictions implied by this fact. Aware of the ruler's personal limitations, the Legalist theorists divide administrative duties into practical units and establish a system of control which guarantees the efficient operation of the government apparatus. Legalist doctrine stresses this aspect of the political organization.

In *The Art of Rulership,* there is the same awareness of the obvious personal limitations of the ruler (9/5a–b):

> When one gets hold of this source of the Way, he is never at his wit's end in responding to things, but when he relies on the talents of men, it is difficult to reach the acme of good government.
>
> Even sage-rulers such as T'ang and Wu would be unable to match the Yüeh people in maneuvering a small craft on the rivers and lakes. Even an outstanding minister such as Yi Yin would be unable to match the Hu people in breaking to harness the fine horses of the north. Even men as broad in understanding as Confucius and Mo Tzu would be unable to match the mountain people in foraging about the thicket and scaling perilous slopes.
>
> Viewing it from this perspective, human intelligence is very limited in its capacity to deal with things. If a person, hoping to light up the whole world and see clearly in all directions, relies exclusively on it rather than on the inevitable outcome of practicing the Way, it will not be long before he reaches a dead-end. Thus it is that individual human intelligence is not adequate to the task of bringing proper order to the world.
>
> Chieh's strength was such that he could split a horn, unbend a hook, plait iron, fuse metal, and maneuver a great ox about; in the water he could kill a giant turtle and on land he could capture a bear. Nevertheless, T'ang leading only three hundred war chariots surrounded him at Ming-t'iao and then captured him at Chiao-men.
>
> Viewing it from this perspective, outstanding strength and boldness are not adequate to the task of retaining control of the world. Since human intelligence is not in itself sufficient to effect proper government and boldness is not in itself sufficient to hold sway, it is clear that individual human talents cannot be relied upon. This being so, where a ruler comprehends circumstances even beyond the four seas without ever leaving his ancestral hall, it is because he takes advantage of things to understand things and he takes advantage of man to understand man.

This rejection of reliance upon individual human abilities is qualified by introducing the notions of "utilizing the people" *(yung chung)* and "each element achieving what is appropriate to it" *(ke te ch'i yi).* That is to say, in *The Art of Rulership* reliance upon the bureaucracy to order the state is extended to reliance upon the collective contribution of the society as a whole. Although "utilizing the people" is in essence the gathering and exploitation of broad human talents, it does not denote an active policy of promoting superior men identified by some arbitrary standard to further the interests of the ruler. Rather, people are given the freedom to grow and express their particular nature and make their personal contribution—very reminiscent of the Taoist interpretation of *wu-wei* and its conviction in the differing and yet equal value of all things. In the *Lao Tzu,* the principle that each element is endowed with unique value has its political application in a passage like chapter 27: "Therefore, because the sage is always adept at rescuing people, he is without rejected people; because he is always adept at rescuing things, he is without rejected things." This same principle, couched in *The Art of Rulership* passages such as "everything large or small, long or short, finds its niche" (9/8a), is applied politically in this assertion (9/7b):

> Where the ruler and minister have different Ways, there is proper order, but where they are the same, there is disorder. If each gets what is appropriate to him and dwells in what is right for him, the one above and those below will know how to deal with each other. . . . For this reason, when the various ministers are like spokes converging side by side at the hub, and irrespective of intelligence or moral character, all do their best, then the ruler has the means to hold control over his ministers, the ministers have the means to serve their ruler, and the Way of ordering the state properly is clear.

The concept of utilizing the people recognizes the vital importance of allowing people to construe themselves naturally and spontaneously. Inasmuch as it advocates full use of the spontaneous contribution of each participant, there is much here which points to Taoist anarchism and its denial of the necessity of authoritarian government. This Taoist element in the political system influences the emphasis placed on other components in the overall political theory. First, while a system of fixed and universally applicable laws is certainly advocated, the ideal society is one in which such laws are on the statute books but are unnecessary, where punishments are listed but are not applied, where jails exist but stand empty (9/2a):

> His [Shen Nung's] intimidating bearing was awesome yet not put to the test, punishments were there yet he did not have to invoke them, and his laws were few in number and not overwhelming. Hence his transformation of the people was godlike. In his territory stretching from Chiao-chih in the south to Yu-tu in the north, T'ang-ku in the east and San-wei in the west, there was no one who would not submit to his rule. At this time the laws were liberal, the punishments were tolerant, and the prisons were empty. The world was one in custom and none were of a wicked mind.

Second, rather than simply relying upon universal enforcement of law to maintain order in the society, the ruler transforms the people by a potency reminiscent of the Confucian ruler's virtue *(te),* which he has managed to accumulate in his own person through nonactivity (9/2b): "Punishments and penalties are inadequate to change social custom; executions are inadequate to put an end to wickedness. Only godlike transformation is estimable and only the most essential vapors can do it in this way."

This notion of "godlike transformation" *(shen hua)* is very close to the traditional conception of virtue—a potency which encourages the natural development and proper operation of the empire. Again the Han Confucian principle of "the mutual influence of human being and nature" *(t'ien jen hsiang ying)* according to which the potency of the ruler penetrates and favorably influences the cosmic order is also evident in this treatise. (9/1b):

> In ancient times when Shen Nung governed the empire, his spirit did not gallop out from his breast, his wisdom did not extend beyond the four directions, and he cherished the benevolent and sincere mind. The sweet rains fell at the proper time and the five grains flourished. In spring they would sprout forth, in summer they would grow, in autumn they would be harvested, in winter they would be stored up. With monthly examinations and seasonal evaluations, at the year's end the record of accomplishments would be offered up, and tasting the grain at the proper season, sacrifice would be made in the Ming T'ang.

Third, the Legalist framework of this chapter implies a certain regimentation imposed on the society from above. In fact, in *The Art of Rulership* this regimentation is internalized with the natural and complementary development of individuals being guaranteed by an external and yet ideally noncoercive political order. The political order, like the family order, is a natural condition. It has the broadest possible bounds and arrests unnatural activity in the society. The spirit of this political theory goes beyond Jeffersonian liberalism in which "that government is best which governs least" and arrives at the anarchist position of "that government is best which governs not at all"—expressed metaphorically as "the court which is overgrown with wild grass" (9/6a). What really tips *The Art of Rulership* away from liberalism in the direction of anarchist theory is the firm conviction that the collective development of individuals in society, unhampered by external coercion, will result in a harmonious society characterized by the freedom of self-determination and the equality of all participants making their uniquely valuable contribution.[47]

Redefinition of the roles of ruler and minister as integral and symbiotic elements in the administrative system. In the political doctrine of *The Art of Rulership,* as in Legalist theory, the roles of ruler and minister are clearly differentiated. The position of ruler is likened to the scales and a carpenter's marking line—fixed and immutable, wholly impartial, universally recognized and respected.[48] It is compared to the unmoving upright on a shadoof (an irrigation device)—unmoving itself but absolutely essential to the operation of the government.[49] Perhaps this analogy can be used to demonstrate the divergence between the original Legalist conception of ruler and the much modified version found in this chapter.

In the Legalist concept of *wu-wei,* the ministers are integral, functioning, and active components in the administrative system; the ruler, as the human embodiment of the authority of the system, is himself separate and distinct from it. It is on this basis that the Way of the ruler is *wu-wei* while that of his ministers is active.

In *The Art of Rulership* we find that this ruler/minister distinction reflects the basic sentiments of its political philosophy. The Way of the ruler is "round"; that of his ministers is "square."[50] That is to say, the ruler and the minister both have functions appropriate to their position (9/7a–b):

> The Way of the ruler is said to be round because revolving and turning, it is without a starting point. He transforms and nurtures like a god, is vacuous and vacant, and follows the natural course of things. Always keeping to the rear, he never takes the lead. The Way of the minister is said to be square because he finds out what is appropriate and dwells in what he is best fitted for. It is by taking the lead in carrying out affairs and by clearly keeping to his defined duties that he realizes his accomplishments.
>
> Where the ruler and minister have different Ways, there is proper order; but where they are the same, there is disorder. If each gets what is appropriate to him and dwells in what is right for him, the one above and those below will know how to deal with each other.

The injection of the essentially Taoist combination of "utilizing the people" *(yung chung)* and "each element achieving what is appropriate to it" *(ke te ch'i yi)* alters the original Legalist thrust in this ruler/minister distinction. The Legalist theorists observe that there is an antagonism between ruler and minister and a constant struggle for power.[51] Hence they insist upon a clear delineation of roles and a system to prevent ministerial usurpation of power and privilege beyond their prescribed offices. *The Art of Rulership* theory describes this distinction between ruler and minister in terms of different things being of different yet equal value. Ruler and minister are both *wu-wei* in the sense that they do not do anything beyond their defined roles; yet both have an active function in the sense that they contribute to the organization and operation of the state. Where the Legalist ruler is distinct from the government apparatus, *The*

Art of Rulership ruler as the unmoving upright on the irrigation device is a functioning but stationary part in the machinery. The ruler-dominated relationship is replaced by a theory of reciprocal and mutually dependent function (9/10a–b):

> When there are strong winds, the waves rise, and where there is thick foliage, the birds gather. This is because the *ch'i* of the one thing gives rise to the other. When the minister does not get what he wants from the ruler, the ruler will also be unable to get what he seeks from the minister. Ruler and minister benefit each other only on the basis of reciprocity. Thus the minister barters with his ruler by offering total commitment to the point of laying down his life whereas the ruler trades with his ministers by offering the dispensation of noble ranks. Just as the ruler cannot reward a minister who has rendered no service, a minister cannot die for a ruler to whom he owes no gratitude. When the favors of the ruler do not flow down to the people, for him to expect service out of them is like whipping an unruly horse. It is like hoping for a ripe harvest without rain. It is a demonstrable impossibility.

Encouragement for the ruler to tap the combined faculties of the people in governing the state. In Legalist political theory, several principles are corollary to *wu-wei.* "Showing nothing" *(wu-hsien),* for example, means refraining from demonstrating one's likes and dislikes. There is also personal secrecy and solitude, keeping one's own counsel, and the encouragement of a personal mystique by avoiding direct contact with others. The purpose of "showing nothing" is to prevent knowledge of the ruler's limitations which may encourage irregularities in the operations of government.

These corollary principles are also a prominent feature of *The Art of Rulership.* On the surface they are reminiscent of their Legalist antecedents. The ruler's personal demonstrations of partiality are discouraged because they give rise to disorder and a breakdown of the established systems (9/15a):

> Where pleasure and anger form in the ruler's heart and desires are manifest in his countenance, then officials charged with specific duties abandon what is proper and pander to the desires of the ruler, and those in authority bend the laws and follow the inclinations of the ruler. Rewards do not tally with accomplishments; punishments do not correspond to the crime. Superior and subordinate become estranged and acrimony grows between ruler and minister. When those in charge of government commit errors through pandering to the ruler, there will be no way of taking them to task. If the guilty are not punished, the bureaucracy will seethe in turmoil that even intelligence cannot settle and praise and blame will sprout forth that even perspicacity cannot illumine.

On the other hand, in refraining from interfering in the smooth functioning of the law and the bureaucratic organization, the ruler makes it possible for these systems to operate with a certainty which will inspire keen observance among his subordinates (9/6a):

> Thus it is that under the administration of a perspicacious ruler, where the state carries out punishments the anger of the ruler is not involved in them; where the court bestows rewards, the ruler plays no part in them. Those who are punished feel no ill-will toward the ruler. This is because it is what their crimes deserve. Those who are rewarded feel no gratitude to the ruler. This is because it is the result of their good service. Because the people know that the source of punishment and reward lies in themselves, they try their best to make themselves fit to carry out their occupations and do not feel indebted to the ruler.
> There are no footprints in the court which is overgrown with wild grass; there are no weeds in the fields which have been well cleared. Thus the most excellent ruler is one of whom his subjects know only that he exists.

Because the ruler keeps himself beyond the probing gaze of his subordinates, he is able to retain an aura of loftiness and omnipotence (9/11 a–b): "The ruler, occupying the position he does, is brilliant like the sun and moon. He is that which all in the world strain their eyes to see, prick up their ears to hear, and crane their necks and stand on tiptoe to gaze upon."

It is at this juncture that *The Art of Rulership* diverges from the Legalist tradition in placing a strong emphasis upon the idea that the ruler must be kept informed from below.[52] While he himself remains secluded and distant, his supporting bureaucracy has been structured in such a manner as to give him constant access to a steady flow of information (9/7a):

> Since the ruler dwells deep in seclusion to avoid the heat and damp, and remains behind layer upon layer of doors in order to protect himself against villainy and insurgency, within he knows nothing about the towns and villages and without he knows nothing about the mountains and valleys. Beyond the curtains and hangings, one's eye cannot penetrate further than a few miles and the ear cannot hear beyond a hundred paces. Even so, he is wholly cognizant of all that goes on within the world because the sources that feed him are immense and those who tap him are numerous. Hence, without going beyond his doors, he knows about the world; without peeping out through his window, he comprehends the heavenly Way.

Here we have the overlap between the concept of *wu-wei* and the notion of utilizing the people *(yung chung)*. By assuming an attitude of *wu-wei,* the ruler makes it possible for the individuals in his society to seek their own realization and the development of their own faculties. At the same time, by tapping the concerted faculties of the populace at large to scan the operations of the state and register any irregularities, the ruler is able to remain in a *wu-wei* posture while keeping wholly informed on current developments (9/12a–b):

> The ruler sees with the eyes of the empire, hears with the ears of the empire, deliberates with the intelligence of the empire, and contends with the strength of the empire behind him. His edicts and commands are able to penetrate to the lowest level and the real condition of his subjects can be known by him above. His bureaucracy has open access to the throne, and his various ministers are like spokes converging at the hub. He does not reward on account of pleasure or punish on account of anger. His awesomeness being established will not be put aside, his intelligence shining forth will not be obscured, his laws and edicts being circumspect will not be unduly harsh, his sight and hearing being penetrating will not be beclouded, and what is actually good and bad being set out before him daily, he will not indulge in conjecture.
>
> In his service the better people use their intelligence to the utmost and the others contribute their full strength. The ruler's favor and bounty sheltering the length and breadth of the land are impartial, and the various ministers laboring assiduously are not remiss in their duties. Those within the realm are content to follow their livelihoods; those in distant quarters are won over by his beneficence. This is so because the ruler, understanding the Way of using people, does not rely on his own abilities.

Hence the ruler rejects any reliance upon his own personal abilities in favor of the collective wisdom and strength of his people. In doing so, on the one hand he is personally *wu-wei* while on the other he has access to the multifarious contributions of his people. The main concern here lies not in furthering the interests of the ruler but in urging that where the ruler permits the free development of the people he guarantees the stability of his own position as ruler. Freedom for the people, far from detracting from the ruler's functioning as an effective head of state, conduces to this end.

Reliance upon universal laws and the ruler's godlike power of transformation. In order to guarantee social and political order, *The Art of Rulership* advocates a synthesis between reliance upon universal laws and the ruler's godlike power of transformation. This notion of "godlike transformation" *(shen hua)* is decidedly Taoist in tone. In the Taoist tradition there is frequent reference to the accumulation of one's vital life forces as a means of attaining realization of the *tao*.[53] This concept is also advanced in *The Art of Rulership* (9/1b): "A person's spiritual souls come from the vapors of heaven; his sentient souls come from the vapors of earth. Returning these to their mysterious apartments and causing each to dwell in its proper residence, if one is able to watch over these and not lose them, he achieves communion above with the Great One.

And the essence of the Great One communes with heaven.'' The formal Legalist system of laws and bureaucratic organization in itself is not enough to guarantee social order (9/2b): ''Punishments and penalties are inadequate to change social custom; executions are inadequate to put an end to wickedness. Only godlike transformation is estimable and only the most essential vapors can do it in this way.'' In fact, severity and constraint in government are inimical to the proper functioning of the state (9/2a): ''Now where water is muddy the fishes gasp, where government is cruel the people are disorderly.''

The Art of Rulership (especially 9/1b–2a and 9/2b–4a) expresses a belief in a potency which can influence the social and cosmic orders. It is the transformation of the people through this potency which is considered the ideal form of government (9/4a): ''The highest ruler is godlike in his transformations. Next comes one who makes it impossible for people to do wrong. And next comes one who rewards those of superior qualities and punishes the troublemakers.''

In summary, then, the concept of *wu-wei* in *The Art of Rulership* is constructed around a Legalist framework. From this Legalist tradition it borrows certain supporting features: an objective and universally applicable system of laws; a bureaucratic organization governed by an objective system of accountability; and a *wu-wei* posture for the ruler. As a consequence of this posture the ruler remains in solitude and seclusion, keeps his own counsel, encourages a personal mystique, refrains from overriding objective standards with subjective preferences, and disdains to make a display of personal attributes, opinions, and ambitions. At the same time, *The Art of Rulership* modifies the Legalist interpretation of *wu-wei* in such a manner that the ruler is in fact deprived of coercive authority over others. While the formal aspects of *wu-wei* might appear Legalistic, the degree to which a spirit of Taoist-influenced anarchism has replaced that of Legalist totalitarianism is striking. This spirit is apparent inasmuch as the ruler, while himself remaining *wu-wei,* orchestrates the natural development of individuals and enables them too to assume a *wu-wei* posture. He follows nature in accepting from subordinates those things which are in keeping with their individual aptitudes and are easy for them to achieve. This spirit is again apparent in its attempt to root out all vestiges of unnatural constraint and external compulsion from the traditional Legalist program of government. While retaining the Legalist conception of laws, it removes the element of coercion by grounding these laws in what is congenial to the people. While retaining the Legalist bureaucracy, it removes the element of coercion by encouraging the use of broad human talents in accordance with individual aptitudes. While retaining a seemingly Legalist conception of the ruler, it removes the element of coercion by insisting that his interests coincide with those of his subjects and are best served by devotion to the well-being of his people. While retaining a Legalist conviction in the efficacy of a solid political structure, it removes the element of coercion by insisting that intervention is necessary only when natural order breaks down.

Although the *Lao Tzu* and *Chuang Tzu* do espouse definite anarchistic sentiments, these sentiments in large part take the form of a protest against constraints imposed on people by authoritarian government. And where these Taoist texts do discuss political theory, the principles are vague and metaphorical and hence defy any attempt at practical implementation. Thus *The Art of Rulership* takes as its task, one could say, the formulation of a political theory with a structure in which the anarchist spirit of Taoism can flourish.

3
SHIH
(Strategic Advantage/Political Purchase)

THE NEXT CONCEPT to be analyzed in this exploration of the political philosophy of *The Art of Rulership* is *shih*, "strategic advantage." This
concept has long been associated with the rise of the Legalist school as
one of its three cardinal precepts: *fa* ("penal law"), *shih* ("strategic
advantage/political purchase"), and *shu* ("art/techniques of rulership"). In spite of its central importance, the historical development of
shih prior to its adoption by the early Legalist thinkers has not, to my
knowledge, been examined in any depth; as a consequence, the full range
of this concept has yet to be clearly delineated. Because it gradually
accrued a wide though not unrelated range of meanings, it has often suffered the common fate of being interpreted in early texts with all its later
connotations. If the meaning of *shih* as used in the earliest sources can be
determined with some accuracy, this definition can be used as a starting
point to trace its later development as it gradually took on additional
dimensions of meaning.

It would appear that at a relatively early period—at least by the time of
Sun Wu in the sixth century B.C.—thinkers who were later to be classified
as "Militarists" had already appropriated the character *shih* to represent
a specific military situation. Having acquired military connotations, this
same character at yet another stage in its development was taken over by
Legalist theorists and given a political dimension in many ways analogous to its earlier military application. Finally, in response to the Legalist
use of *shih* as a special political term, Confucian-oriented texts such as
the *Hsün Tzu* appropriated this concept and shaped it to fit their own
political philosophies. As we shall discover, *shih* as used in *The Art of
Rulership* is much closer to the Confucian variation than to the original
Legalist stock.

DEVELOPMENT OF *SHIH* AS A SPECIAL MILITARY TERM

Hsü Fu-kuan suggests that the expression *shih* was originally a term employed by the Militarist school in discussing contention for advantageous terrain.[1] This assertion is borne out first by references to the Militarists in early texts and again by the contents of extant works representative of the Militarist school, especially those attributed to Sun Wu[2] and Sun Pin.[3]

First, there are references in the early literature which establish a definite association between the Militarist thinkers and this notion of *shih*. The "Debating Military Affairs" *(Yi-ping)* chapter of the *Hsün Tzu* (53/15/5), for example, opens with a debate on military affairs between the lord of Lin-wu[4] and Hsün Tzu before King Hsiao-ch'eng of Chao.[5] In this debate the term *shih* is associated with the Militarists Sun Wu and Wu Ch'i:

> The lord of Lin-wu said: "This is not so. What is valued in military affairs is strategic advantage and benefit; what is put into action is versatility and deception. One adept at deploying the military moves with suddenness and secrecy, and none know from whence he comes. Sun Wu and Wu Ch'i using this philosophy were without equal in the world. How could it be necessary to first win over the people?"[6]

And in the *Lü-shih ch'un-ch'iu* 17/18b it states: "Sun Pin valued strategic advantage." The *Historical Records (Shih-chi)* biography of Sun Pin, pp. 2163–2164, credits him with having said:

> Now, one wanting to unravel a jumbled tangle of silk threads does not tug at it and strike it; one wanting to resolve a conflict does not throw himself punching and jabbing into the fray. If we avoid the enemy's strong points and attack him where he is most vulnerable, and if we change the overall circumstances and control the strategic advantage, the situation will resolve itself. . . .
> The skillful commander who takes his strategic advantage into account can use it to his benefit.

Given the limited number of references to the Militarists in these early texts,[7] it is fair to speculate on the basis of these passages alone that this concept of *shih* was considered to be of central importance to Militarist doctrine. Such speculation is confirmed by examination of the extant Militarist texts.[8]

In the *Sun Tzu,* and particularly in the "Strategic Advantage" chapter, one notes various shades of meaning for this term *shih*. First, as in 10/7a and 10/8a below, there are several instances where, given the general nature of its usage, the term can perhaps be rendered as "conditions" or "circumstances":

In the case of being at a distance from the enemy and where conditions are equally matched, it is difficult to instigate the engagement, and were one to engage the enemy, it is not to his advantage.

Conditions being equally matched, to attack an enemy with one-tenth of his numbers is called "troops in rout."

A second, more complex use of *shih* is that of "disposition," "configuration," "deployment," or "shape." As D. C. Lau has indicated,[9] in the following two passages from the *Sun Tzu* (4/16b and 5/23b) the characters *hsing* ("shape") and *shih* are used as near-synonyms:

That a victorious general committing his men to battle can be likened to the surging of pent-up waters thundering through a gorge is a matter of his army's advantageous deployment *(hsing)*.

Hence that the strategic advantage of the skillful commander can be likened to the avalanching of round boulders down a precipitous mountainside is a matter of his advantageous deployment *(shih)*.

The sometimes synonymous relationship between these two characters is again apparent in the following passage (6/31b):

Now the disposition of troops resembles water: the flow of water avoids high ground and hastens to low areas; the disposition of troops avoids the strong points and strikes at the weak. Water follows the ground in determining its flow; troops follow the enemy in determining their victory. Thus troops have no constant deployment *(shih)* and water has no constant disposition *(hsing)*.

That *hsing* and *shih* can be used in this synonymous manner is due to the fact that they overlap somewhat in meaning. The term *shih* seems to have a strong connotation of physical position—not in the sense of specific location, but rather of a fluid configuration ever responsive to its context. Just as the flow of water is determined by the contour of the terrain, so the physical disposition of *shih* is determined by changing circumstances. "Shape" in the sense of physical terrain is again one of the most significant elements in the acquisition of strategic advantage.[10] Basically, *shih* seems to mean occupation of high ground and the "purchase" or strategic advantage it confers.[11] In 5/8a the *Sun Tzu* employs the metaphors of water, trees, and boulders hurtling down from high ground to express this aspect of *shih:* "That the swiftness of dammed-up waters can even send boulders bobbing about is due to its *shih*." And likewise in 5/23a: "The commitment of troops to battle for one who relies on *shih* is like the avalanching of trees and boulders." *Sun Tzu* 5/10a likens the *shih* implicit in advantageous position to a drawn crossbow: "His *shih* is like a drawn crossbow; his striking distance is like the squeezing of the trigger."[12]

When taken in a military context, this term *shih* refers to deployment of one side in relation to the other. These deployments fall into two categories: "irregular deployments" *(ch'i shih)* and "regular deployments" *(cheng shih)* described in *Sun Tzu* 5/7b as follows: "With battle deployments, there are no more than the regular and irregular, and yet the possibilities of change from one to the other are inexhaustible."[13] Presumably the essential difference between these two kinds of deployment is the enemy's anticipation or lack of it. If a maneuver for advantage is expected by the enemy, it is "regular"; if it catches the enemy unawares, it is "irregular." The critical importance of wresting deployment advantage from the enemy is stated very clearly in *Sun Tzu* 5/20b: "Hence it is in *shih* rather than in man that the skillful commander seeks his victory." This military use of *shih* is perhaps best summarized in the definition which the *Sun Tzu* 1/17b gives for the term: "*Shih* is making the most of beneficial circumstances and tilting the scales in your favor."

In the *Sun Tzu,* then, the term *shih* has at least three dimensions of meaning: (1) "circumstances" or "conditions"; (2) "physical disposition" in connection with the deployment of troops; and (3) occupation of a superior position and access to the potential advantages it confers. In this respect the word can refer either collectively or individually to the superior position, the advantage inherent in the position, and the manipulation of this advantage.

In a work as short as the *Sun Tzu,* the frequency of *shih* and the emphasis placed upon it make it without question one of the central concepts of the text. That this concept continued to be an important aspect of Militarist thought is evidenced by its role in the *Sun Pin Art of Warfare (Sun Pin ping-fa)* and the military chapters of *The Book of Lord Shang (Shang-chün shu)* and *Kuan Tzu.*

Although there are instances in the *Sun Pin Art of Warfare* where *shih* is used with its more general meaning of "conditions" or "circumstances," the tendency to employ it as a specific military term is even more marked than in the *Sun Tzu.* Where there are only two instances in which it may possibly be rendered "circumstances" or "conditions,"[14] and again one more in which it would seem to mean "physical disposition,"[15] the remaining passages insist on the specifically military interpretation of the advantage inherent in a superior position. In several passages it means simply "strategic advantage" or "purchase" (nos. 83, 213–214, and 258):

Sun Pin said, "A military victory lies in the selection of appropriate personnel; courage lies in enforcing strict discipline; skill lies in turning strategic advantage to full account. . . ."

Use fire to throw the enemy into disorder and shower him with arrows. Use the din of the attack drums to spur the troops on, and avail yourself of every strategic advantage to assist them.

The defender can await the enemy after having occupied the best terrain and having made the most of strategic advantages.

Again, as in the *Sun Tzu* 5/7b, the term occurs as a compound expression *chan shih* to mean "battle deployment" (no. 362–363): "Thus, in battle deployment, reinforce those troops on the verge of victory, replace those in the throes of defeat, allow those who are fatigued to rest, and feed those who are hungry."[16] Most significant, however, are the two passages in which it is singled out as one of the terms used to signify factors affecting the outcome of battle (nos. 38 and 111–122):

T'ien-chi then asked, "Are authority, strategic advantage tactics, and deceit the most crucial factors in military operations?" Sun Pin replied, "Not at all. Authority is a means of assembling troops. Strategic advantage is a means of guaranteeing they will fight. Tactics are a means of harassing the enemy. While they can facilitate victory, they are not the most crucial factors." T'ien-chi flushed and said with irritation, "These six factors are utilized by all experts in military operations, and yet you, sir, claim that they are not the most crucial considerations. . . ."

Huang Ti created the sword and then derived the military formation from its characteristics; Yi created the bow and crossbow and then derived the notion of strategic advantage from their characteristics; Yü created the boat and chariot and derived the notion of variability from their characteristics; T'ang and Wu created the lance and derived the notion of wielding authority from its characteristics. These four principles are all based on the application of military weapons. . . . How do we know that the notion of strategic advantage is derived from the bow and crossbow? An archer shoots from between shoulder and chest and kills a person over a hundred paces away who does not even know where the bolt came from. Hence it can be said: the bow and crossbow exemplify strategic advantage. . . . Generally speaking, there are four principles of military operations: military formation, strategic advantage, variability, and authority. A thorough consideration of these four principles is the way to crush a formidable enemy and capture a fierce commander.

Having considered these examples of usage in the *Sun Pin Art of Warfare,* we can conclude with some confidence that the term *shih* played a central role in articulating pre-Ch'in Militarist thought. This conclusion is reinforced by an analysis of the use of this term in the military chapters of *The Book of Lord Shang* and *Kuan Tzu.*

While *shih* does occur once in *The Book of Lord Shang* to mean "conditions,"[17] and occurs also in compound expressions like "physical disposition" *(hsing shih)* in the *Kuan Tzu,*[18] the most frequent usage nevertheless refers to the acquisition of a strategically superior position and its inherent advantage. Consider, for example, this passage in *The Book of Lord Shang* 5/3b (p. 76): "If there is nothing which is beneath one, he will have the advantage of the use of arms. If one can hold this advantage over a long time, his position *(shih)* will become supreme." And again in the *Kuan Tzu* 1:25-10: "Therefore, to understand conditions and calculations clearly is a strategic advantage in the use of troops. A critical factor is timing; of less importance is the calculation of numerical strength."[19]

The final stage in this investigation of *shih* as a key Militarist concept is an examination of its usage in Book Fifteen, *Summary of Military Strategies (Ping-lüeh),* of the *Huai Nan Tzu.* As a compendium of pre-Ch'in thought with considerable borrowings from earlier texts, the *Huai Nan Tzu* reflects an early Han interpretation of the essential elements of many of the early schools. While including a considerable quantity of material which can be identified in sources still extant, it also contains a wealth of early Chinese thought which has been preserved within its pages alone.

Many similar passages make it immediately apparent that the *Summary of Military Strategies* has been considerably influenced by other texts cataloged as belonging to the Militarist school. The importance of *shih* can be inferred from the fact that in the brief description of this treatise in the *Summary of Essentials (Yao-lüeh)* postface to the *Huai Nan Tzu,* the term *shih* occurs twice (21/3b):

> The *Summary of Military Strategies* treatise is to explain the conditions which must obtain for victory in battle and successful attack, the strategic advantage provided by terrain and deployment, and variability possible through deceit and treachery. . . . If one really understands its meaning, in whatever operations he undertakes he will be free from the danger of attack. Taking strategic advantage as his basic stuff and tranquillity and clarity as his ordinary frame of mind, he can avoid his enemy's strong points and attack him where he is vulnerable as if he were driving a flock of sheep.

As in the *Sun Tzu,* there are instances where *shih* might mean simply "circumstances" or "conditions"[20] and places where it might also carry the connotation of "physical disposition" or "deployment."[21] Significantly, however, it continues to favor the special military usage: a strategically advantageous position, the purchase available to the occupant, and the manipulation of this purchase. In this treatise is found what must be the most lucid explanation of *shih* as a military term available to us in any of the early texts (*Huai Nan Tzu* 15/8a–b):

In military preparations there are three kinds of strategic advantage and two kinds of authority. There is the advantage of morale, the advantage of terrain, and the advantage of opportunity:

1. When the general is full of courage and regards the enemy with contempt, when his troops are steeled in their resolve and are pleased at the prospect of battle, when the determination of his army, countless in number, outstrips the skies, when their morale is like a tempest and their battle cries ring like thunder, when utterly committed they fall upon the enemy with all of their might—this is called a morale advantage *(ch'i shih)*.

2. Precipitous passes, narrows, high mountains, known strategic locations, spiraling approaches, basins, snaking roadways, bottlenecks, places where one man can hold a thousand enemy at bay—this is called a terrain advantage *(ti shih)*.

3. Taking advantage of the enemy's fatigue, their ill-preparedness and disorder, their hunger and thirst, their exposure to the elements, pressing in upon them where they are unsure of themselves and giving them no ground where they are most vulnerable—this is called an opportunity advantage *(yin shih)*.

This passage clarifies the important point made in *Sun Tzu* 10/a cited above that *shih* is distinct from the numerical strength of the contending armies. It is not strength of numbers but elements such as "morale," "terrain," and "opportunity" which are indicated by the military usage of *shih*.

By far the majority of instances of *shih* in the *Summary of Military Strategies* can best be rendered "strategic advantage."[22] The crucial importance of *shih* in determining the outcome of battle is clearly stated in 15/11a: "That which determines the victor is the weighing up[23] of strategic advantages." According to this treatise, a truly superior general assesses every factor which might have a bearing on his success or failure: the auspiciousness of the day, the fall of the land, the various human elements. Consequently, he is never routed and never suffers defeat. With the assistance of *shih,* however, even a mediocre general stands a good chance of victory *(Huai Nan Tzu* 15/11a): "Even though there is no certainty of complete success, his chances of victory are indeed good." The preponderant importance of *shih* over all other factors in battle is stressed in the following passage in which it is made analogous to leverage in chopping wood and the crossbow in dispatching the arrow (15/11a):

Now, in chopping firewood with a broadaxe, one need not wait for an opportune moment or auspicious day to cut it down. But if in addressing the axe to the firewood he is without a handle for it, regardless of the extent to which he is in accordance with *chao yao*[24] or how auspicious the day,[25] he will be unable to cut it down. This is because he does not have a leverage advantage. If water is dammed up, it will come cascading down; if an arrow is drawn to the hilt, it will fly a long way. Now, were an arrow to be made from the finest bamboo and decorated with silver and tin, it still would not be able to penetrate the mail of even the thinnest silk or a shield of rotten lotus leaves without some kind of assistance. If, on the other hand, some muscle and the purchase of a crossbow were put behind it, it would pierce rhinoceros hide armor and pass right through a leather shield.

It is this Militarist use of *shih* to connote strategic advantage which at some later date seems to have been taken up by the Legalist thinkers and fashioned into one of the mainstays of their philosophical system. The next step, then, is to trace this concept through the main works of the Legalist tradition and attempt to discover how the notion of *shih* was extended from a principle of effective warfare to a principle of political control. In addition to the Legalist writings *Shen Tao, Shang-chün shu, Kuan Tzu,* and *Han Fei Tzu,* we will also examine the *Lü-shih ch'un-ch'iu* and the *Hsün Tzu*—two texts contemporaneous with the rise of Legalist thought that reflect a different perspective on the development of this term.

DEVELOPMENT OF *SHIH* AS A SPECIAL LEGALIST TERM

As a special Legalist term, *shih* can be rendered "political purchase." The choice of the word "purchase" as an occasional equivalent for *shih* may be clarified with a simple analogy. Whereas the ruler as *individual* is limited in his capacity to regulate the conduct of others, from the strategically advantageous position of the throne he can use his political status as *ruler* to amplify his influence over others. It is this political status and its application as a fulcrum for increasing the ruler's capacity to influence others that constitute his *shih*. (It is significant that the Militarists cite fulcrum-like devices such as the axe handle and crossbow as metaphors for this purchase.) The concept of *shih* thus expressed in its political application indicates the relationship between the position of ruler and other elements of the state, a relationship which can be described in terms of political differentials or "purchase."

SHEN TAO

Modern research into the origin and development of Legalist thought indicates that there were originally three divergent schools which were eventually brought together in the *Han Fei Tzu*. The school of Shen Tao (born about 360 B.C.) is reputed to have stressed "strategic political advantage" or "political purchase" *(shih)*, the school of Shen Pu-hai (d. 337 B.C.?) stressed "techniques of rulership" *(shu),* and the school of Shang Yang (390–338 B.C.) stressed "penal law" *(fa).*[26] The notion that Shen Tao imbued the term *shih* with special Legalist connotations is due largely to the debate set out in the "Critique on the Concept of Political Purchase" *(Nan-shih)* chapter of the *Han Fei Tzu,* the assumption being that if this term had not been popularized by Shen Tao, Han Fei would not have centered his discussion on Shen Tao's comments about it. There are two occurrences of *shih* in the extant writings attributed to Shen Tao.[27] Before examining these two sources, we should consider pertinent references to Shen Tao in other texts which might shed light on his influence on the development of *shih.*

Although the account of Shen Tao's thought in "The World" chapter of the *Chuang Tzu* is predictably Taoist in emphasis, it is significant that in this short description his rejection of "sagacity" is mentioned three times.[28] This is at least consistent with the notion of rule by *shih* rather than sagacity and rule by law rather than moral persuasion. In the "Dispelling Prejudices" *(Chieh-pi)* chapter of the *Hsün Tzu* (79/21/21) we find: "Shen Tzu, being preoccupied with law, was not cognizant of superior character." And again in the "Against the Twelve Philosophers" *(Fei shih-erh Tzu)* chapter (15/6/6): "They [Shen Tao and T'ien P'ien] would say they esteem the rule of law, but in fact they had no law; they did not follow the old precepts but in fact preferred to create their own."

It is rule by law that is the distinguishing feature of Shen Tao's thought. In the *Lü-shih ch'un-ch'iu* 17/17a–b (notably the "Attention to Political Purchase" *(Shen-shih)* chapter), the following passage is attributed to Shen Tao in the context of emphasizing the importance of retaining a firm hold on one's position:

> Shen Tzu said: "Now if a single rabbit hops by, everyone will chase it. This is not because one rabbit is enough for a hundred people to share, but because the question of ownership has not yet been settled. Before this has been settled even a Yao would try his hardest to catch it—how much more so an ordinary person. If someone piles up a bunch of rabbits in the marketplace, passersby will not even give them a glance. It is not that they do not want rabbits, but that the ownership of these rabbits has already been settled. Once the question of ownership has been settled, even the basest people will not wrangle over them. Thus the proper ordering of the empire and the state lies in nothing other than settling the question of what belongs to whom."[29]

On the basis of these references to the thought of Shen Tao in the early literature, we conclude that certain elements in his philosophy are congruent with Legalist doctrine: he wholly rejects the idea of government by morality, he advocates rule by law, and he propounds the principle that the establishment and maintenance of clearly defined political and social roles is a necessary condition for proper government. Although this third feature of Shen Tao's thought does cover the concept of *shih* in a very general sense, it is necessary to turn to the argument as set out in the "Critique on the Concept of Political Purchase" *(Nan-shih)* chapter of the *Han Fei Tzu* for a more precise exposition.

The quotation that is attributed to Shen Tao in this *Han Fei Tzu* debate is very close both in wording and in substance to the *Shen Tzu* 4a–b passage; indeed, it could conceivably be an expansion and elaboration on it. Assuming that Shen Tao was in fact responsible for introducing or at least popularizing the use of *shih* in a political sense, the *Han Fei Tzu* passage represents a starting point in our attempt to gather the full implications of this important Legalist term. For this reason, it is necessary to examine it carefully:

> Shen Tzu said: "The flying dragon mounts the clouds and the *t'eng* snake wanders in the mists. But when the clouds dissipate and the mists clear, the dragon and the snake become the same as the earthworm and the large-winged black ant because they have lost that on which they ride. Where men of superior character are subjugated by inferior men, it is because their authority is lacking and their position is low. Where the inferior are subjugated by the superior, it is because the authority of the latter is considerable and their position is high. Yao the peasant could not govern three men whereas Chieh the emperor could bring chaos on the whole world. From this we know that strategic political position and its purchase are reliable whereas superior character and intelligence are not worth coveting. Indeed, where the crossbow is weak and yet the arrow soars high, it is because it has been lofted up by the wind; where a man is of inferior character and yet his orders are carried out, it is because he is being assisted by the people. When Yao was teaching from an inferior position, the people did not listen to him. But when he assumed the throne and became emperor over the world, his orders were carried out and his prohibitions were observed. Viewing it from this perspective, we can see that while superior character and intelligence are not sufficient to subjugate the people, strategic political position and its purchase can even bring men of superior character to heel."

Shen Tao, presumably addressing himself to the ruler, makes certain assertions. First, since men of superior quality can be subjugated by inferior men and vice versa, it is not the degree of "superiority," moral or intellectual, which affords the individual the capacity to govern others. Second, just as clouds are a necessary condition for the flying dragon to realize itself as a flying dragon, so authority and position are necessary conditions for a man to realize rulership. That is to say, even if a flying dragon has all the other attributes and qualifications of a flying dragon, it is only when he can mount the clouds that he becomes a flying dragon. In the same way, even if a man has all the ability and wisdom of a capable ruler, it is only when he has access to the authority and position of the ruler—that is, when he has *shih,*—that he actually has the opportunity to be a ruler. On the other hand, it is possible for a far less gifted man given the authority and position of the ruler to govern with some degree of success. Finally, whereas superior character may have some bearing on the success of government, it is the authority and position of the ruler which give him political purchase and hence political control.[30]

THE BOOK OF LORD SHANG (SHANG-CHÜN SHU)

Scholarly consensus suggests that *The Book of Lord Shang* is a composite text compiled over a period of at least a hundred years, dating primarily from the third century B.C.[31] It is possible if not probable that the present text does in fact contain fragments from the hand of the historical person Shang Yang (390–338 B.C.).[32]

Considering the theoretical sympathy which exists between Legalist doctrine and principles of military operations, it is not really surprising that a term like *shih* ("strategic advantage"), having strong military associations, was picked up and elaborated upon by the authors of the early Legalist texts. This bond between the Legalists and early Militarist thought is perhaps nowhere more apparent than in the three military sections of *The Book of Lord Shang,* in the existing references to Shang Yang's military writings,[33] and in the military treatises contained in the *Kuan Tzu.*[34]

The character *shih* occurs with some frequency in *The Book of Lord Shang,* and hence provides a basis for analysis of its various usages. First, *shih* occurs three times in direct association with the military: 3/6a–b and 5/3b (twice in the first passage).[35] Second, *shih* occurs most frequently in this text as "prevailing circumstances" or "prevailing conditions." This usage ranges in scope from simply "present circumstances" in 5/11a—"Under these circumstances, corrupt officials are given just the means to accomplish their wicked and perilous deeds"—to "changing circumstances." These changing circumstances make it necessary for the sage-ruler to examine his principles of government constantly and alter them to accommodate the times (2/10a):

> The sage neither imitates antiquity nor follows the status quo. To imitate antiquity is to be behind the times; to follow the status quo is to be handicapped in the face of changing circumstances. The Chou did not imitate the Shang and the Hsia did not imitate the ways of Yü. These three ages were characterized by different circumstances and yet they were all able to rule the world. While there is a set way of becoming king, to hold onto this position is a matter of different principles.

With the reins of government in hand, the sage must continue to give full consideration to changing conditions in exercising his rule (4/11b): "The sage understands the principles underlying the inevitable and recognizes

the proper time and circumstances for those things that must be done."
These changing circumstances are of such overwhelming influence that if
they are inimical to proper government, even the sage-king is powerless
to establish orderly rule. On the other hand, the ruler can, by dealing
with the political situation at its root, create circumstances conducive to
proper order (5/15b–16a):

> To have duties and responsibilities clearly defined is the way to create cir-
> cumstances which conduce to proper order; to leave them undefined is the
> way to create circumstances conducive to disorder. Where circumstances
> conduce to proper order it cannot be otherwise; where they conduce to dis-
> order it cannot be otherwise. If one tries to bring order against the force of
> circumstances he will simply increase the disorder, dut if he seeks to estab-
> lish proper order assisted by the force of circumstances there will be order.
> Thus the sage-king sought to order the orderly and did not attempt to bring
> proper order to the disorderly.[36]

The influence of these prevailing circumstances is not limited to the ruler
alone, of course, but pervades the entire society, transforming thieves
into honest men and honest men into thieves (4/10a): "Where circumstances make it impossible to do evil, even a Robber Chih can be trusted;
but where circumstances are conducive to evil, even a Po Yi will be suspect."[37]

The third important meaning of *shih* in *The Book of Lord Shang* is an
extension of its usage as a special military term. As we have seen, in military parlance *shih* refers to the strategic advantage available to an army
by virtue of its superior position (morale and opportunity as well as terrain) and the manipulation of this purchase to achieve its end—namely,
military victory. In *The Book of Lord Shang,* the concept *shih* is extended to connote the purchase available to things at large as a consequence of their specific attributes and character.

Shih in a political context establishes the connection between political
status and political purchase. Just as the wind is available to the seed-
tuft, so political purchase is available to the ruler (5/9a):

> To understand the Way is to understand political purchase and strategies.
> For this reason, the Former Kings relied on their purchase rather than their
> might and on strategies rather than good faith. . . . A seed-tuft carried aloft
> in a whirlwind will travel hundreds of miles because it avails itself of the
> advantage afforded by the wind. . . . Thus when one relies on this advan-
> tage he will reach his destination however far.[38]

Just as a distinction is drawn between *shih* and military force due to
numerical strength, so in a political context a distinction is drawn between might and *shih,* here meaning political purchase.

Although most of the discussion of *shih* in *The Book of Lord Shang* centers on the position of the ruler, this orientation is probably due to the perspective of the Legalist theorists rather than to any regal monopoly on *shih*. In fact, since *shih* is a natural condition of all political or social status, the *shih* inherent in the political position of minister must be under constant surveillance and check by his ruler (5/9b): "For one conversant with political strategy this is not the case. He divides up and separates the purchase of his ministers and puts restraints on their activities." Although the ruler has no monopoly on *shih,* in the political sphere his purchase is at least theoretically without equal. Jealously prizing his exclusive access to the political advantage of the throne, he must constantly take steps to avert the consolidation of any subordinate's *shih* that might ultimately challenge his position and authority.

The relevant information concerning the concept *shih* which can be drawn from *The Book of Lord Shang* is limited by the brevity of the text. For amplification, it is necessary to turn to another important work in the Legalist tradition: the *Kuan Tzu.*

KUAN TZU

The *Kuan Tzu,* like *The Book of Lord Shang,* is generally considered to be a composite text dating primarily from the third century B.C. The fact that, even in its corrupt and incomplete condition, it still ranks as a lengthy text when compared to *The Book of Lord Shang* (about 130,000 characters as opposed to approximately 20,000) promises a more varied usage of *shih*. An analysis of the text shows that the term occurs only four times with a specific military association (1:22-6 [twice], 1:25-10, 3:93-9); it occurs several times as "prevailing conditions" or "circumstances."[39] There is, moreover, a usage of this term with specific reference to physical terrain.[40] The most significant use of *shih* in the *Kuan Tzu,* however, signifies the purchase available to a thing in consequence of its attributes and status. This use applies to social positions (1:75-1): "If the purchase lies with the son for the duration of a year, even though he proves to be unfilial, the father will be unable to make him obedient." More frequently and more importantly, though, it applies to political status and the advantage associated with it.

Inseparable from this use of *shih* is the connotation of "majesty" or "authority" often expressed as *wei shih*. Since Legalist writings generally, and the *Kuan Tzu* essays in particular, tend to address themselves to the throne, it is not surprising that the status of ruler and the *shih* which is attendant on this position are the main subjects of discussion. This is not to say that other political stations are without their *shih*. The office of minister, for example, has its *shih* (2:36-12): "Thus, in appointing ministers, examine their accomplishments and weigh them against virtue; investigate their industry and scrutinize it in light of the law. Where they measure up to the *ts'an wu*,[41] promote them everywhere. Give them positions with purchase and show clear trust in them." (See *Kuan Tzu chi-chiao*, p. 501.) This *shih* of the minister is again referred to in 3:87-4: "A ruler who loses the 'two [*yin* and *yang*]' and the 'five [standards: colors, sounds, flavors, and the like]' will lose his state; a minister who loses his 'two' and 'five' will lose his political purchase; a commoner who loses his 'two' and 'five' will lose his family."

These isolated passages aside, the preoccupation with the ruler's political purchase demonstrates that political control in this text is generally viewed from the perspective of the ruler and with his interests in mind. The *shih* afforded by the throne is the ruler's exclusive property, and essentially it is this *shih* which makes him ruler. Remaining aloof from his ministers and subordinates, the ruler must make every effort to preserve his *shih* intact (1:74-13):

> Thus if the ruler loses his purchase, his ministers will control him. If the purchase lies with those below, the ruler will be controlled by his ministers. If the purchase remains with him above, then the ministers will be controlled by the ruler. Thus when ruler and minister have exchanged positions, it is a matter of the political purchase lying with those below. If it lies with the minister for the duration of a year, even though he proves to be disloyal the ruler will be unable to take it away.

This too is the thrust of 3:30-7:

> The tiger and leopard are the fiercest of beasts, and when they roam the deep forests and broad marshes, people fearing their nobility show them respect. The ruler has the most purchase in the world, and while he dwells in seclusion, people will fear his purchase. If the tiger and the leopard abandon their remoteness and begin to approach man, however, he will trap them and make light of their nobility. If the ruler abandons his residence and forces himself on the people, they will think nothing of him and look with contempt on his purchase.

Where the ruler fails to retain his *shih* and allows it to be shared among his ministers, his fall is inevitable. When his subordinates cease to obey his edicts, this is an indication that he has lost his grip on his *shih* as ruler (3:54-7):

> That with which the ruler controls his ministers is his authority and his purchase. Thus if the authority and purchase come to lie with those below, the ruler will be controlled by his ministers. If the authority and purchase are retained by him above, the ministers will be controlled by their ruler. Now, obstructing the ruler is not a matter of shutting up his gate and guarding his door. When his commands are not carried out, his prohibitions are not

observed, and his desires are not respected, he has lost his authority and purchase. Thus if authority and purchase lie exclusively with the ruler, the various ministers will be fearful and respectful. If the laws and policies are dispensed by the ministers, the people will cease to obey. Thus in the proper governing of the world by a perspicacious ruler, with his authority and purchase resting exclusively with him, he does not share it with his ministers; with the laws and policies being regulated exclusively by him, they are not dispensed by his ministers. Thus the *Enlightened Laws (Ming-fa)* states: "Authority does not have two homes; policies do not have two sources."

Once the ruler's grip on his *shih* as ruler has slipped beyond a certain point, there is no possibility of regaining his hold. His country and his people are lost to him (3:52-9):

Now, when a ruler cannot disseminate his edicts, when his laws are not obeyed and his ministers do as they please, when his authority has waned and his purchase has already been usurped, when his edicts are not carried out, his ministers are not consulted, and his people are not employed, and when the people within his borders are not under his control, then the country is not his country and the people are not his people.

If, on the other hand, the ruler is successful in retaining his *shih,* it is this *shih* rather than any personal affection or devotion that will function as the most effective instrument of government. It will ensure his control over his ministers and the unveering loyalty of his subordinates (3:51-9):

That the various ministers do not dare to deceive their ruler is not because of any love that they bear him, but because they fear his authority and purchase. That the common people fight among themselves to serve him is not because of any love they bear him, but because they fear his laws and commands. Thus the perspicacious ruler manipulates infallible strategies to govern people who have no alternative but to serve him; he occupies political purchase which must be revered to control ministers who have no alternative but to obey him. As a result, his commands are implemented and his prohibitions are observed, the ruler is revered and the ministers are humble. Thus the *Enlightened Laws (Ming-fa)* states: "That the ruler is revered and the ministers are humble is not a measurement of the affections they bear him, but rather because his purchase is overwhelming."

Thus the emotion which the ruler seeks to inspire in his subjects is *wei*— "awe" or "fear"—rather than love.[42]

The most important instrument available to the ruler in maintaining his *shih* is his exclusive control over life and death (3:52-5 and 3:60-1)

The reason why ministers are afraid of their ruler and will serve him with diligence is because they want to stay alive and hate the prospect of death. If people did not desire life and hate death, they could not be effectively controlled. Now, there has never been a case in which power over life and death has been exclusively in the hands of the chief ministers where the ruler has not been in grave danger. Where good government or disorder is decided by important ministers rather than being determined by law, where the power over life and death lies with subordinates rather than being controlled by the ruler alone—this, then, is a "dependent" ruler. Hence when the ruler turns his authority and his purchase over to others, the disaster of assassination is imminent; when he turns his legal controls over to others, the calamities of disorder and destruction are imminent. Policies such as these are the way of the doomed ruler. Hence the *Enlightened Laws (Ming-fa)* states: "If the ruler gives away his exclusive powers, he will forfeit them."

Controlling the various ministers and holding sole power over life and death is the lot of the ruler; publishing edicts and looking up to control from above is the lot of the minister. Authority, political purchase, respect, and stateliness are the lot of the ruler; humility, modesty, fear, and deference are the lot of the minister.

To check the usurpation of *shih* by persons close to the throne, the ruler must enforce without favoritism a system of constant and unchanging laws for any breach of proper conduct (2:28-5 and 2:33-14):

If a state is without constant laws, the great ministers will venture to encroach upon the ruler's political purchase.

When a perspicacious ruler is on the throne, it is clear that the reason why favorites cannot erode his purposes is because punishments are applicable even to those close to the throne, and the reason why high ministers are not able to encroach upon his purchase is because cliques and factions are punished.

If the faults of those below go unchastened, the *shih* of the ruler will be adversely affected and his authority will wane (2:95-11):

Even so, when the people are dissipated, self-seeking, and do not obey injunctions, when they put on a show of erudition, put their faith in deception, and contend forcibly with one another, then the fault lies with them below. If the fault lies below and yet the ruler fails to deal with it, then men of violence will not be overcome and depravity and disorder will not be checked. If men of violence are not overcome and depravity and disorder are not checked, the purchase of the ruler will suffer and his authority will daily decline.

In these passages we see a clear relationship between the position of ruler and the function of his *shih,* and it is in this clarification of the term that the *Kuan Tzu* (especially chap. 67) is most revealing and informative. While *shih* tends to retain many of its basic Militarist connotations, the area of its application has definitely been extended from the military to the political battleground.

LÜ-SHIH CH'UN-CH'IU

Although the term *shih* occurs in various parts of the *Lü-shih ch'un-ch'iu*, it is the "Attention to Political Purchase" *(Shen-shih)* chapter which really provides insights into its development. The chapter opens with the assertion that the ruler must retain his *shih* in order to maintain his position as ruler (17/15a): "If the ruler loses ground in strategies and yet seeks to make it up in the sincerity of his subjects, this will give rise to uncertainty; if he loses ground in his political purchase and yet seeks to make it up in sovereignty, he will be in peril. Even a fish large enough to swallow a boat, if thrown up on land, will succumb to the insects."[43]

If the ruler loses his *shih,* he will be at the mercy of his subordinates. The chapter not only stresses the critical importance of *shih* to the retention of sovereignty but goes so far as to define sovereignty in terms of *shih* (17/17a): " 'King' is political purchase. To be king is to be without equal in purchase. If there is an equal in purchase, the notion of king ceases to apply." Failure of the ruler to retain his *shih* blurs the distinction between ruler and those around him and results ultimately in a challenge to his authority (17/17a):

> Where their political authority is equally balanced, neither [ruler nor minister] can command the other; where their political purchase is on a par, neither can envelop the other; where their degree of orderliness is on the same level, neither can set the other right. Thus the relative size, importance, quantity, and degree of order obtaining between ruler and minister must be carefully considered. This is the gateway through which calamity and good fortune enter.[44]

Thus the first concern of the ruler in his ongoing struggle to retain his position is to maintain a *shih* differential between himself and those over whom he exercises control (17/16b–17a): "The various nobles do not want to be the ministers of someone else but have no choice in the matter. If the ruler cannot exercise his political purchase with facility, how can he make them his ministers with any ease!"

Having emphasized the importance of *shih* to the ruler, the chapter then turns to a demonstration of how the empire has actually been structured on principles that facilitate the ruler's application of his *shih*. The principle that "large commands the small" is repeatedly asserted (17/16a–b and 17/16b):

> Therefore, for the large to keep the small is auspicious, but the reverse is disastrous; for the important to command the unimportant results in obedience, but the reverse is a bad sign indeed.

> Thus it is easy for a state of ten thousand chariots to command a state of one thousand chariots, it is easy for a state of one thousand chariots to com-

mand one family, it is easy for one family to command one person. If, however, one were to attempt to work in the opposite direction,[45] even a Yao or Shun would be unsuccessful.

This principle of "large commands the small" was, according to the text, applied historically in constructing a system of government that would reinforce the *shih* of the ruler. Certainly the division of the empire into vassal states was carried out as a means of achieving more effective control in the administration of government. It is advantageous for the ruler to preside over many small states (17/15b):

> The territory of the empire being divided into three-hundred-square-mile states was a way of making the administration supremely effective. It is not that they could not be made larger, but that their being small is better than being large and their being few in population is better than being numerous. That many vassals were enfeoffed was not for the benefit of those enfeoffed, but was rather a means of facilitating the ruler's political purchase and preserving his authority. . . .

That this principle for maintaining political control is effective is borne out by historical example (17/15b): "Thus, looking back on previous generations, the prosperity of those whose enfeoffments were many was long-enduring and their names are glorious. Shen Nung ruled the world for seventeen generations because he shared it with the people of the world."

These numerous smaller states existing under the large, controlling hand of the supreme ruler are not to be randomly allocated. Rather, enfeoffment must follow a definite pattern fashioned to facilitate imperial control. First the ruler takes his place at the hub of both the political and the geographical worlds: "Now, the civilized states in contact with each other by boat and carriage who do not require translators make up an area of a thousand square miles. The kings of antiquity, choosing the center of the world, established their states; choosing the center of their capital, built their palaces; and choosing the center of their palaces, erected their ancestral halls." Radiating out from the imperial center, the empire is structured so that the closer the fief is to the center, the larger and more important it is, culminating of course in the size and importance of the ruler's personal domain (17/15b–16a): "As for the enfeoffments made by these kings, the closer they were, the larger; the more distant, the smaller. In the remote coastal regions, there were nobles with territories of only three square miles. These kings preserved their imperial houses intact by having the large command the small, the important command the unimportant, and the many command the few."

Having first emphasized the importance of *shih* to the ruler in his

efforts to remain "large," and then having interpreted the structure of
the state in terms of the principle that "the large commands the small,"
the text next considers the relative importance of having *shih* as opposed
to having superior qualities. The attitude toward *shih* expressed here is
consistent with what has gone before—the greater one's *shih,* the easier it
is to achieve one's ends. Whereas superior virtue is certainly desirable, it
is made perfectly clear that it is *shih* rather than moral character which is
the essential ingredient for success (17/16a):

> The larger that which is used, the easier it will be to acquire that which is
> desired. If T'ang had been without his state of Yi and Wu had been without
> his district of Ch'i, even with perfect qualities of character they nevertheless
> would not have been able to succeed. Even with the superior qualities of
> T'ang and Wu, they nevertheless had to rely on their political purchase: how
> much more so those who are not a T'ang or Wu.

The text makes it clear, moreover, that in order for the ruler to retain the
shih necessary to continue as head of state, he must be fully aware of
political differentials and exert himself in maintaining them (17/17a):
"If the king is aware that the small is better than the large and the few are
superior to the many, then his intelligence will be without equal. And if
his intelligence is without equal, the path of presumers and usurpers will
be far removed." While the king retains the largest and most important
portion of the empire as his personal domain, this royal domain is small
relative to the united whole. It is by using his *shih* as a fulcrum to maintain division in the empire that he is able to keep the large "small" while
making his small "large."

Just as the empire is structured on a pattern facilitating the *shih* of the
ruler, the social and political status of those in the empire has been
established with the same end in mind. The ruler must be vigilant in his
attention to the graduated scheme of social and political positions and
their attendant rights and duties in order to preserve the existing structure (17/17a):

> As for the laws of the former kings, in investing an emperor they saw to it
> that the various nobles would not pretend to his position; in investing the
> various nobles they saw to it that the ministers would not pretend to their
> positions; in investing the legitimate sons they saw to it that the sons of con-
> cubines would not pretend to their positions. Pretending to the position of
> another gives rise to contention, and contention gives rise to disorder. Hence
> if the various nobles lose their positions, the world will be thrown into disor-
> der; if the ministers are without rank, the court will be thrown into disorder;
> if the wives and concubines are not differentiated, the household will be
> thrown into disorder; if the legitimate sons and sons of concubines are with-
> out distinction, the clans will be thrown into disorder.[46]

Before turning to investigate the term *shih* in the *Han Fei Tzu,* it will be useful to examine the specifically Confucian reaction to the growth and popularization of this rival doctrine in the text of Han Fei Tzu's teacher, Hsün Tzu.

HsÜN TZU

In the *Hsün Tzu*'s attitude toward *shih* we enter a new phase in the development of the term. In the lively intellectual exchange of late pre-Ch'in thought, the central ideas of Legalist political theory did not go unchallenged. In the *Hsün Tzu,* perhaps one of the most critical and cogently argued texts of the pre-Ch'in corpus, we have a Confucian rebuttal to the Legalist assertion that it is *shih* rather than moral and intellectual excellence which must be considered the first condition for effective political control.

The usage of *shih* in the *Hsün Tzu* covers the full range of meanings found in the Militarist and Legalist texts. Again *shih* is most frequently used as the special term developed by the Legalist thinkers to connote political status and its attendant advantage. While the *Hsün Tzu* does make use of *shih* with its special Militarist and Legalist implications, this is not to say that it accepts the concept as it is propounded in these traditions. On the contrary, the *Hsün Tzu* employs *shih* to contest their assertions.

The "Debating Military Affairs" *(Yi-ping)* chapter opens with a rejection of the Militarist school's amoral attitude toward the use of arms. Confucian moral precepts are as applicable to the administration of military undertakings as they are to the administration of the state. The terminology used by Hsün Tzu's foil, the Lord of Lin Wu, in advancing his arguments echoes that of the *Sun Tzu* and the *Sun Pin Art of Warfare.* Expressions such as "authority" *(ch'üan),* "plan or strategy" *(mou),* "variability or maneuverability" *(pien),* "deception" *(cha),* and the concept "strategic advantage" *(shih)* all occur frequently in the writings of the Militarists and were undoubtedly meant to have just such an association for the reader. Again, the principles of war advanced by the Lord of Lin Wu and summarily rejected by Sun Ch'ing Tzu (that is, Hsün Tzu) are dressed to give the impression that they are a statement of basic Militarist theory.[47] In this chapter the *Hsün Tzu* dismisses the Militarist emphasis on the primacy of *shih* in military engagements and subordinates it to considerations such as popular support and united strength, suggesting that *shih* itself is a by-product of moral government. The ultimate outcome of war is not determined by temporary military advantages such as deployment of troops and favorable terrain. Rather, it is determined by the will of the people. Thus, from the *Hsün Tzu*'s perspective, *shih* is the popular support enjoyed by the ruler as a *result* of his first concern: moral government.

In addition to setting aside the Militarist emphasis on the primacy of *shih* in the use of arms, the *Hsün Tzu* also argues against the primacy given *shih* in the Legalist conception of effective government. Legalist political philosophy, as we have seen, rejects the Confucian reliance upon moral suasion and loyalty in favor of the manipulation of *shih* and rule by intimidation—thereby repudiating the fundamental Confucian precept exalting persons of superior qualities and employing the able *(tsun hsien shih neng)*. Where the Confucians placed their faith in the transforming influence of the ruler as a consummate *person,* the Legalists stressed the objective conditions of his *position.*

Given the general thrust of the *Hsün Tzu* toward a reworking and crystallization of Confucian doctrine, and given Hsün Tzu's historical position as the standard-bearer of Confucian ideas at a time when Legalist thought was approaching its apogee, it is not entirely unexpected that he took it upon himself to defend evolving Confucian doctrine against this Legalist conception of *shih*. To a certain extent Hsün Tzu does accept the Legalist insistence on the importance of *shih* in maintaining political control. In fact, he even credits the enlightened sages of antiquity with the innovation of political purchase, accepting its contribution to the fabric of order in society (88/23/40):

> Because the sages of antiquity regarded human nature to be evil, considering it prejudiced, unruly, perverse, and erratic, they set up the political purchase of the ruler to control it, they elucidated the notions of social norms and rightness to transform it, they propounded laws and standards to bring order to it, and they stressed punishments and penalties to place curbs on it. The people of the world, as a consequence, all conducted themselves with decorum and in conformity with what is good.

While maintaining certain reservations, Hsün Tzu does acknowledge the effectiveness of Ch'in's program for political domination of the empire —a program based on Legalist principles which include the ruler's manipulation of his political purchase.[48] At the same time, true to his Confucian commitment, Hsün Tzu asserts that in the attainment and preservation of political control, moral and intellectual superiority in the administration of government must take precedence over the manipulation of political advantage (59/16/23):

> If one were to exercise the political purchase of an eminent person and carry out his Way, no one would object. T'ang and Wu stand as examples. If one were to exercise the political purchase of an eminent person and yet not employ his Way, even though he may have as much purchase as an emperor,

in the end he would not even get away with being a commoner. Chieh and Chou stand as examples. Such being the case, the differences between one who acquires the purchase of an eminent person and one who acquires his Way is great indeed.

To illustrate this point, Hsün Tzu suggests that a person who has only limited political purchase can, by virtue of his exemplary character and its authentication in the government of his territory, win over the entire empire.[49] By contrast, he cites the historical examples of the miscreant rulers, Chieh and Chou, who had the birthright of emperor with all the concomitant purchase and yet lost everything because of moral deficiency and the ultimate turning away of their people.[50] Thus although the ruler is the person with access to the most political purchase in the empire, if he strays from the Confucian Way *(tao)* of the True King he would have been better off without any position of authority at all (37/11/1):

> The state is the most efficacious instrument in the world and the ruler is the person with the most political purchase in the world. If he manages this instrument within the perimeters of the Way, he will enjoy great security and honor and will be the source of an increasing number of good deeds. But if he exercises it without reference to the Way, he will suffer great peril and ill-repute and would have been far better off with no country at all.

Hsün Tzu condemns the Legalist injunction that the ruler control his minister by exercising the purchase available to him as ruler as a decidedly inferior method of exacting obedience from subordinates (59/16/11): "Not being able to hold subordinates except by intimidating them with political purchase and terrorizing them with punishments and executions is what is called 'awe inspired by harsh scrutiny.' "

Hsün Tzu's primary objection to the Legalist conception of *shih* is that where the Legalists regard the *shih* itself to be a sufficient condition for political control, Hsün Tzu is convinced that *shih* without popular support is a sinking ship and ultimately untenable. The acquisition and retention of *shih* are a consequence of winning over the people (40/11/70): "The discerning and perspicacious ruler is adept at winning the admiration of the people. Where the people are won over, political purchase follows upon it; where the people are not won over, purchase dissipates. Thus being a king rests in winning over the people." And the people can only be won over by the actions of a morally superior ruler who is devoted to the public good—in short, the archetypal Confucian sage-ruler. While the enlightened ruler devotes himself to his people with the knowledge that popular support also guarantees his own security, the unenlightened ruler concerns himself with *shih* (44/12/5):

The perspicacious ruler considers winning over his people his most urgent task while the unenlightened ruler busies himself with the acquisition of political purchase. Where a ruler exerts himself in winning over his people, the state will be properly ordered while he personally leads a life of ease, his accomplishments will be great, and he will be held in high regard. If he is of high quality he can become a True King, but even if he is of lower quality he can still become a hegemon. But if a ruler does not exert himself in the acquisition of men but rather busies himself in the acquisition of political purchase, the state will be in disorder in spite of his having exhausted himself, his accomplishments will be negligible, and he will be of poor repute. His state will certainly be in grave peril.

Significantly, Hsün Tzu's "unenlightened ruler" bears a striking resemblance to the Legalist portrayal of an effective head of state.

HAN FEI TZU

The *Han Fei Tzu,* compiled in the middle of the third century B.C., has been described as a confluence of the various streams of pre-Ch'in Legalist doctrine. In many respects it represents an aggregation, systematization, and clarification of certain ideas current in the mid–third century B.C. These ideas were such that it required an acutely critical if not cynical mind to bring them together and integrate them into an internally consistent system of political philosophy. One of the central ideas was *shih.*

The *Han Fei Tzu* uses the term *shih* with all the special connotations found in earlier Legalist texts. In fact, *shih* as a special Legalist term finds its most lucid expression in the essays of this work. Since the *Han Fei Tzu* uses the concept *shih* more extensively than any other early text, a close scrutiny of its passages will lead us to a sharper understanding of this term and its importance to Legalist political theory. Indeed, by the time that Han Fei lent his incisive argumentation to the expression of key Legalist concepts, *shih* had come to occupy such an important position in the Legalist program of government that discussion of political control was impossible without it. That the *Han Fei Tzu* devotes an entire chapter to the significance of this term bears testimony to its importance.

There are three main points to be made concerning the usage of *shih* in the text as a whole. First, *shih* occurs in only four passages with any reference to military operations,[51] but these are altogether too general to shed any light on *shih* and its usage as a special military term. Second, *shih* occurs with some frequency as "prevailing conditions or circumstances."[52] Third, and perhaps predictably, the most frequent occurrence of *shih* in the *Han Fei Tzu* is as the special Legalist term referring to the purchase available to a thing in consequence of its status. There is a definite relationship between one's *fen*—social and political status—and the purchase which exists as a condition of this status. The expression *fen shih pu erh* ("where purchase matches status . . .") occurs twice.[53] There are numerous examples of this usage: the social status of commoner is without *shih*,[54] whereas exalted persons,[55] men of principle,[56] the crown prince,[57] court favorites,[58] the consort and concubines,[59] as well as ministers[60] and anyone else in the service of the ruler[61] all have *shih* as a condition of their status. The degree of *shih* is of course graduated and culminates in the position of the ruler himself.

The *Han Fei Tzu*, a ruler's manual for political control, quite naturally concerns itself with the relation between the position of ruler and the function of *shih*. This relation is described in the *Han Fei Tzu* much along the lines found in the earlier Legalist texts, especially the Legalist portions of the *Kuan Tzu* examined above.

In the Legalist tradition, a formal notion of *fen* denoting the rights and duties of a given political position was articulated early on as a theoretical means of dividing up and containing the powers of individual ministers.[62] In the *Han Fei Tzu*, the central principle for bureaucratic control, "accountability" *(hsing ming)*, is based on first defining the rights and duties of an office and then insisting on absolute compliance with this definition in actual performance. When a minister or an official comes forward with advice for the throne, he is called upon to give a full statement of how his policy will benefit the state. If his policy is adopted, he is judged by the accuracy of his forecast. Where there is correspondence between the duties and the actual performance of ministers, and where there is correspondence between the claims and the actual results of policies, generous rewards are appropriate. Where correspondence is lacking, punishments—immediate, public, and severe—are in order.

This principle of accountability, seen from the perspective of the ruler, has the twofold purpose of first placing the responsibility for certain duties or the success of certain policies squarely on the shoulders of a specific minister and, second, protecting the privileges and the purchase of the throne by isolating the purchase available to individual ministers.

The position of the ruler is defined by the retention of the *shih* available to his office (363:2): "The reason why a ruler of a ten-thousand-chariot state and the lord of a thousand-chariot state are in control of the empire and can punish the various nobles is because of their dignity and purchase. Dignity and purchase are the muscle and strength of the ruler." To safeguard his own control, the capable ruler permits no fluctuation in the privileges and duties available to an official (180:16): "A situation in which there is confusion and latitude in rights and duties is a source of disorder. Thus the perspicacious ruler is cautious with respect to it." If the ruler, abandoning his personal control over his purchase and the privileges attendant on his station, instead seeks to meddle in the administrative affairs of his ministers, he will find himself ineffectual in both areas (212:13): "If the ruler does not personally attend to his purchase and to the handles of power, but rather insists on attending to affairs appropriate to his ministers, is it any surprise that he falls asleep over them!"

The ruler, beyond his status as ruler, also has the attributes of an individual person. If, however, he attempts to exercise control on the basis of these personal attributes rather than with the purchase available to his position, he pits his own strength of character against that of every other person in the state (234:8):

> The state is the chariot of the ruler and his purchase is his steed. Not to use political purchase to contain ministers who would usurp the love of the people, to insist on being magnanimous to compete on equal terms with your subordinates for the allegiance of the people—this is to choose to abandon the chariot altogether and to run rather than take advantage of it and the facility of the horses.

To rely exclusively upon his own faculties for maintaining control is not nearly so effective as tapping the collective powers of the empire which are made available to him as a function of his status as ruler (71:8):

> When the ruler relies upon his eyes to be perspicacious rather than trusting to numbers, what he actually sees will be little indeed. This is not the means to avoid being deceived. When he relies upon his ears for keenness of hearing rather than taking advantage of his political purchase, what he actually hears will be little indeed. This is not the way to avoid being duped. The perspicacious ruler gives the world no alternative but to see and hear for him. Thus although he dwells deep within his palace, his perspicacity makes lucid all within his realm.

Clearly it is the political purchase of the ruler rather than his own excellent qualities which is essential for proper government (155:5): "If one has the ability but not the purchase, even though he is a good man he will not be able to keep those who are not good under control." By exercising the political leverage of the ruler, even a man of very average parts can rule effectively (266:2): "Moreover, to transform the people by personally enduring hardships even Yao and Shun found difficult, whereas to rectify one's subjects by exercising purchase even a mediocre ruler would find easy." Conversely, without the purchase of a ruler even an ideal political leader would be ineffective in presiding over the empire (74:13): "Without the purchase afforded by the dignity and respect of the position and without the laws governing rewards and punishments, even a Yao or Shun would be unable to establish proper order."

The function of the ruler's *shih* is to maintain control over his subordinates (337:15): "The people, because they are under their superior's control, fear him; the superior, with his purchase, dominates those beneath him." In his relationship with his bureaucracy, the ruler must trust to his political advantage rather than personal loyalty if he is to retain his position (216:8): "The ruler must rely on purchase rather than faith in his ministers."[63] The people work for the sovereign not in response to any love he may show for them but because they find this course of action to their own advantage (254:4): "That the people work for me does not mean they are working for me because of my love but because of my purchase." Where it is exercised adeptly, political purchase is not only effective in foiling dissolute ministers. It can also be used to arrest conspiratorial malignancy before it can grow to challenge one's position (234:2): "Thus Tzu Hsia said: 'One adept at handling political purchase nips evil in the bud.' "

The *shih* of the ruler is maintained through his exclusive power over life and death (330:14): "The ruler exercises his purchase by maintaining his grip on the handles. As a result, his commands are carried out and his prohibitions are observed. The handles are his control over life and death; political purchase is the means to overwhelm the many." But this same *shih,* if not retained by the ruler as his exclusive property, can be used by others to undermine him (85:5): "If he loans out his authority and purchase, the superior and the subordinate will change places." The ruler is warned repeatedly that he must not relegate his purchase to his ministers (251:13): "How then could the ruler possibly attain success by sharing his purchase with his ministers!" If he allows a minister the smallest concession or special privilege, this relaxation of principle can cost him advantages a hundred times the intended value (179:5): "Authority and purchase cannot be lent to others. If the ruler gives a little the minister will take a lot."

Once the *shih* of the ruler has been wrested from him, there is no turning back. In all likelioood the ruler himself will be expunged and his state will be consumed in turmoil (116:15): "Political purchase and weightiness are the pool of the ruler.[64] If the ruler loses his purchase and his weightiness to the ministers, he cannot retrieve them. When Duke Chien lost them to T'ien Ch'eng and the Duke of Chin lost them to the six ministers, their states perished and they forfeited their own lives."

While the functions of *shih* described in the *Han Fei Tzu* might seem to be substantially the same as that outlined in my analysis of the *Kuan Tzu,* there are at least three areas in which the *Han Fei Tzu* departs from the earlier Legalist texts. First, the *Han Fei Tzu* emphasizes the surveillance and repression of ministers and others close to the throne—an emphasis simply not present in the earlier Legalist literature. From a historical point of view, this might be interpreted as a reaction to an era of intense political struggle in which intrigue, conspiracy, and ministerial usurpation had become crowded concourses of political mobility. The *Han Fei Tzu* interprets political life as an ongoing conflict of individual self-interests. Only the ruler with enough astuteness and resolve to employ every advantage at his disposal can continue in power. All the nobler sentiments—love, trust, honor, mercy—are repudiated as footholds for conspiring ministers and would-be usurpers and are replaced by cold reason and the dexterous manipulation of power. The complete distrust advocated by the *Han Fei Tzu* respects no social institution or relationship. In fact, the closer the individual stands to the hub of power, the greater his threat to the ruler. Thus the ruler must be vigilant if he is to parry the challenges to his position which may be thrust at him from such close quarters.

Second, since the *Han Fei Tzu* represents the consolidation and systematization of Legalist doctrine, it is not surprising that in this text the concept of *shih* is woven into the fabric of a mature political philosophy. It is represented not as an independent principle but in tandem with central Legalist concepts such as "techniques of rulership" *(shu)*, "penal law" *(fa)*, "the handles of reward and punishment" *(erh ping)*, and "accountability" *(hsing ming)*.

Finally, and perhaps most significantly, the concept of *shih* in the *Han Fei Tzu* is not propounded as pure political theory. Rather it is put forward as a central principle in a practical system of political control represented as a superior alternative to the doctrines of its two greatest rivals, the Confucian and Mohist schools. Whereas *shih* is discussed and recommended in *The Book of Lord Shang* and the *Kuan Tzu* on its own merits, in the *Han Fei Tzu* it is repeatedly compared with the notion of rule by virtue. For example (342:11): "Whereas the people will certainly submit to purchase, few can be won over by rightness." This same passage continues by pointing out that Confucius with his benevolence and rightness was only able to win over seventy men to his service. Duke Ai of Lu—a man with little to recommend him—made subjects of everyone within his borders, including Confucius. When the influence of Confucius, the epitome of moral excellence, is weighed against the political purchase of even a mediocre ruler, the scales tip decisively in the ruler's favor. Whereas the moral and intellectual qualities of Confucius failed to make any impression on his ruler at all, Confucius had no choice but to submit to the weight of Duke Ai's political control.

Having demonstrated the effectiveness of purchase as an instrument of government, Han Fei Tzu then proceeds to castigate the scholars of his day—the Confucians and Mohists—for advocating devotion to the principles of benevolence and rightness rather than counseling their rulers to take advantage of their infallible purchase. Such a policy, he admonishes, supposes the ruler to be a man of Confucius' stature and the common people to be on a par with his disciples; it is doomed to certain failure.

In yet another passage,[65] the *Han Fei Tzu* criticizes Confucius for advising the governor of She that "proper government lies in making those close at hand content and attracting those from distant quarters." This is, according to the text, tantamount to "abandoning what his purchase is able to contain in favor of competing with his subordinates for the support of his people by being more magnanimous than them." Such a course is again doomed to certain failure.

While an element of the confrontation between Legalist and Confucian-Mohist doctrine is clear in these passages, in "A Critique on the Concept of Political Purchase" *(Nan-shih)* it becomes the predominant theme. The critique is, for the most part, a Legalist refutation of the common arguments for government by virtue and an apology for its own concept of government by political purchase. The debate consists of three sections.

The first section comprises a statement of the efficacy of political purchase *(shih)* as an instrument of political control ostensibly cited from the writings of Shen Tao. The present *Shen Tzu* 4a–b[66] contains a similarly worded but much abbreviated passage which may have been inflated to serve the author's purposes. This statement argues that whereas the moral and intellectual superiority of the ruler may have an incidental bearing on the success of government, it cannot by any means be considered a sufficient condition for effective political control. This point is demonstrable historically: exemplary figures such as Yao *without* purchase, position, and authority were politically impotent. Far from being a sufficient condition, superior character is not even a necessary condition for political order. This too is demonstrable historically: rulers altogether devoid of moral merit such as Chieh have held sway over persons of considerably more worth than themselves by virtue of their purchase. Shen Tao concludes that it is political purchase and the position which it presupposes that are necessary and sufficient conditions for political control.

The second section presents a rebuttal to Shen Tao's statement from a Confucian perspective, advocating the alternative of government by moral suasion. While it might be conceded that political purchase is a necessary condition for political order, it is by no means a sufficient condition. This is demonstrable analogically and historically. Analogically (using Shen Tao's own analogy, in fact), flying dragons need rising mist and cloud (analogous to *shih*) to raise them aloft, but unwinged insects, even if they encounter these mists, cannot fly. Thus the rising mist and cloud, while being a necessary condition for flight, is not a sufficient condition. Historically (using Shen Tao's historical examples), rulers of exemplary character have been able to use their political purchase to effect order, but there have also been depraved rulers who, in spite of their purchase, have been unable to bring order to the empire. In fact, their purchase magnifies the degree of their injury and the extent of their disruptive influence in the same manner that it promotes the preservation of order under the moral ruler. Thus for a political theorist to advocate the principle of political purchase as a sufficient condition for political order without considering the moral caliber of the ruler is in many cases to facilitate conduct detrimental to the proper ordering of the state.

The third section defends the principle of political purchase by introducing a refinement of Shen Tao's thesis and a refutation of the Confucian arguments. This section presents Han Fei Tzu's own position. To clarify Shen Tao's thesis, he distinguishes two kinds of *shih:* "inevitable natural circumstances" and "political purchase initiated by humans." "Inevitable natural circumstances" refers to a situation not only beyond human control but even beyond human influence. To exemplify this kind of *shih,* the text cites the historical examples of Yao and Shun (archetypal exemplary rulers) and Chieh and Chou (archetypal tyrants). The contention is that, as stated in *The Book of Lord Shang* (5/16a), "where circumstances conduce to proper order it cannot be otherwise; where they conduce to disorder it cannot be otherwise." Since these circumstances cannot be significantly influenced by human agency, it is pointless to consider them in the articulation of a doctrine of political control. Thus the author makes this distinction (299:12): "What I mean by *shih* is simply that which is initiated by man. Superior character has nothing to do with *shih* as I have defined it."

The author then seeks to demonstrate that the concepts of government by moral suasion and government by political purchase are mutually incompatible:

> Using superior character as the Way of government precludes the ruler from instituting controls, but using political purchase as the Way of government requires that the ruler control everything. For the ruler of superior character who cannot institute controls to exercise political purchase which controls everything, is a contradictory position. That the positions of government by superior character and government by political purchase are mutually incompatible is clear.

The point is this: since these two methods of effecting political order are incompatible, it is necessary to choose one of them. What recommends political purchase over moral suasion is the fact that while the former can be employed by the average ruler under all but the most extreme circumstances, the latter is available only to the rare sage-ruler. Cases as rare as

Yao and Shun, or as extreme as Chieh and Chou, are due to circumstances beyond human control and are too infrequent to have a real bearing on the problem of political order. The choice is between, on the one
hand, exercising political purchase and achieving almost perpetual order
or, on the other hand, striving for moral transformation and succumbing
to almost perpetual turmoil with the rare respite of sage-inspired order.
This notion of a system of government devised for the *average* ruler (or
worse) is central to the *Han Fei Tzu* and underscores the pragmatic quality of its political philosophy. Where the Confucians would unrealisti-
cally press their rulers to staggering heights of moral excellence and
encourage them to reach for ideals far beyond their grasp, the *Han Fei
Tzu* is content to propose a program in keeping with the actual quality of
these rulers. Government should be recognized as a craft, and political
purchase should be accorded the status of an indispensable tool of the
trade.

SHIH IN *THE ART OF RULERSHIP*

The use of *shih* in *The Art of Rulership* has a strong link with its use in
historically earlier Legalist texts. This observation is borne out by a striking similarity in wording and metaphor which is immediately apparent
when one compares passages with those in the earlier Legalist works—
especially the *Han Fei Tzu*. This similarity in content and wording also
tends to accentuate their dissimilarities. While *The Art of Rulership*
shares something of a common terminological and doctrinal foundation
with these texts, it also incorporates ideas which can only be described as
differing radically from traditional Legalist thought. These divergent
ideas are both fundamental and consistent.

The passages which make reference to *shih* in *The Art of Rulership* are
at times simple expositions of Legalist precepts and at other times complex fusions of Legalist doctrine and borrowings from rival traditions. In
order to assay their contents and orientation, it is necessary to look at
these passages individually, abstract the Legalist elements, and isolate
the contributions from other sources.

Political purchase (shih) as an effective device for political control. In
The Art of Rulership there are three passages which use the chariot metaphor as an analog for the structure of the state: 9/7a, 9/9b, and 9/13b–
14a. The second of these passages seems to be wholly Legalist in its orientation (9/9b):

> Political authority and purchase are the carriage of the ruler; rank and emol-
> uments are the harness and bit of the ministers. Therefore, because the ruler
> dwells at the focal point of political power and holds firmly to the handles of

rank and emoluments, judges nicely the degree of control, and is appropriate in when and how much to give and take away, all the people exhaust
themselves in his service without feeling fatigued. Now it is not as if the relationship between ruler and minister has the substance of the bond between
father and son or the depth of feeling between flesh and blood relatives, and
yet the minister will work untiringly and risk his life for the sake of the ruler.
Why is this? It is because political purchase makes him do so.

There are several Legalist elements in this passage. Certainly the ruler/
minister relationship is represented wholly from the ruler's perspective
and with his interests in mind. Note also the use of the chariot metaphor
(see *Han Fei Tzu* 234:9, 259:5, 299:1) and the interpretation of *shih* as a
device which provides the ruler with a chariotlike advantage—the ruler
does not compete with his subjects on their level, but rather rides aloft
enjoying his exclusive access to the political advantage of ruler. Also
indicative of Legalist influence is the use of appropriate rewards and
punishments as a device for controlling and directing the ministers. Yet
another Legalist element is the emphasis on the limitations of the bond of
loyalty which can exist between ruler and subject and a rejection of this
bond as an effective means of ensuring diligent and faithful service from
a subordinate (see *Han Fei Tzu* 70:13, 73:13, 267:5). Finally, one notes
the reliance upon the manipulation of the ruler's singularly high position
and its attendant purchase for exacting the utmost service from subordinates.

Symbiotic relationship between ruler and minister. The orientation of
the 9/13b–14a passage in its use of the chariot metaphor is somewhat
more complex:

> The government of a sagacious ruler is like the charioting of Tsao Fu. He
> controls the carriage from the reins and the bit, and he regulates the tight-
> ness of his grip on the reins from his sensitivity to the response of the horses'
> lips. He sets the correct measure in his own breast and holds the regulating
> whip in the palms of his own hands. What he has secured within his own
> mind is externally in accord with the inclinations of his horses. He is able to
> move forward and withdraw as straight as a plumb line, turn a corner as
> roundly as a compass, and even after covering a great distance, he still has
> strength to spare because he truly understands the art.
>
> Now, political authority and purchase are the carriage of the ruler and the
> great ministers are his team of horses. There has never been a case past or
> present of a driver escaping danger who leaves the safety of his carriage and
> loses the responsiveness of his horses to his hands. Therefore, if the carriage
> and the horses are not in accord, even a Wang Liang would be unable to
> take to the road. If the ruler and his ministers are not in harmony, even a
> Yao or Shun would be unable to govern properly. If with a firm grasp of the
> art he drives the chariot of state, then a Kuan Chung or a Yen Tzu would
> serve him to the full extent of his intelligence; if he clarifies the distinction

between the people of different status, then the wickedness of a Robber Chih or a Chuang Ch'iao can be averted.

This passage reveals obvious Legalist associations. Again notice the use of the chariot metaphor (see *Han Fei Tzu* 234:9, 259:5, 299:1) and the legendary charioteers, Wang Liang and Tsao Fu. Note also the emphasis on "art or techniques" *(shu)*. Another Legalist element is the notion that if the ruler abandons his chariot and competes with his subordinates on their own level, he places himself in danger (*Han Fei Tzu* 234:8). Moreover, the passage mentions two Legalist heroes: Kuan Chung and Yen Tzu. Finally, one notes the use of "status" *(fen)* and the importance of retaining the sharp distinction between roles, rights, and duties (see *Han Fei Tzu* 180:16).

This second passage is unmistakably Legalist in its basic orientation. Nevertheless, in the emphasis upon a symbiotic relationship between ruler and minister—that is, a mutually cooperative and beneficial relationship as opposed to one dominated by the ruler's absolute control—one detects a definite Confucian influence.[67] This influence stands in stark contrast to the Legalist attitude of perpetual confrontation (*Han Fei Tzu* 34:10): "The superior and subordinate fight a hundred battles in the course of a day." This Confucian interpretation of the reciprocal relationship between ruler and minister is developed as the central theme in the following passage (9/10a–b):

> When there are strong winds, the waves rise; where there is thick foliage, the birds gather. This is because the *ch'i* of the one thing gives rise to the other. When the minister does not get what he wants from the ruler, the ruler will also be unable to get what he seeks from the minister. Ruler and minister benefit each other only on a basis of reciprocity. Thus the minister barters with his ruler by offering total commitment to the point of laying down his life whereas the ruler trades with his ministers by offering the dispensation of noble ranks. Just as the ruler cannot reward a minister who has rendered no service, a minister cannot die for a ruler to whom he owes no gratitude. When the favors of the ruler do not flow down to the people, for him to expect service out of them is like whipping an unruly horse. It is like hoping for a ripe harvest without rain. It is a demonstrable impossibility.[68]

An interesting comparison can be made between this passage in *The Art of Rulership* and a similar passage in *Han Fei Tzu* (267:4):

> The Way of the perspicacious ruler is not like this. Establishing what the people want in order to seek their good service, he thus confers noble ranks and emoluments to encourage them. Establishing what the people dislike in order to prohibit their evil, he thus metes out punishments and penalties to strike fear into them. Since his rewards can be relied upon and his punishments are certain, the ruler promotes good service from his ministers and

evil is not used against him. Even if there was a Shu Tiao, what could he do to the ruler! Furthermore, the minister bargains with his ruler by offering total commitment while the ruler trades with his ministers by offering the dispensation of noble ranks and emoluments.[69] The intercourse between ruler and minister is not based on the natural love between father and son, but rather is the result of calculation. Where the ruler has the Way of government, a minister will give his best without being tempted by evil, but where the ruler is without it, a minister will obstruct the ruler's vision above and be successful in his own interests below.

On the surface the two passages appear related both in wording and content. A closer examination, however, reveals that while the *Han Fei Tzu* passage is a straightforward explanation of the theoretical basis for the policy of rewards and punishments, *The Art of Rulership* takes as its main theme the reciprocal nature of the ruler/minister relationship.

The Art of Rulership passage follows upon two historical examples— Yü Jang and King Wu—which both illustrate and lay emphasis upon the vital role played by the ruler's magnanimity. A direct connection is established between the generosity of the ruler and his ability to implement his commands. While in the *Han Fei Tzu* rewards and honors are conferred upon subordinates as a mercenary technique for exacting service, in *The Art of Rulership* rewards, honors, and favors generally are construed as a moral obligation of the ruler to his subordinates. Where the ruler exerts himself in the fulfillment of this obligation to his people, his concern is requited with loyalty, devotion, and good service. Conversely, where the ruler demonstrates utter disregard for the comfort and well-being of his people, he is in fact undermining the security of his own position. This notion of moral obligation which has been injected into *The Art of Rulership*'s interpretation of the ruler/minister relationship clearly distinguishes it from its Legalist counterpart.

Moreover, one of the most pronounced features of Legalist literature is that political theory is constructed wholly from the point of view of the ruler's interest. In this passage from *The Art of Rulership,* however, the relationship between ruler and subordinate is described in terms of mutual obligations and responsibilities—if anything, the perspective tends to favor the minister and the people. Not only does it enjoin the ruler to refrain from rewarding unaccomplished ministers but it makes it amply clear that the people will not work for a ruler who fails to fulfill his obligations to them. The tempering of this concept of *shih* with a marked emphasis on ruler/subject reciprocity represents a clear concession to Confucian influence.

Usurpation of the ruler's purchase being symptomatic of decline. While there are many passages in *The Art of Rulership* in which Legalist political theory has been significantly altered by ideas borrowed from rival traditions, it should not be forgotten that there is still much in this treatise which is predominantly Legalist in outlook. The following 9/9b passage, for example, is wholly Legalist in its orientation:

> In a disorderly state it is a different matter. Those praised by the multitude are rewarded even though they have no accomplishments, whereas those who are faithful in their duties are punished even though they are innocent. The ruler is foolish and shortsighted, and the various ministers form factions and are disloyal. The sophists travel about debating and those who cultivate lofty conduct vie with each other for public office. With their cliques they criticize the edict promulgated by the ruler; with their deviousness they contravene the prohibitions of law. Those who cultivate wisdom devote themselves to cunning and deceit; those who cultivate valor devote themselves to contention and strife. The high ministers usurp authority, the low officials seize political purchase, and together, forming cliques and factions, they manipulate the ruler. Even though this state appears to be intact, the ancients would have considered it moribund.[70]

Having previously described an orderly state as one which embodies Legalist principles of political control, this passage then describes the state which, having abandoned these principles, has gone to ruin. And one sure indication of imminent ruin is ministerial usurpation of the ruler's purchase.[71]

Reliance upon political purchase rather than personal qualities. Another familiar principle of Legalist doctrine in *The Art of Rulership* is the notion that in the exercise of political control, the ruler should depend upon his purchase as a ruler rather than upon his attributes and qualities as an individual person (9/14b–15a):

> If a fish large enough to swallow a ship swims off course and goes aground, it will be at the mercy of the insects. This is because it has left its habitat. If a monkey leaves the trees, he will be seized upon by foxes and badgers. This is because it is in an environment not its own.
>
> If the ruler abandons what is proper to him and attempts to vie with his ministers, the officials will seek to hold onto their positions through inactivity and those in office will seek to avoid being discharged by toadying to the ruler. As a result, the ministers will hide their intelligence and not put it to use, passing the burden onto the ruler instead.
>
> Now, the reason why the noble and wealthy are willing to work hard, the astute are willing to look into matters, and the proud and arrogant are willing to show respect is because their political purchase is not equal to that of the ruler.
>
> If a ruler does not entrust things to the able but is instead given to doing things personally, his intelligence will become increasingly taxed and he will take upon himself the burden of responsibility. If he is hard put to cope with his subordinates, he will not be able to facilitate what is right. If his conduct is found wanting by the country, he will no longer be able to exercise exclu-

sive control. Since his intelligence is not sufficient to effect proper government and his awesomeness is not sufficient to enforce punishments, the ruler will not have the means to deal with his subjects.

In this passage certain Legalist elements can be readily identified. The ruler, for example, must not abandon conduct appropriate to his position and contend on a level with his ministers (see *Han Fei Tzu* 85:5). Moreover, the ruler maintains sway over his subordinates by means of his political purchase (see *Han Fei Tzu* 330:14, 337:15). One notes too that the differentiation of roles is stressed (see *Han Fei Tzu* 212:13). And, finally, the ruler's personal attributes are not a sufficient condition for maintaining political control (see *Han Fei Tzu* 234:8).

That the ruler should depend upon his purchase as ruler rather than his personal attributes is reiterated in the following passage, which asserts that even persons of inferior quality can rule by virtue of their access to *shih* (9/16a):

> If one holds firmly to the control handles of authority and purchase, it will be easy for him to transform the people. That Tzu Lu served the ruler of Wei was because the ruler's authority was great; that Kuan Chung and Yen Tzu served the Dukes Huan and Ching of Ch'i as ministers was because the ruler's position was exalted. That the timid can subjugate the brave and the ignorant can control the intelligent is because the purchase in which they lodge themselves is superior.
>
> It is said: "The branch must not be bigger than the trunk and the tip must not be stronger than the root. Why? Because the important and the large should have the means to control the unimportant and the small. This can be likened to the five fingers which being joined to the arm enable one to strike, pull, clutch, and pinch as he so desires."
>
> In other words, the small is adjunct to the large. Holding the advantage in purchase means that although what is held is extremely small, what is dependent upon it is large indeed; although what one keeps to is compact, what is under its control is extensive indeed.
>
> That a pillar of ten girths is able to support a twenty-ton roof or that a five-inch bolt can control the opening and closing of a gate—surely it has nothing to do with their size! It is because the position they occupy is pivotal.

The assertion that the purchase of a thing is due to its strategic location in the overall structure—"it is because the position they occupy is pivotal"—is a notion reminiscent of the *Lü-shih ch'un-ch'iu*'s "Attention to Political Purchase" chapter and is not inconsistent with the general Legalist conception of political purchase.[72] What is unusual in this passage is the appearance of the basically Confucian principle of "transforming the people" *(hua min)*.

Transforming the people. This notion of "transformation" is an ingredient associated with both the Taoist and the Confucian traditions. Conventional Legalist doctrine, however, asserts that the ruler is obeyed because of the political purchase—not because of his moral influence (*Kuan Tzu* 1:76-2): "In his moral actions and awesomeness, the ruler is not unique in being superior to others, but because he is called 'ruler' people go on to exalt him and do not venture to discuss the quality of his moral actions."[73] To ensure proper order in the state, the Legalist ruler manipulates his subordinates with rewards and punishments and opts for rule by law over moral edification (*Han Fei Tzu* 321:4): "Hence to take law as one's method is to suffer at first but benefit in the long run; to take benevolence as one's method is to snatch momentary pleasure but be ultimately frustrated. The sages weighed the merits of these two alternatives and opted for the greater benefit."

Confucian thought, by contrast, takes the moral elevation of the people through dynamic example as the primary task of those in power. For example, the "Greater Preface" to *The Book of Odes (Shih-ching)* states: "With poetry the Former Kings regulated the relationship between husband and wife, developed filial piety and respect, improved upon human relations, enriched edifying instruction and advanced conventions and customs."

Then there is the well-known *Analects* 24/12/19 passage: "Chi K'ang Tzu asked Confucius about government. . . . If you want to be good, the people will be good. The character of the superior is like the wind; the character of the subordinate is like grass. Let the wind blow over the grass and the grass will necessarily bend." In this passage, government is interpreted as the ability to influence, educate, and improve. In the *Hsün Tzu,* the emphasis on study and the commitment to improve and enrich the lives of the people through education have an obvious link with this concept of transforming the people. The task of moral edification is given a high priority in the allocation of responsibilities (30/9/94):

> To discuss social norms and music, to make conduct proper, to spread instruction and transformation, to enrich conventions and customs, and, nurturing things universally, to bring them to a concordant whole—these are the tasks of the senior ministers. To preserve morality intact, to promote loftiness and nobility, to extend refinement to its utmost, to unify the world, to scrutinize the smallest details, and to make all the people in the world submissive and obedient—these are the tasks of the ruler.

Perhaps the most extensive discussion of this transformation in early Chinese literature is to be found in Book Twenty, of the *Huai Nan Tzu: The Great Family (T'ai-tsu)*. In this treatise, "transforming the people" is presented from a decidedly Confucian perspective. It is held up as the desired result of government by moral suasion which, throughout the treatise, is contrasted with the much inferior policy of government by impositional law. The following passage provides a glimpse of this recurring contrast between morality and law (20/8b):

> In the proper government of the individual, the first priority goes not to the cultivation of the physical form but to the cultivation of the spirit. In the proper government of the nation, the first priority goes not to the rectification of the laws but to the cultivation of the people's transformation. . . . To have the people yielding to each other and contending to occupy as low a position as they can, to have them repudiating personal advantage and contending to receive as little as they can, to have them working hard and contending to give of themselves as much as they can, to have them day by day being transformed and reformed by the ruler without knowing how this comes about—this then is the basis[74] of proper government. To have the people striving to do worthy deeds for the sake of rewards, to have them refrain from doing wrong for fear of punishments, to have the common people obeying the laws below because the laws have been set right above—these are the inconsequential aspects of proper government.

It should be borne in mind that given the organismic metaphysics underlying Confucian political philosophy, the role of the people in the process of transformation is far from passive. In fact, while moral edification as the essence of education requires the teacher's commitment, the actual momentum of learning is the consequence of the student's assiduous effort. The function of humane government is to maintain an environment conducive to the people's self-realization and, without imposing constraints on natural development, to facilitate the process of self-growth.

Taoist political thought is similar in this respect. Organizational, noncoercive government simply provides the ambience in which the people can express their own spontaneous growth (*Lao Tzu* 57):

> The Sage states:
> I remain nonactive
> And the people are transformed of their own accord;
> I cherish tranquillity
> And the people are set right of their own accord;
> I do not intervene
> And the people are prosperous of their own accord;
> I am without desires
> And the people return to their natural genuineness of their own accord.

The function of the Taoist ruler in relation to the people is analogous to the constant *tao* in its relation to all existence (*Lao Tzu* 37):

The *tao* is constantly nonactive,
And yet there is nothing which it does not do.
If the nobles and kings would only preserve it,
The myriad things would be transformed of their own accord.

The notion of "transforming the people" *(hua min)* or "the people transforming" *(min hua)* under the sway of the ideal ruler occupies an important place in Confucian and Taoist theory. By contrast, given the Legalist determination to channel the energies of the people to serve the ruler's ends, "transforming the people" is in principle inconsistent with mature Legalist doctrine. And yet "transforming the people" does recur in *The Art of Rulership,* neatly knit into a substantially Legalist fabric (9/8b–9a):

> The key to success or failure in government lies in the ruler. If the inking line is properly set above, the wood will be straightened beneath it. It is not that the inking line does anything in particular to the wood, but rather that the disciplining of the wood in following the inking line makes it so. Thus if the ruler is truly upright, honest officials will be commissioned and villainous persons will hide themselves; but if the ruler is not upright, the wicked will get on in the world and loyal subjects will withdraw into retirement.
>
> Why is it that no one tries to split jade with their hands yet they will try to break melons and gourds in this way? They do not take on the jade or stone because there is nothing to be gained from it. If the ruler holds firmly to integrity and justice as if adhering to a plumb line in measuring the vertical, then those ministers who approach with evil in their hearts will be just like eggs thrown against a rock or fire plunged into water.
>
> Because King Ling of Ch'u was partial to slim waists, there were people who starved themselves by cutting back on their food. Because King Kou Chien of Yüeh was fond of valor, his people would all defy danger in vieing with one another to sacrifice their lives. If we view it from this perspective, it is clear that for the person with the handles of authority and purchase can alter the prevailing attitudes.
>
> When Yao was a common man, he could not even transform the people of one village through his example of benevolence; yet when Chieh was on the throne, his commands were implemented and his prohibitions were effective. Viewing it from this perspective, it is clear that while moral excellence is not enough to govern the world, political purchase can alter custom.

In the second half of this passage, *The Art of Rulership* takes King Ling of Ch'u and King Kou Chieh of Yüeh as historical examples of the overwhelming influence of the ruler. Here the predominant theme is that an upright ruler can act as an edifying force on those under his jurisdiction. King Ling and King Kou Chien as historical examples are not original to *The Art of Rulership;* they occur in both the *Kuan Tzu* and *Han Fei Tzu* as well as in several other early texts.[75] In all these works, as in this passage, these two kings represent the far-reaching influence of the throne. On this much the various texts are in agreement. Their difference, however, lies in the proposed objectives of this influence. By comparing the manner in which these same historical figures are used to illustrate widely divergent ideas one can discover the extent to which *The Art of Rulership* can be regarded as having been colored by Confucian thought.

In the *Kuan Tzu,* King Ling and King Kou Chien appear in a passage which stresses vital importance of agriculture as the fundamental occupation of the state (3:2-10):

> Now, the stability or inner turmoil of an individual depends on the heart; the continuity or destruction of a state depends on the ruler. What is good or bad for the empire may be the consequence of one man's actions. Where the ruler favors the basic industry [agriculture], the people will be fond of clearing uncultivated areas. Where the ruler is fond of money, the people will go in for trading. Where the ruler is fond of buildings and halls, craftsmen and artisans will be skillful. Where the ruler is fond of design and color, the women's work will be elaborate. Because the King of Ch'u was fond of slender waists, beautiful women cut down on their food; because the King of Wu was fond of the sword, the military men of the country embraced death lightly. Since death and starvation are two things universally disliked, why did these people face them of their own volition? Because they were pursuing what the ruler desired.

The ruler's position and influence are such that his desires constitute the directing force of his subordinates. This passage from the *Kuan Tzu* asserts that there is a connection between the ruler's influence and the activities of his people—here agricultural production will mean a strong and stable state. If, however, the ruler distracts the people from the cultivation of the fields, food will be insufficient for the needs of the country and political instability will ensue. Consistent with Legalist doctrine, agriculture is singled out as the most important occupation of the people and as the objective toward which the ruler must exercise his influence.

The *Han Fei Tzu* 28:15 passage provides us with an even more vivid contrast between the Legalist-oriented objective of control and *The Art of Rulership*'s objective of educating and transforming the people:

> The ruler has two pitfalls. If he employs those of superior character, his ministers will take advantage of this to maintain a hold over him. If he promotes people indiscriminately, state undertakings will end in failure. Hence if the ruler is fond of superior character, the various ministers will dress up their conduct in order to meet his approval and will not offer their true abilities in their service to him. If the ministers do not offer their true abilities in the service of the ruler, he then has no way of evaluating them. Because the

King of Yüeh was fond of courage, many of his people embraced death lightly; because King Ling of Ch'u was fond of slender waists, many people in his state starved themselves; because Duke Huan of Ch'i was a jealous man and was fond of his harem, Shu-tiao had himself castrated in order to supervise the harem; because Duke Huan was fond of exotic tastes, Yi Ya boiled his firstborn and served it to him; because Tzu K'uai of Yen was fond of men of superior character, Tzu Chih made it clear that he was not interested in taking over the state.

The gist of this passage is clear: the ruler must not reveal his likes or dislikes to his subordinates. If he does, they will be able to use this knowledge to their own advantage. This problem becomes particularly apparent in the process of official promotions. If the ruler makes it known that he promotes those of superior moral and intellectual character, his ministers will vie with one another to give him the impression that they are men of just such superior character. From the *Han Fei Tzu*'s point of view, this does not mean that these ministers will be encouraged to emulate the ruler's ideal; rather, they will mask their conduct to deceive the ruler in his assessment of their true worth. The policy to be adopted by the *Han Fei Tzu* ruler stands diametrically opposed to that advocated in the quotation from *The Art of Rulership* (9/8b–9a) cited above. In the *Han Fei Tzu,* the ruler is counseled to conceal the objectives of his influence and to refrain from providing his ministers with a model which can be simulated and thus used to delude him. In *The Art of Rulership,* on the other hand, the ruler uses his political purchase to provide his subordinates with a model of proper conduct and to propel them toward his ideal of moral excellence. In the *Han Fei Tzu,* knowledge and imitation of the model are a means of deception; in *The Art of Rulership* they are the basis of education and transformation.

It is clear that the King Ling and King Kou Chien examples in *The Art of Rulership* illustrate an attitude of political control very much at odds with the seemingly similar passages in the Legalist texts. The following excerpt taken from the *Hsün Tzu* 45/12/30 has basically the same thrust as *The Art of Rulership* version:

> The ruler is the gnomon and the people are the shadow. Where the gnomon is upright, the shadow will be upright. The ruler is a basin and the people are water. Where the basin is round, the water will be round.[76] If the ruler is an archer, his ministers are his archer's glove. Because King Chuang of Ch'u was fond of slender waists, there were half-starved people in his court.

From this comparison of the *Kuan Tzu, Han Fei Tzu, Hsün Tzu,* and *The Art of Rulership,* we can see that they all acknowledge the efficacy of political purchase as a force which can be exerted to influence the activities of the people. Of the two Legalist texts, it is suggested in the one that this influence be used to encourage agriculture and in the other that the ruler conceal his likes and dislikes in order to avoid deception by his ministers. These are clearly two important principles of Legalist doctrine. In the *Hsün Tzu* and *The Art of Rulership,* however, the point is made that political purchase can also be used to educate and elevate the people. Given a dynamic model of moral excellence, the people will strive to emulate it. The ruler, by availing himself of his purchase as ruler, can go a long way to determining the character of his subjects. This is a commingling of Legalist and Confucian doctrine.

The principle of transforming the people is fundamentally contrary to the spirit of Legalist thought, but it is a major component of both Taoist and Confucian doctrine. In the Taoist and Confucian traditions, although the working definitions of the ruler's transforming virtue are very different, common ground is shared in that the ruler does not actively transform the people in the sense of imposing on them something that is inconsistent with their natural development. Rather, he functions as a dynamic stimulus for the realization of the people's natural potential. *The Art of Rulership,* having accepted the efficacy of *shih* as a means of implementing political theory, advocates an active approach to the problem of improving the people. Consistent with the Taoist and Confucian traditions, it insists that the ruler use the purchase attendant upon his position to channel the people's energies in a direction beneficial to their own natural development in the belief that personal, social, and political realization are correlative.

Government by purchase versus government by moral suasion. In analyzing the *Hsün Tzu*'s interpretation of *shih,* we noted that Hsün Tzu does succumb to Legalist influence to the extent of acknowledging the effectiveness of political purchase for implementing a program of government—but, at the same time, he objects to the Legalist insistence that political purchase is itself a sufficient condition for political control. In the *Hsün Tzu*'s political theory, purchase is ultimately dependent upon popular support, and popular support is the direct result of rule which embodies Confucian ethical principles. In making this assertion, the *Hsün Tzu* attempts to defend Confucian political philosophy from the Legalist assault.

One of the main features distinguishing the *Han Fei Tzu,* from its precursors in the Legalist tradition is its treatment of government by *shih* not as an isolated theory but as a superior alternative to the rival Confucian principle of rule by moral suasion. *The Art of Rulership*'s interpretation of *shih,* by contrast, represents a Confucian and Legalist synthesis which can perhaps best be viewed as a continuation of Hsün Tzu in attempting finally to resolve this conflict between the Legalist principle of government by *shih* and the Confucian principle of government by morality. On the one hand, the importance and the effectiveness of *shih* are readily acknowledged. On the other, it suggests that this basically Legalist tool of government control be employed to carry out the Confucian task of educating the people and refining their ethical awareness. In other words, the ultimate effectiveness of *shih* is regarded as conditional on the ruler's accord with the Confucian code of moral conduct.

The people as the basis of political purchase. All three passages in the *Han Fei Tzu* which cite the chariot metaphor make the state analogous to the chariot and the political purchase of the ruler analogous to the horses. Of the three instances of this metaphor in *The Art of Rulership*, the one perhaps most in keeping with traditional Legalist precepts relates the proposition of "utilizing the people" *(yung chung)* to the notion of political purchase (9/17a):

> Now, even if Wu Huo or Chieh Fan were to attempt to lead an ox from behind by the tail, they would pull the tail off without budging the ox because they are acting contrary to the way of things. But if one were to pierce the ox's nose with a sprig of mulberry, even a half-grown boy could lead it around the country because he is following the way of things.
>
> Because we harness the water for our use, with a seven-foot oar we can maneuver a boat. Because he takes the people as his purchase, the emperor has only to issue commands to have them implemented and observed.

In this passage the ruler is encouraged to take full advantage of the political purchase available to him as ruler not only because it is the most efficacious means of political control but also because it is "following the way of things." He should not rely on his abilities as an individual to influence others; rather he should manipulate his subjects from the vantage point of his throne. By relying on political purchase rather than personal abilities to enlist the popular support of the people, he is able to tap the concerted strength of all those below him. This gives him power and vision far exceeding that of any individual or group of individuals who may set themselves in opposition to him and challenge his right to rule. While this principle of "utilizing the people" *(yung chung)* can certainly be traced back to an occasional reference in the *Kuan Tzu* and *Han Fei Tzu,*[77] in *The Art of Rulership* it is developed as a central theme. As such, we shall examine it in more detail below. At this juncture it is enough to draw the obvious connection between the concept of political purchase and the popular strength that becomes available to one who can stand above the people and orchestrate their energies.

In conclusion, then, the concept *shih* is used consistently in *The Art of Rulership* as a Legalist term to articulate seemingly Legalist doctrine. Its reiteration of basic Legalist precepts contributes to our understanding of pre-Ch'in political thought. Its contribution, however, does not end there. True to the spirit of eclecticism prevailing in the early Han, there is a sustained effort to select and to synthesize. With respect to *shih,* the two most obvious attempts to blunt radical Legalist theory with Confucian humanism are, first, the reinterpretation of the ideal ruler/minister relationship as being symbiotic, each position responsive to and dependent upon the other, and, second, the acknowledgment of the effectiveness of *shih* as an instrument of political influence to effect the Confucian objective of transforming and elevating the people. This revised interpretation of *shih* stands in sharp contrast to its function in the Legalist system as a tool of political repression.

There is a consistency in *The Art of Rulership* which suggests a complete and integrated system of political theory. While certain elements in this political theory are significant, it is the relative emphasis placed on the various components that determines the ultimate disposition of the system. Further, it is not only what *The Art of Rulership* has taken from the Legalist tradition but how it chooses to deal with what it takes, and again what it chooses to reject, that must be considered in determining its orientation. In the *Han Fei Tzu,* for example, *shih* is frequently discussed in conjunction with the ruthless repression of conniving ministers. There is an almost paranoiac preoccupation with the protection of the ruler's political prerogatives. The purport of *The Art of Rulership,* on the other hand, is one of harmony rather than control, cooperation rather than contention. Having acknowledged the soundness of the concept of *shih, The Art of Rulership* then fits it into an eclectic political philosophy which attempts to combine the effectiveness and practicability of the Legalist doctrine with the more humane considerations of its rival traditions.

4

FA

(Penal Law)

IN THIS CHAPTER I want to discuss the evolution of the character *fa* from its primary meaning of "model or standard" to the notion of "penal law." This is not to say that the early Chinese states lacked a concept of criminal law. On the contrary, scholars are generally in agreement that some form of retaliation against criminal conduct develops early in the life of all emerging societies.[1] The *Tso chuan* alludes to a code of penal law in use during the Hsia dynasty. Certainly by middle Shang times— with the gradual development and expansion of a written language and the emergence of sophisticated methods of political administration—it is likely that some form of criminal law was articulated and written down.[2]

The criticism that Shu-hsiang and Confucius direct at the engraving of penal laws onto tripods implies that penal law up until the sixth century B.C. had been the property and responsibility of the ruling classes. According to these passages recorded in the *Tso chuan*,[3] it was the birthright of nobility to receive (in exactly what form is not clear), interpret, apply, and in turn pass on the laws of their forebearers. The fact that the ruling classes embodied the laws was undoubtedly an important element in the maintenance of the prevailing class structure. It entitled them to the respect and obedience of the common people while demanding from them the expertise necessary to hear litigations and pass judgments.

In the Shu-hsiang letter,[4] a parallel is drawn between the articulation and inscription of Tzu-ch'an's law code and the compilation of the "Penal Code of Yü" *(Yü-hsing)* of the Hsia, the "Penal Code of T'ang" *(T'ang-hsing)* of the Shang, and the "Penal Code of Chiu" *(Chiu-hsing)* of the Chou. The implication is that, like Tzu-ch'an's code, these earlier law codes were fixed. Whether or not they came to be written down is difficult to determine.[5]

By the middle of the sixth century B.C., the details of penal law had become public knowledge with the bronze inscriptions of first the state of Cheng and then Chin.[6] These were followed by the *Classic of Law (Fa-ching)* of Li K'uei (also known as Li K'o and Li Li) (455–395 B.C.). According to the "Treatise on Penal Law" *(Hsing-fa chih)* of the *History of the Chin (Chin-shu)*, this text of Li K'uei constituted the beginnings of codified law and was itself based on a selection of statutes taken from the various Chinese states. It was this code of Li K'uei which formed the basis of Shang Yang's notorious system of political control. The criminal law of Shang Yang became the framework for the penal codes of the Ch'in and then Han dynasties.

In order to determine the evolution of the character *fa* to encompass the notion of penal law, I have examined its usage in the texts which predate the emergence of the Legalist school. At the same time, I have attempted to identify the language in which the concept of penal law was conveyed prior to the extension of the meaning of *fa*. Although the problems of authenticity and chronological order limit the authority with which assertions can be made, it is possible to construct a double hypothesis. First, the vast majority of occurrences of the character *fa* in early texts indicate that prior to the rise of the Legalist tradition the character *fa* was used to convey the meaning of "model or standard." Only well into the Warring States period when the Legalist theorists had taken over this character and injected it with their own meaning did it come to connote "penal law." Second, before the character *fa* evolved to cover the notion of "penal law" this idea was commonly expressed by the character *hsing,* which meant basically "punishments" and, by extension, "penal law." I shall proceed on the basis of this hypothesis to examine the place of penal law in each of the major pre-Ch'in schools of thought: Taoism, Confucianism, and Legalism.

FA IN PRE-CH'IN POLITICAL PHILOSOPHY

THE TAOIST TRADITION

Because the *Lao Tzu* does not deal with penal law directly, it is necessary to extrapolate from the general attitude toward government expressed there. And this attitude of the *Lao Tzu* toward government is summed up succinctly in a passage from chapter 75: "Difficulties in governing the people occur because of the interfering activities of their superiors." These "interfering activities" *(yu-wei)* of those in political control are diametrically opposed to the attitude of "nonaction" *(wu-wei)* central to Taoist political thought. The *Lao Tzu* does not accept laws as an embodiment of objective standards of popular justice adopted by society as a means of preserving social order. Rather, it construes the imposition of laws and regulations as a device employed by various interest groups to consolidate their advantageous positions and achieve their selfish ends. The *Lao Tzu*'s characterization of the existing government expressed in chapter 53 reflects a sense of outrage:

> Their [the rulers'] court is rank with corruption,
> The fields are wholly overgrown with weeds,
> The granaries are utterly empty.
> Their clothing is ornate and embroidered
> And on their belts hang sharp swords;
> They are gorged with food and drink
> And their riches and possessions far exceed their needs.
> They are what are called the ringleaders of brigands. . . .

Given the *Lao Tzu*'s rejection of any universal standard of morality, laws are regarded as being relative to the interests of those who would inflict them on society at large. They are seen as the imposition of unnatural constraints on the spontaneous development of the many in order to serve the few in power. As such, they are nothing short of "a form of aggression on the nature of man."[7] With laws and regulations restricting the natural expression of the people, a tension develops between the oppressive directives of political authority and the people's impetus for natural development. As the government introduces increasingly severe measures to cope with this tension, its action in turn leads to an increasingly strong reaction from the people. This spiral of self-fueling political disintegration is described in chapter 57:

> The more restrictions and prohibitions in the empire,
> The deeper will the people sink into destitution;
> The more sharp weapons possessed by the court,
> The deeper will the nation sink into disorder;
> The more dexterity and adroitness among the craftsmen,
> The more extensive will be the production of nefarious creations;
> The more overt the laws and decrees,[8]
> The more prevalent will be the thieves and brigands.

Thus all "active" measures to effect social order serve only to hasten its dissolution. When government measures reach an extreme of oppression and brutality and the tension between political constraint and natural development becomes unendurable, the people, in spite of the obvious threat of death, rise up to destroy the source of this tension (chapters 72 and 74):

> When the people no longer fear authority,
> Then great calamities will erupt.

If the people do not fear death,
How can death be used to intimidate them?
. . . There is always an executioner who carries out the capital sentence.
Now, to stand in for the executioner in putting others to death—
This is called standing in for the master carpenter in cutting wood.
Among those who would do this, few indeed would escape injuring their
    own hands.

A government obliged to implement cruel punishments is perceived as
having initiated the process of decline which requires these desperate
remedies—and, at the same time, as having rendered these measures incapable of realizing social order. Ironically, invoking capital punishment
is itself the death knell of the political authority which has imposed it on
the people.

The obvious inconsistency between employing laws and punishments
as a means of effecting political control and the general tenor of *Lao
Tzu*'s thought does not help in unraveling the mystery of the relationship
between Taoist and Legalist thought.[9]

In discussing punishment and penal law in the *Chuang Tzu,* I follow
the widely accepted opinion that only the "Inner Chapters" *(nei p'ien)*
can be attributed to Chuang Tzu himself,[10] and that these seven chapters
should be taken as the *Chuang Tzu* core. The primary concern of the
"Inner Chapters" is personal attainment of the Way and the result-
ing enlightened state of mind—a project of personal realization to be
achieved through a process of overcoming the ego-self and attending to
the natural unfolding of one's unique and yet integrated *conatus.* Sociopolitical problems, derived from the unnatural expression of ego-individ-
uality, are secondary if not incidental.[11] An important feature of these
"Inner Chapters" is the assertion that all prescriptive and impositional
mores are a function of one's perspective and, hence, relative. Since law
is usually regarded as being based on some notion of universal morality,
it follows that Chuang Tzu would reject such law as being both arbitrary
and personally inhibiting.[12] Further, one persistent theme in this "Inner
Chapters" section is the desire to live out one's natural span.[13] While
Chuang Tzu would not ascribe any intrinsic value to the arbitrarily proclaimed laws which embody arbitrarily conceived moral standards, there
is more than a hint in these "Inner Chapters" that Chuang Tzu would
recommend an expedient conformity to prevailing conditions and standards.[14] The "realizing person" *(chen jen),* while aware of the fundamental emptiness of politically imposed regulations, does not flagrantly
violate these rules and purposely endanger himself.

There is one further point worth mentioning with respect to these
seven "Inner Chapters." As A. C. Graham observes, "The *Inner Chap-*

ters have as fantastic a menagerie of invalids as the Gospels, but the viewpoint is quite different; they are seen quite without pity and with the same interest and respect as princes and sages.''[15] Many of these invalids are the victims of mutilating punishments—frequently the removal of a foot. Even though they have been thus served by the exercise of penal law, they are more often than not the representatives of the enlightened sage. This being the case, we must assume that Chuang Tzu did not regard the contravention of penal law as grounds for disqualifying a person from the attainment of the highest awareness.

There is another portion of the *Chuang Tzu* we might consider with regard to its attitude toward penal law and punishments—what Graham refers to as the "Primitivist documents."[16] These chapters, quite unlike the "Inner Chapters," concern themselves with social and political problems and contain passages reminiscent of and at times even paralleling the *Lao Tzu*. One theme which these Primitivist chapters share with the *Lao Tzu* is the "decline" theory of history,[17] an interpretation which not only holds that the state of untrammeled simplicity and uncorrupted natural organization is to be preferred over acquired wisdom and unnaturally imposed order, but which further condemns present-day government for the laws, taxes, and corruption which represent nothing more sanctified than the sacrifice of the well-being of the many for the comfort of the few. This devolutionary theory of history, having condemned modern civilization, exalts high antiquity and its natural simplicity as the ideal.

The last section of "Horses' Hoofs" *(Ma-t'i)* depicts an idealized and romanticized village society of high antiquity, slumbering in simplicity eons away from the degenerate influences of culture and civilization. Laws, as one element in the trappings of civilization, are to be rejected along with the contrived morality and artificial social norms of the so-called sages. "Pilfering from Chests" *(Ch'ü-ch'ieh)* states the point clearly (24/10/24): "Only when you have completely obliterated the sagely laws of the world can you begin to communicate with the people." Laws together with tallies, seals, measurements, scales, and all such proud achievements of civilization are condemned as contrived innovations which have corrupted man's original nature. In "Leaving the People Alone" *(Tsai-yu)* 25/11/7 it states: "Since, with much clamor and ado, the rulers from the Three Dynasties on have always relied upon rewards and punishments, how could the people have any time to find contentment in their inborn natures?"

Although the Taoist texts do not deal specifically with the question of penal law, it is possible to make informed speculation on the basis of their attitude toward government in general. The attitudes of *Lao Tzu* and the "core" *Chuang Tzu* are generally consistent:[18] both hold that law is one aspect of the sham called culture and, further, that it is contrary to the notion of *wu-wei* and inimical to the natural development of those residing within its jurisdiction. It is from this concept of *wu-wei* that the Taoist attitude toward penal law can be most effectively derived.

I have argued elsewhere that the political Taoism represented by the *Lao Tzu, Chuang Tzu,* and *Huai Nan Tzu* contains four necessary conditions for a comprehensive anarchism: a theory of human nature such that its realization is a function of its "freedom"; a rejection of coercive authority as a limitation on human freedom and thus an obstacle to human realization; some notion of a noncoercive, nonauthoritarian society that could be realized in the future as the direct and unretarded expression of human nature and its possibilities; and some practical method of evolving from the present authoritarian reality to the nonauthoritarian ideal.[19] The second condition, perhaps the principal characteristic of most Western anarchist theories, is satisfied by the Taoist notion of *wu-wei*. The philological similarities between anarchism and *wu-wei* as terms used to characterize these political doctrines are striking. Both terms refer to an absence of rule or authority. The expression *"wu-wei"* like "anarchy" cannot be used to describe the ideal for *individual* action inasmuch as it refers to a relationship obtaining among things. It is the negation of the authoritarian determination of one thing by another. Metaphysically, *wu-wei* is the negation of predetermined purpose, divine design, Providence; politically, it is the negation of dictatorial authority. It represents personal freedom in the Taoist political scheme.

Significantly, *wu-wei* is a negative way of expressing *tzu-jan*—commonly translated as "natural" or "spontaneous" but perhaps more adequately rendered "spontaneous natural arising." That is to say, it repudiates artificially imposed order while expressing compliance with natural harmony. As it states in the *Chuang Tzu* (29/12/7): "To do something in accordance with *wu-wei* is called 'natural.'" *Wu-wei* is used to characterize the action of the realized person in his relationship to both the human and the natural environments (*Chuang Tzu* 58/22/18): "The sage is attentive to the beauty of the world around him and comprehends the principles of the myriad things. Thus the consummate person *(chih jen)* does not act, the great sage *(ta sheng)* does not do. This is what is meant by 'observing the world around you.'" The "spontaneous" connotations of *wu-wei* enable us to align political Taoism with Western anarchist theorists such as Proudhon and Colin Ward who argue explicitly that anarchism refers not to the contrast between political order and disorder but to the contrast between natural order emanating from below and the artificial order—laws and regulations—imposed from above.[20]

There is an important distinction between Taoist political thought and

Western anarchist theory. Taoism, with its conception of the coextensive relationship between person and state, does not reject the state as an artificial structure; rather it sees the state as a *natural* institution, analogous perhaps to the family. The *Lao Tzu* certainly rejects coercive rule and authoritarian government but, importantly, devotes considerable attention to noncoercive and nonauthoritarian organization under the aegis of the sage-king. This conception of state as a natural institution is implicit in *Lao Tzu* 17:

> The most excellent ruler—the people do not know that he exists;
> The second most excellent—they love and praise him;
> The next—they fear him;
> And the worst—they look on him with contempt.
> When the ruler's integrity is inadequate,
> There will be those who do not trust him.
> Relaxed, the ideal ruler prizes his words.
> When his accomplishments are complete and the affairs of state are in order,
> The common people all say, "We are naturally like this."

Natural action on the part of the ruler is possible in a state where he has a specific organizational function rather than an authoritarian role.

This notion of *wu-wei* as an alternative to imposed law and regulation is further developed in the first treatise in the *Huai Nan Tzu—Tracing the Tao (Yüan-tao)*. First, an amplified and perhaps more concise explanation of *wu-wei* is given with its important political connotations (1/9a):

> Quiescently he does not do, yet all is done; impassively he does not impose order, yet all is properly ordered. "Does not do" means not taking precedence over other things in what one does; "all is done" means accommodating what other things do; "does not impose order" means not changing what is so-of-itself; "all is properly ordered" means accommodating the natural integration of things.

The treatise goes on to describe the institution of rulership and makes the contrast between natural order and the wielding of impositional authority (1/15a):

> The empire is something which I possess, and I am also something which the empire possesses. How could there exist some gap between the empire and me! Why must "possessing the empire" mean collecting authority, grasping onto political advantage, and manipulating the lever of life and death to effect one's edicts and commands? This is not what I mean by "possessing the empire." Quite simply, what I mean is self-realization. If I realize myself then the empire also realizes me. If the empire and I realize each other then we will always possess each other. Again, how could there possibly be any distance between us?

Although Taoist political theory does accept the notion of ruler and political organization as a natural condition, it carries on a sustained opposition to the authoritarian rule symbolized by laws and regulations and points to the contradiction implicit in the project of "enforcing" order. For the Taoists, then, at least ideally, *wu-wei* is perceived as a desirable alternative to penal law.

THE CONFUCIAN TRADITION

Confucius. In exploring the attitude of the Confucian school to penal law, I have found that there is a group of important scholars who share an interpretation which is not wholly consistent with my own. The main features of their interpretation are worth summarizing here.[21] First, Confucius and the early adherents of his teachings advocated a policy of social order to be effected through moral education. This order would be brought about through a government policy of educating the people in appropriate *li*—social norms and institutions. Second, these early Confucians regarded penal law and punishments as being inconsistent with their social norms and institutions and, as such, voiced opposition to penal law generally and to the publication of penal codes specifically. In a word, the attitude of Confucius and his early disciples to penal law and punishments was one of undisguised hostility. Finally, the Confucians gradually became resigned to the necessity of penal laws and punishments to the extent that the "belief that punishments were supplementary to virtue and moral influence became quite popular among Han Confucianists."[22]

While I cannot dispute this interpretation in detail here, I would suggest that this thesis is anachronistic. It assumes that Confucius registered a contrast between penal law and social norms that did not really emerge until several centuries later when the Confucians were called upon to defend themselves against the challenge of the rising Legalists.

There is a major flaw in this popular interpretation which seeks a clear contrast between Confucius' political philosophy and that of the Legalists—the underlying assumption that penal law and social norms are mutually exclusive. It is suggested that early Confucian doctrine advocated only social norms while rejecting penal law and its attendant punishments. It is further suggested that the Legalist position is an absolute commitment to penal laws and punishments to the exclusion of social norms.

Hsiao Kung-ch'üan makes a pertinent observation with respect to social norms and penal laws and the confusion that can arise in dealing with them.[23] He suggests that *li* and *fa* have both a narrow and a broad sense. The narrow meaning of *fa* refers to statutes for hearing litigations and passing judgments. The narrow meaning of *li,* on the other hand, refers to a code of rites and ceremonies governing specified religious and social institutions. At this narrow level, there is little confusion between these two concepts. In a broader sense, however, *fa* and *li* both refer to a system for administering government and regulating the people. The overlapping connotations of these two concepts arose as a result of changing conditions in Chinese society. Society had at one point based its structure on a clan system and simply projected it onto the various social institutions. There came a time, however, when the clan system gave way to feudal society and the powers-that-be found it necessary to replace the notion of "treating relatives with familial affection" *(ch'in ch'in)* with one of "honoring the noble" *(kuei kuei).* As this new system emerged, the designation *li* was retained. But the scope and content of this new system of *li* was much broader and more complex than that which had served the clan, and thus it came to overlap the broader aspects of *fa.*

In the early clan society, then, we have two clearly defined concepts—penal law and regulations governing rites and ceremonies. With the rise of feudalism, the penal laws gradually became more complex and more comprehensive, covering increasingly complicated relationships and institutions. At the same time, *li* were expanded and elaborated upon in response to the new social structure. It was in the gradual inflation of these two concepts of *fa* and *li* that the distinction between them became blurred. Since *li* eventually came to embody the total spectrum of social norms, customs, and mores, and since penal laws are usually devised in response to some prevailing morality, the relationship binding these two notions is immediately evident.

The popular interpretation of Confucius outlined above implies that the Legalists' establishment of penal law precludes a system of *li.* In the Legalist state, *li* are still necessary to order the society and give it a vertical and horizontal structure, but when a person comes into conflict with the law, existing *li* are superseded by the demands of the law. Without *li,* the Legalist state would be devoid of social distinctions. How would one person act toward another? What would the reward of rank mean if it implied no increase in social status? The Legalist position is not an across-the-board replacement of *li* with *fa* but a conviction that *li* alone are insufficient to achieve the Legalist objectives of strong state and political stability. Arguing from this conviction, the Legalists insisted that *li* be supplemented with a comprehensive system of penal laws.

On the basis of these observations I would argue that in both the Confucian and Legalist traditions, penal law and social norms, far from being seen as antagonistic, were in fact regarded as complementary elements in their respective conceptions of effective government. And I believe that this position is borne out by passages in the *Analects* and *Tso chuan* relating to Confucius' attitude toward penal law and punishments.

The Confucius depicted in the *Analects* advocated government by moral suasion and example as the core of his political philosophy. This emphasis on education and moral uplifting did not, however, prevent the practical Confucius from assigning penal law a place in his political thought as an unfortunate but necessary backstop for moral education. Confucius, like Mencius after him, was egalitarian in theory but in practice still clung to typically feudal distinctions respecting social status (14/8/9): "The Master said: 'Common people can be made to do something but not to understand why.'"

In his contrast between the consummate and the unrealized persons, attention to penal law rather than the exercise of special privilege is registered as a characteristic of Confucius' ideal (6/4/11): "While a consummate person cherishes observance of the law, a base person cherishes special privilege." There is an important passage in the *Analects* that juxtaposes the concept of government by moral education with that of government by force (2/2/3):

> Lead the people with administrative policies and regulate them with penal law, and they will avoid conflict but be without a sense of shame. Lead them with virtue and regulate them with social norms, and they will have a sense of shame and moreover seek to do what is good.

In this passage, political leadership based exclusively on regulation and law is contrasted with leadership based on example and moral education. This passage is all too frequently interpreted as offering two alternatives for government.[24] For Confucius, however, society is a creative moral achievement. The thrust of this statement is that political policies and penal laws are not in themselves a sufficient basis for the highest form of social and political leadership. To achieve truly effective and long-lasting political harmony, moral education must receive priority; only where it proves ineffectual should laws and regulations be applied. The relationship between moral education and the fair application of punishment is made clear in 25/13/3: "If affairs are not accomplished, social norms and music do not prosper. If social norms and music do not prosper, punishments and penalties will not hit the mark."

Social norms are conceived of as a tradition of regulations which reinforce the distinctions in a clearly defined feudal hierarchy. Their main function is to divide, separate, and structure. Music, on the other hand, is a harmonizing influence. Its function is to facilitate social cohesion. This passage relates well to the Confucian commitment to the moral instruction of the people as the primary function of the state. When the framework of *li* has been inculcated in the people through education, then and only then can punishments be extended to those deserving of them. As it states in 41/20/2: "The Master said: 'To execute men without having instructed them is called brutality.' " When properly applied, social norms and punishments are seen as two complementary rather than conflicting elements: both are conducive to a properly ordered society.

In addition to the passages cited above, scholars frequently make reference to the following statements in their discussion of Confucius' attitude toward penal law (*Analects* 24/12/19, 25/13/11, 23/12/13):

> Chi K'ang Tzu asked Confucius about government: "What if I kill those without the Way in order to encourage those with the Way?" Confucius replied: "You are the government. Why must you use killing? If you want to be good, the people will be good!"

> The Master said: "Where good men ruled a state for one century, they could transform the violent and dispense with killing. How really true these words are!"

> The Master said: "In hearing litigations, I am as good as anyone. What we must do is make it so there are no litigations!"

Contrary to the interpretation of some scholars,[25] I cannot believe that these passages represent a total rejection of corporal punishment. Simply because Confucius does not regard penal law as the *best* method of achieving social order, it does not follow that he regards execution as an inappropriate punishment for murder. He may argue that where moral government is practiced and people are made morally responsible, they will not commit murder. But Confucius, profoundly pragmatic philosopher that he is, has serious doubts about the possibility of ever attaining this ideal.

The attitude of Confucius to punishments and penal law which can be pieced together from the *Tso chuan* is generally consistent with that revealed in the *Analects*. There is the well-known case of Tzu-ch'an casting tripods and inscribing laws on them. It has been suggested that Shu-hsiang's letter to Tzu-ch'an bitterly denouncing this act represents a very "Confucian" (though predating Confucius) position with respect to law.[26] Yet whenever Confucius mentions Tzu-ch'an in the *Tso chuan* he has nothing but adulation for him,[27] praising him as "worthy to be the foundation of his state."[28] Shu-hsiang is also praised—praised for his fair and impartial application of the country's laws.[29] In the *Tso chuan* (403/Chao 20/7), Confucius, commenting on the administration of the government after the death of Tzu-ch'an, insists upon the necessity of both mildness and severity in government. Only a blending of these two elements will result in effective political control and administration. While Confucius has moral government and a state free of crime and litigation as his ideal, he is at the same time aware of the human effort it would take to approach this ideal. In the *Analects* (25/13/11), for example, he suggests that even good men in government would need a century to instill their moral precepts in the people to the extent that they would no longer have occasion to apply the death penalty. In progressing from the political turmoil of his own age to the realization of his ideal state, Confucius was convinced that moral education and punishment both had roles to play. In *Tso chuan* (483/Ai 11/2), he argues that the only alternative to compliance with laws is disorder and chaos.

Undoubtedly the most problematic passage in the *Tso chuan* with respect to my interpretation of Confucius' attitude toward penal law is the 430/Chao 29/5 passage in which Confucius objects to the laws of Fan Hsüan Tzu being inscribed onto tripods in 513 b.c. It is the similarity between this passage and the Shu-hsiang letter to Tzu-ch'an which has encouraged scholars to associate Confucius' attitude toward penal law with that of Shu-hsiang.[30] H. G. Creel does not accept the *Tso chuan* attribution of this passage to Confucius, asserting that "it is completely at variance with the whole tenor of everything that we have reason to believe to be his philosophy."[31] I must disagree with Creel here. Following Tu Kuo-hsiang,[32] I am not convinced that the thought contained in this passage is inconsistent with Confucius' general sentiments. Instead I suggest another interpretation.

In the first place, Confucius is not objecting to penal law here. Rather, he is objecting to an inferior concept of laws—those promulgated by Fan Hsüan Tzu at the spring hunting ceremony—to supersede a superior system of laws—those established by the son of King Wu of Chou and continued by Duke Wen of Chin. Moreover, Confucius' position is that laws, like social norms, must be responsive to the creative development of the society. Hence the act of articulating laws and inscribing them in bronze undermines the process of constantly reformulating the laws to ensure their appropriateness to prevailing circumstances. And, finally, Confucius objects to the inscription of the laws onto a tripod because he fears misplaced respect. The tripod, an ornament of considerable value, might itself become an object of respect rather than those who embody the law. For Confucius, it is the judgment of the consummate person rather than the letter of the law that must take precedence.

Thus there is no portion of the *Tso chuan* which can be fairly construed as a Confucian rejection of penal laws. On the contrary, consistent with the picture of Confucius abstracted from the *Analects,* there is every reason to believe that Confucius regarded penal law as a necessary if subordinate aspect of proper government.

Mencius. Perhaps the most striking feature of Mencius' attitude toward punishments and penal laws is the degree to which he echoes the sentiments expressed by Confucius. Like Confucius before him, Mencius is committed to the ideal of a political administration grounded in the moral achievement of those who would rule—an ideal that Mencius calls "benevolent government" *(jen cheng)*. Implicit in this notion of benevolent government is the basic Confucian principle that the ruler and his higher officers exert themselves in perfecting their personal natures. The perfection of their moral natures is pursued through a process of interaction with those dependent upon them for direction. And the ordinary people, naturally sympathetic to the dynamic modeling of political leaders, emulate the quality of their humanity and respond to them with moral conduct.

Although Mencius insists that *all* persons have the natural potential to realize their incipient moral endowment,[33] as a member of a highly structured feudal society with clearly delineated social distinctions and limited opportunities he nevertheless clings to the elitist yet perhaps realistic position revealed in a well-known passage (20/3A/4): "Thus it is said: Some people labor with their minds while others labor with their backs. Those who labor with their minds rule; those who labor with their backs are ruled." Theoretically Mencius is egalitarian but, practically speaking, he is still convinced that the contrast between the noble, morally developed person and the inferior, morally stunted person will be a continuing condition of human society. The noble, guided by the moral achievements of their tradition, determine a course of action by commitment to the moral rightness of each situation in which they themselves participate. The inferior, on the other hand, insensitive to the proddings of their own nature, must be directed toward the same course of action by socially imposed standards and penal laws. That both Confucius and Mencius regard internal and voluntary compliance with the dictates of the moral nature to be infinitely preferable to a resentful bowing to external coercion is apparent (12/2A/3): "It is a case of the people's weakness rather than their willing compliance where force is used to subjugate them. But it is with happiness in their hearts and a sincere willingness to comply where virtue is used to win them over. This was the way in which the seventy disciples submitted to Confucius."[34]

The closer the rulers can come to the ideal of benevolent government, the less they have to rely upon external constraints to achieve civil obedience. While tyrannical government sustains itself by severe punishments and oppressive taxes, benevolent government can win popular support without recourse to coercion and material incentives (2/1A/5): "If your majesty extends benevolent government to the people, reducing punishments and penalties and lightening the burden of taxes, . . . you will be able to send them against the stout armor and sharp weapons of Ch'in and Ch'u armed with nothing but clubs." Conversely, where the government in the first instance ignores its moral obligation to ensure that its subjects have a sufficient standard of living and then pursues a policy of merciless suppression when they quite naturally rise in revolt, this is tantamount to setting out to ensnare the people (19/3A/3): "People with a constant means have a constant heart; those without a constant means are without a constant heart. Those without a constant heart will be wanton and dissipated and will know no restraint. To punish them once they have fallen into crime is to have laid a trap for the people."[35]

Another aspect of Mencius' attitude toward penal law which can be gleaned from the *Mencius*—an aspect which is not made explicit in the teachings of Confucius—is found in the following 12/2A/4 passage: "Men of superior character fill the offices at court, men of ability are in government posts, and the state embarks on an era of peace. If the ruler takes advantage of such a time to make his policies and penal laws clear to the people, then the powerful states will have reason to stand in awe of him." In a properly ordered state, the ruler exerts himself in making government regulations and penal law clear to his people.

Like Confucius, Mencius abhors the use of punishments, but where necessary he insists that the full weight and severity of the law be brought to bear on those whose conduct is detrimental to the public good. He has no patience, for example, with warmongers (28/4A/15): "In battles fought for territory, corpses fill the open fields; in battles fought for cities, corpses fill the cities. This is called leading the land to consume human flesh. Death is too good for such a crime! Those adept at war should therefore be subjected to the harshest punishments." Generally, then, Mencius' attitude toward punishments and penal law is a continuation of the view espoused by Confucius. Being totally committed to the ideal of moral government, both philosophers regard penal law as an unfortunate but at times necessary reinforcement for social organization.

Hsün Tzu. In dealing with penal law in Confucius and Mencius, I have had to sift the source material and at times even extrapolate from other more clearly defined concepts in order to piece together a coherent attitude. The *Hsün Tzu* is a different case. Where Confucius and Mencius, committed to the primacy of moral education, could afford to deal with penal law in a perfunctory manner, the emergence and subsequent strength of the Legalist challenge to Confucianism made it imperative that Hsün Tzu define his terms carefully and take up a clear position. As a consequence, Hsün Tzu provides us with a reasonably lucid statement on penal law and punishments.[36]

The opening passage of the "The Way of the Ruler" *(Chün-tao)* chapter illustrates the debt Hsün Tzu owes to his Confucian antecedents. At the same time, it reveals an emphasis which distinguishes Hsün Tzu from the earlier tradition:

> Just as there are disorderly rulers, but no such thing as a disorderly state, so there are persons who effect proper order, but no such thing as laws *(fa)* which can effect it. The principles *(fa)* of Archer Yi have not been lost, but his descendants cannot hit the target in every generation. The laws *(fa)* of Yü still survive, but the House of Hsia does not rule as king for every genera-tion. Thus laws cannot establish themselves and cases cannot determine themselves. Where there is the right person, they survive, but where the right person cannot be found, they are lost. Laws are the source of proper order, but the consummate person is the origin of the laws. Thus where there is the consummate person, even if the laws have been whittled away they will still be enough to meet all contingencies. Where there is no consummate person, however, even if you have a full complement of the laws, they will not be applied at the right time, will not be responsive to changing circumstances, and will only result in disorder.

The principal assertion which identifies Hsün Tzu as a Confucian in his attitude toward penal law is the importance vested in the consummate person as the innovator, interpreter, and executor of the law (and the ancillary role accorded to the objective laws themselves). Hsün Tzu at one point suggests that penal laws are a basic element in the state (52/14/10): "Thus the territory and the people, the Way and the laws, are the foundation of the state." At the same time he is emphatic in subordinat-ing the laws themselves to the people who interpret and apply them.[37] The laws were devised by mortals and require competent trustees to uphold them. The laws can lead to either order or disorder and are them-selves no guarantee of social equanimity. It is the caliber of the people who implement the laws which is in fact the crucial factor (26/9/14): "Thus there has been disorder in spite of good laws, but from ancient times to the present there has never been disorder in spite of the consum-mate person."[38] The priority of people over law is a recurring theme in the text. Even after the laws have been established, tried, and proved effective, "where there is the right person, they survive, but where the right person cannot be found, they are lost."[39]

In putting the human element first and regarding cold and abstract law as a secondary consideration in realizing social order, Hsün Tzu is consistent with the Confucius-Mencius tradition.[40] Another feature of his attitude toward penal law which seems to have been carried over from his Confucian predecessors is evident in his commitment to a social hierarchy and class distinctions. Like Mencius before him, Hsün Tzu on a theoretical level taught the equal potential of all people.[41] Again, like Mencius, on a practical level he is resigned to a continuing contrast between the morally developed and the underdeveloped dimensions of society. Those who are receptive to moral instruction can be regulated by tradition, but the lower reaches of society who are beyond the pale of moral influence must be kept in line by the rule of law (32/10/19): "From the gentleman on up, distinctions must be maintained with social norms and music, but the common people must be controlled with laws and precedents."

There is another characteristic of Hsün Tzu's attitude toward penal law which, although perhaps implicit in the traditional Confucian teachings, was not really articulated until Hsün Tzu. In confronting the positivistic attitudes of the Legalists, Hsün Tzu drew a sharp distinction between the spirit and principle of the law on the one hand and the letter and detail of the law on the other (44/12/4): "Where one does not understand the principle behind the law but works on the basis of its explicit formulation, even where his knowledge is extensive, his administration of affairs is certain to be a disaster."[42] This distinction between principle and explicit formulation marks a crucial difference between the Confucian and Legalist concepts of penal law, and it was probably the Legalist challenge to Confucian doctrine which pressed Hsün Tzu to clarify this point. While the Confucians saw law as reflecting the moral accomplishments of the inherited tradition and insisted that comprehension of rightness *(yi)* must stand behind the application of abstract law, the Legalists held that the laws must remain objective and free from the human element. Hsün Tzu underscores this crucial moral core in the Confucian conception of penal law.

In the following passage, Hsün Tzu stresses the pedagogical responsibilities of government and reiterates Confucius' and Mencius' contention[43] that punishment is only justifiable after those in authority have made every effort to educate the people in the moral precepts underlying the law (35/10/80): "Therefore, if you mete out punishments without having first instructed the people, even though your punishments are everywhere you will still be unable to bring depravity under control. If you fail to mete out punishments after having instructed the people, dissolute people will not be discouraged."

Although Hsün Tzu's attitude toward punishments does not diverge substantially from that of Confucius and Mencius, he does state his position in clearer terms than either of his predecessors. Generally he follows the commonsense Confucian dictum of reward or punishment according to the deed. In response to a hypothetical suggestion that the ancients, having brought stability to the world, developed a system of symbolic punishments as an alternative to using corporal punishments, Hsün Tzu replies in very certain terms (66/18/37):

> This suggestion is incorrect. If the age were in fact peaceful and there were no more criminals, there would be no more use for symbolic punishments than there would be for corporal punishments. But if there were criminals and all they did was commute their punishments, even murders would not have been punished. And if the most serious crimes received the lightest punishments, the ordinary person would not know right from wrong. There could be no greater disaster! Now, the basic purpose for punishing people is to put a stop to violence and to show up evil as evil and, moreover, to deter any recurrence of the crime. Where murderers are not executed and people who harm others are not punished, this is showing favor to violent criminals and magnaminity to thieves. It is certainly not showing up evil as evil! Thus symbolic punishments are not the product of some ancient golden age but an innovation of a modern period of disorder.[44]

Punishment is unquestionably directed at the eradication of evil elements. But rather than stopping here, it is also thought to be a positive aid to moral education. When Hsün Tzu advocates the use of severe punishments,[45] his primary reason for doing so is because he believes they will instill an abhorrence of the crime in the people and reinforce their sense of right and wrong. The Legalists, by contrast, accept the deterrent function of punishments but show little interest in the moral edification of the people.

It is now possible to list certain characteristics as typical of the Confucian position on penal law and punishments:

1. Good laws by themselves are not a sufficient condition for proper social order. Proper order is the consequence of benevolent government undertaken by a moral ruler who is at best aided by a system of laws. Hence it is the character of the ruler which is the critical factor in the attainment of political stability.
2. Penal laws are an abstraction from the moral accomplishments of the tradition. For this reason, political leaders of superior character are necessary to interpret the spirit behind these laws. This subjective element is essential in the service of justice, which can never be realized through the mechanical enforcement of a code of laws. Subjective evaluation comes first; laws are simple guidelines.

3. Laws and the consequent punishments can be justifiably applied only after every effort has been made to provide the people with moral education.
4. Laws and the consequent punishments have both a deterrent and an educational function.
5. Laws, as mere guides, must always remain open to interpretation in order to conform fully with the spirit of the law. As such, they must remain flexible to meet ever-changing circumstances.
6. Although the higher echelons of society, by virtue of a moral awareness nurtured in their enactment of traditional social norms, can generally be led by an appeal to cultivated moral sensibility, the lower strata require the coercive pressure of penal law to keep them in line. Whether a person should be led by social norms or be pushed by law depends on his degree of moral awareness. Given the Confucian commitment to educate society at large in moral precepts and the Confucian determination to win general appreciation for social norms, a case can be made for at least a theoretical ideal of equality before the law.
7. In the ideal society, penal laws do exist but the moral development of the people is such that these regulations are never violated.
8. On the practical side, given the less-than-ideal society with which the Confucian thinkers had to contend, they follow the general principle that the punishment should fit the crime.
9. Inasmuch as penal laws are an expression of the moral accomplishments of the inherited tradition, the ruler is bound by law to the same degree that he is bound by his own moral awareness.

THE LEGALIST TRADITION

In analyzing the Legalist position on "penal law" *(fa)*, I rely primarily on the concept as presented in *The Book of Lord Shang (Shang-chün shu)*, taking account of any obvious discrepancy between that work and the *Han Fei Tzu.*[46] In dealing with penal law in the Legalist tradition, *The Book of Lord Shang* is given priority for several reasons. First, frequent reference is made throughout the corpus of early Chinese literature to Shang Yang and his doctrine of penal law and punishments—a doctrine almost invariably identified as *fa.*[47] These references, coupled with Shang Yang's historical position in the Legalist tradition, encourage the opinion that he was himself the father of the doctrine of *fa.* I suspect it was he who took this character *fa*—which had until then probably connoted "model or standard"—and, injecting it with new meaning and giving it a broader application, popularized it as the main tenet underlying his entire political philosophy. Whereas there is some debate regarding the authenticity of *The Book of Lord Shang* and its various parts,[48] most scholars agree that the text does contain the basic tenets of Shang Yang's political doctrine. Again, the sections of the text, while possibly dating from different periods and originating from different hands, are generally consistent and even at times repetitious in their content.[49] From this work reaching back to the inception of the *fa* doctrine, it might be possible to construct a consistent and reasonably complete outline of its main characteristics.

Second, the *Han Fei Tzu,* while ascribing the establishment and development of the *fa* political philosophy to Shang Yang and generally referring to him with undisguised reverence, nevertheless maintains that the Shang Yang program of government based almost wholly upon this concept of *fa* has definite limitations.[50] Han Fei absorbs the basic principles and the spirit of Shang Yang's political philosophy, but in accommodating administrative concepts from other thinkers to construct his Legalist amalgam, he cannot help but modify certain aspects of the original *fa* doctrine. In basing this discussion on *The Book of Lord Shang* conception of *fa* and then noting any *Han Fei Tzu* divergence from this source, I hope to arrive at a comprehensive characterization of the Legalist position on penal law and punishments.

Shang Yang. Shang Yang's political theory and administrative methods serve both a point of view and a purpose. Characteristic of the Legalist theorists, Shang Yang's program of government is addressed to the ruler, and it is in the service of his interests that the text directs itself. And the ultimate purpose served is political survival. That is to say, under the conditions prevailing among the states of pre-Ch'in China, failure in the struggle against rival contenders meant certain political extinction. History had taught that there was no safety in the halfway measures of alliance and coexistence. Because this single and overwhelming purpose of international domination colors Shang Yang's political philosophy from start to finish, it is essential to keep it always in sight when analyzing his thought.

For Shang Yang, political domination of the Chinese states could be accomplished only through military conquest.[51] In an era in which internecine struggle had become convention, this conclusion was neither unrealistic nor extreme. To raise an army of some consequence, the ruler would require the interdependent resources of a strong economy and a large population. And to transform the rabble into front-line troops, the ruler would have to impress order onto the population and use his position as ruler to direct the public effort toward realization of this national purpose. This was the problem to which Shang Yang addressed himself, and his answer was *fa.*

Shang Yang saw the ruler's task of subjugating, regulating, and shap-
ing his people as comparable to the blacksmith forging his metal or the
potter fashioning clay (4/8b, pp. 64–65): "Therefore the root of dominating the people lies in holding control over them. This is analogous to
the blacksmith working his metal or the potter his clay. If the root is not
firmly established, the people will be like birds of the air or beasts of the
wild, and who is able to control them?"[52]

Penal law, as the source of order in the state, is the very basis of government (5/15a, p. 94): "Laws and edicts are the destiny of the people,
the root of achieving proper order, and the means of containing the people." The strict application of the law is conducive to success in the two
fundamental and complementary occupations of the state—agriculture
and warfare (5/5b, p. 79): "Therefore a perspicacious ruler pays careful
attention to the laws, and none of the people within his borders have
wicked minds, sophists and recluses are conscripted into the front lines,
and all the people are eagerly engaged in farming and warfare."

By adhering to the law and enforcing severe punishments, the ruler
instills fear into the hearts of his people, and people who are deathly
afraid of their superiors make good soldiers (1/13a, p. 18):

> A state which employs intelligence and cleverness but is without real strength
> will certainly perish. Timorous people encouraged by punishments will cer-
> tainly be brave, and brave people encouraged by rewards will give their lives.
> Where timorous people are brave and brave people are ready to give their
> lives, the state will have no equal.[53] A state with no equal is strong, and the
> strong will certainly rule the world.

Shang Yang focuses on this concept of law as a central principle around
which his political philosophy is constructed. But Shang Yang does not
stop at abstract theorizing with imaginary rulers implementing hypothetical laws. Rather, he is very specific about the source, the nature, and the
content of his legal regimen. In response to the frequent conservative
complaint that any alteration in the existing laws will be to the detriment
of public order, Shang Yang insists that different periods of history have
required different laws. To rely upon outmoded regulations to maintain
order in modern times is setting a course for certain disaster.[54] Shang
Yang concedes that in high antiquity when people were simple and honest, it was possible and even practical to rule them by encouraging virtue,
but the complexities of modern times demand government by law and
punishments.[55] Not only must law be responsive to changing circumstances, but further, it must take popular custom into account (3/2b–
3a, p. 37):

> Therefore the sage in governing a state does not imitate antiquity or follow[56]
> established procedures of the day; according with the times he lays down

policy, and assessing popular customs he lays down laws. If laws are set up without carefully examining the real conditions of the people, he will not succeed; if the government is administered in accordance with the times, it will not come up against opposition.[57]

As this passage makes abundantly clear, the ruler is not considerate of prevailing customs as a kindness to his people. Rather, he is aware that where laws are not consistent with the lifestyle of the people, they will be resisted and will prove ineffective. Shang Yang does not attempt to buttress law with a concept of divine sanction or the authority of antiquity's hoary sages. Instead he attributes good laws to the intelligent ruler. And these laws are "good" because they reflect insight into prevailing customs and a sensitivity to the changing conditions of his age. In promulgating new laws or reformulating the old, the ruler must proceed within the limits of human nature. He must punish on the basis of what people dislike and reward on the basis of what they like (3/4a, p. 39):

> It is because the people[58] have likes and dislikes that they can be governed, and the ruler must pay close attention to them. These likes and dislikes are the root of rewards and penalties. Now it is human nature to like rank and emoluments and to dislike punishments and penalties. It is to control the aspirations of the people and determine what they want that the ruler sets up the system of rewards and punishments.

The nature of the laws is one of the most frequently discussed subjects in the text. The laws in order to function effectively must be clear and simple (5/16a–b, p. 95):

> One cannot establish laws that only the intelligent can understand because the people are not all intelligent. One cannot establish laws that only those of superior character can understand because the people are not all of superior character. Thus the sage in establishing laws is sure to make them clear and easily understood and is precise in his terminology so that ignorant and intelligent alike are able to understand them.

Once the laws have been articulated in clear and easily grasped language, debate over their moral worth by self-styled social advocates must be actively discouraged (3/8a, p. 46): "Once the law has been laid down, do not allow 'good words' to injure it. Where one employs men who show results, the people will say little; where one employs 'good' men, the people will have a lot to talk about." Where law constitutes the one and only standard, the deceitful are rendered impotent (5/11b–12a, p. 90): "If officials have no standard beyond the law, even when they are cunning they will have no chance for depravity; if the people have no vehicle beyond warfare to achieve recognition for their abilities, even when they are treacherous they will have no chance for conspiracy."

The law must always be equitable, absolutely objective in its application, and strictly enforced (4/6a, pp. 60–61):

> What is meant by "making punishments uniform" is that punishments should know no rank or class. From minister of state or general down to the officials and common people, if anyone should fail to observe the edicts of the king, should violate prohibitions of the state or disrupt the ruler's institutions, his crime warrants death without pardon.[59]

By being fastidious in application of the law, the state impresses on its people that there is a necessary connection between crime and punishment. Anyone guilty of a crime will in due course be called upon to answer for it. And the punishment as the painful complement of law must be severe enough to dissuade others from pursuing the same course of criminal behavior. The Confucians follow the general principle that the punishment should fit the crime, but the Legalists advocate severe punishments for even the most minor infraction of the law (2/2a, p. 22): "Therefore, in applying punishments, if minor offenses are dealt with severely and hence cease to occur, then serious crimes will have no breeding ground." The Legalist reasoning is that by treating minor violations as the inception or intent of serious crimes and punishing them accordingly, the state is able to arrest the escalation and proliferation of criminal activities. In so containing serious crime, the state ultimately renders the application of the most severe measures[60] unnecessary (3/10a, p. 48): "If in applying penalties minor offenses are dealt with severely,[61] then minor offenses will not occur and serious crimes will not arise. This is called using punishment to abolish punishment. And when punishment has been abolished, the affairs of government can be accomplished."

While a program of complementary rewards and punishments is proposed as a means of encouraging popular compliance with governmental measures, it is in fact the punishments which receive most attention. Shang Yang suggests a ratio of nine punishments to one reward as the proper proportion for social order (1/13a, p. 18): "In a state that rules the world, punishments number nine to every one reward. In a strong state there are seven to three. And in a disintegrating state there are five to five."[62] When penal laws and punishments are applied and strictly enforced, the society will gradually evolve toward its ideal condition. This ideal condition is frequently described in paradoxical terms (3/8b, p. 47; 1/13b, p. 18): "This is called using laws to abolish laws. . . . This is called using punishment to abolish punishment. Using punishment to abolish punishment, the state will be well-ordered; using punishment to breed punishment, the state will be in turmoil."

The ideal rulership characterized by these paradoxes is spelled out in the final paragraph of the text (5/16b, p. 96):

When the sage rules the empire, that he does not have any executions is not because he is without the death penalty. Rather, in promulgating laws and edicts he makes them clear and easily understood and establishes judicial ministers and officials to act as teachers in guiding the people to an understanding of them. The people all know what to pursue and what to avoid. In pursuing prosperity and avoiding calamity, they are self-ordering. Therefore the perspicacious ruler, taking advantage of this order, adds the final touches, and as a consequence the empire attains a state of lasting order.

According to the *Han Fei Tzu,* the ideal condition described in this passage was realized under the rule of Duke Hsiao of Ch'in and his able chancellor, Shang Yang (71:12):

Therefore everyone guilty of depravity was apprehended and those punished were many. The people were exceedingly resentful and their complaints were heard daily. Duke Hsiao did not listen, but carried through the laws of Lord Shang. When the people came to understand that those guilty of crimes were certain to be punished, informers[63] became numerous. Thus none of the people violated the laws and no punishments were meted out. For this reason, the state was well-ordered, the army was strong, the territory was extended, and the ruler was revered.

These, then, are the main principles underlying Shang Yang's doctrine of *fa*. But general principles and abstract theory are only the first of three dimensions of Shang Yang's political philosophy. The second dimension is represented by chapter 26 and its detailed blueprint for a Legalist state. This chapter outlines plans for a special arm of the bureaucracy contrived for the sole purpose of implementing the laws. This judicial branch has certain features. Specially trained "judicial ministers" *(fa kuan)* are empowered to memorialize the throne to propose laws and legal reforms. The ruler personally presides over the law and dispenses laws and reforms to the *fa kuan*. The *fa kuan* are responsible for passing the laws down through the bureaucracy and bringing them to public notice. A constant supply of *fa kuan* is maintained by a special and rigorous law course for students. No one save the ruler is empowered to alter the law. The *fa kuan* are responsible for clarifying the law and must answer all enquiries in a prescribed manner. Measures such as secret archives and duplicate files must be implemented to guarantee the objectivity and impartiality of the law. *Fa kuan* are attached to various levels in the power structure from the palace on down so that everyone is made aware of the laws and heeds them.

The third dimension of Shang Yang's political philosophy is his political regime. This regime, which he himself extablished under Duke Hsiao of Ch'in, reached its culmination in the unification of China under Ch'in Shih Huang Ti. Whatever repugnance Shang Yang's brand of brutal despotism may arouse, the efficacy of his plan for political survival through internal consolidation and foreign conquest is nothing less than historical fact. One of the livelier sinological debates of our time concerns the relative influence of Confucian and Legalist ideas in the formative years of imperial China. Whatever the eventual outcome of this debate, the profound and lasting impact of Shang Yang's conception of *fa* on the Chinese empire is beyond question.

Han Fei Tzu. Now that we have outlined the conspicuous features of the concept of penal law as found in *The Book of Lord Shang,* the next step in determining its Legalist development is to compare these features with its representation in the *Han Fei Tzu.* The most striking consequence of such a comparison, far from being any obvious divergence between the two texts, is rather their basic consistency. Han Fei takes over Shang Yang's conception of *fa* almost entirely intact.[64] This fact is especially significant when one considers that although Shang Yang's political philosophy had already been current for over a century by Han Fei's time, its central principle *fa* could still be absorbed wholesale into Han Fei's political doctrine without notable revision. The only really significant difference between *fa* in *The Book of Lord Shang* and the *Han Fei Tzu* is that while it constitutes the unchallenged core of Shang Yang's thought, in the *Han Fei Tzu* its importance is somewhat diminished by the introduction of what Han Fei regards as equally essential principles: "the techniques of rulership" *(shu)* and "political purchase" *(shih).* The *Han Fei Tzu* states categorically that techniques of rulership are as necessary to the ruler as *fa* and moreover, that neither is sufficient in itself (304:6): "Where the ruler is without the techniques of rulership *(shu)* he will be deceived; where the subjects are without law *(fa)* they will be disorderly. One cannot be without either one of these—both are instruments of the emperor."

Having discovered a general consistency in the Legalist interpretation of *fa,* we can now abstract the following characteristics as typical of the Legalist position on penal law and punishments:

1. Good laws are a necessary condition for proper social order. A ruler without laws is the same as no ruler.[65] Because the emergence of a sage-ruler is a rare event and cannot be relied upon, Legalist doctrine establishes a system which does not depend directly upon the character of the ruler.[66]
2. The essential purpose of laws and the consequent punishments is to intimidate and deter.
3. Every effort must be made to promulgate laws clearly and concise-

ly in a manner which guarantees that every person in the state is
wholly aware of their contents and implications.

4. For the Legalists, penal laws have been divested of moral significance and religious sanction. Law replaces morality and functions
as the exclusive standard of good. What is in accordance with the
law is good; what violates the law is bad. Because the law itself
serves as an objective and impartial standard, the object is to
remove any reliance upon subjective interpretation.[67] The function
of law ideally is analogous to the operations of an automatic and
self-regulating machine.

5. The Legalists advocate that severe punishments should be strictly
applied for even the most minor infraction of the law.

6. All persons in the state (with the sole exception of the ruler himself) are subject to the rule of law, regardless of their status or
influence.

7. The ruler is himself beyond the law, and the law is controlled by
the ruler to serve his interests.

8. Laws must be constantly reviewed and modified to meet changing
circumstances. The power to do this rests solely with the ruler. The
laws must be reformulated from time to time, but they cannot be
interpreted to accommodate particular cases. This reformulation
reflects a continual reassessment of the most effective means of
achieving the ruler's purposes.

9. The ideal is a conditioned society in which law is universally understood and followed to the extent that litigations cease to arise.

10. There is a conviction that a basic antagonism exists between the
national and collective purpose on the one hand and the interests
of the individual on the other. This antagonism is frequently expressed in a contrast between "public welfare" *(kung tao)* and
"private interests" *(szu li)*.

FA IN *THE ART OF RULERSHIP*

In the preceding portion of this chapter we traced the evolution of *fa*
through the seminal stages of Chinese thought and isolated many of the
main features of this important concept as it is found in the Taoist, Confucian, and Legalist traditions. With respect to the role of penal law and
punishments in government, we have encountered an outright Taoist
rejection of such contrived measures as being symptomatic of a spiraling
political decline. The Confucians,[68] while grudgingly admitting the necessity of law as a guardrail on socially acceptable conduct, strive for a
society which encourages a voluntary devotion to the project of moral

development. The Legalist thinkers, possibly the first group to assign this character *fa* the connotation of penal law, develop a theoretically consistent and practicable system of government grounded in the conviction that the people and the governing bureaucracy are best regulated by impartial and universally applicable laws.

We now consider the political thought of *The Art of Rulership* to determine its sources and orientation. The syncretic pattern typical of other related concepts is very much the prevailing current here. While Taoist, Confucian, and Legalist attitudes are blended to constitute the basic stock of *The Art of Rulership,* one's first impression is that this concept of penal laws and punishment, couched in a series of short discussions, is by no means consistent. In fact, the several statements when juxtaposed appear to produce flagrant contradictions.[69] This is only a first impression, however, for the notion of penal laws and punishments as represented in *The Art of Rulership,* when understood as relative to several qualitatively different levels of government, can in fact be construed in a consistent way.

The Art of Rulership describes three different levels of government, each with its particular degree of efficacy (9/4a): "The highest ruler is godlike in his transformations. Next comes one who makes it impossible for people to do wrong. And next comes one who rewards those of superior qualities and punishes the troublemakers."[70] This single passage can be used to explicate *The Art of Rulership*'s position on penal law. The highest and most desirable level of government is one in which the charismatic influence of the ruler has transformed the people such that they do what is right of their own accord. The second level of government is one in which control consists solely in prohibiting actions which threaten social and political harmony. Note that the government's function here is not to inform the people what they *should* do but rather, as a facilitator of societal growth, to restrain disruptive conduct by ensuring that the people do not have an opportunity to sabotage social harmony. The third and lowest level—the application of rewards and punishments—is the government telling the people what they should and should not do by establishing a system of incentives and deterrents.

The highest of these three levels and its notion of "godlike transformation" *(shen hua)* requires some explanation. Late Warring States and Western Han literature repeatedly attributes an accumulated magical potency to the exemplary sage-ruler. This potency is frequently associated with a capacity to elevate and transform his subjects in an imperceptible fashion beyond their understanding or even knowledge. This transformation is wrought through a veiled influence which is likened to divinely inspired change.[71] This notion of *shen hua* is a popular subject in the *Huai Nan Tzu* in general.[72] In this specific passage from *The Art of Rulership,* the highest level of *shen hua* is described in the context of the golden age in the development of Chinese civilization.[73] Even though laws and punishments were still in force during this golden age, under the tutelage of a sage-ruler like Shen Nung there was no cause to apply them (9/2a): "His intimidating presence was awesome yet not put to the test, punishments were there yet he did not have to invoke them, and his laws were few in number and not overwhelming. Hence his transformation of the people was godlike."

Because of the transforming influence of Shen Nung's spiritual essence,[74] the application of rigorous laws and severe penalties was wholly unnecessary (9/2a): "At this time the laws were liberal, the punishments were tolerant, and the prisons were empty. The world was one in custom and none were of a wicked mind." By contrast with this golden age, in recent times the authorities have lost the transforming potency of Shen Nung and instead have concentrated on the incidental measures of government, unaware that harsh and oppressive policies exacerbate social strife and political instability (9/2a): "Now where water is muddy the fishes gasp; where government is cruel the people are disorderly."

Only when the government can reform itself at the root and effect a transformation among its people by the potency of its "spiritual essence" *(chih ching)* can there be a return to this golden age. The alternative, an exclusive reliance upon punishments and executions, will never lead to a substantive and lasting improvement in social order (9/2b): "Punishments and penalties are inadequate to change social custom; executions are inadequate to put an end to wickedness. Only godlike transformation is estimable and only the most essential vapors can do it in this way." The author cites the historical examples of Sun Shu-ao, Yi Liao, and Ch'ü Po-yü[75] to illustrate the potential of godlike transformation and to emphasize the futility of depending upon laws and punishments. He concludes that (9/3a):

> Things like armor and grimaces of wrath are a far cry from an effective defense against arms; things like contracts and ceremonial gifts, punishments, penalties, and instruments of execution are of little use in resolving difficulties; the method of relying on your eyes to see and your words to command is fraught with difficulties in effecting proper order.

By concentrating the potency of his spiritual essence, the ruler becomes capable of influencing the course of the entire cosmos and directing the world about him. Measured against such far-reaching influence, a project as inconsiderable as the successful implementation of laws and edicts is no more than a matter of course (9/4a):

With the sage-kings of antiquity, when the most essential vapors were embodied within, likes and dislikes did not lie on the outside. Their words were spoken to express what was truly on their minds and they issued commands to show their purposes. Setting these out in social norms and music and recounting them in song and verse, their deeds have been known to each succeeding generation and have spread to every corner of the world. They could even shape and transform birds, beasts, and insects. How much more so could they administer the law and implement edicts.

This ideal of social order effected through *shen hua* would appear to be a synthesis between Taoist elements and the Han Confucian notion of the mutual influence of human being and nature. From the Taoist side, *The Art of Rulership* inherits the decline theory of history which idealizes the pristine ignorance and uncorrupted natural harmony of high antiquity. While this section of the chapter does not deny the practical necessity of some form of political administration, it is made very clear that the best government is the least government (9/2b): "Hence the sage governs easily because his affairs are few, and the people are easily satisfied because his demands on them are few. He is benevolent without giving, he is trusted without speaking, he gets without seeking, he accomplishes without doing." Where Ch'ü Po-yü is cited as a historical example of this most effective form of government, his response to the question "How do you govern the state?" is simple (9/3a): "I govern it by not governing it." This portion of the text also contains many allusions to the classical Taoist works,[76] and some of the basic terminology appears to have been drawn from the Taoist tradition.[77] Moreover, historical examples of superlative rulers are generally taken over from Taoist sources.[78]

The Han Confucian contribution too is readily identifiable. Perhaps the most salient Han characteristic is the notion of the mutual influence of human being and nature, a doctrine which received wide currency during the Western Han. The essential vapors which are gathered and stored in the breast of the ruler are able to transform the people and ensure the regularity of the climate and the success of the crops. This notion of the ruler being able to transform his people through his inner magical potency is reminiscent of the traditional Confucian concept of "virtue" *(te)*.

The godlike transformation described in the opening portion of *The Art of Rulership* is posited as an ideal approach to government. As we have seen in analyzing related concepts,[79] one of the strongest features of *The Art of Rulership*'s political philosophy is that it attempts to provide a practical framework within which the ruling authority can pursue such lofty and even nebulous ideals. While asserting that the godlike transformation is real and attainable, this treatise recognizes the inherent difficulties in attempting to institutionalize such an elusive principle. Consequently it attempts to provide a realistic structure of political administration which can function as a controlled environment in which abstract principles can be nurtured and encouraged. This practicable level of government is characterized as "making certain the people have no chance to do wrong" *(shih pu te wei fei),* an expression which as a principle of political control has strong Legalistic associations.[80] Laws are depicted as a device available to the ruler for controlling his underlings (9/14b):

> Since laws and measurements are the ruler's means of controlling his subordinates,[81] to discard them is like trying to gallop without a harness and bit and will ultimately reverse the situation and enable the various ministers and common people to manipulate the ruler. For this reason, those who have mastered the art of statecraft control others whereas those who have not are controlled by others.

People in the present time have seldom achieved a level at which they will voluntarily regulate their lives on the basis of what is good and right (9/16b): "There is not one man in ten thousand who is devoted to goodness and takes joy in proper conduct such that he will voluntarily abide by laws and regulations without being pressed by prohibitions and punishments." Therefore it is prudent for the ruler to dissuade his people from doing wrong rather than depending upon them to do right (9/14b): "In government, it is better to make it so that one's subjects have no chance to do wrong than to rely upon their putting themselves right."

The author of *The Art of Rulership,* like Shang Yang and Han Fei, has no use for the sophists and itinerant intellectuals who question, criticize, and thereby undermine the rule of law (9/9b): "The sophists travel about debating and those who cultivate lofty conduct vie with each other for public office. With their cliques they criticize the edicts promulgated by the ruler; with their deviousness they contravene the prohibitions of law."[82] Those who would offer advice on the operations of government must be carefully regulated by the rule of law (9/9a): "Those who discuss state business must be closely scrutinized by the law and those who cultivate conduct must be tested in office. . . . Words are not allowed to exceed real achievement; actions are not allowed to overstep the law."

As we discovered in the discussion on *wu-wei,* it is the automatic and mechanical functioning of the system of laws that enables the ruler to assume his *wu-wei* posture. Using the familiar analogy of the scales to represent the objective and impartial system of laws, the text attributes the success of the system to a strict policy of *wu-wei* (9/4b):

> Now the scales, the compass, and the square once fixed cannot be changed. They do not compromise their integrity for the sake of Ch'in or Ch'u nor do

they change their semblance for the sake of the Hu or Yüeh people. Being constant, they do not vary; being used for a special purpose, they do not adapt themselves. Having once been cast, they are passed on through ten thousand generations and operate through nonaction.

Like the Legalist philosophers, the author of this treatise regards a strictly enforced code of laws to be more crucial to the continued existence of the state than the ruler himself. In fact, the salient characteristic of a "doomed state" is that it lacks an applied regimen of penal laws (9/13b): "It is not the case that what is called a 'doomed state' has no ruler, but that it has no laws." By contrast, a state with a notorious ruler is not necessarily marked for imminent extinction (9/4b–5a): "It may be that a nation has a doomed ruler, but there is no such thing as the useless Way; it may be that man has reached the end of his tether, but principles never fail to be applicable." As we shall see, law takes precedence over the ruler because the source of the laws is the will of the people. The ruler is only an administrator.

While insisting that the principle of penal law itself is constant, *The Art of Rulership* follows the Legalist tradition in accepting the necessity of reformulating the individual laws (9/13b): "It is not the case that to act at variance with the laws is quite the same as being without them, but to have laws and not use them is tantamount to not having any laws at all." Altering the law is not to be confused, however, with interpreting the laws to serve the moment. *The Art of Rulership*'s interpretation of government is adamant in its insistence upon a system of objective and impartial laws. To emphasize the importance of impartiality, these laws are frequently made analogous to measuring instruments like scales and squares (9/4a–b): "Because the crosspiece of a pair of scales shows no bias toward either the right or left in weighing, it can be level. Because a plumb line shows no bias toward inside or out in measuring, it can be straight. Because the ruler in administering the law shows no bias toward those he likes or dislikes, his words can be command." Law neither acknowledges class distinctions nor bends under the pressure of political influence (9/13a):

> Once the laws have been fixed, those who live up to the demands of the law are rewarded while those who are shown to be wanting by the marking line are punished. For the exalted and noble, punishments are not lightened; for the lowly and base, punishments are not made more severe. Where one violates the law, even if he be a man of superior character, he must be punished. Where one lives up to the standards set, even if he be a man of little worth, he must be deemed to have committed no offense.

While the impartiality of the law is a prominent feature of the Legalist tradition, *The Art of Rulership* goes one step further in regarding penal law as the exclusive standard to be used by the government in assessing social conduct. In the preceding analysis of the Legalist position on penal law, it has been noted that while the concept of law is put forward as a universal standard, the conspicuous exception to this standard is the ruler himself. Ultimately, as the final arbiter of the law it is within his power to change government policy and alter the laws. In *The Book of Lord Shang* and *Han Fei Tzu,* law is recommended to the ruler as an effective means of subordinating and regulating his people—a system of political control contrived with the express purpose of protecting the absolute power of the ruler. By contrast, in the following passage we are given *The Art of Rulership*'s raison d'être for government and its bureaucracy (9/13a):

> The purpose of setting up a bureaucracy in antiquity was to prevent the people from doing just as they pleased. That they set up a ruler was to check the bureaucracy and prevent it from being dictatorial. Law, records, social norms, and a code of moral conduct are to prevent the ruler from making decisions based on his own whims.[83]

While the first portion of this passage is entirely consistent with the Legalist tradition, the assertion that the laws and social norms have been established to contain the powers of the ruler is an important modification. In *The Art of Rulership,* law is elevated to an absolute and exclusive standard which supersedes the will of the ruler. Whereas the Legalist theorists in all likelihood regarded any discussion of the relative authority of law and the will of the ruler to be both unnecessary and injudicious, *The Art of Rulership* states categorically that the rule of law is the only rule in the land. In his role as custodian and administrator of the law empowered by the people to carry out its injunctions, the ruler has an explicit obligation to conform to the standards which he himself enforces (9/13b):

> What one has in oneself he does not condemn in others; what one lacks in oneself he does not demand in others. That which is established below is not abandoned above; that which is prohibited for the people is not practiced by oneself. . . . The ruler in establishing laws first makes himself a model and example, and thus his commands are carried out in the world.

Given that the ruler's authority is limited by the absolute power of the law, the question arises as to the ultimate source and basis of the laws. It is apparent that whoever controls the laws in some sense controls the ruler. This, then, is another important innovation in *The Art of Rulership* (9/13a):

Law comes from rightness, rightness from the various kinds of right measure, and right measure is consistent with the human heart and mind. This is the crucial factor in proper order. Thus one who penetrates to the root will not be misled at the periphery; one who sees the crucial factor will not be confused by details. Laws do not drop from the heavens nor spring forth from the earth. Arising out of human society, they are reflexive in regulating the society itself.

The Art of Rulership's political philosophy does not accept the Legalist assumption that the rule of law should be grounded in the arbitrary dictates of an absolute ruler. Rather, the law is conceived of as an exclusive standard of conduct based upon moral realizations which are in turn consistent with what is congenial to and accepted by the majority. The laws are not impressed on society from above; they are generated from within the society to regulate itself. The human condition takes precedence over the will of the ruler, and the whole image of the ideal ruler is transformed from that of a despot to a servant of his people dedicated to their benefit and responsible for their welfare (9/7a):

> Putting the whole world under his bounty instead of bringing his own intelligence into play, the ruler follows what the people find beneficial. Now, by lifting his heel, he is able to benefit the empire. Hence he takes his place above, and yet they do not find him heavy. . . .

In *The Art of Rulership*, law is described as being grounded in "rightness" *(yi)*. In the final section of this treatise there are numerous examples describing the moral ingredient in penal law.[84] For example (9/21b): "Minor officials observe the law, but the superior man controls on the basis of what is right. Someone who knows only about law but not about rightness is no better than a minor official and is not equal to the task of governing." In giving this concept of *fa* a moral dimension, *The Art of Rulership* takes a decisive turn in the direction of Confucian theory—which, as we have seen, regards penal law as a coercive means of enforcing morality that is to be invoked only when education and voluntary compliance break down.

In conclusion, then, the concept of *fa* in *The Art of Rulership* is constructed on a Legalist framework. The following elements have been assimilated from the Legalist tradition:

1. Law in the hands of the ruler is used as an instrument of political administration.[85]
2. Law should function on the principle of preventing people from doing wrong rather than encouraging them to do good.
3. Law can be enforced by manipulating human likes and dislikes.

4. Those inclined to question the law must be actively discouraged from doing so.
5. The system of laws and its mechanical operation is fundamental to the ruler assuming a *wu-wei* posture.
6. The system of laws takes precedence over the ruler in terms of importance to the state. Whereas the individual qualities of the ruler have only a limited bearing on the future of the state, the condition of the laws is absolutely crucial.
7. Laws must be strictly enforced.
8. Laws, should their effectiveness become impaired, can be reformulated to accommodate changing conditions.
9. Laws cannot be interpreted. They stand as an impartial standard which must be universal in its application.

While accepting these characteristics from the Legalist tradition, the political philosophy presented in *The Art of Rulership* introduces some radical modifications: making the will of the ruler subordinate to the rule of law; asserting that law has been established to contain the political authority of the ruler; insisting that the ruler has an obligation to abide by the law and be exemplary in his personal conduct; transferring the ultimate authority of the law from the will of the ruler to what is congenial to the people and grounding the laws in rightness; and regarding the formal structure of government as being nothing more than a realistic framework in which the ideal of godlike transformation *(shen hua)* can be cultivated and the people can be guided to a thorough and lasting transformation.

These modifications in what initially appears to be a Legalist-oriented method of political control go much further than simply giving basic Legalist precepts a new slant. The changes are so essential that in the synthesis the Confucian and Taoist contributions loom larger than the Legalist framework on which they are tacked. The very purpose of having government is altered. While the Legalist framework gives the system structure, the direction, disposition, and orientation of the system are changed to serve much less totalitarian and much more humanitarian ends. Penal law is downgraded to a subordinate institution with the main service of providing a practical basis for the real work of government—the education, elevation, and ultimate transformation of its people. Penal law has a greenhouse function: creating a controlled environment in which the government's task of godlike transformation can proceed. By insisting that these laws have their basis in the moral achievements of the people, a principle found at the core of traditional Confucianism, the original Legalist notion of penal law is further altered. Again, the absolute power of the ruler characteristic of Legalist doctrine has been considerably reduced. In Legalist thought, much of the ruler's power is derived from the fact that the law is the embodiment of his will. In *The Art of Rulership*, by contrast, the ruler is deprived of absolute power. Not only is his will superseded by the will of the people as the basis of law, but the ruler himself is made answerable to the law. Perhaps of even greater significance is the assertion that laws were originally devised to contain the arbitrary powers of the ruler.

With such fundamental changes in the two central features of the Legalist political philosophy—the role of the law and the role of the ruler—the political doctrine of *The Art of Rulership* relinquishes any pretentions at constituting a Legalist system of government. The concept of *fa* is fundamentally a synthesis of ideas propounded by the pre-Ch'in philosophers—a synthesis achieving its own unique contribution in developing a theory of government which seeks to temper high ideals with a sensible pragmatism.

5

YUNG CHUNG

(Utilizing the People)

IN CHAPTER 2 we saw that a ruler's ability to assume a *wu-wei* attitude is correlative to his ability to orchestrate the collective efforts of his people. In this chapter, I want to pursue this notion of using the collective and concerted strength of the people—a notion frequently referred to as *yung chung*—and outline its role in the political theory of *The Art of Rulership*.[1] While *yung chung* can be traced directly to a Legalist antecedent, its close association with non-Legalist elements, especially the notion of "each element achieving what is appropriate to it" *(ke te ch'i yi),* makes a preliminary examination of the historical background to *yung chung* imperative. Since *The Art of Rulership* develops its political theory on an indisputably Legalist framework, a comparison of the *Han Fei Tzu's* notion of *yung chung* with relevant portions of *The Art of Rulership* will be of particular interest.

YUNG CHUNG IN THE LÜ-SHIH CH'UN-CH'IU AND HAN FEI TZU

The expression *yung chung*[2] refers to the specific policy of the ruler who utilizes the collective physical and mental resources of the people to effect political order as an alternative to either relying upon his own talents or exploiting the abilities of a few capable men.[3] In other words, the starting point of this concept of *yung chung* is the not unreasonable conviction that the talents of the individual—*any* individual—have their limitations.

This concept of *yung chung* does occur in the *Lü-shih ch'un-ch'iu* where, consistent with its generally pro-Confucian and anti-Legalist orientation, it asserts that because political power and stability are ultimately dependent upon the will of the people, and because the concerted strength of the people far exceeds that of even the most talented individuals, it is characteristic of the enlightened ruler to win over the people and rely on their support. The *Lü-shih ch'un-ch'iu* (4/9b) states:

> Using the concerted courage of the many, one does not stand in awe of even Meng Pen; using the concerted strength of the many, one does not stand in awe of even Wu Huo; using the combined vision of the many, one does not stand in awe of even Li Lou; using the combined wisdom of the many, one does not stand in awe of even Yao and Shun. Using the many—this is the great treasure of the ruler.

This pervading emphasis on the welfare and priority of the people that is found in the *Lü-shih ch'un-ch'iu* represents a direct challenge to the ruler-centered authoritarianism of the Legalists.[4] It is in the late Legalist tradition, however, with its rigid devotion to the interests of the ruler, that this concept of "utilizing the people" takes on a decidedly new significance. Where the *Lü-shih ch'un-ch'iu* advocates using the people in the interests of the people, the *Han Fei Tzu* advocates exploiting the people in order to manipulate them and enhance the ruler's own power.

In the *Han Fei Tzu*'s exposition of *yung chung*, this principle of utilizing the people follows from the Legalist rejection of "exalting persons of superior qualities and employing the able" *(tsun hsien shih neng)*. It denies the wisdom of this Confucian policy on the basis of a conflict of interests. Moreover, it denies the ultimate dependability of this reliance upon individual talents on the basis of impracticability, in particular looking askance at the Confucian ideal of government by the sage-king.[5] The weakness inherent in a ruler who relies upon individual talents in general and exercises his own abilities in particular is clearly described (331:9):

> The strength of the individual is not equal to that of the many; the intelligence of the individual cannot understand all things. It is better to employ an entire state than rely on one man. Therefore, where intelligence and strength are equal the larger will prevail. Where one succeeds, he will be personally exhausted; where he fails, he will be guilty of error. The inferior ruler makes full use of his own talents; the average ruler makes full use of the strength of others; the superior ruler makes full use of the intelligence of others.

Rather than compete with the people, the ruler is prevailed upon to orchestrate the individual contributions of the population as a whole (258:13):

> In putting out a fire, were the fire chief to grab pots and jugs and run to the fire, he would have the use of only one man. If, on the other hand, picking

up a whip and taking command he superintends the men, he will have
legions under his control. Therefore the sage does not join the rabble or personally undertake matters of little consequence.[6]

Using mythohistorical examples of persons renowned for their exceptional wisdom or strength, the *Han Fei Tzu* makes the point that even
such famous exemplars of individual talent as Yao, Wu Huo, Meng Pen,
and Hsia Yü are very much restricted by the fact that ultimately they are
still only individuals (146:6):

> Therefore, even with the intelligence of Yao, if one is without the assistance
> of the people he will not accomplish great things; even with the strength of
> Wu Huo, if one does not get the assistance of others he cannot lift himself
> up; even with the might of Meng Pen and Hsia Yü, if one is without laws or
> political techniques he will not prevail for long.

The *Han Fei Tzu* even goes so far as to attack the precursors of its own
political theory for relying on individual ability rather than establishing a
system of personnel management whereby the strength of the people can
be used reflexively to control them. Having censured Tzu-ch'an for exercising his own sagacity in discovering wrongdoers, the *Han Fei Tzu* concludes (287:14):

> Moreover, where things are many an intelligent man himself is limited. Since
> the limited cannot prevail over the many, intelligent men cannot keep
> abreast of all things. Therefore they must make use of things to govern
> things themselves. While subordinates are many, superiors are few. That the
> few do not prevail over the many means that the ruler himself cannot keep
> abreast of all his ministers. Therefore he must make use of the people in
> order to keep informed about people. This being the case, without tiring his
> own person, affairs will be properly ordered, and without using his own
> intelligence, villains will be apprehended.

Shen Pu-hai's insistence that an official should not offer information on
matters beyond his office is overruled by the necessity of the ruler's having access to all information (*Han Fei Tzu* 305:15): "Because the ruler
sees with the eyes of the entire state, there is none who can see more
clearly; because he hears with the ears of the entire state, there is none
who can hear more keenly. Now, if those who know do not speak up,
whose ears and eyes can he use?"

There are several characteristics of the *Han Fei Tzu*'s concept of *yung
chung* that form a basis for comparison with *The Art of Rulership*'s
interpretation of this same principle. First, the starting point in Legalist
thought is service to the interests of the ruler. This being the case, the
concept of *yung chung* is grounded in a rejection of the efficacy of indi-

vidual abilities because it is impractical to expect that the ruler himself will always be a person of exceptional talents or to expect that he will always have access to exceptional ministers. Exceptional talent is a variable and, as such, cannot be relied upon as essential material in a constant and self-regulating governmental apparatus. Even when exceptional talent is available, the talents of one man are inevitably inferior to the combined talents of the many.

Second, the *Han Fei Tzu* rejects the policy of relying upon superior men where "superior" refers to anything like the Confucian or Taoist notions of self-realization. The development of natural abilities is encouraged only when those abilities are congruent with the specific offices of the individual in promoting the overriding interests of ruler and state. Natural proclivities which extend beyond the prescribed duties implicit in the Legalist principle of "accountability" *(hsing-ming),* far from being encouraged, are strenuously curtailed.

Finally, the *Han Fei Tzu* regards the exploitation of the collective strength and intelligence of the people as a *means* that can be used to the specific end of channeling their energies toward the advancement of the ruler's interests. While the *Han Fei Tzu* does contain several passages offering a seminal discussion of *yung chung,* it is a qualified *yung chung* which must limit the extent of its utilization of the people to those talents that will further the ruler's ends.

YUNG CHUNG IN *THE ART OF RULERSHIP*

In comparing the limited development of *yung chung* in the *Han Fei Tzu* and the much expanded and radically altered version found in *The Art of Rulership,* our task is eased considerably by the fact that the discussion of *yung chung* found in these two texts and even in the *Lü-shih ch'un-ch'iu* seem to have been derived from a common source.[7] That is to say, the discussion of *yung chung* in *The Art of Rulership* seems to be a modified and somewhat extended rendition of text similar to that found in the *Han Fei Tzu.*

A considerable portion of *The Art of Rulership*—especially 9/5a–12b—is devoted to a discussion of *yung chung.* This portion of the text begins with the assertion (9/5a) that "when one gets hold of this source of the Way, he is never at his wit's end in responding to things, but when he relies on the talents of men, it is difficult to reach the acme of good government." As in the *Han Fei Tzu, The Art of Rulership*'s representation of *yung chung* is grounded in a rejection of the efficacy of individual talents and, specifically, in an awareness of the obvious personal limitations of the ruler (9/5a):

Since human intelligence is not in itself sufficient to effect proper government and boldness is not in itself sufficient to hold sway, it is clear that individual human talents cannot be relied upon. This being so, where a ruler comprehends circumstances even beyond the four seas without ever leaving his ancestral hall, it is because he takes advantage of things to understand things and he takes advantage of man to understand man.[8]

No individual—not even a sage-ruler—can possibly be best in all things. And even when the ruler is individually unsurpassed in a certain respect, he still cannot match the combined strength of the multitude. Given this conviction in the severe limitations of individual human talents, the ruler's alternative—and, at the same time, his guarantee of success—is seen to lie in orchestrating the collective energies of the people (9/5b): "Where concerted strength is applied it is equal to any task; where the intelligence of the many is employed, it will succeed in all things."

It is at this point that *The Art of Rulership* makes a radical departure from the *Han Fei Tzu.* This rejection of the ruler's reliance upon individual human abilities is qualified by introducing a corollary notion of "each element achieving what is appropriate to it" *(ke te ch'i yi).* This notion has its basis in the principle that in nature each particular has its own unique aptitude, function, and value (9/5b): "Now, the two famous horses, Hua Liu and Lü Erh, would cover several hundred miles in one day. But if one set them to catching rabbits, they would be outdone by a wild dog or a wolf. This is because their faculties and abilities are different."[9] Since each particular makes its own unique contribution, no one thing has any more right to exist than any other (9/11b):

> The superior ruler in the use of men is like the skilled workman in the disposing of his wood. Large pieces are used for boats and beams; small pieces are used for oars and joists; long pieces are used for eaves and rafters; short pieces are used for gargoyles and decorative designs. All of these pieces irrespective of their size find their niche, and all of the carpenter's instruments and templates have their application.[10]
>
> Of all things in the world, nothing is as deadly as the herb aconitum. And yet a good doctor will put it in a pouch and keep it on hand because he has a use for it. Even among the resources of nature's thriving forests there is nothing which can be discarded—how much less so in the sphere of man!

The effective ruler is able to recognize the potential of each individual and to coordinate his own expectations with the natural capacity and expression of the individual (9/8a): "A deaf person can be made to chew the animal sinew used in covering bows, though he cannot be made to hear. A dumb person can be made to work in the horse stables, though he cannot be made to speak. This is because their physical persons are not whole and their abilities have their limitations."[11] In terms of production, this means that the ruler is able to respond to individual talents in employing his people (9/5b–6a):

> In ancient times in the construction of a carriage, the varnisher did not do the ornamental drawing and the engraver did not wield the adze. A worker did not have more than one skill, a scholar did not combine two offices. Each kept to his own province and did not interfere with others; each person found his niche and each thing found its place. As a result, products were not of inferior quality and duties were not neglected.
>
> Where the debt is small it is easy to repay; where duties are few they are easy to fulfill; where a person's burden is light he is easy to encourage. With the ruler making only limited demands and his subordinates presenting him with accomplishments easily achieved, sovereign and ministers will never become tired of each other.

When this principle is carried into the political sphere, it means that the effective ruler is adept at assigning administrative responsibilities which are commensurate with individual capabilities (9/8a and 9/11b–12a):

> That which has a specific form can occupy a position appropriate to it and that which has a specific ability can undertake a task appropriate to it. When the strength of a person lifting a burden is equal to the task, he does not feel it too heavy to raise; when the ability of a person pursuing a task matches it, he feels no difficulty.

> Each person has his talents and each thing has its disposition. Some people are overburdened when entrusted with one responsibility; others are at ease handling a hundred times as much. For this reason, a person proficient in making minute calculations will certainly be lost on the great computations of the world; a person who does not make a mistake in the calculation of small things will be perplexed in the accomplishment of large matters. Analogously a badger cannot be made to pounce on an ox, and a tiger cannot be made to catch mice.
>
> Now, with people, some have talents which make them want to establish peace in the world, bring together the territories beyond the frontier, preserve an imperiled state, and revive a defunct line. They set their minds on righting the administration, correcting what has gone awry, settling problems and straightening out difficulties, yet all you do is demand of them details of court ceremony and other such trifling and innocuous duties. Some have talents which only enable them to be glib of tongue, to lead people astray, to flatter and fawn, and to find great pleasure in rhetoric. They follow vulgar customs and debase themselves to please the eyes and ears of the common herd, and yet you entrust them with the pivot on which the order and disorder of empire depend. This is like splitting a hair with an axe

or using a knife to fell a tree—in both cases it is using the instrument for the wrong purpose.

Further, there is an assumption that when each particular is allowed to express its own natural potential without being distorted by external constraints, these elements will collectively function in a thoroughly integrated natural order. The ruler takes advantage of this principle by gauging his assignments in such a manner as to make full use of an individual without offending his natural propensities (9/8a): "When everything large or small, long or short, finds its niche, then there is equality in the empire without anything being able in any way to surpass another. Because the sage uses both big and small, long and short, there is no wasted ability." This principle finds political application in another assertion (9/7a–7b):

> Where the ruler and the minister have different Ways, there is proper order, but where they are the same, there is disorder. If each gets what is appropriate to him and dwells in what is right for him, the one above and those below will know how to deal with each other. . . . For this reason, when the various ministers are like spokes converging side by side at the hub, and irrespective of intelligence or moral character, all do their best, then the ruler has the means to hold control over his ministers, the ministers have the means to serve their ruler, and the Way of ordering the state properly is clear.

The Art of Rulership's interpretation of *yung chung,* tempered with the notion of each element achieving what is appropriate to it, recognizes the vital importance of allowing each particular to express its own naturalness and uniqueness. If we understand the primary objection of the anarchist to be coercive authority—that is, one person or group obliging another to act in a certain way—and the primary objective of the anarchist to be the eradication of this kind of authority from all areas of political life, then inasmuch as *The Art of Rulership* advocates full use of the spontaneous contribution of each participant in an organization committed to the nonmediated action of personal initiative, there is much here that points to a Taoist anarchism. In early Confucianism and Taoism, personal realization is coextensive with familial, social, and political realization and, as such, some form of political organization, like the family, is regarded as a natural condition. The raison d'être for the political structure outlined in *The Art of Rulership* seems to be nothing other than to provide a framework for the collective realization of all members in the society to the extent that this is practically possible. And the function of this political apparatus focuses on organization rather than authority.

The decidedly Taoist interpretation of *yung chung* in *The Art of Rulership* demonstrates the internally consistent nature of its political philosophy as a whole. *Yung chung* is knit into an integrated program of government and strongly influences the disposition of the other components in the overall political theory.

The Art of Rulership interpretation of *yung chung* is consistent, for example, with its synthetic conception of *wu-wei*. On the Legalist side of this synthesis, it is consistent with the ruler relying on the energies of his subordinates rather than exercising his personal skills. The rejection of reliance upon his own talents allows the ruler as individual to remain aloof and beyond the view of his subordinates. His personal attributes and limitations are inconsequential to the effective operation of the state. In terms of the Taoist contribution to the synthesis, this theory of utilizing the people—with its corollary, each element achieving what is appropriate to it—is consistent with *wu-wei* as the political principle of refraining from using political authority to constrain natural human behavior. It accommodates the fundamental Taoist conviction in the completeness of the actualizing totality—the recognition that whereas particular things have different and seemingly antagonist courses of development, as a whole they constitute an integrated natural order which requires no constraint. It is consistent with the Taoist proposition that each thing is necessary and has its unique value and, moreover, that all things are thus on an equal footing in relation to the whole. These interpretations of *yung chung* and *wu-wei* both reflect the relativity of all value judgments and preclude the establishment of a scheme of values which, when applied at a political level, determines an individual's suitability to participate in the political life of the state. Fundamentally incompatible with an elitist principle of promoting men of superior talent, this interpretation of *yung chung* allows that all persons take part in the social and political dimensions of life in accordance with their natural propensities. In fact, it is the natural propensities of the people that ultimately determine the actual content and concerns of the political apparatus.

Yung chung is also entirely consistent with the concept "political advantage or purchase" *(shih)* as it is presented in *The Art of Rulership*. Two distinct modifications of *shih* appear in this treatise. There is in the first place a significant turning away from the ruler-dominated relationship between ruler and minister characteristic of Legalist theory in favor of a reciprocating harmony in which each position responds to the other. Moreover, *shih* is seen as an effective device for maintaining a desirable political organization which conduces to universal personal realization rather than as an instrument to enforce a Legalist program of totalitarian repression.

The concept *shih* requires that the ruler avail himself of the political purchase concomitant with his station to sustain the existing apparatus rather than exercise control on the basis of his personal talents. That is to say, his position as ruler entitles him to "utilize the people" *(yung chung)* and to marshal the physical and intellectual resources of the state in order to maintain stability. By tapping the collective strengths of all his subordinates to aid him in his organizational role, the ruler acquires power and vision which go far beyond any individual or group which might threaten the political organization and his position at its head. The degree to which these two concepts of *yung chung* and *shih* have been integrated is apparent inasmuch as the ruler must utilize the people in order to maintain his status as ruler and the *shih* attendant upon it; and it is his *shih* as ruler which entitles him to enlist the support of the whole.

Yung chung as interpreted in *The Art of Rulership* is further consistent with its interpretation of "penal law" *(fa)*. The most prominent feature distinguishing the concept of law outlined in this treatise from its Legalist antecedent is the proposition that law is grounded in the human heart and mind. Employing the people according to their aptitudes and relying on their collective strengths are principles complementary to the conception of law as an unfortunate but perhaps necessary guarantee that the people have the freedom to express themselves both individually and collectively in a way determined by what is appropriate to themselves. Law, ideally on the statute books but seldom if ever invoked, is best seen as a backstop for extremes of activity that would violate the underlying spirit of *yung chung*—the collective realization of individuals in the society.

CONCLUSION

There are important similarities, but also differences, between the earlier *Han Fei Tzu* notion of *yung chung* and *The Art of Rulership*'s development of this concept. First, both interpretations reject the efficacy of individual talents in favor of the collective contribution of society as a whole. Whereas in the *Han Fei Tzu* each individual's contribution is carefully superintended to promote the interests of the ruler, in *The Art of Rulership* this contribution is synonymous with the spontaneous expression of each particular nature in its dialogue with the organismic whole.

Further, both interpretations reject the promotion of superior men where "superior" connotes a universally applicable code of normative values. Whereas in the *Han Fei Tzu* an individual could conceivably qualify as superior through strict adherence to the prescribed obligations of his office and hence be entitled to advancement in the system, in *The Art of Rulership* the individual participates in the political life of the state according to his aptitude.

Finally, the *Han Fei Tzu* delineates the concept of *yung chung* to provide the ruler with a technique that can be used to exploit the collective strength and intelligence of the people as a means to control their energies and channel their efforts to an end determined by his own personal interests. *The Art of Rulership*, however, seeks to exploit the people's natural wealth of talent as an end in itself. In the *Han Fei Tzu*, the education and development of the people for their own sake is repeatedly discouraged as constituting a threat to the ruler's authority. Division of labor is encouraged not because of an appreciation of varied talents but rather because division among subordinates is a necessary element in the exercise of control. While *The Art of Rulership* theorist would suggest that the strongest state is one in which each person is allowed to make his own unique contribution to the whole, the *Han Fei Tzu* follows *The Book of Lord Shang* in saying that a strong state is one in which the people are made weak. By keeping the people weak the ruler can harness them and regulate their activities by a system of external constraints.

This difference between the *Han Fei Tzu* and *The Art of Rulership* stems from the strong Legalist conviction that a great tension exists between private and state interests and the opposite and equally strong conviction in *The Art of Rulership* that individual and social fulfillment are coextensive. Whereas the entire government apparatus in Legalist thought is constructed to serve the interests of the ruler, *The Art of Rulership*, rejecting the notion that there is a basic antagonism between the peoples' welfare and the interests of the state, insists that the means of serving the ruler and the ruled is one and the same. In the political theory of *The Art of Rulership*,—especially in the wedding of "utilizing the people" and "each element achieving what is appropriate to it"—there is a fundamental conviction that if everyone is allowed to follow the spontaneous and natural course of his development, the result will be an integrated social order. Politically this means that the ruler allocates his offices in such a manner as to take full advantage of individual talents while making every effort to avoid demands on his subordinates that will distort their natural inclinations. His expectation is that this attitude will result in a strong and stable society rooted in the unique strength of each individual.

The similarities which the *Han Fei Tzu* and *The Art of Rulership* share with respect to this principle of *yung chung* are superficial, but their differences are crucial. In the *Han Fei Tzu*, the ruler controls the people; in *The Art of Rulership*, the people hold sway over the ruler to the extent that they define the character of his administration. *The Art of Rulership*'s ruler is not free to use the people as he likes; he must accommodate the government to the natural expression of the people and must in the disposition of his administration pursue congruency with their natural proclivities.

In this essential difference lies the principle of control over the power of the sovereign which pervades this entire treatise and colors its interpretation of the other Legalist concepts. Hsiao Kung-ch'üan identifies this same effort to limit the ruler's control as a central theme in the *Lü-shih ch'un-ch'iu:* "His [Liu Pu-wei's] greatest contribution would appear to be his proposals for all kinds of methods by which to restrict the ruler, preventing him from indulging his whims and passions."[12] To accomplish the end of setting limits on the powers of the ruler, Liu Pu-wei invokes theories based on the Confucian notions of kingly rule and the ultimate importance of the people. *The Art of Rulership,* on the other hand, reflects its historical context and the popularity of Taoist ideals in proffering a syncretic and heavily Taoist solution to this same problem of delimiting the ruler's powers.

There is another interesting parallel between the political philosophies propounded in *The Art of Rulership* and the *Lü-shih ch'un-ch'iu:* both texts present an alternative to Legalist totalitarianism. The *Lü-shih ch'un-ch'iu* reexamines the Confucian tradition in search of this alternative and ultimately establishes the principles of "valuing life" and seeking "the whole life"—seeing political organization as a necessary condition for ensuring the good life for the individual.[13] *The Art of Rulership,* on the other hand, constructs its alternative to Legalism by borrowing heavily from Taoist precepts. The concept of *yung chung* and in fact the entire *The Art of Rulership* treatise has been developed, I think, with the express intention of providing a political structure conducive to the advancement of certain principles, primarily Taoist, at a practical level. The author of this text, aware of the pragmatic inadequacy of earlier Taoist political theory, concedes the minimal amount of political structure necessary to guarantee the maximum degree of individual freedom. I believe that this element in the political theory outlined in *The Art of Rulership* is in fact an attempt at a "practicable Taoism"—a somewhat tamed Taoism which is willing to trade certain claims to unconstrained freedom for simple practicability.

6

LI MIN

(Benefiting the People)

IN THE PRECEDING PAGES we have encountered one recurring theme: throughout *The Art of Rulership* there is a sustained attempt to subordinate the interests of the ruler to the welfare of the people. This theme, notably the converse of traditional Legalist doctrine, seems to take its mode of expression from the concept under discussion.

The exploration of *wu-wei* in Chapter 2, for example, emphasized *The Art of Rulership*'s assertion that the interests of the people and those of the ruler coincide. Where Legalist theory discerns an underlying antagonism between ruler and subject, *The Art of Rulership* insists that in benefiting the people, the ruler benefits himself. Again, while the Legalist distinction between the ruler and minister reflects a constant struggle for power and privilege, *The Art of Rulership*'s distinction is based on the principle that different things have differing yet equal value.

In the analysis of the concept "political purchase" *(shih)* in Chapter 3, we saw that the relationship between the ruler and his subordinates is a symbiotic bond involving mutual obligations and responsibilities. There is a strong emphasis on the notion that the people will only exert themselves for a ruler who has their welfare at heart. The tempering of this special Legalist term *shih* with ruler/subject reciprocity is one aspect of the priority given to the welfare of the people.

In Chapter 4, dealing with "penal law" *(fa)* and punishments, we discovered that *The Art of Rulership* so modifies the Legalist conception of penal law that it drastically alters its very raison d'être. Whereas Legalist doctrine recommends penal law to the ruler as an effective means of protecting his absolute power, *The Art of Rulership* insists that the rule of law is universal and the ruler himself is answerable to it. Whereas Legalist law reflects the arbitrary inclinations of the ruler, *The Art of Rulership* says that it is society which fashions laws to regulate itself. Further, these laws take on a moral dimension in that they are regarded as an exclusive standard of conduct grounded in a notion of rightness *(yi)* reflective of what the society at large regards as congenial.

The analysis of "utilizing the people" *(yung chung)* in Chapter 5 also illustrates this commitment to the primacy of the people's welfare. In the *Han Fei Tzu,* the ruler's policy of *yung chung*—in this case, "exploiting the people" is perhaps a better rendering—is set against the inadequacy of his reliance on his own abilities. The point is that the ruler's own interests can best be served by orchestrating the collective energies of his people. On turning to *The Art of Rulership*'s development of this concept, we find that the primary concern had shifted from the interests of the ruler to the collective realization of the people. In fact, rather than political leadership determining the occupation of the people, it is the natural direction of the people that determines the disposition and concerns of government.

In the political philosophy of *The Art of Rulership,* these central concepts mesh together and complement each other to round out a consistent and functional schema of political organization. It is the mechanism of laws and punishments which make it possible for the ruler to assume the ideal *wu-wei* attitude. Again, his ability to assume such an attitude is correlative to his ability to orchestrate the collective efforts of the people as each person seeks his own niche. In the overall system, the ruler finds himself in the position of having to accommodate his government to the inclinations of the people and of being governed himself by what the people in general find agreeable.

In the political theory of *The Art of Rulership,* this theme of giving primacy to the welfare of the people can be characterized as "benefiting the people" *(li min)*. Before exploring the historical background of this concept to determine the orientation of *The Art of Rulership*'s interpretation, I want to examine its philosophical dimensions.

As is the case with a great many moral precepts, virtue is the result of an externally manifested social conformity to a given standard of conduct. When "love," for example, is directed at others, it is an acceptable moral precept. When it is turned inward, however, and directed at oneself, it is not only deprived of its moral attractiveness but can become morally repugnant. The same is true of *li:* benefit or profit. While benefiting others is generally regarded as virtuous conduct, a preoccupation with benefiting oneself is not. Apparently the injection of self into a code of moral precepts transmutes socially redeeming conduct into socially abhorrent behavior.

In its extended meaning of benefit, the character *li* has both a positive meaning and a derived pejorative connotation. In its positive sense, *li* frequently occurs as the rhyming antithesis of *hai* ("harm") and means to benefit something.[1] In its pejorative sense, *li* is frequently contrasted with *yi* ("rightness")—that is, dedication to the furtherance of private interests as opposed to an effort to exert one's moral sense and do what is right in each unique situation.[2] This contrast seems to have originated in the Confucian tradition with such passages as *Analects* 7/4/16: "The superior person understands what is right while the inferior person understands what is personally profitable." In any case it spread rapidly to become a characteristic comparison in early Chinese literature.

In *The Art of Rulership,* as in most other early texts, *li* is applied socially to represent the positive meaning of "benefit" and applied personally with the pejorative sense of "self-interest." In fact, as we shall see, *The Art of Rulership* uses this bidirectional characteristic of moral principles as flux in fusing the basically Legalist notion of manipulating the natural human devotion to self-interest with the Confucian-Mohist principle of *li min*—benefiting the people.

SELF-INTEREST *(SZU LI)*

The Art of Rulership contains the following assertion (9/16b):

> There is not one man in ten thousand who is devoted to goodness and takes joy in proper conduct such that he will voluntarily abide by laws and regulations without being pressed by prohibitions and punishments. But if the ruler issues commands which brook no disobedience so that those who accord with them will benefit while those who defy them will bring grief on themselves, before there is time for a shadow to move, everyone will be in line with the rule of law.

This statement has two significant implications. It implies first that people, at least in recent times, are motivated by personal profit and second that the ruler can use this insight into human nature to manipulate the energies of his people for his own purposes. Such an attitude can lead to a very close affinity with the Legalist tradition. *The Book of Lord Shang,* for example, arrives at a similar insight into human nature which it then turns to political advantage (2/7a, pp. 28–29):

> The nature[3] of man is such that having measured alternative things he takes the longest, having weighed them he takes the heaviest, and having evaluated them he takes what is personally beneficial. Where the perspicacious ruler pays close attention to these three, national order can be established and the talents of the people can be exploited.[4]

The *Han Fei Tzu* follows *The Book of Lord Shang* in recognizing the political power to be gained from manipulating the human propensity for self-interest (314:3): "The means whereby the sage achieves proper order are three. The first is called profit. . . . Profit is his means of winning over the people." Another passage in *Han Fei Tzu* has a similar purport (167:10): "You, sir, do not know how to effect proper government. Because awesomeness is enough to subjugate others and personal profit is enough to encourage them, one is able to govern them properly."

In fact, the central Legalist concept of reward and punishment is rooted in the conviction that people can be led by feeding their instinct for self-interest (*Han Fei Tzu* 26:15):

> The means by which the perspicacious ruler guides and controls his ministers is simply the "two handles." These two handles are punishments and bounty. What is meant by punishments and bounty? Maiming and execution are punishments; dispensations and rewards are bounty. Because those who act as ministers fear punishments and penalties but are attracted by profit from dispensations and rewards, if the ruler keeps the use of punishments and bounty in his own hands, the various ministers will fear his awesomeness and hasten to receive his profits.

This observation is reiterated in *Han Fei Tzu* 367:2:

> But the things which the people like and dislike are controlled by the ruler. The people like personal profit and emoluments but dislike punishments and penalties. Where the ruler manipulates the people's likes and dislikes to command their strength, there is no reason for him to fail in his undertakings.[5]

While *The Art of Rulership* does seem to incorporate this basically Legalist notion of manipulating people's self-interest,[6] it modifies it substantially by asserting that the ruler's interests coincide with those of his people. That is to say, in benefiting his people the ruler is benefiting himself. While in Legalist theory the accent is unquestionably on punishments and coercion, *The Art of Rulership* puts more store in the notion of willing compliance. There the ruler is encouraged to use the natural disposition of his subjects toward their own self-interest as a device for gathering popular support (9/17a):

> If the ruler prevents that which the people consider injurious while encouraging that which they consider beneficial, his authority will prevail like the opening of a dike or the breaking of a dam. Hence if one goes downstream with the current, he will easily get to his destination; if one gallops along with the wind at his back, he will easily cover a great distance.[7]

The Legalist element of the primacy given to maintaining the ruler's political position and authority is tempered by the consideration that private and public benefit are coextensive. Since the disposition and direction of government are determined by what is beneficial to the people, there can be no point of conflict.

It might be suggested that, generally speaking, the Legalist theorists, ever preoccupied with the ruler's interests, show little concern for the welfare of the people. This is of course true. But where it is expedient, the Legalist thinkers are not averse to benefiting the people.[8] For example, Legalist theory puts great store by law and order because it is regarded as a necessary condition for political strength and stability. That law and order generally makes life more pleasant for the people is a convenient coincidence, but certainly not a primary motive. Thus the Legalists diverge from the mainstream of Chinese political theory in their conception of the *purpose* of government. The spirit of the following passage from *The Book of Documents (Shu-ching)* was accepted by Confucius as the basis of his political doctrine and transmitted down through the Confucian-Mohist traditions (080087): "It is the people who are the root of the state. Where the root is secure, the state will be at peace." The Legalist thinkers, on the other hand, were adamant that the sole purpose of government is to serve the ruler's interests. If benefiting the people is conducive to this end, Legalist doctrine says benefit them, but where the interests of the ruler and people are at cross purposes, there is no question whose interests must be served.

Section 15 in the accompanying translation of *The Art of Rulership*, which is devoted to a discussion of "benefiting the people" *(li min)*, contains two principles: the ruler can organize the people by manipulating their instinct for self-interest, and the ruler can consolidate and expand his influence by benefiting the people. While the first assertion is purely Legalist, the second synthesizes the Legalist's preoccupation with the ruler's interests and the Confucian belief that the ruler's interests and those of the people are one and the same.

BENEFITING THE PEOPLE *(LI MIN)*

The concept that the people are the root of the state is a relatively early position in the development of Chinese political thought. In *The Book of Documents (Shu-ching)* we find the following statements (040299[9] and 210279[10]):

Heaven hears and sees as my people hear and see.
Heaven is sympathetic to the people. What the people want, heaven is certain to pursue.

Again, in the following *Tso chuan* passage, the position of the ruler is defined in terms of his obligations and responsibilities to his people. The welfare of the people is unambiguously placed ahead of the personal interests of the ruler (165/Wen 13/3):

> Duke Wen of Chu divined about moving to Yi. The diviner said: "It will be beneficial for your people, but not for you." The duke said: "If it will benefit my people, it is to my benefit. Heaven in giving birth to the people set up a ruler in order to benefit them. When the people are benefited, I will certainly share in it." His advisors said: "Your life could be prolonged—why not forget it?" The duke replied: "My life lies in nurturing my people; whether I die sooner or later is only a matter of time. If the people will benefit, we move. Nothing could be more propitious." They thereupon moved to Yi, and in the fifth month Duke Wen of Chu died. The superior person comments: "He knew his duty."

This traditional concept that the people are the root of government was absorbed into the Confucian doctrine at its inception to become the foundation of its political philosophy. Acknowledging this basic principle, the Confucians then insist that government must function for the sake of its people and, moreover, that the ruler's power and stability are correlative to the degree of his success in advancing the people's interests. This Confucian emphasis on the welfare of the people is demonstrable by a survey of their representative texts:

Analects 41/20/2:

> The Master said: "Promoting that which the people find to their benefit—is this not being bountiful at no cost to oneself?"[11]

Mencius 31/4B/16:

> Mencius said: "There has never been a person who succeeded at subjugating others with his goodness. Only in using this goodness for the welfare of others is one able to subjugate the empire. And there has never been a True King without the empire's sincere allegiance."[12]

Hsün Tzu 26/9/21:

> Tradition has it: "The ruler is the boat, the common people are the water. While the water can support the boat, it can also capsize it." This is what it means. If the superior man wants security, therefore, nothing is better than being equitable in his government and loving his people.[13]

Lü-shih ch'un-ch'iu 4/7a:

> Among great acts of rightness, none is greater than benefiting others, and in benefiting others, nothing is greater than instructing them.

A popular Confucian metaphor for the relationship between the ruler and his people is that of parent and child, the welfare of the child being the parents' most vital concern (*Great Learning [Ta-hsüeh]* 10):[14] "*The*

Book of Odes (Shih-ching) says: 'How happy is this ruler, the father and mother of his people.' That which the people like, he likes; that which they dislike, he dislikes—that is what is meant by father and mother to the people.''[15]

While the notion of government for the people is certainly a feature of the pre-Ch'in Confucian tradition, it was by no means their exclusive property. Early on it was absorbed and elaborated upon by the Mohists until it became the central principle of their political thought (*Mo Tzu* 11/9/53):

> Who would you name as persons who, while being wealthy and occupying high position, received rewards for being superior in character? I would say that the sage-kings of the Three Dynasties in ancient times—Yao, Shun, Yü, Wen, and Wu—were such men. What did they do to receive the rewards? In governing the empire, they loved the people without distinction, further benefited them, and finally led the people of the empire in esteeming and exalting heaven and serving the spirits. Because they loved and benefited the people, heaven and the spirits rewarded them, enthroning them as the Son of Heaven and making them father and mother to the people.[16]

In the several centuries from Confucius down to the Western Han, Confucian thought underwent a process of doctrinal development. This development has left seminal Confucian ideas and Han Confucian ideas so radically distinct that there is some question as to whether calling some of the early Han thinkers "Confucian" is not more misleading than enlightening. Nonetheless, one important thread of continuity is the concept of government for the people. Among Western Han Confucians, Chia Yi can be taken as representative in his emphasis on the ruler's obligation to govern for the benefit of the people (*Chia t'ai-fu hsin-shu* 9/B 43a):

> I have heard that with respect to government, the people are the root of everything. They are the root of the state, the ruler, and the officialdom. Whether the state is stable or unstable depends on the people; whether the ruler is held in awe or viewed with contempt depends on the people; whether the officials are noble or base depends on the people. This is what is meant by the people being the root of everything.

The same text (9/B 48b) adds: "The people are that on which the state stands and the root of the various nobles. They cannot be treated lightly." In fact, this entire "Great Government" *(Ta-cheng)* chapter of Chia Yi's *New Text (Hsin-shu)* is devoted to the thesis that the people are the root, the destiny, and the strength of the nation.

Tung Chung-shu defines the ruler's position in terms of his ability to win the support of the people (5/1a and 7/14a):

A king *(wang)* is one to whom the people flock *(wang);* a ruler *(chün)* is one who does not lose the masses *(ch'ün)*. Therefore one who can cause the myriad people to flock to him and can gain the support of the masses is without equal in the world.

Moreover, where heaven's giving birth to the people is not for the sake of the king, its enthroning the king is for the sake of the people. Therefore heaven will employ one whose virtue is such as to make the people peaceful and happy but will dismiss one whose wickedness is such as to cause them injury.[17]

In the *Huai Nan Tzu* itself, the concept of *li min* can be found in every corner of the text and is unquestionably one of its main themes (2/12b and 13/3a):

In antiquity during an era of the highest virtue, the merchants were contented with their shops, the farmers were pleased with their occupation, the ministers were comfortable in their offices, and the recluses cultivated their *tao*. At this time, the winds and rains did not cause damage and destruction, the grasses and trees did not die prematurely, the nine ceremonial vessels were heavy, pearls and jade were lustrous, the Lo river gave forth the *Tan-shu* and the Yellow River produced the *Lü-t'u*. Therefore Hsü Yu, Fang Hui, Shan Chuan, and P'ei Yi each attained the *tao*. How was this? It was because the ruler of the age was of a mind to benefit the empire, and hence the people were able to enjoy themselves each in his own way.

The administering of a nation has its constants, and takes benefiting the people as its root. Political instruction too has its constants, and takes obedience to command as its root. If something is beneficial to the people, it need not be in imitation of the ancients; if it is everywhere commensurate with present circumstances, it need not follow old ways.[18]

The Art of Rulership, as one treatise in the *Huai Nan Tzu* anthology, is certainly no exception. *Li min,* in the sense of giving primary consideration to the welfare of the people, is an aspect of almost every major concept in *The Art of Rulership*'s political thought. Whereas *li min* is only an implication of the other main concepts in the political system and receives only incidental treatment in those portions of *The Art of Rulership* having a different focus, Section 16 is given over wholly to a discussion of this one theme, culminating in the following description of the former kings (9/19a–b):

The former kings in making things whole in accordance with the proper time, in enriching the country and benefiting the people, in settling unpopulated areas and attracting those from distant reaches, showed that in their Way nothing was overlooked. It is not that they, the heart, could be the eyes and feet in seeing and carrying things out. But so long as the heart never loses sight of wanting to benefit the other organs, those organs will fulfill their functions of their own accord. The heart in its relationship to the nine orifices and the four appendages is not able to do the job of any one of them, and yet in moving, listening, and looking all of them depend on it for direction. This is because it never loses sight of wanting to benefit them.

This attitude of *li min* is a lofty ideal, but what are the practical measures necessary to realize it? The first consideration, the economic health of the people, begins with frugality as standard government policy (9/10b): "The Way of the ruler is to cultivate his person by dwelling in quietude and to lead his subjects with frugality and moderation."[19] Since extravagance on the part of the ruler is always a direct drain on the resources of the people, it encourages social unrest (9/10b):

> If the ruler has a penchant for predatory birds and ferocious animals, rare and exotic things, and is anxious and agitated, if he is not sparing with the efforts of his people, enjoys horses and hunting and takes to the field at whatever time he pleases, then the duties of his bureaucracy will be thrown into disorder and there will be little material wealth in spite of hard work, the people will be miserable and distressed, and their means of livelihood will go untended. Where the ruler is fond of high pavilions, deep ponds, sculptured and engraved ornamentation, beautifully colorful patterns, fine linen and embroidery, precious stones and jewels, then his taxes will be exhorbitant and the energies of the common people will be utterly depleted.[20]

An extravagant court and poverty among the people are certain signs of bad government and impending political decline (9/11a):

> When the age is in decline, however, it is a different matter. The ruler, having once gained the wealth of possessing the empire and having occupied the purchase attendant upon his position, will then exhaust the energies of the common people in catering to his own desires. His mind is wholly preoccupied with buildings, pavilions, ponds, gardens, ferocious animals, precious stones, and exotic objects. Consequently the poor people do not even have husks and chaff to eat and yet the tigers, wolves, and bear fill themselves on fine meats; the common people are sparsely clothed in coarse rags and yet palaces and halls are draped with silk and embroidery. The ruler gives priority to those undertakings which serve no useful purpose, and the people of the empire become haggard and gaunt. Thus it is that he causes the people of the empire to become discontented with their lot in life.[21]

Because of the ideal ruler's concern for the welfare of his people, his reign, far from being the acme of personal luxury and comfort, is a time of singular hardship and sacrifice (9/10b–11a):

> In accepting the empire it was not as if Yao coveted the wealth of the myriad peoples or the ease of being ruler. Seeing that the common people struggled

among themselves, the strong dominating the weak and the many oppressing the few, Yao then personally comported himself in accordance with moderation and frugality, and elucidating the virtue of mutual love, he brought the people together in harmony. Thus it was that his roofing thatch was not trimmed, his rafters were not cut and finished, his royal carriage was not ornamented, his mats were not hemmed, his pottage was not seasoned, and his grain was not polished. Going on his royal progress and spreading his guidance, he labored assiduously in the empire and traveled to each of the five sacred peaks. Surely it was not that the lifestyle of the emperor would be anything but enjoyable, but that he took the whole empire for the sake of the empire and not because he derived any personal benefit from it. When he became old and weary and abdicated in favor of Shun, it was just like stepping back and kicking off his sandals.

It is not possible for the ideal ruler to delight in the luxuries available to his office if his people are deprived of a reasonable existence (9/17a–b):

> It is not that high pavilions and storied buildings, connecting halls and towers, are not magnificent. But where his people do not even have caves or thatched huts in which to find shelter, a perspicacious ruler does not enjoy them. It is not that fat meats, rich wines, sweetmeats, and delicacies are not delicious. But where his people do not even have husks and chaff or bare staples to put into their mouths, the perspicacious ruler finds no relish in them. It is not that a peaceful bed and soft matting are not agreeable. But where his people dwell in remote frontier settlements, brave every kind of peril, and finally perish in the marshes with their bones bleaching in the sun, the perspicacious ruler finds no comfort in them.[22]

The ruler comports himself in a manner consistent with the conditions prevailing among his people and takes pleasure in leisure activities only when times are good (9/17b):

> The ruler of antiquity was concerned about the hardships of his subjects to the extent that if there were people starving in his state, at each meal he would have only one single dish, and if there were people freezing in winter he would not attire himself in fur garments. Only when the harvest was good and the people had plenty would he then set up the bells and drums and display the shields and axes. And with ruler and subject, superior and subordinate, all enjoying these together, there was no sorrowful person left in the whole state.[23]

Not only should the ruler's leisure activities reflect the conditions prevalent among his people, but more important, the taxes levied to support these leisure activities should be commensurate with the economic capabilities of his subjects (9/17a): "The ruler in levying his taxes on the people must first calculate the year's yield, assess the accumulated stores of the people, and know the extent of surplus or shortage in the yearly harvest before exacting enough to cover his carriages, clothing, and food and to satisfy his wants."[24]

On the positive side, the ruler derives pleasure from the prosperity of his people. Thus he does everything in his power to encourage economic strength and vitality in his domain.[25] This policy begins with an attitude of personal moderation (9/18a): "Thus when a benevolent and perspicacious ruler is moderate in his taxes and his own expenditures, his people will enjoy the bounty of heaven and earth and not suffer the miseries of hunger and cold."[26] He employs the people wisely and instructs them in the most effective way of exploiting their resources (9/18b):

> Food is the foundation of the people, people are the foundation of the state, and the state is the foundation of the ruler. The ruler of men should take advantage of the seasons of heaven above, make full use of the earth's plenty below, and deploy the energies of the people wisely in between. As a result, all living things will reach maturity and the five grains will thrive. He should teach the people to raise the six domestic animals, to plant trees at the proper times, to labor diligently in the cultivation of the fields and to plant mulberry bushes and hemp widely, to use each kind of terrain and soil to its best advantage so that on hills and slopes which will not produce the five grains, they grow bamboo and wood. In the spring he should teach them to prune out what is rotten and dry, in summer to gather the fruit and berries, in autumn to lay in the vegetables and grains, and in winter to cut and gather firewood. This then becomes the basis of the people's livelihood.

While encouraging his people to take full advantage of earth's bounty, the ruler lays down a program of sensible conservation of the environment (9/18b–19a):

> In hunting, the laws of the former kings did not permit the extermination of the whole herd or flock or the trapping of the young. They did not allow the draining of ponds to fish, the burning of woods to hunt, the spreading of nets in the wild prior to the autumn's wild dog sacrifice, the setting of nets in the water prior to the spring's otter sacrifice, the stretching of bird-nets in valleys and river gorges before the autumn falconry, the logging of hill forests before the autumn shedding of leaves, the burning off of fields before the hibernating of the insects. They did not allow the killing of pregnant animals, the collecting of fledglings and bird eggs, the taking of fish less than a foot in length, or the consumption of piglets less than a year old.
>
> Thus grasses and trees billowed forth like rising steam, birds and animals rushed to their domains like a flowing spring, and birds of the air swarmed to them like clouds of smoke because they had that which brought all this about.[27]

In this analysis of the concept *li min*, it is apparent that the position taken in *The Art of Rulership* is for the most part consistent with pre-

Ch'in Confucian texts. What is of particular interest is the degree to which this concern for the general human condition is a feature representative of Western Han Confucianism. Not only is the concept of government for the people one of the strongest themes in the *Huai Nan Tzu* anthology; it is the first principle in the political philosophies of other early Han thinkers—notably Chia Yi and Tung Chung-shu.

With respect to *li min,* it has been possible to detect a minor Legalist contribution in the notion of controlling the people by manipulating the human preoccupation with self-interest. Once formulated, this Legalist thesis is immediately tempered by the Confucian proposition that in fact the interests of the people and their ruler coincide. Hence any governmental concession to the interests of the people reinforces the strength and stability of the government itself.

This concept of *li min* is overwhelmingly Confucian in its orientation and without question represents the most important Confucian contribution to the political system propounded in *The Art of Rulership.* On one level, this concept is discussed as an independent idea, but in a more profound sense the notion of government *for* the people constitutes the unifying spirit of its entire political philosophy.

HUAI NAN TZU
BOOK NINE
The Art of Rulership

The Art of Rulership

This translation is based on a critical text established by collating the following six redactions of the *Huai Nan Tzu: Pei-Sung hsiao-tzu pen,* the *Tao-tsang pen,* the *Wang P'u (Liu Chi) pen,* the *Chung-li ssu-tzu pen,* the *Mao I-kuei pen,* and the *Chuang K'uei-chi pen.* I have relied upon the research of Yü Ta-ch'eng and Harold D. Roth for an analysis of the extant editions.

Rhymed passages are indented, and the rhyming characters are indicated in parentheses at the end of the phrase or sentence. An important source for the rhymes of this period is the *Han-Wei-Nan-pei-ch'ao yün-pu yen-pien yen-chiu* by Lo Ch'ang-p'ei and Chou Tsu-mo.

I have divided the text where it seemed most appropriate. This treatise, while for the most part internally consistent, does not always have one continuous theme readily identifiable in each of the sections. Often one section is a series of related ideas, one leading to the next, all falling loosely under one subject heading. That I have been reasonably accurate in dividing the text is supported by a general correspondence between my attempts and the divisions found in the *Wen Tzu* and the *Ch'ün-shu chih-yao.* The margin numbers correspond to the *SPTK* pagination.

SECTION 1[1]

The art of the ruler is to deal with things through nonaction and
to disseminate wordless instructions *(chiao).*
Limpid and still he does not move; even when moved he is not
agitated *(yao):*
taking advantage of the course of things he delegates
responsibility to subordinates and, holding them to account, he
does not wear himself out *(lao).*

1a

Even though he is aware of how things should be done, he allows
himself to be guided by the imperial tutors *(tao);*
even though he himself is able to speak, he allows his diplomats
to proclaim the ceremonial words *(tz'u);*
even though he himself is able to walk, he allows his escort to
lead the way *(tao);*
even though he himself is able to hear, he allows the
administrators to select the right advice *(mou).*[2]

Therefore in his deliberations he does not decide on any wrong
courses of action and in his movements he does not err *(shih).*[3]
His words are refined and elegant and his actions are a worthy
model for the world.[4]
His comings and goings are timely *(shih)*
and whether he acts or not is consistent with the implicit
principles of things *(li).*
Beauty and ugliness do not stir up his likes and dislikes, and
punishments and rewards are not accompanied by anger or
pleasure *(hsi).*[5]
He lets each name name itself and each class classify itself.[6]
Things proceed from what is naturally so and nothing arises from
him personally *(chi).*

Therefore a king of antiquity would attach a veil of pearls to his
cap to prevent himself from seeing too clearly *(ming);*
he would have yellow silk plugs in his ears to prevent himself
from hearing too keenly *(ts'ung).*[7]
The emperor being surrounded by screens was to erect a barrier
around himself *(chang).*[8]

When what is to be governed is distant, one should focus on what is close
at hand; when what is to be ruled is great, one should preserve the small.[9]

For him to be wild and willful in the use of his eyes would lead to excess;
to be wild and willful in the use of his ears would lead to confusion; to be
willful in the use of his mouth would lead to disorder. These three gate-
ways must be carefully guarded.

Where one seeks to regulate something *(kuei chih),*
he is in fact going contrary to it *(li chih);*
where he seeks to embellish something *(shih chih),*
he is in fact harming it *(tsei chih).*[10]

SECTION 2[11]

A person's spiritual souls come from the vapors of heaven; his
sentient souls come from the vapors of earth *(p'o).*[12]
Returning these to their mysterious apartments and causing each
to dwell in its proper residence *(chai),*
if one is able to watch over these and not lose them *(shih),*
he achieves communion above with the Great One *(yi).*
And the essence of the Great One *(ching)*
communes with heaven *(t'ien).*[13]
The Way of heaven is mysterious and silent *(mo)*
and is without any movement[14] or fixed pattern *(tse).*
It is too great to be measured to its ends *(chi)*
and too deep to be fathomed *(ts'e).*
Constantly[15] being a companion to the process of transformation,
it is beyond his comprehension *(te).*

In ancient times when Shen Nung governed the empire,[16] his spirit
did not gallop out from his breast *(chung),*
his wisdom did not extend beyond the four directions *(yü),*
and he cherished the benevolent and sincere mind *(hsin).*
The sweet rains fell at the proper time and the five grains
flourished *(chih).*
In spring they would sprout forth, in summer they would grow
(chang),
in autumn they would be harvested, in winter they would be
stored up *(tsang).*
With monthly examinations and seasonal evaluations,[17]
at the year's end the record of accomplishments would be offered
up *(kung),*
and tasting the grain at the proper season,
sacrifice would be made in the Ming T'ang *(t'ang).*[18]

The institution of the Ming T'ang was such that it had a roof and
no walls *(fang),*
but the elements could neither enter it nor do it harm *(shang).*
With a halting manner he would enter it.
Nurturing his people in justice *(kung),*

they became plainly honest and sincere.
Without contending one with the other,
they found that they had plenty;
without wearing themselves out they achieved their ends *(kung).*[19]

And taking advantage of the stock of the heavens and earth they lived in perfect accord with their natural environment *(t'ung)*.

His intimidating presence was awesome yet not put to the test, punishments were there yet he did not have to invoke them,[20] and his laws were few in number and not overwhelming. Hence his transformation of the people was godlike. In his territory stretching from Chiao-chih in the south to Yu-tu in the north, T'ang-ku in the east and San-wei in the west, there was no one who would not submit to his rule.[21] At this time the laws were liberal, the punishments were tolerant, and the prisons were empty. The world was one in custom and none were of a wicked mind.

The government in a declining age is a different matter:
Those above are fond of taking without any conception of proper limit *(liang)*
while subordinates are self-assertive and wholly given over to avarice *(jang)*.
The people, impoverished and distressed, contend angrily *(cheng)*, and working themselves to the bone, never achieve anything *(kung)*.
Cleverness and deception sprout forth,
bandits and thieves are increasingly evident *(chang)*,
ill-will appears between superiors and subordinates, and edicts and orders are not implemented *(hsing)*.
The authorities do not devote their efforts to returning to the right path. Going against the roots, they cultivate the nonessentials; cutting back on their bounty, they increase their punishments. And yet by doing such things they are trying to establish proper order! This is no different from holding a catapult and hoping to attract a bird, or wielding a cane to tame a dog. It will just make matters worse.

SECTION 3[22]

Now where water is muddy the fishes gasp; where government is cruel the people are disorderly.

Those who breed tigers, leopards, rhinoceroses, and elephants put them in pens, provide for their desires, feed them at the right time, and give them room to vent outbursts of temper.[23] But notwithstanding this, that the animals do not live out their natural span of years is because they are physically under duress.
Where superiors escalate their cleverness *(ku)*,
their subordinates will be that much more deceptive *(cha)*;

where superiors escalate their interference *(shih)*,
their subordinates will be that much more self-seeking *(t'ai);*
where superiors intrude on the people without respite,
their subordinates will be that much more unsettled *(ting);*
where superiors escalate their demands,
their subordinates will wrangle all the more among themselves
(cheng).[24]
Working at the nonessentials rather than straightening things out at the root is like prodding a pile of dirt to put down the dust or bringing an armload of firewood to extinguish a fire.

The sage governs easily because his affairs are few, and the people are easily satisfied because his demands on them are few.
He is benevolent without giving *(jen)*,
he is trusted without speaking *(hsin)*,
he gets without seeking,
he accomplishes without doing *(ch'eng)*.
Solitarily he preserves what is genuine *(chen)*,
embraces virtue, and promotes sincerity *(ch'eng).*[25]
And the world follows him just as the echo responds to the sound *(sheng)*
and the shadow to the form *(hsing).*[26]
This is because he cultivates the root.

Punishments and penalties are inadequate to change social custom; executions are inadequate to put an end to wickedness. Only godlike transformation is estimable and only the most essential vapors[27] can do it in this way.

Now, a loud shout cannot be heard beyond a hundred paces, but where the mind is focused it will make itself understood several hundred miles away.[28]

In the winter the myriad things seek out the sun while in summer they seek the shade. There is nothing which causes this yet it is so.[29]
With the appearance of the most essential vapors *(hsiang)*
things come without being summoned and depart of their own accord without being dismissed *(wang)*.
Dark and abstruse *(ming ming)*,
no one knows who produces them and yet their achievements are naturally realized *(ch'eng)*.
The wise are not able to speak of them and the eloquent are not able to describe them *(hsing)*.

In ancient times Sun-shu Ao reposed peacefully and yet gave the men of Ying no opportunity to use their weapons.[30] Yi Liao of Shih-nan toyed with his pellets and yet even with the trouble existing between the two families there was no opening for either side to express their views.[31] Things like armor and grimaces of wrath[32] are a far cry from an effective defense against arms; things like contracts and ceremonial gifts, punishments, penalties, and instruments of execution are of little use in resolving difficulties; the method of relying on your eyes to see and your words to command is fraught with difficulties in effecting proper order.

When Ch'ü Po-yü became prime minister, Tzu Kung went to see him and asked, "How do you govern the state?" He replied, "I govern it by not governing it."[33] Chien Tzu, wanting to attack Wei, sent Shih An to go and make a preliminary examination of the situation. Returning, he reported: "With Ch'ü Po-yü as prime minister, the time is not yet right to attack." How could any kind of fortifications have such an effect![34]

It was when the mute Kao Yao became minister of justice that the world was free of cruel punishments.[35] This was because he had something of greater value than the spoken word. It was when the blind Shih K'uang became prime minister that Chin was free of disorderly government.[36] This was because he had something of greater value than sight.

It was orders without words and seeing without looking that were the methods that made Fu Hsi and Shen Nung fit to be mentors.

In being transformed, the people follow what the ruler does rather than what he says.

Duke Chuang of Ch'i spoke against strife while in deed being fond of courage. As a result, the state was raked by turmoil which led in due course to his assassination at the hands of Ts'ui Chu.[37] And King Ch'ing Hsiang spoke against promiscuity while in deed being fond of women. As a consequence, his people were extremely unruly which led ultimately to the problem of Chao Ch'i.[38]

The effects of the most essential vapors, such as the spring vapors giving life and the autumn vapors extinguishing it, occur even faster than the speed of a post horse or a courier.[39]

The ruler is like an archer. Where his aim is off to the slightest degree, he will miss the mark by yards. Because of this, he is cautious in how he moves the people.

On hearing Jung Ch'i-ch'i play one chord on his lute, Confucius was delighted for three days. This was because he was moved by its harmony.[40] On hearing Tsou Chi strum his lute once, King Wei of Ch'i grieved all night long. This was because he was moved by its plaintive sound.[41] Whereas one is able to arouse delight and grief in others by articulating his feelings in the sound of the lute and lyre, he cannot alter customs and conventions by proclaiming laws and establishing rewards. This is because [in the latter case] his sincerity of mind is not projected abroad.[42]

Hearing Ning Ch'i's melancholy song which came from beneath the ox cart, Duke Huan [of Ch'i] sighed and took a second look. This shows how deep the most essential vapors touch others.[43]

4a

It is said: With music, if one hears its sound, he will know what kind of customs there were, and if he sees the customs, he will know how the people were transformed.[44]

That Confucius studying the lute under Master Hsiang understood the purposes of King Wen[45] was because on seeing the faintest outline he could fill in the rest clearly.[46] That Chi Tzu of Yen-ling on hearing the music of Lu knew the customs of the Yin and Hsia dynasties was because on classifying what was close at hand he could infer what was far away.[47] The culture produced in high antiquity and lasting a thousand years is still with us—how much more so the influence of this on the people of that era.

At the time of King T'ang of Yin there was a seven-year drought.[48] When he offered himself as sacrifice on the outer reaches of Sang-lin, the clouds from all quarters of the world gathered and rain fell for hundreds of miles around. Embracing simplicity and offering his sincerity, he moved the heavens and earth. If his spirit can make itself understood[49] even in the realm beyond, how could his orders being carried out and his prohibitions being observed have caused him any difficulty?

With the sage-kings of antiquity, when the most essential vapors were embodied within, likes and dislikes did not lie on the outside.[50] Their words were spoken to express what was truly on their minds and they issued commands to show their purposes. Setting these out in social norms and music and recounting them in song and verse, their deeds have been known to each succeeding generation and have spread to every corner of the world. They could even shape and transform birds, beasts, and insects. How much more so could they administer the law and implement edicts.

The highest ruler is godlike in his transformations. Next comes one who makes it impossible for people to do wrong.[51] And next comes one who rewards those of superior qualities and punishes the troublemakers.

SECTION 4[52]

Because the crosspiece of a pair of scales shows no bias toward either the right or left in weighing, it can be level *(p'ing)*.
Because a plumb line shows no bias toward inside or out in measuring, it can be straight *(cheng)*.
Because the ruler in administering the law shows no bias toward those he likes or dislikes, his words can be command *(ming)*.

It is by depending upon a given method and dispensing with the human element that in weighing things the scales are precise to the smallest fraction of an ounce, that in straightening things the plumb line is accurate to a hair's breadth,[53] and that in redressing any waywardness or deviation the ruler is wholly free of personal prejudice or bias. Deviousness cannot make him bend, slander cannot disturb him, he gives no ground for gratitude or ill-will. Such rulers, in relying on art, dispense with the human element. Hence cleverness plays no part in government.

Now, a boat floating on water and a vehicle rolling along the land are both natural to their circumstances.[54] Why, on running into a tree and breaking the carriage axle or running onto the rocks and staving in the boat, does one not feel ill-will toward the tree or the rocks but rather holds the skill of the driver or boatman to blame? The answer is because there is no deliberate intention on the part of the tree or the rocks.

Where the Way is accompanied by intelligence, there is confusion; where good deeds are accompanied by a motive, there is treachery; where the mind is accompanied by the eye, there is bedazzlement.[55]

No weapon is as piercing as a fixed purpose—compared to it, even the Mo-yeh sword is inferior;[56] no invaders are as great as the *yin* and *yang*—compared to these, even the attack drums are insignificant.[57]

Now the scales, the compass, and the square once fixed cannot be changed. They do not compromise their integrity for the sake of Ch'in or Ch'u nor do they change their semblance for the sake of the Hu or Yüeh people. Being constant, they do not vary; being used for a special purpose, they do not adapt themselves. Having once been cast, they are passed on through ten thousand generations and operate through nonaction.[58]

SECTION 5[59]

It may be that a nation has a doomed ruler *(chu)*,
but there is no such thing as the useless Way *(tao)*;   5a
it may be that man has reached the end of his tether *(ch'iung)*,
but principles never fail to be applicable *(t'ung)*.
Viewing it from this perspective, nonaction is the source of the
Way *(tsung)*.

When one gets hold of this source of the Way *(tsung)*,
he is never at his wit's end in responding to things *(ch'iung)*,
but when he relies on the talents of men *(ts'ai)*,
it is difficult to reach the acme of good government *(chih)*.

Even sage-rulers such as T'ang and Wu[60] would be unable to
match the Yüeh people in maneuvering a small craft[61] on the
rivers and lakes *(hu)*.
Even an outstanding minister such as Yi Yin[62] would be unable to
match the Hu people in breaking to harness the fine horses of the
north *(t'u)*.[63]
Even men as broad in understanding as Confucius and Mo Tzu
would be unable to match the mountain people in foraging about
the thicket and scaling perilous slopes *(tsu)*.

Viewing it from this perspective, human intelligence is very limited in its
capacity to deal with things. If a person, hoping to light up the whole
world and see clearly in all directions, relies exclusively on it rather than
on the inevitable outcome of practicing the Way, it will not be long
before he reaches a dead-end.[64] Thus it is that individual human intelligence is not adequate to the task of bringing proper order to the world.[65]

Chieh's strength was such that he could split a horn, unbend a hook,
plait iron, fuse metal, and maneuver a great ox about; in the water he
could kill a giant turtle and on land he could capture a bear. Nevertheless, T'ang leading only three hundred war chariots surrounded him at
Ming-t'iao and then captured him at Chiao-men.[66]

Viewing it from this perspective, outstanding strength and boldness are
not adequate to the task of retaining control of the world. Since human

intelligence is not in itself sufficient to effect proper government and boldness is not in itself sufficient to hold sway, it is clear that individual human talents cannot be relied upon. This being so, where a ruler comprehends circumstances even beyond the four seas without ever leaving his ancestral hall, it is because he takes advantage of things to understand things and he takes advantage of man to understand man.[67]

> Where concerted strength is applied,
> it is equal to any task *(sheng);*
> where the intelligence of the many is employed,
> it will succeed in all things *(ch'eng).*

That household wells do not host giant turtles is because they are too cramped; that flower gardens do not produce huge trees is because they are too small.[68]

A person will be unsuccessful in lifting a heavy tripod if he has inadequate strength. But when it comes to removing it, he does not necessarily have to rely on one person with a great deal of strength.

A community of a thousand people has no broken bridges,[69] and a settlement of ten thousand people has no abandoned projects.

Now, the two famous horses, Hua Liu and Lü Erh,[70] would cover several hundred miles in one day. But if one set them to catching rabbits, they would be outdone by a wild dog or a wolf. This is because their faculties and abilities are different. During the night an owl can snatch a flea or mosquito out of the air and discern even the tip of an autumn hair. But during the day, stretching its eyes wide open,[71] it cannot even see a mountain or hill. This is because it is contrary to its nature for it to do this.[72]

The *t'eng* snake springs up into the mists; the flying *ying* dragon ascends into the sky mounting the clouds; a monkey is nimble in the trees and a fish is agile in the water.

In ancient times in the construction of a carriage, the varnisher did not do the ornamental drawing and the engraver did not wield the adze.

> A worker did not have more than one skill,
> a scholar did not combine two offices *(kuan).*
> Each kept to his own province and did not interfere with
> others *(kan);*[73]
> each person found his niche and each thing found its place *(an).*[74]
> As a result, products were not of inferior quality and duties were
> not neglected *(man).*

Where the debt is small it is easy to repay; where duties are few they are easy to fulfill; where a person's burden is light he is easy to encourage.[75] With the ruler making only very limited demands and his subordinates presenting him with accomplishments easily achieved, sovereign and ministers will never become tired of each other.

The Way of the ruler is like the impersonator of the spirit at the sacrifice to the *ling* star.[76] Being solemn and mysteriously silent, he auspiciously receives his blessing.

> One who embodies the Way does not make himself up because he
> is ugly *(shih)*
> or serve as a standard for the good *(chi).*[77]

It is a cape not too big for one man to wear nor too small for ten thousand.

If the ruler exercises the same caution before bestowing favors as he does in being severe, the Way of proper government will prevail. "To bestow favors" is to set store in largess. When those who do not give good service are richly rewarded and those who do not exert themselves receive high rank, ministers with defined duties will grow negligent and persons who do not hold office will press for appointment. "To be severe" is to punish without grounds.

> When the innocent are executed *(wang)*
> and the upright are punished *(hsing),*

the welldisciplined will not be encouraged toward good conduct and the wicked will think nothing of defying their ruler.

> Bestowing favors is a source of villainy *(chien)*
> and being severe is a source of strife *(luan).*

And villainy and strife are the prevailing winds in a doomed state. Thus it is that under the administration of a perspicacious ruler,

> where the state carries out punishments, the anger of the ruler is
> not involved in them *(nu);*
> where the court bestows rewards, the ruler plays no part in them
> *(yü).*

Those who are punished feel no ill-will toward the ruler. This is because it is what their crimes deserve. Those who are rewarded feel no gratitude to the ruler. This is because it is the result of their good service.

> Because the people know that the source of punishment and
> reward lies in themselves *(shen),*
> they try their best to make themselves fit to carry out their
> occupations and do not feel indebted to the ruler *(chün).*[78]

There are no footprints in the court which is overgrown with wild grass; there are no weeds in the fields which have been well-cleared. Thus the most excellent ruler is one of whom his subjects know only that he exists.[79]

SECTION 6[80]

Now, the upright on the shadoof,[81] being fixed vertically, does
not move,
and yet the crosspiece in moving up and down is controlled by it
(yen).
The ruler being still and silent is not restless,
and yet the bureaucracy takes its measure from him *(yen)*.
This can be likened to the standard bearer of an army—if he signals indiscriminately, chaos will ensue.

Cleverness is inadequate to the task of bringing about a great peace; intelligence is inadequate to the task of dispelling danger.

Rather than praising Yao and reviling Chieh, we do better to put aside the ability of eyes and ears and return to cultivating the Way.[82]

If the ruler is limpid, still, and nonactive,
the heavens will provide him with the proper seasons *(shih)*.[83]
If he does not appropriate what is not his,
is frugal, and keeps to moderation,
the earth will yield him up its bounty *(ts'ai)*.
If he is content with being stupid while praising the virtues of
others,
sages will lend him their counsel *(mou)*.[84]

It is to the low ground that the myriad things repair *(kuei)*
and to the empty that the empire gives its gifts *(yi)*.[85]

(When the ruler listens to state affairs, his vision should be clear and unobscured, and his mind should be open and free of preconceptions. As a result, the various ministers will converge on him side by side like spokes at the hub, and irrespective of intelligence or moral character, all will strive to do their best. He can then commence to set out his code of social conduct and establish it as his basis.)[86]

This is (for the ruler) to mount a chariot which is the
overwhelming support of the people *(ch'e)*,

and to drive horses which are the intelligence of the people *(ma)*. 7a
Even on a remote or treacherous stretch of road *(t'u)*,
there is no fear of his not knowing which way to go *(huo)*.

Since the ruler dwells deep in seclusion to avoid the heat and damp, and
remains behind layer upon layer of doors in order to protect himself
against villainy and insurgency,
    within he knows nothing about the towns and villages *(ch'ing)*
    and without he knows nothing about the mountains and valleys
    (hsing).
Beyond the curtains and hangings, one's eye cannot penetrate further
than a few miles and the ear cannot hear beyond a hundred paces.[87] Even
so, he is wholly cognizant of all that goes on within the world because the
sources that feed him are immense and those who tap him are numerous.
Hence, without going beyond his doors, he knows about the world; without peeping out through his window, he comprehends the heavenly
Way.[88]

When the ruler avails himself of the intelligence of the people,
gaining the empire is a task hardly worth doing *(yu)*,
but when he relies exclusively on his own mind,
the preservation of even his own person cannot be
guaranteed *(pao)*.[89]

Putting the whole world under his bounty instead of bringing his own
intelligence into play, the ruler follows what the people find beneficial.
Now, by lifting his heel, he is able to benefit the empire.[90] Hence he takes
his place above and yet they do not find him heavy;[91] he dwells in front
of them and yet they do not find him an obstacle; though they raise him
up, they do not feel that he is too high; though they support him, they do
not grow tired of it.[92]

The Way of the ruler is said to be round *(yüan)*
because, revolving and turning, it is without a starting point
(tuan).
He transforms and nurtures like a god *(shen)*,
is vacuous and vacant, and follows the natural course of things
(hsün).
Always keeping to the rear,
he never takes the lead *(hsien)*.[93]
The Way of the minister is said to be square *(fang)*[94]
because he finds out what is appropriate *(tang)*
and dwells in what he is best fitted for.

It is by taking the lead in carrying out affairs *(ch'ang)*
and by clearly keeping to his defined duties *(ming)*
that he realizes his accomplishments *(kung)*.[95]

Where the ruler and minister have different Ways, there is proper order, but where they are the same, there is disorder.[96] If each gets what is appropriate to him and dwells in what is right for him, the one above and those below will know how to deal with each other.[97]

When the ruler listens to state affairs, he should be empty of mind and weak of resolution,[98] and his mind should be clear and unclouded. For this reason, when the various ministers are like spokes converging side by side at the hub, and irrespective of intelligence or moral character, all do their best, then the ruler has the means to hold control over his ministers, the ministers have the means to serve their ruler, and the Way of ordering the state properly is clear.

Because King Wen though himself intelligent was given to
consulting others *(wen)*,[99]
he became sagely *(sheng)*.
Because King Wu though himself redoubtable was given to
consulting others *(wen)*,[100]
he became victorious *(sheng)*.[101]

If one rides on the intelligence of the people,
there is nothing which cannot be carried *(jen)*;
if he employs the strength of the multitude,
there is no task to which he is not equal *(sheng)*.

A weight of eight tons[102] could not be lifted even by Wu Huo.[103] But if the people were to act in concert, a hundred men would have more than enough strength.
Hence if one relies on the strength of one man,
even a Wu Huo cannot be counted upon *(shih)*,
but if he takes advantage of the intelligence of the people,[104]
then ruling over the whole world is a task hardly worth
doing *(yu)*.

Yü[105] diverted the course of the Yangtze and dredged out the Yellow River in order to benefit the world, but it was not within his ability to make the waters flow westward. Chi cleared the land in order to encourage farming among the people,[106] but it was not within his ability to make grain grow in winter.[107] It is not that anything humanly possible has been left undone, but that this was not possible in the nature of things.

Now to attempt what circumstances render impossible[108] instead of following what natural principles make inevitable is something even a saint or a sage would be unable to achieve success in—how much less so the ruler of our present age!

Where the cartload is heavy and the horses are emaciated, even a Tsao Fu would not be able to drive far;[109] but where the cart is light and the horses are good, even a person of mediocre abilities can drive along at a fast pace.[110]

It is not as if the sage could possibly go against what natural principles make inevitable in accomplishing things, or run contrary to what is natural in making the bent straight or the contracted outstretched! He always takes advantage of what a thing can be used for and uses it accordingly.   8a

Where concerted strength is applied,
no task is too great *(sheng);*
where the intelligence of the people is engaged,
no undertaking will go unfinished *(ch'eng).*[111]

A deaf person can be made to chew the animal sinew used in
covering bows *(chin),*
though he cannot be made to hear *(wen).*
A dumb person can be made to work in the horse stables *(yü),*
though he cannot be made to speak *(yü).*[112]
This is because their physical persons are not whole and their abilities have their limitations.

That which has a specific form can occupy a position appropriate to it and that which has a specific ability can undertake a task appropriate to it.

When the strength of a person lifting a burden is equal to the task, he does not feel it too heavy to raise; when the ability of a person pursuing a task matches it, he feels no difficulty.
When everything large or small, long or short, finds its
niche *(yi),*[113]
then there is equality in the empire[114] without anything being able
in any way to surpass another *(kuo).*

Because the sage uses both big and small, long and short, there is no wasted ability.[115]

SECTION 7

The ruler sets high store in integrity and conscientiousness. Where men of conscientiousness and integrity are in authority and preside over affairs with propriety, sychophants and villains will have no avenue of approach.
It is like the square and round being unable to overlap *(kai)*
and the bent and straight being unable to admit each other *(ju)*.

That birds and animals do not run together is because they are a different class of creature.[116] That the tiger and deer do not gambol about together is because they are unequal in strength.

When a sage gets his way and is on the throne, those sychophants and villains who want to intrude on him are like a sparrow encountering a hawk or a mouse running into a badger—they are at the end of the line!

Now in every move,[117] the ruler must exercise great care.[118] If the one who is entrusted is the right person, the state will be wellordered, the relations between superiors and subordinates will be harmonious, the various ministers will be devoted to him, and the common people will bend to his will; but if the one who is entrusted is the wrong person,
the state will be in peril *(wei)*,
superiors and subordinates will be at variance *(kuai)*,
the various ministers will feel ill-will *(yüan)*,
and the common people will be disorderly *(luan)*.
Therefore, if any move is inappropriate *(tang)*
it will be a bane on him for the rest of his life *(shang)*.

The key to success or failure in government *(tao)*
lies in the ruler *(chu)*.
If the inking line[119] is properly set above,
the wood will be straightened beneath it.
It is not that the inking line does anything in particular to the wood *(yen)*,
but rather that the disciplining of the wood in following the inking line makes it so *(jan)*.
Thus if the ruler is truly upright,
honest officials will be commissioned *(shih)*

and villainous persons will hide themselves *(ni);*
but if the ruler is not upright,
the wicked will get on in the world and loyal subjects will
withdraw into retirement.[120]

Why is it that no one tries to split[121] jade with their hands yet they will try
to break melons and gourds in this way? They do not take on the jade or
stone because there is nothing to be gained from it.

If the ruler holds firmly to integrity and justice as if adhering to a plumb
line in measuring the vertical, then those ministers who approach with
evil in their hearts will be just like eggs thrown against a rock or fire
plunged into water.

Because King Ling of Ch'u[122] was partial to slim waists, there were people who starved themselves by cutting back on their food. Because King
Kou Chien of Yüeh[123] was fond of valor, his people would all defy danger in vying with one another to sacrifice their lives. If we view it from
this perspective, it is clear that the person with the handles of authority
and political purchase can alter prevailing attitudes.[124]

9a

When Yao was a common man, he could not even transform the
people of one village through his example of benevolence *(li),*
yet when Chieh was on the throne, his commands were
implemented and his prohibitions were effective *(chih).*[125]
Viewing it from this perspective, it is clear that while moral excellence is
not enough to govern the world, political purchase can alter custom.[126]
This is what is meant when the *Shu-ching [Book of Documents]* states:
"If the ruler enjoys good fortune, the myriad people benefit by it."[127]

SECTION 8

Most of the people in the world are dazzled by name and reputation, and
few make the effort to find out what is actually the case. Thus recluses
become exalted because of their fame and itinerants attain prominence
because of their eloquence. If we examine the grounds on which they
become exalted and attain prominence, it is for the simple reason that the
ruler, being ignorant as to the line between benefit and injury, is impressed by the opinion of the many.

A properly ordered state is a different matter. Those who discuss state
business must be closely scrutinized by the law and those who cultivate

conduct must be tested in office. The ruler takes up their claims and demands of them that they actually perform accordingly, and the ministers render good service by adhering to what they have said they will do. Words are not allowed to exceed real achievement; actions are not allowed to overstep the law. None of the various ministers, being like spokes in a wheel converging at the hub, would dare monopolize the ruler. (Where a certain matter does not fall under the rule of law and yet can be of benefit to the state and its administration)[128] The system of *ts'an wu* must be consulted in order to discern their purposes.[129] He must make good use of people and remain everywhere attentive to determine how their position changes. He is not biased toward any one position and does not take any one side against another. The ruler stands at the center without any bias and sheds light on the length and breadth of the world, the various ministers are impartial and upright and none would dare to be devious. The bureaucracy renders an account of their duties and devotes itself to delivering meritorious service.[130] When the ruler is perspicacious above and the rulers exert themselves to the utmost below, then all traces of villainy and deviousness will be erased and daily progress will be made in his various undertakings. For this reason, . . . and the courageous will give their all in military service.[131]

In a disorderly state it is a different matter. Those praised by the multitude are rewarded even though they have no accomplishments, whereas those who are faithful in their duties are punished even though they are innocent. The ruler is foolish and shortsighted, and the various ministers form factions and are disloyal.[132] The sophists travel about debating, and those who cultivate lofty conduct vie with each other for public office. With their cliques they criticize the edicts promulgated by the ruler; with their deviousness they contravene the prohibitions of law.[133] Those who cultivate wisdom devote themselves to cunning and deceit; those who cultivate valor devote themselves to contention and strife. The high ministers usurp authority, the low officials seize political purchase, and together, forming cliques and factions, they manipulate the ruler. Even though this state appears to be intact, the ancients would have considered it moribund.[134]

    Without superintending official duties,
    nor bearing arms *(ping),*[135]
    nor yet cultivating the fields,
    a person could gain the reputation of a worthy sage *(sheng).*
    This is not the way to educate the state.[136]

Ch'i Chi and Lü Erh are the fastest horses in the world.[137] But if they do not respond to the harness commands for going forward and stopping, even a moron would not mount them.[138]

Now, there are clues to be had even with the subtle turning point between proper government and disorder, and yet none of the rulers of the age are able to see them. This is why the Way of proper government is obstructed.

Political authority and purchase are the carriage of the ruler; rank and emoluments are the harness and bit of the ministers. Therefore, because the ruler dwells at the focal point of political power and holds firmly to the handles of rank and emoluments, judges nicely the degree of control, and is appropriate in when and how much to give and take away, all the people exhaust themselves in his service without feeling fatigued.

10a

Now it is not as if the relationship between ruler and minister has the substance of the bond between father and son or the depth of feeling between flesh and blood relatives, and yet the minister will work untiringly and risk his life for the sake of the ruler. Why is this? It is because political purchase makes him do so.[139]

In antiquity Yü Jang was an official in the household of Chung-hsing Wen Tzu, but when Chih Po attacked the Chung-hsing family and appropriated their lands, Yü Jang turned his back on his lord and went into the service of Chih Po. When Chih Po was defeated by Viscount Hsiang of Chao in battle at Chin-yang, he was killed and disgraced,[140] and his state was divided into three. Yü Jang, attempting to take revenge on Viscount Hsiang of Chao, painted his body to look like a leper, swallowed ashes to change his voice, and pulled out his teeth to alter his appearance. As the same person serving these two masters with one and the same heart, he in the one case abandoned his master while in the other case he wanted to follow his master into the grave. Surely this cannot be simply a difference of choice or partiality. It was the difference in the way he was treated by his masters.[141]

When the tyrant Chou ruled the empire and received the homage of the various nobles at court, every corner that human footprints reached and oars plied offered submission. Even so, King Wu with only three thousand armor-clad soldiers captured him at Mu-yeh. This was certainly not because the Chou people died out of a sense of duty while the Yin people turned against their master. It was because their ruler was bountiful and righteous and his orders were carried out.[142]

When there are strong winds, the waves rise; where there is thick foliage, the birds gather. This is because the *ch'i* of the one thing gives rise to the other.

When the minister does not get what he wants from the ruler, the ruler will also be unable to get what he seeks from the minister. Ruler and minister benefit each other only on a basis of reciprocity. Thus the minister barters with his ruler by offering total commitment to the point of laying down his life whereas the ruler trades with his ministers by offering the dispensation of noble ranks. Just as the ruler cannot reward a minister who has rendered no service, a minister cannot die for a ruler to whom he owes no gratitude.[143]

> When the favors of the ruler do not flow down to the people,
> for him to expect service out of them is like whipping an unruly
> horse *(ma)*.
> It is like hoping for a ripe harvest *(chia)*
> without rain *(yü)*.
> It is a demonstrable impossibility *(shu)*.

SECTION 9[144]

The Way of the ruler is to cultivate his person by dwelling in quietude and to lead his subjects with frugality and moderation. If he is quiet, his subjects are not disturbed; if he is frugal, his people will have no cause to complain. Should his subjects be disturbed it would mean political disorder; should his people have cause to complain it would mean that his bounty is not generous. Where there is political disorder, those of superior character will not proffer their counsel, and where the ruler's bounty is not generous, those of valor will not die for him.

If the ruler has a penchant for predatory birds and ferocious animals, rare and exotic things, and is anxious and agitated, if he is not sparing with the efforts of his people, enjoys horses and hunting and takes to the field at whatever time he pleases, then the duties of his bureaucracy will be thrown into disorder and there will be little material wealth in spite of hard work, the people will be miserable and distressed, and their means of livelihood will go untended. Where the ruler is fond of high pavilions, deep ponds, sculptured and engraved ornamentation, beautifully colorful patterns, fine linen and embroidery, precious stones and jewels, then his taxes will be exorbitant and the energies of the common people will be utterly depleted.

In accepting the empire it was not as if Yao coveted the wealth of the myriad peoples or the ease of being ruler.[145] Seeing that the common people struggled among themselves, the strong dominating the weak and the many oppressing the few, Yao then personally comported himself in accordance with moderation and frugality, and elucidating the virtue of mutual love, he brought the people together in harmony. Thus it was that his roofing thatch was not trimmed, his rafters were not cut and finished,[146] his royal carriage was not ornamented, his mats were not hemmed, his pottage was not seasoned, and his grain was not polished. Going on his royal progress and spreading his guidance, he labored assiduously in the empire and traveled to each of the five sacred peaks. Surely it was not that the lifestyle of the emperor would be anything but enjoyable but that he took the whole empire for the sake of the empire and not because he derived any personal benefit from it. When he became old and weary and abdicated in favor of Shun,[147] it was just like stepping back and kicking off his sandals.

11a

When the age is in decline, however, it is a different matter. The ruler, having once gained the wealth of possessing the empire[148] and having occupied the purchase attendant upon his position, will then exhaust the energies of the common people in catering to his own desires. His mind is wholly preoccupied with buildings, pavilions, ponds, gardens, ferocious animals, precious stones, and exotic objects. Consequently, the poor people do not even have husks and chaff to eat and yet the tigers, wolves, and bear fill themselves on fine meats; the common people are sparsely clothed in coarse rags and yet palaces and halls are draped with silk and embroidery. The ruler gives priority to those undertakings which serve no useful purpose, and the people of the empire become haggard and gaunt. Thus it is that he causes the people of the empire to become discontented with their lot in life.

SECTION 10[149]

The ruler, occupying the position he does, is brilliant like the sun and moon *(ming)*.
He is that which all in the world strain their eyes to see, prick up their ears to hear,[150]
and crane their necks and stand on tiptoe to gaze upon *(wang)*.

11b

Unless he is calm and tranquil, he will have no way of manifesting his virtue. Unless he is peaceful and still, he will have no way of extending his influence a long way. Unless he is liberal and expansive, he will have no way of providing shelter for all things. Unless he is compassionate and generous, he will have no way of winning over the people. And unless he is just and impartial, he will have no way of making judgments.

The superior ruler in his use of men is like the skilled workman in the disposing of his wood. Large pieces are used for boats and beams; small pieces are used for oars and joists; long pieces are used for eaves and rafters; short pieces are used for gargoyles and decorative designs. All of these pieces irrespective of their size find their niche, and all of the carpenter's instruments and templates have their application.[151]

Of all things in the world, nothing is as deadly as the herb aconitum.[152] And yet a good doctor will put it in a pouch and keep it on hand because he has a use for it. Even among the resources of nature's thriving forests there is nothing which can be discarded—how much less so in the sphere of man![153]

That the court does not promote some person and the local people do not praise him is not because he is unworthy, but rather because the job they have put him into is not in keeping with his true vocation.

When a deer is climbing on a mountain, even a roe deer is not able to follow it, but once having come down from the mountain, even a shepherd boy can give it chase. This is because individual abilities have their strengths and weaknesses. You cannot expect a person of broad abilities to have quickness and skill, therefore, and you cannot entrust a person of limited intelligence with great enterprises.

Each person has his talents and each thing has its disposition *(hsing)*.
Some people are overburdened when entrusted with one responsibility; others are at ease handling a hundred times as much *(ch'ing)*.[154]
For this reason, a person proficient in making minute calculations will certainly be lost on the great computations of the world *(shu)*;
a person who does not make a mistake in the calculation of small things will be perplexed in the accomplishment of large matters *(chü)*.

Analogously a badger cannot be made to pounce on an ox, and a tiger cannot be made to catch mice.

Now, with people, some have talents which make them want to establish peace in the world, bring together the territories beyond the frontier *(wai)*,
preserve an imperiled state, and revive a defunct line *(shih)*.
They set their minds on righting the administration, correcting what has gone awry *(hsieh)*,
settling problems and straightening out difficulties *(na)*,
yet all you do is demand of them details of court ceremony and other such trifling and innocuous duties. Some have talents which only enable them to be glib of tongue, to lead people astray, to flatter and fawn, and to find great pleasure in rhetoric. They follow vulgar customs and debase themselves to please the eyes and ears of the common herd,[155] and yet you entrust them with the pivot on which the order and disorder of empire depend. This is like splitting a hair with an axe or using a knife to fell[156] a tree—in both cases it is using the instrument for the wrong purpose.

SECTION 11[157]

The ruler sees with the eyes of the empire,
hears with the ears of the empire *(t'ing)*,
deliberates with the intelligence of the empire,
and contends with the strength of the empire behind him *(cheng)*.
His edicts and commands are able to penetrate to the lowest level and the real condition of his subjects can be known by him above. His bureaucracy has open access to the throne, and his various ministers are like spokes converging at the hub.[158] He does not reward on account of pleasure or punish on account of anger.

His awesomeness being established will not be put aside *(fei)*,
his intelligence shining forth[159] will not be obscured *(pi)*,
his laws and edicts being circumspect will not be unduly harsh, his sight and hearing being penetrating will not be beclouded, and what is actually good and bad being set out before him daily, he will not indulge in conjecture.[160]

In his service the better people use their intelligence to the utmost and the others contribute their full strength. The ruler's favor and bounty sheltering the length and breadth of the land are impartial, and the various ministers laboring assiduously are not remiss in their duties. Those within the realm are content to follow their livelihood; those in distant quarters are won over by his beneficence. This is so because the ruler, understanding the Way of using people, does not rely on his own abilities.

> One who makes use of a carriage and horse can travel several
> hundred miles without tiring his feet *(li);*
> one who avails himself of a boat and oars can cross rivers and
> seas without even knowing how to swim *(hai).*[161]

Now, no ruler really desires other than to gather in the collective intelligence of the world and make use of every ounce of the people's strength. Nevertheless, few of the various ministers who make their purposes known and offer their utmost in service avoid placing themselves in grave peril. Even when counsel comes from a rudely clad bumpkin or woodcutter, if it is sound it should not be disregarded. Even when it comes from the prime minister or the ruler of a state issuing policy from the ancestral temple, if the counsel is unsound it should not necessarily be followed. In the discovery of where the truth lies, honor and status are simply irrelevant. Thus when a perspicacious ruler listens to his ministers, if someone's counsel can be used he is not ashamed of his lowly position. As long as his counsel can be implemented,[162] he does not demand eloquence of him.[163]

For the obtuse ruler, it is a different matter. Even when his favorites and intimates are depraved and without integrity, he is unable to see it. Even when[164] the lowly and those distant from him[165] exhaust their energies and do their utmost in his service, he is unable to appreciate it. He drives those who come with counsel into a corner with his own eloquence and metes out punishment to those who come with admonition. A ruler who is like this and yet who wants to light up the world and see everything around him is no different from a person who stuffing up his ears still hopes to distinguish the sharp from the flat, or a person who covering his eyes still hopes to distinguish blue from yellow. He is certainly a long way from being sharp of hearing and keen of sight!

SECTION 12[166]

Law is the rod and measure of the empire and the level and marking line of the ruler. The laws are published with an eye to punishing those who violate them; rewards are set up with an eye to rewarding those who deserve them.[167] Once the laws have been fixed, those who live up to the demands of the law are rewarded while those who are shown to be wanting by the marking line are punished.[168] For the exalted and noble, punishments are not lightened; for the lowly and base, punishments are not made more severe. Where one violates the law, even if he be a man of superior character, he must be punished. Where one lives up to the standards set, even if he be a man of little worth, he must be deemed to have committed no offense. Thus the path of impartiality will be open while that of special interests will be blocked off.[169]

The purpose of setting up a bureaucracy in antiquity was to prevent the people from doing just as they pleased. That they set up a ruler was to check the bureaucracy and prevent it from being dictatorial. Law, records, social norms, and a code of moral conduct are to prevent the ruler from making decisions based on his own whims. Where the people are not allowed to do just as they please, the Way will be relied upon exclusively, and the Way being relied upon exclusively, principles are followed through. Thus they return to a state of nonaction. Nonaction does not mean being completely inert, but rather that nothing is initiated from the ego-self.

The centimeter comes from the millimeter, the millimeter from the shape, the shape from the shadow of the gnomon, and the shadow from the sun.[170] This is the root of measurement. Music comes from the notes, notes from the pitchpipes, and the pitchpipes from the wind. This is the source of sound. Law comes from rightness, rightness from the various kinds of right measure, and right measure is consistent with the human heart and mind.[171] This is the crucial factor in proper order. Thus one who penetrates to the root will not be mislead at the periphery; one who sees the crucial factor will not be confused by details.   13b

Laws do not drop from the heavens nor spring forth from the
earth *(sheng)*.
Arising out of human society,
they are reflexive in regulating the society itself *(cheng)*.[172]

What one has in oneself he does not condemn in others *(jen)*;
what one lacks in oneself he does not demand in others *(jen)*.[173]
That which is established below is not abandoned above;
that which is prohibited for the people *(min)*
is not practiced by oneself *(shen)*.[174]

It is not the case that what is called a "doomed state" has no ruler but that it has no laws. It is not the case that to act at variance with the laws is quite the same thing as being without them, but to have laws and not use them is tantamount to not having any laws at all.[175] The ruler in establishing laws first makes himself a model and example, and thus his commands are carried out in the world. Confucius said, "Where the ruler himself is upright, without even articulating his commands they will be carried out; where he is not upright, even issuing commands they will not be followed."[176] Thus if prohibitions are observed by the ruler himself, his commands will prevail among the people.

SECTION 13[177]

The government of a sagacious ruler is like the charioting of Tsao Fu.[178] He controls the carriage from the reins and the bit, and he regulates the tightness of his grip on the reins from his sensitivity to the response of the horses' lips. He sets the correct measure in his own breast and holds the regulating whip in the palms of his own hands.[179] What he has secured within his own mind is externally in accord with the inclinations of his horses. He is able to move forward and withdraw as straight as a plumb line, turn a corner as roundly as a compass, and even after covering a great distance, he still has strength to spare because he truly understands the art.[180]

Now, political authority and purchase are the carriage of the ruler and the great ministers are his team of horses. There has never been a case past or present of a driver escaping danger who leaves the safety of his carriage and loses the responsiveness of his horses to his hands. Therefore, if the carriage and the horses are not in accord, even a Wang Liang would be unable to take to the road.[181] If the ruler and his ministers are not in harmony, even a Yao or Shun would be unable to govern properly.[182] If with a firm grasp of the art he drives the chariot of state, then a Kuan Chung or a Yen Tzu would serve him to the full extent of his intelligence;[183] if he clarifies the distinction between people of different status, then the wickedness of a Robber Chih or a Chuang Ch'iao[184] can be averted.[185]

If leaning over the edge one peers down to the bottom of the well, even a person of exceptional sight can not see the reflection of his pupils. If, however, he makes use of a bronze mirror to reflect himself, he can examine the smallest detail.

The eyes and ears of the perspicacious ruler are not fatigued nor is his spirit spent. He observes the form of things as they present themselves; he responds to new situations as they occur. So long as that near at hand, namely himself, is not in disorder, then that far away, namely things and events, will be properly ordered. Thus, because he does not resort to what is contingently so but rather uses what is necessarily so, in his innumerable undertakings he is wholly free from oversight.[186]

Now, in charioteering, when the bodies of the horses are attuned to the carriage and the heart of the driver is in harmony with his team, in driving them through rough terrain and to distant quarters, and in maneuvering them about,[187] they will follow his every whim. But even where one has horses as fine as Ch'i Chi and Lü Erh,[188] if it is given to servants and slaves to drive them,[189] the horses on the contrary will do as they please and the drivers will not be able to control them.

14b

In government, it is better to make it so that one's subjects have no chance to do wrong than to rely upon their putting themselves right. Therefore it is said: "Rather than relying on people not to seek after something, do not make the thing covetable; rather than relying on them not to contend over something, make the ownership of the thing indisputable." If this is done, then with individual human ability being put to one side, the way of impartiality will prevail. Those who have more than enough will not[190] go beyond the proper measure and those who do not have enough will manage to be useful. Thus the whole world can be equally put to good use.[191]

If the ruler ignores actual achievements and pays attention to reputation, and if he ignores the public good which has been done and pays attention to cliques and factions, then those of unusual talents and a good appearance will be promoted out of turn[192] while those who carry out their duties faithfully will be blocked and not receive advancement. Under such conditions, popular customs will be in chaos in the society at large and ministers with meritorious service will have to contend for recognition in the court.

Since laws and measurements are the ruler's means of controlling his subordinates, to discard them is like trying to gallop without a harness and bit and will ultimately reverse the situation and enable the various ministers and common people to manipulate the ruler. For this reason, those who have mastered the art of statecraft control others whereas those who have not are controlled by others.[193]

SECTION 14[194]

If a fish large enough to swallow a ship swims off course and goes aground, it will be at the mercy of the insects.[195] This is because it has left its habitat. If a monkey leaves the trees, he will be seized upon by foxes and badgers. This is because he is in an environment not his own.

If the ruler abandons what is proper to him and attempts to vie with his ministers,[196] the officials will seek to hold onto their positions through inactivity and those in office will seek to avoid being discharged by toadying to the ruler.[197] As a result, the ministers will hide their intelligence and not put it to use, passing the burden onto the ruler instead.

Now, the reason why the noble and wealthy are willing to work hard, the astute are willing to look into matters, and the proud and arrogant are willing to show respect is because their political purchase is not equal to that of the ruler.

If a ruler does not entrust things to the able but is instead given to doing things personally, his intelligence will become increasingly taxed and he will take upon himself the burden of responsibility. If he is hard put to cope with his subordinates, he will not be able to facilitate what is right. If his conduct is found wanting by the country, he will no longer be able to exercise exclusive control.[198] Since his intelligence is not sufficient to effect proper government and his awesomeness is not sufficient to enforce punishments, the ruler will not have the means to deal with his subjects.[199]

Where pleasure and anger form in the ruler's heart and desires are manifest in his countenance,[200] then officials charged with specific duties abandon what is proper and pander to the desires of the ruler, and those in authority bend the laws and follow the inclinations of the ruler. Rewards do not tally with accomplishments; punishments do not correspond to the crime. Superior and subordinate become estranged and acrimony grows between ruler and minister.

When those in charge of government commit errors through pandering to the ruler, there will be no way of taking them to task. If the guilty are not punished, the bureaucracy will seethe in turmoil that even intelligence cannot settle,[201] and praise and blame will sprout forth that even perspicacity cannot illumine.[202]

Failure to set what is fundamental right and return to spontaneous government[203] will make the ruler more and more burdened with hard work and give the ministers an increasingly easy time of it. It is like skinning an animal for the chief cook[204] or cutting wood in place of a master carpenter.[205] If one attempts to race with a horse, he can tear his tendons and still not keep up with it, but if he mounts a chariot and takes up the reins, the horse will submit[206] to his harness.

Now, if with Po Lo[207] choosing the horses and Wang Liang[208] at the reins, the perspicacious ruler mounts the carriage, the fact that he can travel several hundred miles without the effort of driving or choosing the horses is because availing himself of the abilities of others he uses them as his aides.[209]

15b

> The ruler is nonactive in carrying out the concerns of his office *(shou)*
> and when he does take action he does it free of likes and dislikes *(hao)*.

Were he to show dislike, he would provoke slander; were he to demonstrate partiality, he would invite flattery.[210]

The old Duke Huan of Ch'i was fond of exotic tastes, so Yi Ya boiled his firstborn son to gain his confidence. The ruler of Yü was fond of precious things, so Duke Hsien of Chin baited him with jade and horses. The King of the Hu was fond of music, so Duke Mu of Ch'in seduced him with female musicians.[211] These men all fell under the control of others because of greed. Thus this passage: What is firmly planted cannot be uprooted.[212]

Now, though fire is hot, water extinguishes it; though metal is hard, fire melts it; though wood is stiff, axes cut it down; though water flows, earth dams it up. The creator and transformer alone is what nothing can overcome.

> To keep desires inside and not let them come out is called being sealed up *(chiung)*;
> to keep evils outside and not let them enter is called being closed off.
> Where the internal is sealed up and the external is closed off *(pi)*,
> what could there be that is not of proper measure *(chieh)*?
> Where the external is closed off and the internal is sealed up *(chiung)*,
> what could there be that will not be accomplished *(ch'eng)*?[213]
> Only by not utilizing a thing is one able to use it *(chih)*;
> only by not doing something is one able to do it *(chih)*.
> Where the spirit is fatigued, it dissipates *(yüeh)*;
> where the senses are excessively indulged, they get spent *(chieh)*.

The ruler in possession of the Way extinguishes thought and
dispenses with intentionality *(yi)*.
Waiting in limpidity and vacuity *(tai)*,
he uses words that do not boast and takes action that does not
rob subordinates of responsibility *(shih)*.[214]
He makes demands of fulfillment according to claims made.
He lets them get on with their duties *(szu)*
without telling them how *(chao)*;
he expects them to fulfill their duties without instructing them
(chiao).
He takes "not knowing" as his Way *(tao)*
and the question "what am I to do?" as his treasure *(pao)*.
Acting in this way, each of the various officials will then have his
appointed tasks *(shou)*.[215]

SECTION 15[216]

If one holds firmly to the control handles of authority and purchase, it
will be easy for him to transform the people. That Tzu Lu served the
ruler of Wei was because the ruler's authority was great;[217] that Kuan
Chung and Yen Tzu served the Dukes Huan and Ching of Ch'i as ministers was because the ruler's position was exalted.[218] That the timid can
subjugate the brave and the ignorant can control the intelligent is because
the purchase in which they lodge themselves is superior.

It is said:
   The branch must not be bigger than the trunk and the tip must
   not be stronger than the root. Why?[219] Because the important and
   the large should have the means to control the unimportant and
   the small. This can be likened to the five fingers which being
   joined to the arm enable one to strike, pull, clutch, and pinch as
   he so desires.
In other words, the small is adjunct to the large.[220]

Holding the advantage in purchase means that although what is held is
extremely small, what is dependent upon it[221] is large indeed; although
what one keeps to is compact, what is under its control is extensive
indeed.

   That a pillar of ten girths *(mu)*
   is able to support a twenty-ton roof *(wu)*
or that a five-inch bolt can control the opening and closing of a gate—

surely it has nothing to do with their size! It is because the position they occupy is pivotal.[222]

Even though Confucius and Mo Ti cultivated the political art of the former sages, were wellversed in the theories of the six arts,[223] and what they expressed orally they embodied in their conduct, even then, those who cherished and followed their teachings and became their disciples were no more than a few dozen.[224] If, however, they had occupied the throne of the emperor, the whole empire would have become their followers.

King Chuang of Ch'u, afflicted by the death of his minister, Wen Wu-wei, at the hands of Sung, rose[225] to his feet and threw down part of his sleeve.[226] With a continuous procession of officials taking to the road, they formed an army beneath the walls of Sung.[227] This was because he had a handle on important authority. King Wen of Ch'u being fond of wearing a *hsieh chih* ceremonial cap, the whole state of Ch'u followed the fashion. King Wu-ling of Chao attending court with a belt of shells and bird plumage, the whole of the state of Chao was transformed by him.[228] If, however, a commoner or peasant were to attend court wearing this ceremonial cap or belt of shells and bird plumage, he would not escape ridicule.

16b

There is not one man in ten thousand who is devoted to goodness and takes joy in proper conduct such that he will voluntarily abide by laws and regulations without being pressed by prohibitions and punishments. But if the ruler issues commands which brook no disobedience so that those who accord with them will benefit while those who deny them will bring grief on themselves, before there is time for a shadow to move, everyone will be in line with the rule of law.

If a person were to take a stance grasping the blade of his sword,[229] even a Pei-kung Tzu or Ssu-ma K'uai K'uei[230] cannot be made to meet the challenge of the enemy, but if he were to grasp the hilt and raise the tip, even a person of average skill would be able to take the victory.

Now, even if Wu Huo or Chieh Fan were to attempt to lead an ox by the tail from behind, they would pull the tail off without budging the ox because they are acting contrary to the way of things. But if one were to pierce the ox's nose with a sprig of mulberry, even a half-grown boy could lead it around the country because he is following the way of things.[231]

Because we harness the water for our use, with a seven-foot oar we can maneuver a boat. Because he takes the people as his purchase, the emperor has only to issue commands to have them implemented and observed.

If the ruler prevents that which the people consider injurious while encouraging that which they consider beneficial, his authority will prevail like the opening of a dike or the breaking of a dam. Hence if one goes downstream with the current, he will easily get to his destination; if one gallops along with the wind at his back, he will easily cover a great distance.[232]

When Duke Huan of Ch'i presided over the government, he got rid of meat-eating animals, grain-fed birds, and snaring nets. With three deeds he pleased the people.[233] Chou of Yin killed Prince Pi Kan and incurred the resentment of his relations; he broke open the legs of men wading through the morning stream and provoked a revolt by the common people.[234] With two deeds he lost the empire. Thus it is not that rightness is able to benefit all the people in the world, but that in benefiting one it wins over the whole world. It is not that tyranny inflicts injury on all the empire's people, but that in injuring one it stirs the whole world to revolt. Duke Huan with his three deeds united the various nobles, whereas Chou of Yin with his two deeds forfeited even the right to live as a commoner. Thus it is that one's actions are something he must be exceedingly careful about.

SECTION 16[235]

The ruler in levying his taxes on the people
    must first calculate the year's yield,
    assess the accumulated stores of the people *(chü),*
    and know the extent of surplus or shortage in the yearly
    harvest *(shu)*
    before exacting enough to cover his carriages, clothing, and food
    (shih)
    and to satisfy his wants *(yü).*
It is not that high pavilions and storied buildings, connecting halls and towers, are not magnificent. But where his people do not even have caves or thatched huts in which to find shelter, a perspicacious ruler does not enjoy them. It is not that fat meats, rich wines, sweetmeats, and delicacies are not delicious. But where his people do not even have husks and chaff or bare staples to put into their mouths, the perspicacious ruler

finds no relish in them. It is not that a peaceful bed and soft matting are not agreeable. But where his people dwell in remote frontier settlements, brave every kind of peril, and finally perish in the marshes with their bones bleaching in the sun, the perspicacious ruler finds no comfort in them.

The ruler of antiquity was concerned about the hardships of his subjects to the extent that if there were people starving in his state, at each meal he would have only one single dish, and if there were people freezing in winter he would not attire himself in fur garments.[236] Only when the harvest was good and the people had plenty would he then set up the bells and drums and display the shields and axes.[237] And with ruler and subject, superior and subordinate, all enjoying these together, there was no sorrowful person left in the whole state.

The use of metal, stone, pipes, and strings by the ancients was to express their joy. Weapons, armor, battleaxes, and broadaxes were to give a more polished expression to their anger. The ceremonies of libations and offerings were to represent their gladness.[238] Funeral garments and sedge footwear, beating of the breast, and weeping were to demonstrate their grief. These are all instances of the general truth that what fills one inside will be given formal expression outside.

Under the reign of a misguided ruler, in taxing the people
   he does not take into account what they can support *(li)*,
   and in making demands on those below he does not assess their
   accumulated stores *(chi)*.
The men and women are prevented from following their
   occupations of farming and weaving *(chih)*
   in order to meet the ruler's demands.
The people exhaust their strength and their wealth, and minister and ruler hate each other. When circumstances reach the point where the people in the face of great hardships do not know where their next meal is coming from,[239] he nevertheless orders the striking of the great bell and the beating of the drums, the sounding of the reeds and flutes, and the strumming of the lutes and zithers. As incongruous as suiting up in armor to enter the ancestral temple or attiring oneself in rich brocade to march off to war, he has completely lost sight of the reason for music.[240]

For the people in eking out their livelihood, one man tilling the soil can cultivate no more than one and a half acres of land, and the annual yield from average land does not exceed four piculs. Women and children, the old and the infirm, will have to be fed from this. From time to time there are the misfortunes of flood, drought, and natural calamity. And in addition, out of this income must be paid the various taxes and war surcharges of the ruler. Looking at it from this perspective, a human life is wretched indeed!

In reckoning for the whole empire, from three years of cultivating there is one year's surplus. In proportion, from nine years there should be three years' stores set by; from eighteen years there should be six and from twenty-seven there should be nine.
> Even in the face of the calamities of flood, drought, and natural disaster *(yang)*,
> none of the people will be destitute or drift away from their homes *(wang)*.[241]
> Therefore the condition of a state without nine years' stores laid by can be described as short,
> without six years' reserves as critical *(chi)*,
> and without three years' stores as desperate *(fa)*.[242]
Thus when a benevolent and perspicacious ruler is moderate in his taxes and his own expenditures,[243] his people will enjoy the bounty of heaven and earth and not suffer the miseries of hunger and cold.
> But if an avaricious and tyrannical ruler causing grief for those under him poaches on the preserves of his people to gratify insatiable desires *(yü)*,
> the common people will be unable to wear the harmonious vapors of the heavens and tread among the bounties of the earth *(te)*.

Food is the foundation of the people, people are the foundation of the state, and the state is the foundation of the ruler.[244]

> The ruler of men should take advantage of the seasons of heaven above *(shih)*,
> make full use of the earth's plenty below *(ts'ai)*,
> and deploy the energies of the people wisely in between *(li)*.
> As a result, all living things will reach maturity and the five grains will thrive *(chih)*.
> He should teach the people to raise the six domestic animals *(ch'u)*,
> to plant trees at the proper times *(shu)*,
> to labor diligently in the cultivation of the fields and to plant mulberry bushes and hemp widely *(ma)*,
> to use each kind of terrain and soil to its best advantage *(yi)*

so that on hills and slopes which will not produce the five
grains *(ku)*
they grow bamboo and wood *(mu)*.
In the spring he should teach them to prune out what is rotten and dry, in
summer to gather the fruit and berries, in autumn to lay in the vegetables
and grains, and in winter to cut and gather firewood.

This then becomes the basis of the people's livelihood *(tzu)*.

In life there is no shortage of necessities and in death there are no
abandoned corpses *(shih)*.[245]

In hunting, the laws of the former kings did not permit the extermination
of the whole herd or flock or the trapping of the young. They did not
allow the draining of ponds to fish, the burning of woods to hunt, the
spreading of nets in the wild prior to the autumn's wild dog sacrifice, the
setting of nets in the water prior to the spring's otter sacrifice, the
stretching of bird nets in valleys and river gorges before the autumn
falconry, the logging of hill forests before the autumn shedding of
leaves, the burning off of fields before the hibernating of the insects.
They did not allow the killing of pregnant animals, the collecting of fled-
glings and bird eggs, the taking of fish less than a foot in length, or the
consumption of piglets less than a year old.[246] Thus grasses and trees bil-
lowed forth like rising steam, birds and animals rushed to their domains
like a flowing spring, and birds of the air swarmed to them like clouds of
smoke because they had that which brought all this about.   19a

In the political administration of the former kings,
   when the clouds gather from the four seas [in spring], they would
   repair the boundary demarcations *(ch'iang)*.
   When the toads croak and the swallows alight [in the third
   month], they would open up the roads.
   When the *yin* vapors fall on the various streams [in the tenth
   month],[247]
   they would repair the bridges *(liang)*.
   When the *chang* star culminates at dusk [in the third month],
   they would devote themselves to the planting of rice *(ku)*.
   When the *ta huo* star culminates at dusk [in the fourth month],
   they would plant millet and beans *(shu)*.
   When the *hsü* star culminates at dusk [in the eighth month],
   they would plant wheat *(mai)*.
   When the *mao* star culminates at dusk [in autumn],
   they would harvest[248] and lay in their crops *(hsü)*
   and cut firewood *(mu)*.[249]

Above they would report to heaven *(t'ien)*
and below they would announce it to the people *(min)*.

The former kings in making things whole in accordance with the proper
time, in enriching the country and benefiting the people, in settling unpopulated areas and attracting those from distant reaches, showed that
in their Way nothing was overlooked. It is not that they, the heart, could
be the eyes and feet in seeing and carrying things out. But so long as the
heart never loses sight of wanting to benefit the other organs, those
organs will fulfill their functions of their own accord.[250] The heart in its
relationship to the nine orifices and the four appendages is not able to do
the job of any one of them, and yet in moving, listening, and looking all
of them depend on it for direction. This is because it never loses sight of
wanting to benefit them.

When Yao did good deeds, this attracted other good deeds; and when
Chieh did evil deeds, this attracted other evil deeds. Where good accumulates there is success, but where evil accumulates, disaster knows no
bounds.[251]

SECTION 17[252]

Speaking of man generally, while in his mind he wants to be circumspect,
yet in his purposes he wants to be great; while in his intelligence he wants
to be round, yet in his conduct he wants to be square; while in his abilities
he wants to have many, yet in his affairs he wants to have few.

What is meant by "in his mind he wants to be circumspect" is that he
considers a situation and prepares for it before disaster strikes, he guards
against error, is vigilant in dealing with matters in their embryonic
stages, and does not give rein to his desires.

"In his purposes he wants to be great" means that he takes the ten thousand states under his aegis,
    unifies all the different customs *(su)*
    and broods over all the people as though they belong to one
    family *(tsu)*.
    With right and wrong converging as spokes he acts as the
    hub *(ku)*.

"In his intelligence he wants to be round" means
    he is free turning like a ring *(yün)*

without a starting point and without an end *(tuan)*,
he flows outward to the four quarters *(ta)*,
and is as inexhaustible as a deep spring *(chieh)*.
The myriad things arise side by side *(ying)*
and he fails to respond to none of them *(hsing)*.

"In his conduct he wants to be square" means
he is upright and unbending *(nao)*,
pure white and unsullied.
He does not compromise his integrity even in adversity *(ts'ao)*
and does not assert himself at the expense of others.

"In his abilities he wants to have many" means he is competent in both
civil and military affairs
and is consistent with proper deportment in his every
movement *(yi)*.
In his policies and in his promotions and dismissals he is just
right *(yi)*,
and being free of any opposition,
he achieves happy results in all his undertakings *(yi)*.

"In his affairs he wants to have few" means he has a firm grasp on the
handles and the art of political control.
Securing the crucial he responds to the many *(chung)*,
and grasping the essential he administers to the broad and
far-reaching.
He dwells in tranquillity and holds onto the center *(chung)*,
and turning around at the pivot *(shu)*
as if matching tally sticks *(fu)*,
he responds fittingly to the myriad with the one.

Therefore one whose mind is circumspect takes precautions over
matters when they are still in their embryonic stages *(wei)*;
one whose purposes are great is all-encompassing *(huai)*;
one whose intelligence is round is all-knowing *(chih)*;
20a
one whose conduct is square has that which he will not do *(wei)*;
one whose abilities are many can do everything *(chih)*;
one whose affairs are few makes sure that what he holds onto is
the essential *(ch'ih)*.

Of old, when the emperor would hold court, the high ministers would
proffer honest admonition, the learned scholars would chant the odes,

the music masters would sing their criticisms, the common people would communicate their opinions, the court historians would chronicle errors in judgment, and the court chefs would reduce the number of dishes at meals, but still this was not considered enough.[253] Thus Yao set up a drum for those offering bold admonition, Shun established a notice board for criticisms, T'ang instituted an independent judicial authority, and King Wu provided a small drum to forewarn him against rashness.[254] Before an error could show itself there was already a safeguard against it.[255] The sage's attitude toward goodness is that there is nothing so small that he will not promote it; his attitude toward mistakes is that there is nothing so trivial that he will not correct it.

Yao, Shun, T'ang, and Wu all faced south with an easy mind and ruled.[256] At this time, at the sound of the gong they would begin eating, at the sound of the *yung* music they would clear the food from the table, and after eating the rice they would sacrifice to the kitchen range.[257] Before traveling, they had no recourse to shamans and prayer masters. Ghosts and spirits would not dare call down evil upon them and mountains and streams would not dare to inflict calamity on them. Thus they can be said to have been the most exalted of men.

Nevertheless in fear and trembling *(li)*
they became more cautious with the day *(rih)*.
Viewing it from this perspective, the mind of the sage is circumspect. This is what the *Shih-ching (Book of Odes)* means in saying, "Oh, this King Wen, so careful and scrupulous he offered illustrious service to Shang Ti and therein embraced good fortune."[258]

When King Wu conquered Yin,[259] he distributed the grain stores of Chü-ch'iao granary and the monies of the Lu-t'ai coffers, set up a memorial tomb for Pi Kan, honored Shang Jung's village, worshiped at the ancestral shrine of Ch'eng T'ang, and liberated Chi Tzu from his incarceration.[260]

Leaving the people to dwell in their own homes and till their own fields *(t'ien)*,
he did not ask whether a person is known to him or not *(shin)*,
allowing himself to be attracted only to those of superior character *(ch'in)*.
He made use of people and things which had not previously been his *(jen)*
with no misgivings as though they had been his all along.[261]
Viewing it from this perspective, the purposes of the sage are great.

Comprehensively King Wen reviewed successes and failures,
what was morally right and morally wrong in history,
the reasons why Yao and Shun prospered *(ch'ang)*
and the reasons why Chieh and Chou perished *(wang)*,[262]
and recorded all of this in the Ming T'ang *(t'ang)*.[263]
On the basis of this, extending his sphere of knowledge and
erudition,
the sage is able to respond to things without any fixed formula
(fang).[264]
Viewing it from this perspective, the intelligence of the sage is round.

Emperors Ch'eng and K'ang,[265] carrying on the work of Wen and Wu
and the observation of the Ming T'ang institution, examined the historical traces of preservation and destruction and the way that success and
failure change one into the other. They would not speak unless in keeping with the Way and would not act unless in keeping with rightness.
They did not speak lightly, nor did they act lightly. They would act only
after having chosen the course of conduct they considered good. Viewing
it from this perspective, the conduct of the sage is square.

The capacity of Confucius[266] was such that his intelligence surpassed that
of Ch'ang Hung,[267] his courage exceeded that of Meng Pen,[268] his feet
were faster than a nimble rabbit, his strength was such that he could hold
up a portcullis.[269] His talents were indeed numerous.[270] But he is not
known to the world for his courage or his skills. Solely through practicing the Way of filial piety he became the uncrowned king.[271] This would
indicate that his affairs were indeed few. With respect to the 242 years of
the Ch'un-ch'iu period which had seen fifty-two states destroyed and
thirty-six cases of regicide, by singling out the good and condemning the
unseemly he established the Way of the True King. This would indicate
that his discussion was indeed broad. Even so, when he was surrounded
in K'uang,[272] his countenance did not change and he did not stop his
strumming and singing. Even when in a death trap[273] in peril of his life,
still upholding his principles of rightness, he was not overcome by fear.
This would indicate that he was clear about his lot. As commissioner of
police in Lu, when hearing cases he always came to a judgment, and in
compiling the *Ch'un-ch'iu [Spring and Autumn Annals]* he did not speak
of ghosts and spirits or presume to offer arbitrary judgments based on
personal inclinations.

21a

To begin with, the intelligence of the sage is considerable. Because in his
sphere of activities he holds onto the essential, when he acts he is certain

of success. The moron is limited in intelligence from the start. Because he takes on too many things, when he acts he is certain to fail.[274]

Wu Ch'i and Chang Yi not having the intelligence of a Confucius or Mo Tzu still contended with rulers of large states. This is the reason why they were drawn and quartered.[275]

One who instructs and transforms with what is proper will not only find the going easy, but will certainly succeed. One who attempts to beguile society with trickery will not only encounter difficulty, but will certainly fail. Now if one is going to establish a model of conduct and set up some preferences in this world, to reject a method which is both easy and certain of success[276] in favor of one which is both difficult and certain of failure is something only the foolish and confused would do. These six opposites [circumspect = small, great = large, round, square, many, and few],[277] then, must be carefully examined.

SECTION 18

To know everything there is to know about the myriad things and yet not know the Way of man cannot be called intelligence; to love all the various living things and yet not love mankind cannot be called benevolence. Benevolence means loving one's own species; intelligence means being beyond perplexity. The compassion of a benevolent ruler is manifest even at the moment he orders a mutilation punishment;[278] evidence of the discernment of an intelligent ruler is manifest even when encountering[279] the most baffling of affairs.

Putting oneself in the place of others and looking inward at one's nature, not imposing on others what one does not desire oneself,[280] understanding the remote from the near at hand, and understanding others from oneself—this is putting into effect what benevolence[281] and intelligence are in agreement upon. Correcting small matters and thereby preserving matters of import, punishing small offenses and thereby bringing about a great peace—this is the practice of extending the heart of compassion.[282] These are judgments that only the intelligent person can make. Thus benevolence and intelligence are sometimes in conflict and sometimes in agreement. Agreement is their normal condition; conflict is an anomaly. The significance in either case is the same.

Minor officials observe the law, but the superior man controls on the basis of what is right. Someone who knows only about law but not about rightness is no better than a minor official and is not equal to the task of governing.

Farming as an occupation is exhausting, and weaving is vexing. But where the people do not reject their occupations even though they are vexing and exhausting, it is because they know they will thereby earn their food and clothing.[283] The nature of man is such that he cannot do without food and clothing, and the production of food and clothing necessarily begins in farming and weaving. This is a truth seen by everybody.[284] Things generally are like farming and weaving in that they always begin with bitter toil but bring benefit in the end.

22a

Although things which can be prepared against are many, simple people perceive only a few; although those matters which can be weighed up are numerous, simple people weigh up only a few. This is the reason why the simple encounter many misfortunes.[285] The intelligent prepare for everything which can be prepared against and weigh up all affairs which can be weighed up. This is the reason why the intelligent encounter few misfortunes. Thus the intelligent person starts by doing something which appears wrongheaded but proves to be right in the end, whereas the simple person begins in joy but ends in grief. Having won honor today, that one should pursue rightness tomorrow is easy to understand. But having done rightness today that one will receive honor tomorrow is difficult to grasp.[286]

If you ask a blind man what "white" is like, he will reply that it is a light color. If you ask him what "black" is like, he will reply that it is a dark color. But if you take something white and something black and show them to him, he will make the wrong choice. It is with the eye that man sees black and white; it is with his mouth that he speaks of them. A blind man has the means for speaking of them, but he has no means for knowing them. Thus, in speaking of black and white, he is the same as others, but in distinguishing them he is different.[287] People irrespective of their intelligence and character know that being filial to one's parents and doing one's best for one's ruler is rightness, but those who can identify conscientious and filial conduct when examples are set out in front of them are rare indeed.

As a rule, any person will act in accordance with what he thinks is right. So it is in what a person considers to be right that distinguishes the simple from the intelligent.

Generally speaking, it is in his nature that man considers nothing as exalted as benevolence and nothing as urgent as intelligence. If a man has benevolence as his basic substance and implements it by means of intelligence,[288] and with these two as his foundation, he were to augment them with valor, eloquence, agility, diligence, keenness, insight, perspicacity, and judgment, all these things would then add something to the foundation. But since a morally uncultivated person carefully develops his skills while having no benevolence or intelligence to act as his mainstay, even if he augments these skills with many meritorious qualities he will only add to the detriment. For this reason, to be lacking in benevolence while being courageous and bold is a madman holding a sharp sword.[289] To be lacking in intelligence while being eloquent and glib is a fine horse in the hands of a man in two minds about which way to go.[290] Even if one has talent and ability, if it is used in the wrong places and for the wrong things it is only good for abetting deceit and camouflaging wrongdoings. For such a person it is better to have few skills than to have many.

> Those with ambitions above their stations cannot be given access
> to facilitating purchase *(shih);*
> those of inferior character cannot be given sharp weapons *(ch'i).*

A fish swimming about in the water is happy, but if the dam is broken and the water drains off, the fish becomes food for insects. If one conducts repairs on the dike and replaces the water which has leaked out, the fish will derive benefit from it.

There is that by which a state is preserved; there is that by which a man stays alive. That on the basis of which a state exists is benevolence and rightness; that on the basis of which man lives is doing good. If a state is without rightness, even though it is large it will certainly perish. If a man is without a resolve to do good, even though he is courageous he will certainly suffer injury.[291]

Unless commissioned by the ruler, one can play no part in the government of the state.
> But as for being filial to mother and father *(mu),*
> fraternal to brothers and sisters and winning the trust of
> friends *(yu),*
it is possible for a person to do these without any directives from above. It is perverse to demand of someone something over which he has no control instead of that which it is possible for him to do.

When a person living in obscurity wants to gain the ear of the ruler, he must first turn in upon himself. There is a way to gain the ear of the ruler. If one does not acquire name and reputation, he will not be heard by the ruler. There is a way to acquire reputation. If one does not win the trust of his friends, he will not acquire reputation. There is a way to gain the trust[292] of friends. If in serving his parents one fails to make them happy, he will not gain the trust of his friends. There is a way to make one's parents happy. If in cultivating his person a man is not sincere, he will not be able to serve his parents. There is a way for a man to be sincere in his person. If the mind is not of single resolve, he will not be able to achieve unwavering sincerity.[293]

When we seek the Way in the difficult when it lies in the easy and when we seek confirmation in the distant when it lies in the near-at-hand, we do not get what we are after.

Notes

INTRODUCTION

1. During the 1930s there was one pioneering assault on a portion of the text by Evan Morgan, but this attempt offers a rendering far removed from the original. Apart from Evan Morgan's *Tao, The Great Luminant,* there is only B. Wallacker's translation of one book: *The Huai-nan-tzu, Book Eleven: Behavior, Culture and the Cosmos.*

2. The theory that an early version of our modern *Huai Nan Tzu* was submitted to the Han court in 140 B.C. is based on the Hu Shih equation of the "Inner Documents" *(nei-shu)* mentioned in the *History of the Han (Han-shu)* biography of Liu An with the modern text. He bases this equation on a second reference to the text in the "Record of Literary Works" *(Yi-wen chih)* of the *History of the Han:* "The Inner Huai Nan in Twenty-one Books" *(Huai Nan nei erh-shih-yi p'ien).* Yen Shih-ku, an early T'ang commentator on the *History of the Han,* observes that the "inner chapters:" *(nei-p'ien)* discuss the *tao.* This remark is consistent with the opening book of the present text: *Book One: Tracing the Tao (Yüan-tao).*

Kanaya in *The World of Lao Tzu and Chuang Tzu,* pp. 94 ff., and the corresponding "History of the *Huai Nan Tzu*" *(Enanji no rekishi)* chapter of his *Researches into Ch'in and Han Thought,* and Kusuyama, pp. 33 ff. (also p. 24), reject this 140 B.C. date for the *Huai Nan Tzu.* They contend that the nature of the text is such that it was probably written one book at a time over many years until Liu An's suicide in 122 B.C. It was then edited into twenty books and the *Summary of the Essentials (Yao-lüeh)* postface was appended as a summary of this editing. The text first came to be called *Huai Nan Tzu* in the "Record of Classics and Documents" *(Ching-chi chih)* of the *History of the Sui (Sui-shu).*

There is another reason for questioning the 140 B.C. date. In the Kao Yu commentary to *Huai Nan Tzu* 6/9a—"At the present time the Son of Heaven is on the throne"—he glosses "the Son of Heaven" as "Emperor Wu of the Han" *(Wu Ti).* It therefore appears that Kao Yu, at least, thought this was written *during* the reign of Wu Ti. The year 140 B.C. was only Wu Ti's first year on the throne.

3. For a discussion of authorship, see Togawa et al., pp. 344–345, n. 47–48; Kanaya, *The World of Lao Tzu and Chuang Tzu,* pp. 41 ff.; and Kusuyama, pp. 26 ff.

4. See Chan, *Source Book,* p. 305. He suggests that "his originality is negligible." Watson, *Early Chinese Literature,* p. 190, says that "one of its few original contributions is a brief description of the creation of the universe." Hsiao Kungch'üan (Mote trans.), p. 582, having cited several passages from *The Art of Rulership* and the historical sources for these ideas, concludes: "None of these points contains the slightest modicum of newness, and they demand no further discussion." This appears to be a widely held opinion.

5. The *Summary of the Essentials (Yao-lüeh)* description of *The Art of Rulership* treatise in *Huai Nan Tzu* 21/3a is perhaps the earliest source of this association. The editor of the *Huai Nan Tzu* describes this treatise in purely Legalist terms. More recently, Kusuyama, pp. 43 and 124, and Kanaya, *The World of Lao Tzu and Chuang Tzu,* pp. 145–148, discuss it under a Legalist heading. While these two scholars do detect a Taoist influence in the treatise, they regard this influence as a more pronounced version of the Taoist element contained in *Han Fei Tzu.* Bodde and Morris, p. 15 n., state quite categorically that "the chapter here quoted [*The Art of Rulership*] represents the Legalist school."

CHAPTER 1

1. See *Analects* 32/15/39 and 36/17/2; cf. *Hsün Tzu* 8/3/36.
2. *Analects* 5/3/14, 15/8/18, 19, 20, and 22.
3. I use the word "culture" in its broadest sense to indicate the sum total of social institutions, customs, and values created by people to regulate and refine their relationships. It is their formal expression—in social manners, music, literature, art, and the like—of a system of values which distinguishes civilized man from his primitive antecedents.
4. See *Analects* 34/16/8.
5. Ibid. 5/3/24, 13/7/23, 16/9/9, and 29/14/35.
6. Ibid. 13/7/20.
7. Ibid. 11/7/1.
8. Ibid. 15/8/19, 35/17/5, and 41/20/1.
9. Ibid. 5/3/25, 12/7/14, and 31/15/11.
10. Ibid. 4/3/9.
11. See *Tso chuan* 346/Chao 2/1: "The social norms *(li)* of Chou have been fully retained in the state of Lu."
12. See *Analects* 12/7/5 and 35/17/4.
13. Although the calendars of Chou and Yin took the eleventh and twelfth months of the lunar calendar respectively as the first month of the year, only the Hsia was reputed to have a calendar which began the year with the first month of the lunar calendar.
14. The state carriage of Yin was made of wood and simple in design. This phrase implies that Confucius preferred the austere appearance of this vehicle to the ornate and perhaps extravagant coaches of the Chou period.
15. In the *Analects* one can detect a strong sense of mission associated with the preservation and transmission of the Chou culture. See 5/3/24, 13/7/23, 16/9/9, and 29/14/35.
16. See *Analects* 2/1/15 and 39/19/6.
17. My construction of Confucius' conception of history relies almost entirely on the *Analects*—the *Tso chuan* sheds little light on this aspect of his thought.

There is a rival characterization of his conception of history which, though ascribed to Confucius, has a strong Han flavor. In the "Evolution of the Rites" *(Li-yün)* chapter of the *Record of Rites (Li-chi)*, Confucius contrasts the utopian "Great Unity" *(ta-t'ung)* era of high antiquity with the less glorious but more recent "Lesser Prosperity" *(hsiao-k'ang)* era. The most striking points of this contrast can be itemized as follows:

Great Unity *(Ta-t'ung)*

1. Ruled by "the heroes of the three eras" (glossed as the "five emperors")
2. No "us/them" distinction—love and concern were not graduated but extended to all without distinction
3. Promotion to office on the basis of merit
4. Relationships governed by good faith and sincere affection—natural and spontaneous social bonds
5. Property shared by all
6. People labored for the common good
7. No thieves or rebels

Lesser Prosperity *(Hsiao-k'ang)*

1. Ruled by Yǔ, T'ang, Wen, Wu, Ch'eng, and the Duke of Chou
2. Love and and concern extended exclusively to members of one's own family
3. Hereditary offices and titles
4. Social norms *(li)* grounded in rightness *(yi)* as a whole system of social values devised to regulate human relationships—social institutions and formal organization
5. Private property
6. People labor for private gain
7. Thieves and rebels arise because of unnatural social values

While this portrayal of Confucius in the *Record of Rites* is not consistent with the *Analects* and cannot be accepted as representative of his conception of history, it is included here in some detail as a basis for comparison. The knitting together of the almost Taoist "Great Unity" utopia and the Confucian "Lesser Prosperity" society has an eclecticism which points to the Western Han.

18. The conception of history expounded in the *Hsün Tzu* shares much with that of Confucius. See *Hsün Tzu,* chap. 5, especially 13/5/28. In this discussion, Hsün Tzu makes two important points: (1) The essential principles around which good government is constructed are timeless and constant. (2) The proposition that the intrinsic value of a culture can be measured by its age is rejected. Rather, Hsün Tzu insists that since the early Chou period can be clearly understood, its customs and culture can be adapted for present-day application. It is the constant and essential principles rather than the cultural dressing which are of supreme importance.

19. By "*Lao Tzu* literature of the Taoist school" I am referring to three bodies of work. The first is the *Lao Tzu*. The second is those parts of the *Chuang Tzu* which Graham has identified as the "Primitivist documents"—chaps. 8, 9, 10, and 11/1–28. Graham, p. 477, dating this Primitivist school at about 205 B.C., sees a primitive utopia as one of their main themes: "The Primitivist looks back to a tribal Utopia in which men lived as spontaneously as the animals, there was no distinction of gentleman and knave, and leaders had names followed by *shih,* implying that their position was that of head of a clan or family. Ever since the Yellow Emperor the original spontaneous harmony has progressively deteriorated, hastened first by the invention of moral rules, later by disputation to settle

disagreements over moral rules." In answer to the tradition of *Chuang Tzu* being so composite and varied, Graham, pp. 480–481, poses a question: "Does the Primitivist belong to the tradition of Chuang-tzu, or rather to that of Lao-tzu?" He then responds: "The Primitivist is indeed one of the earliest datable witnesses (with Han Fei tzu) to the sudden and extraordinary impact of *Lao-tzu* when it began to circulate in the late third century B.C. In particular the picture of an idealized village life has an extended parallel with *Lao-tzu* 80 (chap. 10/31–32). Probably we should think of the Primitivist as an exponent of Lao-tzu's ideal government, only incidentally interested in Chuang-tzu."

Third is the chapters of the *Chuang Tzu* which Graham identifies as the "Individualist documents": chaps. 28, 29, and 31. Following Kuan Feng, Graham makes a distinction between "Individualist" and "Taoist." These chapters contain much "utopia" material which Graham, p. 482, again concludes has close ties with the Primitivist portion of the *Chuang Tzu* text: "Of especial interest are the striking resemblances to the Primitivist essays, which suggest that the two sets of documents must be very close in date. The Primitivist too uses Robber Chih as the exemplary criminal, but nowhere else in the *Chuang-tzu* is he mentioned. Themes which Robber Chih shares with the Primitivist are the tribal Utopia of long ago and the progressive degeneration under the sage Emperors."

20. It is true that the Confucian tradition depicts the territory of the legendary emperors as being small, but where their formal holdings were incidental, their magico-political influence gave them sway over both the Chinese states and the barbarian hinterland.

21. See *Lao Tzu* 49.

22. See the discussion of Creel's distinction between "purposive" and "contemplative" Taoism in note 23 to Chapter 2.

23. See *Lao Tzu* 10, 19, and 57.

24. Ibid. 15, 19, 28, and 57.

25. Ibid. 10, 20, 28, 49, and 55.

26. Ibid. 3, 20, and 65.

27. This is represented metaphysically in *Lao Tzu* 42 and elsewhere in the text.

28. See *Chuang Tzu* 23/10/4 and particularly 25/10/32.

29. This discussion is based on *The Book of Lord Shang* and the *Han Fei Tzu*, which contain a generally consistent conception of history. As is the case with most Legalist precepts, it is *Han Fei Tzu* which provides us with the most mature and well-rounded exposition. In particular, see the "Five Vermin" *(Wu-tu)*, "Facing South" *(Nan-mien)*, "Eminence in Learning" *(Hsien-hsüeh)*, and "The Mind of the People as a Standard" *(Hsin-tu)* chapters.

30. The fullest account of Shang Yang's career is to be found in the *Historical Records (Shih-chi)* 68. Compare *Policies of the Warring States (Chan-kuo ts'e)*, "Policies of Ch'in" *(Ch'in-ts'e)*.

31. See *Historical Records (Shih-chi)* 68, p. 2235.

32. Reading *hsiu* as *hsün*.

33. See Ching Chih-jen, pp. 35 ff., and Hsieh Yün-fei, pp. 72 ff.

34. See in particular his *Han Fei Tzu chiao-shih*, pp. 942 ff., where he discusses Han Fei's philosophy of history.

35. Because the *Han Fei Tzu* does on occasion depict high antiquity as primitive squalor, there is a tendency for scholars to infer that since humanity has progressed out of this condition, it has "evolved." This is to misinterpret the *Han Fei Tzu*'s conception of history. While the text describes the human condition as at

one stage having been primitive, it also says that at this time good food was abundant and grew wild. People did not have to work; there was no struggle for survival. Because of the abundance of material things, people did not have to vie with each other and proper order reigned. See, for example, *Han Fei Tzu* 339:14:

> In ancient times, the menfolk did not plow the fields. The fruit of the bushes and trees supplied ample food. Their wives did not weave. The skins of animals supplied ample clothing. Without exerting themselves, their provisions were sufficient. Because people were few and goods were abundant, people did not contend for them. Thus generous rewards were not dispensed nor heavy punishments applied, and yet the people were properly ordered of their own accord.

Again there are passages which can be construed as implying a process of devolution (341:12): "In high antiquity, people competed on the basis of moral virtue; in antiquity, they competed with wisdom and planning; today they vie with their spirit and physical prowess." Han Fei neither condemns antiquity nor praises the present. His attitude is simply that people in the past had their problems and their ways of dealing with them. This is a new world with new problems calling for new solutions.

36. I say "based on" rather than "an elaboration of" because these two books, although interesting enough in themselves, are at times very different from if not at odds with the original texts. This is perhaps even more the case with *The Beginning Reality (Ch'u-chen)* treatise than *Tracing the Tao (Yüan-tao)*. The extent to which these two treatises are based on the *Lao Tzu* and *Chuang Tzu* texts can perhaps be illustrated by the fact that approximately seven hundred characters of *The Beginning Reality*—about fifteen percent of the whole—constitute passages which can be found in the present *Chuang Tzu*. That these two treatises are a variation on their respective sources can be demonstrated by the opening portion of *The Beginning Reality*. It cites the *Chuang Tzu* 5/2/49 passage which in context is an illustration of the imprecise nature of language. Whereas the notion of "having a beginning" *(yu shih che)* would generally be assumed to indicate a definable point in a process, by prefacing this expression with an inexhaustible number of "nevers" *(wei shih)*, it is shown to be very imprecise indeed. This *Huai Nan Tzu* passage restates the *Chuang Tzu* discussion; but rather than associating it with the *Chuang Tzu* concept of relativity, it interprets it *literally* as stages which can be defined in the genesis of things. The author makes a heroic attempt to make each cosmogonic stage progressively more recondite and obscure as he describes (1) beginning, (2) never beginning to have a beginning, and (3) never beginning to never begin to have a beginning. Not only does this *Huai Nan Tzu* passage add nothing to the *Chuang Tzu*'s intended meaning, but it attempts to give precise definition to examples initially posited to demonstrate the imprecision of language!

37. In the sequel to this passage, there is the typically Taoist contrast between the return to the pristine untrammeled nature and the retarding cultivation of Confucian virtues. Compare this with the "Evolution of the Rites" *(Li-yün)* description of the Great Unity *(ta t'ung)* and Lesser Prosperity *(hsiao k'ang)* eras discussed in note 17 above. See also the opening section of *Book Eleven: Equalizing Customs (Ch'i-su)* of the *Huai Nan Tzu*.

38. Although most of the ideas in this chapter reiterate the pre-Ch'in Taoist themes, some elements are undeniably Han. There is a strong emphasis on the "mutual influence of human being and nature" *(t'ien jen hsiang ying)* theme, for

example, and the analogy of the human body for the sphere of heaven is prominent. Again there are long passages describing human interference in the activities of *yin* and *yang* and human destruction of the balance existing among the "five processes" *(wu hsing)*.

39. I omit the phrase *hsi pu hsien yü yin* here as being an erroneous interpolation. In place of these five characters I substitute the two characters *ku che* in the interests of parallel structure.

40. Compare *The Fundamental Constancy (Pen-ching)* 8/4a–b account of human inventions and innovations.

41. This conclusion is conceivably directed against the Taoists. Compare *Lao Tzu* 20: "Repudiate study and there will be no anxieties." And again *Lao Tzu* 64: "Therefore the Sage . . . studies not studying."

42. Omitting the character *pu* in the phrase *"to pu chia rih chih ku."*

43. I follow Wang Nien-sun in reading *pen ch'in* as *k'ua ch'in.*

44. Compare, for example, 13/3a with *The Book of Lord Shang* 1/2b (pp. 3–4). In fact, much of the first chapter of *The Book of Lord Shang* is contained in this *Perennial Discussions (Fan-lun)* treatise in the *Huai Nan Tzu.*

45. See 9/17b–18a.

46. See 9/13a and 9/19a.

47. Compare *Tso chuan* 456/Ting 10/3 in which Confucius contends that even entertainment must have as its purpose the illustration of virtue.

CHAPTER 2

1. Creel, in his research on Shen Pu-hai, has gone to great lengths to prove that *wu-wei* was a concept first developed in the Shen Pu-hai branch of Legalist thought; see *What Is Taoism?,* "On the Origin of *Wu-wei*," pp. 48–78, and *Shen Pu-hai,* pp. 176–179. Creel concludes that subsequent to its development as a technical Legalist term, *wu-wei* was absorbed by the Taoists and reinterpreted in a way consistent with the basic tenets of Taoist thought. Creel's arguments are based on an assumption that the Shen Pu-hai fragments are genuine and, moreover, on a tentative and highly subjective attempt to arrange pre-Ch'in texts in a chronological order. Creel makes a point of the fact that *wu-wei* does not occur in *The Book of Lord Shang* without even mentioning the *Kuan Tzu* in which *wu-wei* does occur as a special term. Again, the expression *wu-wei* occurs in what is being called the *Huang-ti ssu-ching* recently unearthed from tomb no. 3 at Mawangtui, and which has been tentatively dated at about 400 B.C. The examples of *wu-wei* in the *"Shih ta-ching"* 140 and the *"Yüan-tao"* 168 sections of this text are decidedly Taoist—the latter passage even has an echo in the *Tracing the Tao (Yüan-tao)* treatise of the *Huai Nan Tzu* and also the *Wen Tzu* "The Tao Source" *(Tao-yüan)* chapter. See *Acta Archaeologica Sinica (K'ao-ku hsüeh-pao)* 1(1975):28 ff. In early Chinese thought, for each tradition or school there are very few representative texts, and these are often composite in nature. The early history of their transmission is often shrouded in an almost impenetrable shadow of textual problems. Given the combination of scant data and tenuous chronology, no attempt to determine the historical origin of *wu-wei* can amount to much more than strained speculation. There is a traditional and seemingly logical opinion that the development of the Taoist doctrine somehow contributed to the emergence of Legalist political theory. While this opinion is certainly not

unassailable, it has not yet been discredited. Loewe, p. 199, makes the general comment that Creel's *Shen Pu-hai* "may be criticized on the grounds that its method of argument is questionable and its sense of history unsatisfactory." Lau, in his review of Creel's *What Is Taoism?*, specifically points out the inadequacy of Creel's evidence for ascribing the earliest usage of *wu-wei* to Shen Pu-hai rather than the Taoists.

2. Cf. *Analects* 2/2/3 and 24/12/19.

3. Cf. *Analects* 25/13/6 and 30/14/42.

4. See his "Philosophy of *Wu Wei*," p. 84. This assertion is of course true of Confucius and Mencius, but not of Hsün Tzu. The word "Confucianists" is perhaps too general.

5. See *Record of Rites (Li-chi)* 16/9a.

6. See *Ssu-shu chang-chü chi-chu* commentary.

7. Expanded on the basis of *K'ung Tzu chia-yü* 1/14a–b.

8. See Lau, *Mencius,* pp. 20–21.

9. See Lau, *Mencius,* pp. 19–22, for a discussion of Hsün Tzu's interpretation of "nature" *(hsing).*

10. Creel in *What Is Taoism?*, p. 61, suggests that Hsün Tzu in its usage of *wu-wei* is Taoist rather than Confucian: "And this Taoist *wu-wei* became so influential that we find it, and not the *wu-wei* of Confucius, in the Confucian book *Hsün Tzu.*"

11. See "The Philosophy of *Wu Wei*," pp. 99–100.

12. The thought contained in the *Tracing the Tao (Yüan-tao)* and *The Beginning Reality (Ch'u-chen)* treatises in the *Huai Nan Tzu* can be regarded as an amplification of the *Lao Tzu* and *Chuang Tzu* respectively. As such, the interpretation of *wu-wei* in these two treatises reflect these sources. See 1/3a, 7b, 8a, and 14b, and 2/4b–5a, 5a, and 11a.

13. Creel in *What Is Taoism?*, p. 55, suggests that *"wu-wei* is treated as a technique of government in fifty percent of its occurrences in the *Lao-tzu."* Ch'en Ku-ying, p. 28, on the other hand, states: "Apart from the use of the term *wu-wei* to describe the *tao* in Chapter 37 . . . every other instance of this term in the text is concerned with political affairs in the sphere of man." The passages in the *Lao Tzu* which contain the expression *wu-wei,* exclusive of chap. 37, are either specifically political or general statements which can have a political application.

14. "Nonintervention" *(wu-shih)* occurs four times: chaps. 48, 57 (twice), and 59. "Nondeployment" *(wu-hsing)* occurs once: chap. 69.

15. For "true knowledge" see *Lao Tzu* 47, 56, 71, and 81; for "obstructive erudition" see 3, 10, and 19.

16. For example, see *Lao Tzu* 21.

17. I am using the notion of "identity" here in the way that Francis Cook uses it to discuss Fa Tsang's conception of dependent origination *(pratītyasamut-pāda).* See Cook, chap. 4: "Identity."

18. See *Chuang Tzu* 3/2/3–9, 9/4/18–21, 14/5/52–55, 15/6/1–4, 16/5/19–21, 19/6/95–97, 28/11/69–74, 33/13/passim, 44/17/50–54, 87/31/37–40; *Hitting the Mark in the Everyday (Chung-yung)* 20, 22; *Hsün Tzu* "A Discourse on Heaven" *(T'ien-lun)* chapter.

19. *Chuang Tzu* 15/6/1–2. There appears to be an amplification of this same passage in the *Huai Nan Tzu* 18/17b: "If one knows the operations of nature and knows the practices of man, then he will have the means to sustain himself in the world. If one knows nature but does not know man, he will have no way of com-

municating in the ordinary world. If one knows man but does not know nature, then he will have no way of achieving freedom in the *tao.*" Compare *Chuang Tzu* 18/6/66–74 and 75/27/1–10.

20. A careful reading of the *Chuang Tzu* suggests that the author of this text (especially the "Inner Chapters" seems to be aware of problematic and ambiguous use of language in the *Lao Tzu* and resolves some of the problems by a careful choice of terminology. For example, specific language is developed to indicate the consummate human being: *chen jen, chih jen,* and so on. *Hsiao-yao-yu* ("wandering in unconditioned freedom") is a happy exchange for *wu-wei.*

21. See *Lao Tzu* 77.

22. For a full treatment of this background, see Lau's *Lao Tzu: Tao Te Ching,* especially the appendixes on "The Problem of Authorship" and "The Nature of the Work."

23. Creel, *What Is Taoism?,* pp. 37–47, suggests that the political application of Taoist principles is purposive—"the attempt to utilize an essentially mystical doctrine for the furtherment of personal ambitions and political purpose" (p. 45). In interpreting this chapter of the *Lao Tzu,* Creel in *Shen Pu-hai,* p. 193, concludes that *Lao Tzu* was "no longer a protest against the regimentation of the Legalist system, but the most powerful instrument for such regimentation."

Since Taoist political theory is propounded as a microcosm of their metaphysics in which the operation of the political state is seen as correlative to the functioning of the cosmos, it follows that the ideal ruler can only be "purposive" if in fact there is some purpose in his cosmic counterpart, the *tao.* The Taoism of the *Lao Tzu* does acknowledge a certain natural "so-ness" which exists in all things and propels them toward their own realization. But the political theory of the *Lao Tzu* is certainly not purposive in the sense of advocating a specific and artificially contrived political program which enables one to seize and exercise political control. The Taoist sage-ruler does not pursue a policy of *wu-wei* because *wu-wei* is the most effective way of guaranteeing political success. Rather, his purpose—that is, the actualization of his own potential—can only be achieved through emulation of the *tao,* and emulation of the *tao* means expressing one's own so-ness while maintaining an attitude of *wu-wei* with respect to other phenomena. The political theory of the *Lao Tzu* can be accused of being impracticable, but to project selfish desires and base ambitions onto it is a distortion which, in my opinion, does violence to the spirit of the text.

24. Cf. *Kuan Tzu* 3:31–8.

25. As is frequently noted, the *Chuang Tzu* is a composite text and, as such, contains passages which offer different and at times even contradictory interpretations of basic Taoist tenets. Nevertheless, the *Chuang Tzu* text is still very important in representing *wu-wei* as an aspect of the sublimated state of mind.

Graham makes a tentative division of the *Chuang Tzu* into:

1. Chuang Tzu's own writings   Chaps. 1–7
2. Primitivist documents   Chaps. 8–10, 11/1–28
3. Individualist documents   Chaps. 28, 29, 31
4. Syncretist documents   Chaps. 12/1–6, 7–12, 12–18; 13/1–45, 60–64; 14/1–5; 15/all; 33/all.

In the writings which Graham and most scholars would ascribe to Chuang Tzu himself, *wu-wei* occurs only three times to characterize the *tao* (16/6/29) and to describe the sublime state of mind (3/1/47 and 18/6/70).

In the Primitivist documents, *wu-wei* is a political policy applied to the government of the world. This is in keeping with the characteristic Primitivist sympathy with the *Lao Tzu*. As Graham, p. 481, observes: "Probably we should think of the Primitivist as an exponent of Lao-tzu's ideal of government, only incidentally interested in the *Chuang-tzu*."

Graham describes the Individualists as being "as unmystical as a Mohist." It is not surprising that *wu-wei* does not occur in these three chapters.

In the Syncretist passages of the text, the notion of *wu-wei* is generally put forward as an aspect of the ideal ruler—an ideal ruler in whom Taoist, Legalist, and Confucian virtues are commingled. The beginning of chap. 12 and particularly the beginning of chap. 13 are good examples of the Syncretist's eclecticism. The opening passage of chap. 13, for example, knits together the Legalist notion of "accountability" *(hsing-ming),* the Confucian objectives of fame and accomplishment, passages from the core *Chuang Tzu* chapters, and allusions to the *Lao Tzu*. With respect to the notion of *wu-wei,* it is represented as a very purposive (in Creel's sense) technique of government. It is not only a policy guaranteed of success in the world of politics but, moreover, will thrust one to the forefront even among recluses. A particularly Legalist element in this passage is the idea that only the ruler may pursue a policy of *wu-wei;* his subordinates must be very active *(yu-wei)* indeed. References to *wu-wei* in the remaining portions of the text are predominately in description of the sublime level of mind.

26. See 16/6/29 and 40/15/8.

27. See 40/15/8 and 46/18/11.

28. See also 64/23/78 and 28/11/54.

29. See also 3/1/47, 26/11/13, 31/12/68, 38/14/52, and 59/22/48.

30. Graham, p. 481, isolates *Chuang Tzu* 8–10 and 11/1–28 as belonging to the Primitivist school; he characterizes this tradition as "one of the earliest datable witnesses (with Han Fei tzu) to the sudden and extraordinary impact of *Lao-tzu* when it began to circulate in the late third century B.C.

31. See 38/14/52, 56/21/36, and 93/33/60.

32. See 26/11/13 (*Lao Tzu* 13), 46/18/11 (*Lao Tzu* 21, 37, 39, and 48), 57/22/9 (*Lao Tzu* 48), 64/23/70 (*Lao Tzu* 37 and 48), 72/25/64 (*Lao Tzu* 37 and 48).

33. As Watson observes in his introduction to *Mo Tzu: Basic Writings,* p. 7: "The Taoists, it is true, talk much of freedom of thought and action, but it is a freedom which ignores or transcends the social order, not one that functions effectively within it."

34. The impracticability of the Taoist position is fiercely attacked in the *Striving with Effort (Hsiu-wu)* treatise in the *Huai Nan Tzu.* It interprets this Taoist notion of *wu-wei,* not altogether unreasonably, as a total repudiation of human culture and a naive idealization of primitivism. In doing so, it affirms human wisdom and describes the active contributions of the legendary sage-emperors who taught the people what to eat, where to live, how to provide for themselves, how to avoid illness, and how to respond to each other in a civilized manner. Rejecting the basic Taoist interpretation of history as gradual decline in favor of their concept of historical and cultural evolution, it dismisses the notion of primitive utopia as a romantic interpretation of animal squalor. The author of *Striving with Effort,* having pointed out the flaws in the Taoist conception of *wu-wei,* then proceeds to offer his own interpretation (19/3a). For this author, *wu-wei* is complying with the natural tendency of things and exploiting them to human advantage, whereas "activity" *(yu-wei)* is any departure from this principle (19/3b). In fact, what is labeled *wu-wei* in this *Striving with Effort* treatise is exactly what the Taoists have rejected as *yu-wei*—the active exploitation of the natural condition. As Miyamoto, pp. 28–35, observes, the concept of *wu-wei* in this treatise is simply

following a scientific methodology in order to achieve the most effective exploitation.

35. Although the development of Legalist doctrine (which found its culmination in the *Han Fei Tzu*) owes a debt to *The Book of Lord Shang* as one of its primary sources, it is on the basis of this lack of "political technique" *(shu)—wu-wei* being one of the most important *shu*—that the *Han Fei Tzu* criticizes the political theory of Shang Yang. See the "Fixing Laws" *(Ting-fa)* chapter of the *Han Fei Tzu.*

36. The passage 1:17-2 is very similar to *Lao Tzu* 38 in wording, whereas 2:85-11 would seem to be an explanation of 1:17-2. Again, 1:82-3 can be compared to *Lao Tzu* 7, 25, 37, and 41. The remaining six occurrences are all contained in "The Art of the Mind: Part I" *(Hsin-shu shang).*

37. This passage serves as commentary to the initial statement in the opening lines of this chapter.

38. Although this might also be said of the Confucian interpretation of *wu-wei,* the ideal Confucian ruler is still responsible for selecting and promoting virtuous ministers and, as such, is an integral part of the administrative system. In Legalist doctrine, however, the fact that the minister's role is one component in the operation of the government apparatus while the ruler exists outside the administration indicates the sharp distinction between these two roles.

39. Creel, having collected fragments attributed to Shen Pu-hai from various sources, has found that the term *wu-wei* with strong Legalist connotations occurs six times within this very limited material. By comparison, *wu-wei* occurs only seventeen times in the entire *Han Fei Tzu,* eight of which are in the "Unraveling the *Lao Tzu*" *(Chieh-Lao)* chapter and have nothing to do with Legalist thought. Again Creel points out that the *Han Fei Tzu* 238:10 passage attributes the Legalist interpretation of this *wu-wei* concept to Shen Pu-hai directly. See Creel, *What Is Taoism?,* p. 63.

In the *Han Fei Tzu* (238:10) passage cited here, the failure of the parallel structure is indicative of textual corruption. I have reconstructed the text where possible.

40. Liang Ch'i-hsiung, *Han Tzu chien-chieh,* vol. 2, p. 319.

41. Ch'ien Mu, pp. 501–502.

42. The concept of *wu-wei* is probably the principal "technique of rulership" *(shu)* in Legalist theory, and the *shu* branch of political thought is traditionally traced to Shen Pu-hai.

43. The fact that Shen Pu-hai ("Shen Tzu") and "the elder of Cheng" occur side by side in the same chapter of the *Han Fei Tzu* seems to indicate that, in the mind of the author of this chapter, these were two different people. On the other hand, this chapter of the *Han Fei Tzu* was not written until at least a century after the death of Shen Pu-hai.

44. See Chapter 6 on the concept of "benefiting the people" *(li min).* The notion of benefiting the people is combined with a typically Legalist agrarian emphasis, and the economic theory necessary for equitable government is discussed. The point is made that the taxation of the ruler must relate to the conditions of the harvest. Again, the concept of benefiting the people is not confined to this one book in the *Huai Nan Tzu* but is a recurrent theme throughout the text (10/9b, 13/3a, 19/2a). Although this theme has its roots in the early Confucian texts, by early Han times it had become one of the leading tenets of the new Confucianism.

45. See *Mencius* 7/1b/7, 8; 36/5a/5; 56/7b/14; and see *Hsün Tzu* 53/15/1 and 26/9/19.

46. See also 9/1a and 9/9a.

47. See Novak's distinction between liberalism and anarchism.

48. See 9/4a–b.

49. See 9/6b.

50. See 9/7a.

51. Rubin, p. 62, observes: "The idea that the relations between the state and the people are antagonistic is a feature that distinguishes the Legalist theory from other trends of political thought in both the East and the West." While this comment seems to overstate the uniqueness of this feature of Legalist thought, it is correcting in identifying this antagonism as one of its most prominent characteristics.

52. The *Han Fei Tzu* 239:5 insists that the ruler must remain secluded and shrouded in secrecy. In 305:16 there is the notion of taking advantage of the combined faculties of the people to see and hear. While these two elements are certainly present in the *Han Fei Tzu,* here it is the complementary nature of these two ideas which receives emphasis.

53. See, for example, *Chuang Tzu* 42/17/20 and 58/22/18.

CHAPTER 3

1. See Hsü Fu-kuan, vol. 2, p. 143.

2. Kuo Hua-jo, p. 2, concludes that the *Sun Tzu* by Sun Wu was a summary of the salient features of warfare current during the Spring and Autumn period. It was a distillation of experience gained when Wu attacked Ch'u and a product of Sun Wu's study of military affairs with King Ho-lü of Wu, Wu Tzu-hsü, and others. Having undergone more than a century of oral transmission, the *Sun Tzu* was edited and added to by Sun Pin, a descendant of Sun Wu, to form the present thirteen chapters *(p'ien)*. Although this has represented scholarly consensus, with the recent unearthing of the *Sun Tzu Art of Warfare (Sun Tzu ping-fa)* fragments and the *Sun Pin Art of Warfare (Sun Pin ping-fa)* (a text previously unknown), this opinion is being reassessed. On the basis of this Yin-ch'üeh-shan find in 1972, the *Sun Tzu Art of Warfare* is being reattributed to Sun Wu alone and is being restored to its Spring and Autumn position. See *Cultural Relics (Wen-wu)* 12 (1975):20–24. This relatively early dating of at least some portions of the *Sun Tzu Art of Warfare* is attested by the similar summary passages found in *The Book of Lord Shang* military chapters (see Duyvendak, *The Book of Lord Shang,* pp. 244–252).

3. Ch'ien Mu dates Sun Pin as 380–320 B.C. The 1972 discovery of portions of some thirty chapters of the *Sun Pin Art of Warfare (Sun Pin ping-fa)* in the Han tomb of Yin-ch'üeh-shan has provided us with perhaps some of the eighty-nine chapters attributed to Sun Pin in the *History of the Han (Han-shu)* "Record of Literary Works" *(Yi-wen chih)*. The unearthing of this text along with fragments of the *Sun Tzu Art of Warfare* enables us to make a distinction between these two representatives of the Militarist school and their two treatises. The text of the *Sun Pin Art of Warfare* chapters has been transcribed in *Cultural Relics (Wen-wu)* (1975).

4. This lord of Lin-wu is identified by commentators as a Ch'u general.

5. King Hsiao-ch'eng of Chao (r. 265–245 B.C.).

6. Cf. *Sun Tzu* 7/14b–15a.

7. See also *Han Fei Tzu* 347:3 and *Huai Nan Tzu* 15/3a.

8. Kuo Mo-jo, vol. 5, p. 205, on the basis of the contents of the *Wu Tzu*, argues that it is the product of the late Warring States period or early Han. Chang Ping-lin, p. 802, notes that the military weapons mentioned in the *Wu Tzu* are anachronistic and dates it as late as the Six Dynasties. Since the *Wu Tzu* is a compilation of dubious authenticity, and *shih* occurs in it only twice, I shall pass over it in favor of the more reliable *Sun Tzu* and *Sun Pin Art of Warfare*.

9. See Lau, "Some Notes on the *Sun Tzu*," pp. 332–333.

10. For the use of the expression *hsing-shih* as a compound term, see the titles of chaps. 2 and 64 in the *Kuan Tzu*, as well as *Kuan Tzu* 1:58-4, where it seems to mean "the shape of things" or "prevailing conditions." It also occurs in the *Kuan Tzu* 1:22-6, where it seems to refer to the physical arrangements for defense such as walls, moats, and fortifications, which must be constructed in strategically advantageous locations. The expression *hsing-shih* occurs also in the *Huai Nan Tzu* 15/3a: "Things generally give omens. Only the Tao is without them. The reason that it is without omens is because it is without a constant shape or disposition *(hsing-shih).*"

11. The word "purchase" is used in the sense of a grip that enables one to apply influence or pressure in order to accomplish something. It can refer to the actual contrivance used for increasing this influence or to the advantage gained by applying this device. I have purposely avoided using "power" or "force" as equivalents for *shih* because I believe that *shih* usually refers to something quite different from the actual strength required to accomplish something. It is a kind of power, but "power" is too vague here.

12. See also the *Sun Pin Art of Warfare (Sun Pin ping-fa),* no. 111–122, and *Huai Nan Tzu* 15/11a and 15/14a.

13. For a discussion of the meaning of this passage, see Lau, "Some Notes on the *Sun Tzu*," p. 331. Supporting my interpretation of *shih* as a special military term is a passage in the *Sun Tzu Art of Warfare* fragments where *ch'i shih* is used as a compound expression (no. 145-6). See *Cultural Relics (Wen-wu)* 12(1974):11 and, for a discussion, p. 18. This passage is too corrupt to venture a translation.

14. Although passage no. 243 in the *Sun Pin Art of Warfare (Sun Pin ping-fa)* is too corrupt to offer a definite interpretation, *shih* seems to mean "conditions" or "circumstances." There is also no. 257-60:

> The aggressor, on the other hand, arrives only after having braved narrow defiles [and] if he tries to retreat they will venture to strike off his head. And even if he does advance, why will he not dare to engage the enemy? Because he is strategically disadvantaged and occupies unfavorable terrain. Where you have strategic advantages *(shih)* and favorable terrain, the rank and file will advance of their own accord [and] will themselves retreat. Those who can be said to be adept at warfare are those who can gain strategic advantages *(shih)* and occupy favorable terrain.

15. See the *Sun Pin Art of Warfare (Sun Pin ping-fa)* no. 349: "And that some things have a surplus while others are deficient is an example of things being of various dispositions *(shih).*"

16. See also the *Sun Pin Art of Warfare (Sun Pin ping-fa)* no. 359: "Thus, in battle deployment *(chan shih),* a large formation . . . broken, and a small formation . . . dispersed." In no. 32 a similar expression, "military deployment" *(ping*

shih), is used: "King Wei [of Ch'i] then exclaimed, 'Excellent! You speak on military deployments with inexhaustible insight.' "

17. See *The Book of Lord Shang* 3/6a: "In carrying out these three things there are two conditions."

18. See note 10 above.

19. The first reference is *SPTK;* the second is Chu Shih-ch'e's *Shang-chün shu chieh-ku ting-pen,* which is excellent for textual problems.

20. See *Huai Nan Tzu* 15/5a: "Therefore virtue and rightness are sufficient to win over the people of the world; human industry is sufficient to deal with the pressing needs of the world; selection and promotion are sufficient to secure the goodwill of superior men; planning and considering are sufficient to know conditions of strength and weakness. This is the root of certain victory."

21. See *Huai Nan Tzu* 15/3a: "Things generally give omens. Only the *tao* is without them. The reason that it is without omens is because it is without a constant shape or disposition."

22. See, for example, *Huai Nan Tzu* 15/9b and 15/10b: "None will venture to resist your military advantage *(shih)*. . . . Strategic advantage *(shih)* has the edge over manpower."

23. This character *ch'ien* occurs in books annotated by Hsü Shen as a substitute for the taboo, *ch'üan*.

24. *Chao yao* is the name of the seventh star of the Big Dipper, which forms the last portion of the handle. Book 5 of the *Huai Nan Tzu* is a system of social-ceremonial directives based on the point indicated by the *chao yao* star. When *chao yao* points in one direction, it indicates that it is the first month of spring. When it points in another direction, it indicates that it is the second month and so on. See *Huai Nan Tzu,* bk. 5 passim, and Needham, vol. 3, p. 250.

25. The expression *hsing te* refers to the twelve *"ch'en"* or branches and the ten *"rih"* or stems.

26. See Fung Yu-lan, *A History of Chinese Philosophy* vol. 1, p. 318. That Shen Pu-hai and Shang Yang stressed "techniques of rulership" *(shu)* and "penal law" *(fa)* respectively is stated clearly in the "Fixing Laws" *(Ting-fa)* chapter of the *Han Fei Tzu,* but no such early evidence exists for the association of Shen Tao with the concept *shih.*

27. See Thompson, fragments 13 (p. 236) and 71 (p. 274). Fragment 13 is similar to *Han Fei Tzu* 297:8 and *Huai Nan Tzu* 9/9a.

28. See *Chuang Tzu* 92/33/46: ". . and ridiculed the world's esteeming those of superior character." And 92/33/47: ". . and criticized the great sages of the world." And 92/33/50: ". . and had no use for the sages and those of superior character."

29. Similar passages attributed to Shen Tao are contained in *Yi-lin* 2/15a and *TPYL* 907 (p. 4022). Again, similar passages *not* attributed to Shen Tao can be found in *The Book of Lord Shang* 5/15a and in *Yin Wen Tzu* 5b.

30. It is perhaps worth noting that since Legalist thought is generally meant for the ears of the ruler himself (to the extent that many of the "techniques of rulership" *(shu)* are to remain his exclusive property), the rather obvious question of how to acquire the position *(wei)* and authority *(ch'üan)* of a ruler does not really arise. It is how to maximize your political purchase that is of central concern.

31. Lo Ken-tse, p. 510, dates *The Book of Lord Shang* between 260 and 233 B.C.; Ch'en Ch'i-t'ien, *Chung-kuo fa-chia kai-lun,* p. 234, attributes eleven sections to Shang Yang or "possibly Shang Yang" and twelve to a later period

extending into the Western Han. Duyvendak in *The Book of Lord Shang,* pp. 141 ff., dates it primarily as third century B.C. with some possibly original fragments. Kao Heng, in his introduction to *Shang-chün shu chu-i,* takes a position similar to that of Duyvendak.

32. See Duyvendak, *The Book of Lord Shang,* p. 131, and Kao Heng, *Shang-chün shu chu-i,* pp. 10–11.

33. The *History of the Han (Han Shu)* "Record of Literary Works" *(Yi-wen chih)* lists Kung Sun Yang under the "Militarist School," and the "Treatise on Penal Law" *(Hsing-fa chih)* says: "The state of Wu had its Sun Wu, Ch'i had its Sun Pin, Ch'in had its Shang Yang. They all captured opposing commanders and secured victory, and handed down their written works."

34. See, for example, chaps. 17, 26, and 28.

35. See the discussion above on the development of *shih* as a special military term.

36. I follow Chu Shih-ch'e, who reads the two characters *shih* ("age") in this passage as *shih* ("circumstances") on the basis of the *Ch'ün-shu chih-yao* 36/7b, which quotes this passage. See also *Han Fei Tzu* 299:11, which cites part of this passage.

37. Cf. *The Book of Lord Shang* 5/9b.

38. There is considerable textual variation on this passage. I follow the Yen Wan-li version in Chu Shih-ch'e, p. 86.

39. In this text, as in *The Book of Lord Shang,* the range of this usage is considerable. At one extreme one finds simply "present circumstances" in 3:95-6:

Kuan Tzu replied: "If we accord with what is appropriate and take advantage of prevailing circumstances *(shih),* we will be able to get the most out of things; if we make plans and do what is expedient, our attainments will be considerable. A True King takes advantage of prevailing circumstances *(shih);* a sage takes advantage of changing conditions. And both are always appropriate to the things around them." [Following Yü Sheng-wu in reading *yen* as *ho;* following Kuo Mo-jo in reading *yu* as *yi;* see Wen I-to, pp. 1200–1201.]

At the other extreme one finds "unalterable prevailing circumstances." The 3:51-9 passage following is similar to 5/15b–16a cited above in suggesting that prevailing circumstances can demand proper order: "When the perspicacious ruler is on the throne and enjoys circumstances which guarantee proper order, the various ministers will not dare to do wrong." The assertion that prevailing circumstances are of such overwhelming influence that they can make honest men of thieves—found in *The Book of Lord Shang* 4/10a (and 5/9b) and also cited above —can again be found in the *Kuan Tzu* 1:58-4: "Therefore, when circumstances do not allow wrongdoing, even dissolute persons will be on their best behavior."

40. Chapter 76 of the *Kuan Tzu* discusses five types of "regional conditions" *(kuo shih)* (3:82-8): "Duke Huan asked Kuan Tzu: 'Could you please tell me about regional conditions?' Kuan Tzu replied: 'There are mountainous regions, regions of low-lying lands, regions of mixed mountainous and flat terrain, regions of floodlands, and regions of swampland. These are the five types of regional conditions.' "

The expression "natural circumstances" *(t'ien shih)* also occurs in 3:38-7: "During the reign of Kung Kung, seventy percent of the land was covered with water while only thirty percent was dry. Taking advantage of the natural circumstances, he seized and ruled the empire." For these two passages, see Wen I-to, pp. 1139 and 1159.

41. There is a clear definition of this term, *ts'an wu,* in *Huai Nan Tzu* 20/4b–5a. (See the accompanying translation of *The Art of Rulership,* note 129.) In accord with the nature of heaven above and earth below, the Former Kings established the *ts'an*: the family, the nation, and the officialdom. To give structure to these institutions, they laid down the proper relationships between ruler and minister, father and child, husband and wife, senior and junior, and between friends. These relationships are called the *wu.*

42. See, for example, 3:51-9 and 3:54-7.

43. Compare *Han Fei Tzu* 289:10, in which a similar passage is attributed to Shen Pu-hai: "Shen Tzu [Shen Pu-hai] said, 'If the ruler loses ground in strategies and seeks to make it up in the sincerity of his subjects, this will give rise to uncertainty.' "

44. Compare *Hsün Tzu* 26/9/15:

Where everyone's status is of equal standing, there will be no subordination; where their political purchase *(shih)* is the same, there will be no unified direction; where everyone is on a par, no one will command anyone else. As soon as you had the heavens and the earth, there was a distinction made between "above" and "below," and as soon as you had a perspicacious king on the throne, his state included regulations governing status. That two persons of equal nobility cannot serve each other and that two persons of the same lowly station cannot command each other is a natural principle.

Thompson, fragment 98 (p. 287), cites a fragment attributed to Shen Tao from the *Yi-lin* 2/15a: "Two persons of equal nobility do not serve each other and two persons of the same lowly station do not command each other."

45. Following Pi Yüan's commentary in reading *ch'ang shih chi tz'u* as *ch'ang shih fan tz'u.*

46. I follow T'ao Hung-ch'ing, p. 125, in interpreting the character *yi* as *ni*: "to be similar to, to approximate, to pretend."

47. See Chiang Shang-hsien, p. 344. Again Wei Chang-t'ung, pp. 118–119, gives examples of how the *Sun Tzu* is in fact misrepresented in this debate.

48. See 54/15/32.

49. See 40/11/65.

50. See 60/16/35.

51. See 12:14, 50:8, 171:6, and 163:2.

52. As in the earlier Legalist texts we have examined, the meaning of this term can range widely. At one extreme we have simply "present circumstances" (136:13): "If," said Hui Tzu, "you put a monkey in a cage, it will be no different from a pig. Thus where circumstances *(shih)* are not conducive to a thing, it does not give it room to express its ability." (Compare *Huai Nan Tzu* 2/13b.) At the other extreme we have the shape of circumstances in which two things participate. While this may sound like a convoluted way of saying "relationship," it is important to remember that just as *shih* in its original military usage describes the situation of two armies—that is, the two armies *and* their relationship to one another—so the meaning of *shih* here indicates the two states *and* the relationship in which they stand (41:13 and 308:7): "Now, Yü's having Kuo is like a carriage having a running board. The running board depends on the carriage, but the carriage also depends on the running board. The relationship *(shih)* obtaining between Yü and Kuo is exactly this."

53. See 284:10 and 332:11.

54. See 346:8.

55. See 156:4.

56. See 235:15.
57. See 80:2.
58. See 68:14.
59. See 84:2.
60. See 238:5 and 242:10.
61. See 325:4.
62. For example, *The Book of Lord Shang* has a chapter entitled "Fixing Privileges and Duties" *(Ting-fen). Fen* is also an important expression in the "Commentary on Enlightened Laws" *(Ming-fa-chieh)* chapter of the *Kuan Tzu.*
63. Cf. *The Book of Lord Shang* 5/9a.
64. See 116:8: "The control of the government being invested in the ruler himself is called 'weightiness' *(chung).*" This is a commentary on *Lao Tzu* 26.
65. See 284:15. I follow the Ku Kuang-ts'e commentary in reading *pu* as *hsia.*
66. See Thompson, p. 234.
67. Hsü Fu-kuan, pp. 143–144, also detects a Confucian influence here.
68. The term "favors" *(te)* is used in this passage in a manner reminiscent of the "Handles of Reward and Punishment" *(Erh-ping)* chapter of the *Han Fei Tzu,* where it stands in contrast to "punishments" (25:15): "The two control handles are punishments and favors. What is meant by punishments and favors? Execution and disgrace are called punishments; honors and rewards are called favors."
69. I emend this passage on the basis of the *Huai Nan Tzu* 9/10a–b.
70. Cf. *Kuan Tzu* 3:56-2.
71. A similar wholly Legalist warning against allowing ministers to encroach upon the political purchase of the ruler appears in Book Thirteen: *Perennial Discussions (Fan-lun)* (13/6b):

Old Duke Chien of Ch'i abandoned the control handles of the state and gave exclusive authority to his great ministers. The high ministers arrogated his prestige and usurped his purchase, private families formed factions and impartiality no longer prevailed. As a result, he made it possible for Ch'en Ch'eng and Ch'ih Yi Tzu P'i to succeed in their conspiracy. That the posterity of the Lü clan was cut off and the Ch'en clan succeeded to the state was the result of weakness and timidity.

Here the author castigates Duke Chien of Ch'i for allowing his ministers to gain control of the government. Consistent with Legalist predictions for such a course of action, the purchase of the ruler was gradually eroded and the ruler himself was ultimately expunged.
72. See also *Huai Nan Tzu* 9/9b–10a: "Hence, because the ruler dwells at the focal point of political power. . . ."
73. The notion of transformation does occur in the *Kuan Tzu:* 2:35-5, 2:27-10. That these passages are included in the *Kuan Tzu* does not automatically mean, however, that they represent orthodox Legalist theory. For example (2:27-10): "Where the ruler constitutes a moral example, the people are transformed; where his moral qualities are what they should be, the bureaucracy is properly ordered. The essential task of ordering the bureaucracy properly and transforming the people lies with the ruler." This notion of transforming the people was not only repudiated by later Legalist thinkers but was even challenged within the pages of the *Kuan Tzu* itself by the radical principle that the ruler's moral attributes are of no concern to his subordinates.
74. I follow Wang Nien-sun in reading *sheng* as *pen.*

75. See the notes to the accompanying translation for a list of these references.
76. I follow Liang Ch'i-hsiung, *Hsün Tzu chien-shih,* p. 165, in his reading of this passage.
77. See *Kuan Tzu* 1:73-8; 3:36-6; 3:42-1; *Han Fei Tzu* 305:16; 331:9; 288:4.

CHAPTER 4

1. For example, Hu Shih in his *Chung-kuo ku-tai che-hsüeh shih,* p. 86, warns against assuming that the notions of *fa* ("penal law") and *hsing fa* ("punishments and penalties") are synonymous; he points out the relatively late date of the former as opposed to the ancient origins of the latter. Since society itself is often defined in terms of social contract, it follows logically that violation of this contract by any member would result in some form of retaliation by other members of the group.
2. See Creel, *Origins of Statecraft,* pp. 161 ff., for a discussion of early law codes.
3. *Tso* 360/Chao 6/1 and 430/Chao 29/5.
4. This letter is discussed later in the chapter; see "The Confucian Tradition."
5. That *hsing* was used to represent a fixed and tangible code of laws is borne out by its usage in the *Tso-chuan.* In 501 B.C., for example (*Tso* 453/Ting 9/2): "Ssu Ch'uan of Cheng killed Teng Hsi and used his bamboo criminal code *(chu-hsing).*"
6. Tzu-ch'an was reputedly the first to inscribe written laws onto a pair of tripods in 536 B.C. with his famous *Book of Punishments (Hsing-shu)* (*Tso* 360/Chao 6/1). This inscription was followed by that of Fan Hsüan Tzu of Chin in 513 B.C. (*Tso* 430/Chao 29/5).
7. Welch, p. 26.
8. If my hypothesis that the "law" dimension of the character *fa* is a later extension of its original meaning, the implication is that this passage of the *Lao Tzu* is relatively late—at least later than the emergence of the Legalists. Given the nature of the *Lao Tzu* as an edited collection of epigrammatic statements, it was undoubtedly in a fluid state for some time before it was fixed in its present form. This occurrence of *fa* could have been inserted relatively late. Again, this is the only example of this usage of *fa* in the text. (In chap. 25 it means "to model or imitate.") While this version of this phrase is admittedly the most widely accepted, it should be noted that there is an alternative version (Ho-shang Kung) which interprets this as: "The more display is made of precious things, the more prevalent will be the thieves and brigands."
9. The expression *"Fa-chia"* refers to such a disparate group of theorists and such a broad spectrum of ideas that it frequently needs qualification. Again, as Creel in *Shen Pu-hai,* p. 140 ff., suggests, even the character *fa* under discussion here may have had a different significance in the thought of Shen Tao and Shen Pu-hai than it had for Shang Yang and Han Fei Tzu. This is certainly borne out by an analysis of the historical development of this concept. It is further possible that the thought of Shen Tao (and perhaps that of Shen Pu-hai) is the source of the earliest association between the Legalist and Taoist traditions. Yang Hung-lieh, pp. 69-71, follows Takeuchi Yoshio *(Rōshi shin kō)* in suggesting that there is much in the *Lao Tzu* which came to influence the development of the Legalists. They date *Lao Tzu* as having been compiled during the several decades between

the reigns of King Lieh of Chou (r. 375–368 B.C.) and King Hsien of Chou (r. 368–320 B.C.). Takeuchi claims that the doctrine of the Legalists originated with *Lao Tzu* and that Shen Tao (c. 350–275 B.C.) was the first proto-Legalist. Yang Hung-lieh considers the following chapters of the *Lao Tzu* to contain ideas similar to the central concepts of Shen Tao: chaps. 3, 18, 19, 20, 48, 64, and 65. There is also a passage in the *Yi-lin* 2/15b attributed to Shen Tao which is very similar to *Lao Tzu* 18. The last two phrases of this Shen Tao passage are probably commentary; they are identical with *Lao Tzu* 18. For further discussion, see Takeuchi's *Chūgoku shisō shi,* pp. 72–75.

10. Although *fa* occurs some thirty-four times in the *Chuang Tzu* text as a whole, it does not refer to penal law in any of the "Inner Chapters" but does so in some of the remaining occurrences. This fact supports the contention that the "Inner Chapters" date from an earlier period, perhaps prior to the spread and popularization of Legalist ideas.

11. The opening portion of "Responding to Emperors and Kings" *(Ying ti-wang)* is perhaps an exception, but even here the prescribed method for proper government is simply the personal attainment of the Way.

12. Although law is *usually* based on some notion of public morality, it is at times grounded in a set of standards which seem to bear little relation to moral principles. The Legalists represent such a case—the arbitrary whims of the ruler constitute the single and exclusive standard of right and wrong.

13. See, for example, "The Human World" *(Jen-chien-shih)*: the dialogues between Yen Hui and Confucius, Yen Ho and Ch'ü Po-yü, and the anecdote about Tzu-kao, governor of She.

14. See, for example, 16/6/17, and the Ai T'ai-t'o passage in 13/5/31 ff.

15. Graham, pp. 470–471.

16. See Chapter 1, notes 25 and 30.

17. See Chapter 1.

18. See Chapter 2, note 25, with respect to the *Chuang Tzu.* Because it is a composite text representing several diverse and often incompatible schools of thought, it can only be cited with some qualification as to which tradition of thought is being discussed.

19. See Ames, "Is Political Taoism Anarchism?"

20. See Guerin, pp. 42 ff., for a discussion of Proudhon, Malatesta, and Voline. See also Ward, p. 387.

21. See Bodde and Morris, pp. 17–18; Ch'ü, pp. 226–279; Hu Shih, *Chung-kuo ku-tai che-hsüeh shih,* pp. 87 ff.; Yang Hung-lieh, pp. 47–51; Munro, pp. 110–112. In listing three Confucian arguments against penal law, Munro cites two quoted from Shu-hsiang's letter in *Tso* Chao 6. While Munro, p. 110, states his conviction that the early Confucians opposed penal laws as a means of social control, he seems to be aware of the conflicting textual evidence when he admits (p. 112): "It should be noted that Chou Confucians did not totally reject penal law and 'punishments,' but sometimes acknowledged their supplementary role as a control technique." Rubin, p. 65 (see also pp. 18–20), observes: "I noted above that Confucius opposed publication of the laws. Believing that successful government depended exclusively on the moral qualities of the leader, he asserted that penal laws (and these were the form of the oldest legislation in China) were not necessary and could only bring harm."

22. See Ch'ü, p. 271.

23. Hsiao Kung-ch'üan (Mote trans.), pp. 182 ff., especially 182–183, 194–198.

24. As Ch'en Ta-ch'i, pp. 303–305, observes, whereas "administrative policies *(cheng)*" and "penal law" *(hsing)* are listed together and are certainly contrasted with "virtue" *(te)* and "social norms" *(li)*, the distinction being made between these two attitudes toward government lies in the fact that the former is more temporary and expedient, simply forcing the people into a regulated mode of conduct. The latter attitude, on the other hand, leads to a permanent situation inasmuch as it teaches the people to want to pursue a moral course of behavior. While these methods differ in their effect on the people, it is possible for them to be applied simultaneously to different strata of people in the society with the result of syncretizing their conduct. Ch'en therefore insists that these two methods are best interpreted as being complementary rather than exclusory. See also Yang Hung-lieh, pp. 47–51.

25. Chan in his *Way of Lao Tzu,* p. 231, for example, interprets 24/12/19 as Confucius' opposition to capital punishment.

26. Bodde and Morris, pp. 16–17: "Although Shu-hsiang himself cannot be formally counted a Confucian, his letter nevertheless epitomizes what may be termed the 'purist' Confucian view of law."

27. See 336/Hsiang 31/7, 385/Chao 13/5, 430/Chao 20/7.

28. Confucius expresses a similar opinion of Tzu-ch'an in the *Analects;* see 8/5/16 and 27/14/9.

29. See *Tso chuan* 387/Chao 14/4.

30. See Bodde and Morris, p. 16, n. 31; Needham, vol. 2, p. 531. While the Shu-hsiang and Confucius passages are similar inasmuch as they are both critical of the inscription of laws on the bronze ceremonial *ting,* the reasons for their objections are somewhat different. Shu-hsiang's main criticism is that penal law, once articulated and fixed, cannot cover all eventualities and can be manipulated by the unscrupulous to serve their own ends. The existence of such a code will increase litigation and turn the focus of traditional law from justice based on moral precepts to victory based on clever argumentation. Law becomes a device for the wrongdoer rather than a guarantee for the honest man.

Confucius, on the other hand, objects to the inscription of Fan Hsüan Tzu's laws on the *ting* because such an action undermines the social and political hierarchy which structures the state. It is important to note here that Confucius fears that both common people and persons of high social status will be deflected from their respective obligations by the investment of value in the tripod. Hitherto penal law and its interpretation had been the responsibility of the ruling elite; further, that the ruling class had been able to maintain its position was due to the respect that this hereditary birthright had fostered in the common people. Thus to inscribe these laws on the bronze tripods was to take the laws out of the hands of the governing class and divest them of one important claim to authority. This is tantamount to erasing the distinction between noble and base and challenging the existing social structure. This Confucius would not do.

31. Creel, *Origins of Statecraft,* p. 162, n. 8: "Both of these philosophical disquisitions [the Shu-hsiang and Confucius passages] look as if they could be scholarly additions to the text, such as certainly are present in the *Tso-chuan.* The two are remarkably similar. The latter one is put into the mouth of Confucius, where it is wholly out of place. . . . I have shown the dubious character of these two passages in detail, in a paper entitled 'Legal Institutions and Procedures During the Chou Dynasty,' to be published shortly."

32. See Tu Kuo-hsiang, pp. 127 ff.

33. See 46/6B/2: "Everyone can be a Yao or a Shun."

34. Cf. *Analects* 2/2/3.

35. Cf. 4/1A/7. See also *Analects* 41/20/2: "The Master said: 'To execute men without having instructed them is called brutality.' " And see *Hsün Tzu* 35/10/80: "Therefore, if you mete out punishments without having first instructed the people, even though your punishments are everywhere you will still be unable to bring depravity under control."

36. In the *Hsün Tzu,* the concept of penal laws is most frequently represented with the character *fa* and punishments with the character *hsing.* Of course, "penal law" is not a satisfactory rendering for all occurrences of *fa.* As we have observed above, by the end of the Warring States period, the term *li* had been inflated from its original specific meaning of ancestral rites to overlap much of the broader implications of *fa.* Although *fa* in its narrow sense had come to represent penal law, in its broader meaning it refers to a system of regulations devised for the purpose of maintaining social control—perhaps not unlike the concept of "common law." While *li* and *fa* as systems can perhaps be distinguished by the stratum of society to which they apply, the fact that both are directed at the preservation of social order suggests that they did share some common ground. Tu Kuo-hsiang, p. 128, in his discussion of *li* in the *Hsün Tzu,* goes so far as to conclude that *li* and *fa* are often used synonymously. In this discussion of Hsün Tzu's attitude toward penal law and punishments, it is the use of *fa* in the narrow and specific sense of "penal law" which is of primary concern.

37. See 20/8/24 for a passage in which Hsün Tzu defines the Way in terms of man and man alone: "This Way is not the Way of heaven or of earth. It is the Way by which the people should be led and the Way by which the consummate person leads."

38. See also 41/11/87 and 52/14/12.

39. See "The Way of the Ruler" *(Chün-tao)* passage cited above in the text. Compare this with the "Critique on the Concept of Political Purchase" *(Nanshih)* chapter of the *Han Fei Tzu* which advocates the absolute rule of law and indifference to the ruler's capacity.

40. Hsün Tzu seems to go one step beyond both Confucius and Mencius in the relative weight given the position of ruler. The overwhelming emphasis on the position of ruler almost suggests that when the ruler is incapable of achieving social order, all is lost. This focus on the position of ruler is a strong argument for placing Hsün Tzu as a source for at least some aspects of Han Fei's Legalism.

41. See the *Hsün Tzu* 89/23/53: "With respect to basic human nature, your Yao, Shun, Chieh, and Shih are all one and the same. The nature of the consummate person and the inferior person is identical."

42. See also 26/9/11.

43. Cf. *Analects* 41/20/2 and *Mencius* 4/1A/7 and 19/3A/3.

44. *Han Fei Tzu* 273:15: "Those who spare the weeds waste the grain; those who are kind to robbers injure good people. Now, to be lax in punishments and everywhere kind is to benefit the depraved at the expense of the good. This is not the way to effect proper order."

45. As, for example, in 34/10/63 and 66/18/37.

46. Because of the composite nature of the *Kuan Tzu* and the wide spectrum of philosophical positions represented from one chapter to the next, the construction of a consistent interpretation of penal law and punishment is an impossible task. Some portions of the text are definitely Legalistic in orientation (see Yang

Hung-lieh, pp. 84–87), but there is little here with respect to *fa* that is not also found in *The Book of Lord Shang*.

Hsiao Kung-ch'üan (Mote trans.), pp. 333 ff., discusses the concept of *fa* in the *Kuan Tzu*. First he assumes that the *Kuan Tzu* is earlier than *The Book of Lord Shang*. Further, he treats the *Kuan Tzu* as a homogeneous text and arrives at the not unexpected conclusion that *Kuan Tzu*'s concept of *fa* has a moral dimension whereas that of Shang Yang and Han Fei does not. While Shang Yang and Han Fei regard penal law and the authority of the ruler as the basis for political control, the *Kuan Tzu* still looks to the family system and human relations. In the *Kuan Tzu* there are perhaps passages which bear out Hsiao's conclusions, but there are also sections which describe *fa* in terms comparable to Shang Yang and Han Fei with all this implies. By treating the text as homogeneous, Hsiao mixes the more Confucian portions with the Legalist and arrives at an interpretation somewhere between the two.

47. See *Han Fei Tzu* 159:5, 167:14, and 304:4; *Huai Nan Tzu* 16/14b, 20/17b, and 21/8a. For a full collection of these passages, see Kao Heng, pp. 195 ff.

48. See Duyvendak, *The Book of Lord Shang*, pp. 141–159, especially pp. 143–145.

49. See Chang Hsin-ch'eng, pp. 769–771.

50. See the "Fixing Laws" *(Ting-fa)* chapter of the *Han Fei Tzu*.

51. The militarist associations of Shang Yang's political philosophy and those of Legalist doctrine in general cannot pass without remark. We have seen that the central concept *shih* ("strategic advantage") was probably developed as a special militarist term before being absorbed into the Legalist tradition. Again, as Rubin (pp. 77–78) observes: "It is within the army that the principles of governing through a system of rewards and punishments, later proclaimed by the Legalists as the sole method of ruling society in general, are filst worked out." In *Han Fei Tzu* 303:4, *Huai Nan Tzu* 20/17b, and *History of the Han (Han-shu)*, "Treatise on Penal Law" *(Hsing-fa chih)*, Shang Yang is discussed together with militarists such as Wu Ch'i, Sun Pin, and Sun Wu. Moreover, the *History of the Han (Han-shu)*, "Record of Literary Works" *(Yi-wen chih)*, lists Shang Yang as a militarist. In the *Hsün Tzu* 55/15/43 Shang Yang is described as "one popularly known as being adept in the use of the military."

Ch'ien Mu, pp. 227–230, insists that Shang Yang's ideas are to a great extent derived from Li K'uei and Wu Ch'i. Among those ideas which Ch'ien Mu regards as being common to the three theorists is the emphasis on *fa*. Ch'ien Mu suggests that the *Li Tzu* (10 *p'ien*) entered under the "Militarist" heading in the *History of the Han (Han-shu)* "Record of Literary Works" *(Yi-wen chih)* is probably Li K'uei—making Li K'uei, Wu Ch'i, and Shang Yang all members of a Legalist/ Militarist tradition. This theory, given the spirit of Shang Yang's political philosophy, is worth careful consideration.

Further evidence which would support an association of these theorists includes the obvious echoes in the "Methods of War" *(Chan-fa)* chapter of *The Book of Lord Shang* from the *Sun Tzu*. In *Historical Records (Shih-chi)* 65, p. 2168, when Wu Ch'i became prime minister of Ch'u in 384 B.C., his administration is described in the following Legalistic terms: "He made the laws clear and reviewed official edicts. He weeded out unnecessary offices and got rid of the system of employing these imperial relatives, using these resources to build up the armed forces." Again, in *Han Fei Tzu* 67:9, Wu Ch'i recommends that King Tao of Ch'u consolidate his authority by appropriating the powers held by privileged classes. This is very much a Shang Yang principle. The position of importance given warfare in Shang Yang's thought contributes further to this Legalist/Militarist association.

52. The first reference is to *SPTK;* the second is to Chu Shih-ch'e.

53. I follow Duyvendak, *The Book of Lord Shang,* p. 201, n. 4, in inserting the phrase "the state will have no equal."

54. See *The Book of Lord Shang* 1/2a, p. 3. Cf. *Huai Nan Tzu* 13/5b.

55. See *The Book of Lord Shang* 2/10b, p. 32.

56. Reading *hsiu* as *hsün.*

57. See *The Book of Lord Shang* 2/7b, p. 29.

58. I follow T'ao Hung-ch'ing in reading *jen chün* as *jen sheng.*

59. This aspect of Shang Yang's doctrine of *fa* has often been cited as a redeeming feature in his totalitarianism. Some scholars would go so far as to suggest that the principle of objective and universally applicable law would not only guarantee fair treatment for prince and pauper alike but would further serve to contain the discretionary powers of the ruler himself. This is neither theoretically the case nor is it borne out by historical example. First, the perspective assumed by Legalist political thought is invariably that of the ruler. The principle of universal law was posited not to curb the ruler's authority but to guarantee his political survival (see, for example, 4/10b, p. 67). Further, the notion that "laws must meet changing conditions" coupled with the position of the ruler as final arbiter of the law gives him the freedom to interpret and even alter the laws at will. Shang Yang's purpose in propounding the concept of equality before the law was not to serve popular justice; it was to serve the ruler in achieving his own ends.

As I suggested in discussing the Confucian concept of *fa,* the feudal structure of society had tended to give the higher echelons of society extralegal privileges. Shang Yang's principle of "equality before the law" seeks to increase the powers of the sovereign at the expense of these privileged classes. Far from being prompted by egalitarian sentiments, however, this principle was simply an unintentional by-product in the process of consolidating central authority.

60. While it might be argued that the death penalty for a minor infraction is the same as the death penalty for a serious crime, the Legalists would reply that death can be brought on with varying degrees of imagination. Moreover, the execution of one person is considerably kinder than the extermination of an entire family—see 4/6a (p. 61) and 4/9a–b (p. 65) for examples. For a list of common punishments employed by Shang Yang, see Bodde, *China's First Unifier,* p. 168.

61. The phrase *"ch'ing ch'i chung che"* is omitted here. See Duyvendak, *The Book of Lord Shang,* p. 258, n. 4.

62. See also 2/11a, p. 33.

63. I follow Wang Hsien-shen in reading *kao* for *szu.*

64. Ts'ao Ch'ien, pp. 24–26, outlines Han Fei's debt to Shang Yang under the following headings: (1) concept of historical progress, (2) law changing with the times, (3) rejection of the old morality, (4) nationalism, (5) policy of weakening the people, (6) antithetical tension between the interests of superior and subordinate, (7) incompatibility of public and private interests, (8) emphasis on punishments, (9) emphasis on agriculture, (10) legalism, (11) militarism, (12) informers, and (13) group responsibility. Ch'en Ch'i-t'ien, *Han Fei Tzu chiao-shih,* p. 934, insists that in spite of Han Fei's criticisms of Shang Yang, his conception of *fa* was by and large derived from the earlier theorist. Ching Chih-jen, p. 23, concurs

with Ch'en Ch'i-t'ien: "As regards the concepts of *fa* and 'rewards and punishments' *(hsing shang),* that Han Fei for the most part took them over from Shang Yang is beyond question."

65. See *The Book of Lord Shang* 2/11b, p. 34: "To have a ruler but no laws is just as injurious as having no ruler at all."

66. See *Han Fei Tzu* 300:5:

Further, the Yaos, Shuns, Chiehs, and Chous who only appear once every thousand generations are thought to come one after the other. In fact, those who govern the world are consistently of average parts. Those for whom I discuss this concept of "political purchase" are these average rulers. . . . If they preserve the law and reside in a position of political purchase, proper order prevails; if they turn their backs on law and abandon their political purchase, disorder will set in.

67. See *Han Fei Tzu* 368:1: "The most perspicacious in administering the laws rely on legal measures rather than people."

68. Note that Hsün Tzu does represent a special case and cannot be grouped with Confucius and Mencius without qualification.

69. For example, consider this passage (9/2b): "Solitarily he preserves what is genuine, embraces virtue, and promotes sincerity. And the world follows him just as the echo responds to the sound and the shadow to the form. This is because he cultivates the root. Punishments and penalties are inadequate to change social custom; executions are inadequate to put an end to wickedness." Now consider this passage (9/13b): "It is not the case that what is called a 'doomed state' has no ruler, but that it has no laws."

On first reading these two passages seem very much at odds, but when they are understood in light of the "decline theory" of history (see Chapter 1) as two levels of government—one in antiquity's golden age and one that is practicable in modern times—the text appears to be more consistent.

70. Compare this with *Huai Nan Tzu* 20/8b: "In the proper government of one's person, the first priority goes to the cultivation of the spirit and only next to the cultivation of the physical form. In the proper government of the nation, the first priority goes to the cultivation of the people's transformation and only next to the rectification of laws."

71. For the association between godlike power and the capacity to effect change, see *Mencius* 51/7A/13 (this same phrase is repeated in *Hsün Tzu* 57/15/102 and 110/32/32), *Hsün Tzu* 1/1/5 and 7/3/27, and *I-ching* 45/*Hsi* B/2. Most of these examples attribute a magical power to the sage-rulers of old. That the transformation is often characterized as inscrutable is demonstrated in *Mencius* 57/7B/25 and *Hsün Tzu* 95/26/17.

72. See especially chaps. 1, 2, 10, and 20.

73. See Sections 2 and 3 of the accompanying translation.

74. The influence of Shen Nung's spiritual strength is not limited to the human world but pervades the cosmos, guaranteeing regular seasons and bountiful crops. This notion of mutual influence between the spheres of man and nature is a characteristic element of Western Han thought. See also the anecdote about King T'ang of Yin in 9/4a.

75. See notes 30 and 33 to the translation.

76. See the notes to Section 3 in the accompanying translation of this treatise for examples of these allusions.

77. For example: "spiritual essence" *(chih ching)* can be found in the *Chuang Tzu* 42/17/20 and 58/22/18; "unspoken teaching" *(pu yen chih chiao)* in *Lao Tzu* 2, 43, 73 and *Chuang Tzu* 12/5/2 and 57/22/7.

78. For example: Hsiung Yi Liao and Sun Shu-ao (9/2b–3a) can be found in the *"Hsü-wu-kuei"* chapter of the *Chuang Tzu;* Ch'ü Po-yü (9/3a) is mentioned in "The Human World" *(Jen-chien-shih)* chapter of the same text. See the notes on Section 3 of the translation.

79. For example, see Chapter 2.

80. See *Han Fei Tzu* 355:2: "The sage in governing the state does not depend on the people's doing what is good of their own accord, but rather makes certain that they have no chance to do wrong. . . . Therefore he attends to the laws rather than to virtue."

Ch'en Ch'i-t'ien, *Han Fei Tzu chiao-shih,* p. 17, n. 7, suggests that "depending on the people's doing good of their own accord" is a reference to the Confucian principle of "transformation through virtue" *(te hua).* There is a second passage in *Han Fei Tzu* 70:12 which has a similar purport: "Looking at it from this perspective, the sage in governing the state is certain to operate on the principle of giving his people no choice but to act on his behalf rather than relying on them to act out of love for him. To expect people to act out of their love for him is dangerous; to rely on their doing what they have no other choice but to do is safe indeed." *The Book of Lord Shang,* 4/11a, p. 67, also has a similar passage: "What is meant by perspicacity is that nothing escapes him, so that the various ministers do not risk treachery and the people do not dare to do wrong. For this reason the ruler can recline on his couch and listen to his music, yet the empire is properly ordered."

81. The fixing of measurements was always considered to be an important responsibility of the ruling authority. See, for example, *Analects* 41/20/1: "He was scrupulous about weights and measures and examined standards and measurements with care."

82. This is the general meaning, but the text is problematic.

83. Cf. *Lü-shih ch'un-ch'iu* 4/10b: "The reason for the ruler's being enthroned arises out of the people. For him to disregard the people after he has been enthroned is for him to gain the branches while losing sight of the root."

84. Because of reservations about the final portion of this chapter—it is quite possibly a later accretion—I have tried to avoid basing any crucial aspect of the analysis on this section of the text alone. Here I cite this passage as only a supporting example.

85. There is no contradiction in asserting that the ruler uses law to control his subordinates and, at the same time, that the ultimate source and authority for law is the public will. While the laws must be responsive and answerable to the human condition, on a practical level they are nevertheless formulated, articulated, promulgated, and enforced by the ruling power.

CHAPTER 5

1. Miyamoto, p. 9, refers to this concept as *chi-li chung-chih;* Hu Shih in *Huai Nan Wang shu,* p. 71, calls it *chung-chih chung-li;* Hsü Fu-kuan, p. 142, following the *Lü-shih ch'un-ch'iu,* calls it *yung chung.*

2. This notion of *yung chung* also occurs in the *Kuan Tzu,* but its occurrences

are restricted to the "Commentary on Shape and Circumstances" *(Hsing shih chieh)* chapter which Chang Hsin-ch'eng, p. 763, suggests is relatively late and which Rickett, p. 121, concludes was written subsequent to the *Huai Nan Tzu*—probably the first century B.C. Again the two main passages in this chapter which discuss this concept of *yung chung* (3:36-6 and 3:42-3) have *sheng jen* for *chung jen* in most texts, although most commentators insist that *sheng* is a misreading of *chung*. See Rickett, p. 148, n. 120, for a discussion of this chapter.

3. Apart from the occurrences of *yung chung* found in the *Han Fei Tzu* and *Kuan Tzu,* this expression is also used as a section heading in the *Lü-shih ch'un-ch'iu*. This concept of *yung chung* must be distinguished from the *yung jen* theme —*yung shih* in *Lü-shih ch'un-ch'iu*—which also has some prominence in these early texts. This notion of *yung jen* refers to the effective employment of individual ministers and, in the Legalist tradition, involves certain principles: accommodating a man's abilities in assigning him office; appointing a man to a specifically defined office and making him responsible for the performance of carefully detailed duties; promoting and demoting officials on the basis of their success in carrying out prescribed duties; taking into account practical experience in the appointment of officials. See the "Effective Use of Personnel" *(Yung jen)* chapter of the *Han Fei Tzu* and the "Effective Use of People" *(Yung min)* chapter of the *Lü-shih ch'un-ch'iu.*

4. See Hsiao Kung-ch'üan (Mote trans.), pp. 559 ff.

5. In the "Critique on the Concept of Political Purchase" *(Nan shih)* chapter of *Han Fei Tzu* (300:5), for example, the point is made that since sages are few and far between, political expedience demands a theory of government operational under at least the average ruler.

6. This passage also occurs in *Han Fei Tzu* 250:8, but most of the major commentaries are agreed that this is an erroneous interpolation. See Liang Ch'i-hsiung, *Han Tzu chien-chieh,* vol. 2, p. 332.

7. I base this observation on several factors. First, there is a pool of mythohistorical figures from which these texts draw in order to illustrate the inefficacious nature of individual talents. This pool includes Wu Huo (*LSCC* 4/10b; *HFT* 146:6; *HNT* 9/7b); Meng Pen (*LSCC* 4/10; *HFT* 146:6); Yao/Shun (*LSCC* 4/10b; *HFT* 146:6); Li Lou (*LSCC* 4/10b; *HFT* 146:6); Chieh (*LSCC* 4/10b; *HNT* 9/5a). Second, there is recurring reference to a distinction between "intelligence" *(chih)* and "strength" *(li)*: *Shen Tzu* 8a; *Han Fei Tzu* 331:9, 146:6, and *Huai Nan Tzu* 9/5b, 7b, 8a, 12a–b. And third, there are several parallel passages. Consider, for example, *Shen Tzu* 8a, *Han Fei Tzu* 305:15, and *Huai Nan Tzu* 9/12a. Then compare *Han Fei Tzu* 287:14 and *Huai Nan Tzu* 9/5a–b. While these texts may share a common source for their respective discussions of *yung chung,* they differ considerably in the relative weight given this concept in their political philosophies.

8. Cf. *Han Fei Tzu* 288:1.

9. This principle of the unique and equal value of all things is an extension of Taoist relativism. See, for example, *Chuang Tzu* 2/1/34 and 6/2/67. The "Utilizing the People" *(Yung chung)* chapter of the *Lü-shih ch'un-ch'iu* supports its concept of using the collective strength of the people by suggesting that everyone has their strengths and weaknesses: "All things certainly have their strong points and their shortcomings. Man is the same. . . . Even Chieh and Chou had characteristics worth revering and adopting—how much more so the man of superior character!"

This notion of each thing having its particular strengths and weaknesses is Confucian rather than Taoist, however, inasmuch as it assumes a standard of excellence. The strengths and weaknesses of a ruler, for example, exist relative to a preconceived notion of what a ruler should be. When you turn to *The Art of Rulership,* this notion of strengths and weaknesses is replaced by an assertion that since the concepts of quality and value are relative to a given purpose, there really is no way of comparing things qualitatively. Thus, rather than suggesting that things have strong points and shortcomings, it simply contends that all things are different and hence, in terms of quality and value, incommensurable.

10. See similar passages in *Chuang Tzu* 29/12/17 and in *Huai Nan Tzu* 9/8a. See also *Lao Tzu* 27:

Hence the sage is always adept at turning others to account,
And therefore is without inefficacious people;
He is always adept at turning things to account,
And therefore is without worthless things.
This is called "in accord with natural perspicacity."

11. The concept of ruling the people by accommodating the development of their natures is not an attitude new to the *Huai Nan Tzu.* Rather, it is a succinct characterization of Taoist political philosophy. In effecting proper order in the human world, this attitude demands acknowledgment of the natural condition (*Chuang Tzu* 32/12/72):

Sagely government? This is for the ruler in deciding on his appointments to make no mistakes about talent. It is being fully abreast of affairs and accommodating the activities of the people. His words and actions are for his own sake, yet the world is transformed. With the wave of his hand or the nod of his head, the people from every direction will all come rushing to him. This is what is called "sagely government."

12. Hsiao Kung-ch'üan (Mote trans.), pp. 563–564.

13. Ibid., pp. 559 ff.

CHAPTER 6

1. An example of this usage appears in *Mo Tzu* 22/15/1: "The reason for a benevolent man's doing something must be to foster the benefit of the world and do away with its ills. This is why he undertakes things."

2. At times *li* is also contrasted with *shan* ("good, goodness"). See *Mencius* 53/7A/25. While *li* and *yi* do not usually constitute a rhyme, Lo Ch'ang-p'ei, p. 161, does cite one Eastern Han example.

3. Reading *sheng* as *hsing.*

4. See also *The Book of Lord Shang* 2/4a, pp. 26–28, and 3/4a-b, p. 39.

5. Although this last phrase appears to be corrupt, this would seem to be the meaning.

6. See *The Book of Lord Shang* 4/9a-b, p. 65, for an example of this attitude.

7. That this section by itself could be construed as describing Confucian theory is borne out by a similar idea and metaphor found in *Mencius* 27/4A/10:

Those who lose the people lose their hearts. There is a Way of winning the empire: to win over the people is to win the empire. There is a Way of winning over the people: to win their hearts is to win the people. There is a Way of winning their hearts: simply accumulate that which the people desire on their behalf and refrain from giving them what they dislike. The people

flocking to the benevolent is like water rushing downhill or wild animals scampering into the bush.
For similar passages, see *Hsün Tzu* 45/12/32 and 57/15/102.

8. See, for example, *Han Fei Tzu* 72:9:
It is in fact the sage who examines the realities of right and wrong and investigates the basic nature of chaos and proper order. Thus, in governing the state properly, he rectifies clearly articulated laws and implements severe punishments in order to save sentient beings from chaos, to rid the world of its calamities, to prevent the strong from outraging the weak and the many from riding roughshod over the few, to allow the aged to see out their years and the young and orphaned to reach maturity, to ensure that the borderlands are not invaded, that ruler and minister are intimate, that father and son look out for each other, and that all escape the disasters of death on the battlefield and capture by the enemy. This then is the highest degree of accomplishment, and yet stupid people do not understand it as such, and regard it as tyranny.
See also *The Book of Lord Shang* 1/12a–b, pp. 17–18, and 2/11a, p. 33.

9. A similar passage is cited in *Mencius* 36/5A/5. When juxtaposed with the concept of "Heaven's Mandate" *(T'ien ming)*, this statement means that the king's rule is in fact a mandate from his people.

10. Cf. *Tso chuan*, 334/Hsing 31/4 and 339/Chao 1/2, and *Discourses of the States (Kuo-yü)* 1679 and 11638.

11. See also *Analects* 23/12/7.

12. See also *Mencius* 19/3A/64 and 27/4A/10.

13. See a similar passage in *Hsün Tzu* 107/31/30.

14. See also *Mencius* 12/2A/5, *Hsün Tzu* 65/18/22 and 75/19/109, *Great Learning (Ta-hsüeh)* 9.

15. Ode 172.

16. See also *Mo Tzu* 12/9/66, 22/15/1, 33/19/62, 53/31/107, 62/37/44.

17. For further discussion of Tung Chung-shu see the chapter in *Hsü Fu-kuan*. The first passage here can be used to illustrate what I suspect to be a strong *Hsün Tzu* influence on Tung Chung-shu. Compare, for example, the passages in *Hsün Tzu* 29/9/75 and 46/12/43.

18. For passages with a similar theme, see also 7/7b, 10/9b, 15/4a, and 19/2a.

19. The Confucian texts too extol moderation. See, for example, the *Analects* 1/1/5: "The Master said: 'In governing a thousand-chariot state, the ruler must be earnest in his affairs and have the confidence of the people. He must be frugal in expenditures and love his people and conscript them only at the appropriate times.' " See also *Analects* 23/12/8 and *Mencius* 19/3A/3 and 52/7A/23. Frugality is of course also a central tenet of the Mohist doctrine—the "Regulating Expenditures" *(Chieh-yung)* chapter is devoted to this one theme. Moreover, the condemnation of music and elaborate funerals is based primarily on this principle of governmental thrift.

20. Compare *Mencius* 2/1A/4 to this 9/10b and the following 9/11a passage. King Hui of Liang is condemned for his thoughtless extravagance—"allowing animals to devour men." The ruler can only enjoy his luxury when it is willingly sponsored by his people (*Mencius* 1/1A/2).

21. See also 9/2a.

22. Compare *Shuo yüan* 20/5a, which contains a passage attributed to *Mo Tzu* that may have come from the lost "Regulating Expenditures" *(Chieh-yung)* chapter: "Therefore, in food we must make sure that everyone has sufficient before

worrying about delicacies; in clothing we must make sure that everyone is warm before worrying about fashion; in shelter we must make sure that everyone is comfortable before worrying about pleasure. What can be regarded as the important principle of conduct here is that the essentials must take priority over luxuries."

23. Compare *Mencius* 5/1B/1:

Let me explain to you about pleasure. Now say that Your Majesty had a musical performance here. If the common people on hearing the sound of your bells and drums and the tune of your pipes and flutes, with aching hearts and furrowed brows, all said to each other: "Since our king is fond of music, how can he push us into these dire straits? Fathers and sons do not see each other; brothers, wives, and children are separated and scattered."
. . . This is precisely because you do not share your pleasure with the people.

Now say again that Your Majesty had a musical performance here. If the common people on hearing the sound of your bells and drums and the tune of your pipes and flutes, with bright eyes and happy faces, all said to each other: "Our king must be free of illness, or how could he have a musical performance?" . . . This is precisely because you share your pleasure with the people.

Now were Your Majesty to share your pleasure with your people, you would be a True King.

To appreciate this passage, the reader should be aware of the homographic relationship between "pleasure" *(lo)* and "music" *(yüeh)*. Moreover, one does well to bear in mind the traditional Chinese understanding of the virtue of music. Music was regarded as more than entertainment. It was thought to be an effective means of synchronizing, harmonizing, and reconciling the various social relationships. Its function was to bring together. In this passage from the *Mencius,* the notion of the ruler enjoying music while the families of his people are being separated and scattered does more than spotlight the ruler's lack of concern for his people. It underscores his inability to grasp the essential purpose of music. See also *Mencius* 1/1A/2.

24. This same concern over an equitable system of taxation which will take into account the condition of the harvest is an important theme in the *Mencius* (18/3A/3):

Lung Tzu said: "In administering the land, nothing is better than the *chu* system and nothing is worse than the *kung* system." The *kung* system is calculating the average yield over a period of several years as the basis of a set tax. Now, in a bumper year when the fields are full of grain and a considerable amount could be exacted without being considered oppressive, the government takes only a small portion. In a bad year when there is not even enough to fertilize the fields, they insist on the full measure. If the one who should be father and mother to his people makes them scowl with anger because after having toiled bitterly for a full year they cannot get enough to care for their parents and have to go out and borrow in order to make up the difference, if he causes the old and young to be left abandoned in the gutters, how can he be said to be father and mother to his people?

See also *Mencius* 12/2A/5.

25. Cf. *Analects* 25/13/9: "Jan Yu said: 'When the people are numerous, what else can be done for them?' The Master replied: 'Make them prosperous.' " See also *Mencius* 2/1A/7, 6/1B/4, and 52/7A/23.

26. Cf. *Mencius* 19/3A/3: "Therefore a ruler of superior character must be respectful and frugal, genteel and modest, and must take from his people only within limits."

27. This attitude of conservation is reminiscent of *Mencius* 1/1A/3:

If you do not interrupt the important agricultural periods, grain will be more than can be eaten. If fine nets are prohibited from fish pools and ponds, fish and turtles will be more than can be eaten. If hatchets and axes are only permitted in the hill forests at given seasons, there will be more lumber than can be used. If the grains, fish, and turtles are more than can be eaten and the lumber is more than can be used, the people can care for the living and bury the dead without remorse. And caring for the living and burying the dead without remorse is the beginning of the Kingly Way.

THE ART OF RULERSHIP

1. This first section appears as a block in the *Ch'ün-shu chih-yao* 41/3b–4a. In *Wen Tzu* B/12a–b this entire section appears together with a portion of Section 2 below.

2. I follow the Kao Yu commentary, which states that some texts read *chien* as *mou*. The character *mou* rhymes with *ts'u*. With respect to this entire passage, compare the *Shen Tzu* cited in the TPYL 76, p. 358 (Thompson, p. 294) and also *Ch'un-ch'iu fan-lu* 6/5b–6a.

3. Compare *Chia t'ai-fu hsin-shu* A/83a and *Ta Tai li-chi* 3/4b, which have the same passage.

4. Cf. *Ta Tai li-chi* 5/5a.

5. Reading *hsi nu* as *nu hsi* for the *hsi* rhyme.

6. Cf. *Huai Nan Tzu* 10/5b; *Han Fei Tzu* 17:16 and 30:14; *Huang-ti ssu-ching*, p. 31; and *Shih Tzu* A/6a.

7. Cf. *Ta Tai li-chi* 8/4a and *Yen Tzu ch'un-ch'iu* 7/11b.

8. See *Lao Tzu* 47 for similar purport.

9. I follow Wang Nien-sun. See *Lao Tzu* 63 and 64 for similar purport.

10. Compare the beginning of *Chuang Tzu* (chap. 11) and *Lao Tzu* 29.

11. This section is contained in *Wen Tzu* A/12a–b and A/10b–11a.

12. Cf. *Record of Rites (Li-chi)* 11/27, 7/1a, and 7/1b.

13. I follow *Wen Tzu* B/12a. See Wang Nien-sun's commentary in LWT 9/2a.

14. I follow Kao Heng's discussion on the *Lao Tzu* in *Lao Tzu cheng-ku*, pp. 51–52.

15. I follow *Wen Tzu* B/12a.

16. Shen Nung is a legendary ruler who, according to tradition, reigned from 2838 to 2698 B.C. He is particularly remembered as the sage who developed and taught husbandry. He is also the father of Chinese medicine, having devoted himself to the study of herbs and their properties.

17. Cf. *Ta Tai li-chi* 1/3a and *K'ung Tzu chia-yü* 1/9b.

18. The Ming T'ang was a sacred structure visited by the emperor in carrying out various sacrifices linked to the calendar. For lengthy (yet not altogether accurate) discussions on the Ming T'ang institution, see Granet, pp. 177 ff., and Soothill, passim.

19. I follow Yang Shu-ta, p. 56. This passage is probably an interpolation.

20. Cf. *Hsün Tzu* 57/15/90 and 102/28/20.

21. This passage occurs either in part or in whole in the following texts: *Ta Tai li-chi* 7/2a; *Shuo yüan* 19/12a–b; *Mo Tzu* 35/21/6; *Shih Tzu* B/4b; *Lü-shih ch'un ch'iu* 22/8b–9a; *Chia t'ai-fu hsin-shu* B/56b; *Huai Nan Tzu* 19/1b. Yu-tu, T'ang-ku, and San-wei are also mentioned in *Huai Nan Tzu* 4/4b and 4/8b.

22. This section is found in *Wen Tzu* A/10b–11a and A/11a–b.

23. Cf. *Teng Hsi Tzu* 2b–3a, *Chuang Tzu* 11/4/60, and *Lieh Tzu* 2/4b.

24. This passage is reminiscent of *Lao Tzu* 57.

25. Cf. *Chuang Tzu* 14/5/42 and 55/21/17; *Lao Tzu* 47.

26. Cf. *Chuang Tzu* 28/11/64 and *Huang-ti ssu-ching* p. 20.

27. The expression *chih ching* is a special term in this treatise connoting a powerful though intangible inner potency which, when concentrated and retained intact, can be directed at others to influence their activities and effect their transformation. It also occurs in *Chuang Tzu* 58/22/18 and in *I-ching* 43/Hsia/9. The notion of inner potency finds many shapes in the Chinese tradition—note, for example, the currency of the concept *te* in most of the important schools of Chinese thought. This aspect of Chinese philosophy seems to have received particular attention in the early Han in its association with the concept of "the mutual influence of human and nature" *(t'ien jen hsiang ying)*. We can find reference to *chih ching* (and other such expressions used to represent "inner potency") throughout the *Huai Nan Tzu*—for example, 6/1a, 6/1b, 6/2a, 6/2b, and 7/1a. In the 20/2b–3a passage, it describes an analogous relationship between "fertilization" as an invisible influence and the sage with his "superlative sincerity" *(chih ch'eng)* transforming the people. In 20/8b–9a it contains an extended discussion on how the most efficacious method of influencing and transforming the people is through the "essential vapors."

28. Cf. *Record of Rites (Li-chi)* 42/2.

29. Cf. *Teng Hsi Tzu* 6a.

30. These historical figures and their circumstances appear also in other early texts. In *Tso chuan* 493/Ai 16/3 (479 B.C.) there is an account of a rebellion in Ch'u staged by Po Kung, son of the late heir to the Ch'u throne, Chien. In plotting the rebellion, he said to a fellow conspirator, Shih Ch'i, that five hundred men would be sufficient to effect their coup. In response to Shih Ch'i's reservations about raising this body of men, Po Kung replied that Hsiung Yi Liao, a fearless officer, was alone worth any five hundred men. They approached Yi Liao and tried to win him to their cause. When he refused their promises of wealth, they held a blade to his throat. Still he would not budge. Convinced that he would not reveal their plot for personal gain, they released him. In the subsequent insurrection Po Kung killed the two high ministers, Tzu Hsi and Tzu Ch'i, and took King Hui of Ch'u captive. In the end, the rebellion was suppressed.

In the *Chuang Tzu* (apart from the 67/24/65 passage from which the *Huai Nan Tzu* passage seems to be taken), Hsiung Yi Liao also appears as an advisor to Duke Ai of Lu (51/20/9 ff.). Although Duke Ai observes basically Confucian virtues and values, he has difficulty avoiding calamity. Yi Liao advises him to abandon conventional values and adopt the Taoist attitude toward life.

The "two families" refer to the two conflicting branches of the Ch'u royal house; "toying with pellets" represents Yi Liao's disregard for his own safety in remaining aloof from the warring factions of the royal family.

Sun-shu Ao appears in the *Historical Records (Shih-chi)* 119, pp. 3099 ff., as a prime minister under King Chuang of Ch'u. Sun-shu Ao's government is so effective that he can prevent wrongdoing without invoking punishment. In a short period he was able to rid the state of corrupt officials and robbers and to provide the people with an environment of sufficiency and contentment.

These two figures represent men who were able to succeed through nonaction. The methodology of this approach is described in the *Historical Records (Shih-chi)* 119, p. 3100. The allusion in this *Huai Nan Tzu* passage is perhaps based on *Chuang Tzu* 67/24/65.

31. The character *hai* here is an error for *jung*. See *Lao Tzu* 50.

32. Similar expressions occur in *Teng Hsi Tzu* 6a and in *The Book of Lord Shang (Shang-chün shu)* 5/8b.

33. Ch'ü Po-yü appears in *Chuang Tzu* 10/4/54. He is a minister of Wei who, when consulted about how to teach a crown prince lacking in virtuous qualities, emphasizes the dangers involved. To be virtuous and parade one's own talents before him is perilous; to follow him in untoward activities is a course equally fraught with danger. In this passage he is a wise Taoist-oriented counselor who offers advice similar to that given Yen Hui by Confucius at the beginning of this "Human World" *(Jen-chien-shih)* chapter. He appears frequently in early literature as a wise and particularly introspective minister (*Analects* 29/14/25; *Huai Nan Tzu* 20/9b–10a). In *Chuang Tzu* 71/25/51 he is spurned for this introspection. In sixty years whatever he has called right he has then had to change and call wrong. He does not have the scope just to leave things alone and refrain from projecting value judgments on them.

34. Cf. *Lü-shih ch'un-ch'iu* 20/11a and *Shuo yüan* 12/17a.

35. Kao Yao is traditionally identified as the minister of justice and associated with the institution of punishments under the sage-ruler Shun. The "Kao Yao Mo" chapter of the *Shang-shu* is partially devoted to him. See also *Tso chuan* 387/14/4 and *Shih-ching* 79/299/5.

36. Shih K'uang was a music master of Chin who lived during the sixth century B.C. Throughout Chinese literature he appears time and again epitomizing musical skill and auditory sensitivity. See, for example, *Tso chuan* 287/Hsiang 18/4; *Hsün Tzu* 101/27/129; *Han Fei Tzu* 40:6; *Chuang Tzu* 5/ 2/44, 21/8/5 and 28, 24/10/28. (In this last passage it mentions his blindness.)

37. Ts'ui Chu was a minister of Duke Chuang of Ch'i in the sixth century B.C. who in 548 B.C. arranged the assassination of his ruler after having provided his own home as a rendezvous for the ruler's indelicate encounters. He then put Duke Ching on the throne and became prime minister himself. Later he was put to death for his regicide and his body was exposed in the marketplace. See *Ch'un-ch'iu* 304/Hsiang 25/1, 2 and *Tso chuan* 305/ Hsiang 25/2.

38. King Ch'ing Hsiang reigned in Ch'u from 298 to 263 B.C. See *Historical Records (Shih-chi)* 40, pp. 1728 ff. There is no mention in the *Historical Records* of his fondness for women or of this man, Chao Ch'i. The Kao Yu commentary identifies Chao Ch'i as a minister of Ch'u. There is a Chao Tzu

who does figure into the record of both King Ch'ing Hsiang and his father, King Huai, but this is Chao Sui. In the *Historical Records* account of this period, Chao Tzu's basic advice is to form alliances with other states against Ch'in. By following this advice Ch'u is constantly plagued by Ch'in incursions and suffers repeated military defeats at the hands of Ch'in. See *Historical Records* 40, pp. 1726 ff. Perhaps the allusion here is to this Chao Sui written as Chao Ch'i in error.

39. Cf. *Meng Tzu* 10/2A/1.

40. For a more thorough account of Confucius' encounter with the hermit Jung Ch'i-ch'i on Mount T'ai, see *Lieh Tzu* 1/4b and a similar passage in *K'ung Tzu chia-yü* 4/7a–b.

41. For this story of Tsou Chi, see *Historical Records (Shih-chi)* 74, p. 2344. For a more detailed account, see *Historical Records (Shih-chi)* 46, p. 1889. According to Ch'ien Mu, this event occurred in the first year of King Wei (357 B.C.).

42. The notions of "sincerity" *(ch'eng)* and "sincerity of mind" *(ch'eng-hsin)* are elaborated upon in *Huai Nan Tzu* 20/3a–b:

Thus, for the sage in nurturing his mind, nothing is as good as sincerity. And attaining the highest sincerity, he can influence and transform other things. . . . When a sage-ruler is on the throne, expansively formless and serenely silent, his bureaucracy seems to have no occupation and his court seems vacant. There are no recluses and hermits, no corvée labor and unjust punishments. Everyone in the world looks up to his virtue and imitates his principles, and the barbarian nations transmitting word of him from one state to the next all come to pay tribute. It is not a case of going from door to door and convincing one household after another; simply by extending his sincere mind, its influence spreads throughout the world. . . . That an arrow can be shot a long distance or can penetrate a hard object is due to the strength of the crossbow, but that it can hit the target or split a small object is accountable to a precise mind. To reward the good and to punish acts of violence is the function of official edicts, but that these edicts can be implemented is accountable to pure sincerity. Hence, even though the crossbow is strong, unassisted it cannot hit the target; even though the edicts are enlightened, unassisted they cannot be implemented. There must be something imparted to them from out of the essential vapors which enables them to extend the Way. Thus, if extending the Way everywhere to the people, the people fail to follow it, it is because the sincere mind has not reached out to them.

43. A full account of this story is found in *Lü-shih ch'un-ch'iu* 19/20a–b. This account is repeated almost verbatim in *Huai Nan Tzu* 12/5b–6a with Ning Yüeh in place of Ning Ch'i. References to this story are also to be found in *Yen Tzu ch'un-ch'iu* 4/30b; *Historical Records (Shih-chi)* 83, p. 2473; *Ch'u-tz'u* 1/40a. Ning Ch'i wanted to serve in the government of Duke Huan of Ch'i, but being lowly and poor he had no way of gaining audience. After traveling to Ch'i as a merchant, Ning Ch'i found an opportunity to sing as the duke passed by his cart. The duke was so moved by his song that he interviewed him and gave him a post in his administration.

44. There is a similar passage in *Lü-shih ch'un-ch'iu* 6/6b.

45. King Wen (1231–1135 B.C.) was the father of King Wu, first ruler of the Chou. Also known as Hsi Po, he ruled over the territory of Ch'i. He constantly remonstrated against the excesses of Chou, last ruler of the Shang, and was impri-

soned for two years because of it. According to legend, he was a man of such quality and character that the military conquest of Shang by his son was almost unnecessary. He had already won the allegiance of the people with his personal virtue.

46. There are similar passages in *Han-shih wai-chuan* 5/6a–b and *K'ung Tzu chia-yü* 8/6a. By playing a piece of music, Confucius could infer who wrote it—such was the extent of his sagacity.

47. This passage is perhaps an allusion to *Tso chuan* 328/Hsiang 29/8. The Duke of Wu, Chi Cha, pays a state visit to Lu and asks to hear the music of Chou. After watching a series of performances of music from each place and era, he makes his comments. Yen Ling was a city of Wu in which Chi Cha had been enfeoffed. Elsewhere in the *Huai Nan Tzu* 7/9a, it says of Chi Cha: "When Chi Cha of Yen Ling would not accept the throne of Wu, those who contended over border lands were ashamed."

48. References to this drought can be found throughout the corpus of early Chinese literature. See, for example, *Kuan Tzu* 3:73-11; *Chuang Tzu* 45/17/73; *Hsün Tzu* 36/10/102; *Lun-heng* 15/10a, 11a, 16b, 17/14a, 15b; 18/8b, 20/3b, 27/3b; *Mo Tzu* 5/15/18; *Shuo yüan* 1/15b; *Lü-shih ch'un-ch'iu* 15/2a. Tradition has it that T'ang reigned from 1766 to 1753 B.C. as the founder of the Shang dynasty. He overthrew the notorious Chieh at Ming-t'iao. The severe drought and consequent famine lingered over China for seven years, and the suffering of the people is described throughout early Chinese literature. It is also recorded that T'ang did everything within his power to alleviate this suffering and stands in literature as a paragon of selflessness.

49. Compare the *Wen Tzu* parallel here.

50. There is something obviously wrong with the *Huai Nan Tzu* version of this passage. The *Wen Tzu* echo has a variant reading in which the characters *wang* and *ming* would have a similar pronunciation in Han times, rhyming except for the tones. This translation reflects a tentative emendation.

51. *The Book of Lord Shang (Shang-chün shu)* advocates a similar principle in 4/10b.

52. This section is found as a block in *Wen Tzu* B/19b. The second part of it is also found in *Teng Hsi Tzu* 5b–6a.

53. Cf. *Kuan Tzu* 1:47-9.

54. Cf. *Teng Hsi Tzu* 5b.

55. Cf. *Teng Hsi Tzu* 6a. The last few phrases are perhaps based on *Chuang Tzu* 89/32/38.

56. Allusions to the legend of this famous sword appear throughout the early texts. According to *Wu Yüeh ch'un ch'iu* 4/20a–b, Kan Chiang was commissioned by King Ho Lü of Wu to forge two swords. Mo-yeh was the name of Kan Chiang's wife. When he attempted to cast the swords, the gold and iron would not fuse. Mo-yeh then cut her hair and clipped her nails and threw them into the furnace. The metals then commingled, and Kan Chiang fashioned swords from it. The *yang* sword he called Kan Chiang and the *yin* sword he called Mo-yeh. Kan Chiang then hid the Kan Chiang sword and presented the Mo-yeh sword to King Ho Lü.

This legend occurs with considerable variance in the *Sou-shen chi* 11/1b–2b (fourth century A.D.). On the basis of this tradition, the sharpness of the Mo-yeh sword has become legendary.

57. This passage is perhaps based on *Chuang Tzu* 63/23/51.

58. I follow the *Teng Hsi Tzu* 6a passage here.
59. Most of this section is contained in two blocks of *Wen Tzu* B/20a and B/11a–12a.
60. For T'ang see note 48 above. King Wu (1169–1116 B.C.) was the first ruler of the Chou. He rose up in rebellion against the oppressive tyranny of Chou, last ruler of the Shang. Because of the compelling circumstances, his conquest of China has always been interpreted as liberation rather than usurpation. Having conquered the empire, he disbanded his army and established a feudal system in China, dividing the territory into eighteen large states and seventy-two smaller ones. He ennobled the military and civil supporters who had been responsible for placing him on the throne.
61. I follow Wang Nien-sun in his emendation.
62. Yi Yin was the most prominent of T'ang's good counselors. As the *Mo Tzu* (9/8/22 and 13/10/23) relates the story, he was raised up from the position of servant and cook to become prime minister. *Mencius* 37/5A/7 rejects this account, contending that Yi Yin was a landholder known for his virtue and that T'ang had to ask him three times to become his prime minister. He also appears in *Lü-shih ch'un-ch'iu* 14/4b which begins with the story of his miraculous birth. Yi Yin recurs throughout early Chinese literature as an exemplary sage-minister.
63. The *t'ao-t'u* in this passage is a wild horse of the north. *Yüan*, according to the Hsü Shen commentary cited in the *Ch'ün-shu chih-yao* 41/4b, is the name of a state which was southwest of Yi-chou (an ancient province in what is now Szechwan) and which produced fine horses. The LWT text has *ch'i-yüan-ma* here, treating *yüan* as the name of this state. The *Ch'ün-shu chih-yao* has *ch'i-yüan-ma*.
64. I follow *Wen Tzu* B/20a in reading *yüan* for *ta*.
65. Compare the *Ch'ün-shu chih-yao* 41/4b–5a version of this passage.
66. Chieh, last ruler of the Hsia, appears throughout early Chinese literature as the model miscreant. Not only does his unbounded extravagance bring great suffering to his people, but, even more villainous, he derives sadistic pleasure from this suffering. The story of T'ang's distress at Chieh's conduct and the progress of his insurrection is described in *Lü-shih ch'un-ch'iu* 15/1b. In this account, before crossing swords with T'ang, Chieh flees. He is intercepted at Ta-sha where T'ang has him dismembered. A second account—indeed, the most popular—has Nan-ch'ao as the place where Chieh dies (see, for example, *Lü-shih ch'un-ch'iu* 8/5a). In *The Art of Rulership*, the decisive battle occurs at Ming-t'iao and Chieh is captured at Chiao-men. The Kao Yu commentary states that some texts have *ch'ao* for *chiao*, and the fact that they probably constituted a rhyme does suggest that they refer to one and the same place. *Hsün Tzu* 56/15/76 and *Policies of the Warring States (Chan-kuo ts'e)* 30/446/4a are similar to *The Art of Rulership* account in locating the battle at Ming-t'iao. *Huai Nan Tzu* 13/10a also states that T'ang captured Chieh at Chiao-men. For a thorough discussion of the location of this battle and the subsequent events, see B. Karlgren, "Legends and Cults," pp. 333 ff.
67. Cf. *Han Fei Tzu* 288:1.
68. Cf. *Shuo yüan* 16/9b.
69. Although the meaning of the expression *chüeh-liang* here is unclear, the general intent of the passage is not in doubt.
70. These are two of the eight fine horses of King Mu of Chou.
71. I follow Wang Yin-chih (LWT 9/8a–b) and *Chuang Tzu* 43/17/37.

72. Cf. *Chuang Tzu* 43/17/36 and *The Book of Lord Shang (Shang-chün shu)* 4/12a, p. 68.

73. I follow Yang Shu-ta, p. 58, and the *Wen Tzu* echo here.

74. Cf. Thompson, fragment 17 (p. 238).

75. I follow the *Wen Tzu* echo.

76. The *ling* star rules over husbandry.

77. I follow Wang Nien-sun, LWT 9/9a, in his reading of this phrase.

78. Cf. *Han Fei Tzu* 285:15.

79. Cf. *Lao Tzu* 17.

80. Portions of this section are echoed in *Wen Tzu* B/30b, B/12b, and *Ch'ün-shu chih-yao* 41/5a–b.

81. A shadoof is the "well sweep" widely used for irrigation purposes in the Orient. See Hsü Kuang-ch'i, vol. 1, pp. 347–348, for an explanation of this device. Hommel, pp. 119–120, describes it as follows: "Tuan-mu Tz'u, a sage of the sixth century B.C., attests to the antiquity of the well sweep. He describes it as being made of wood, the after part heavy and the fore part light and it can raise water like a pump. . . . Between two upright posts set firmly in the ground and propped by slanting beams, the large balance-beam is pivoted. One end is weighted with a heavy stone which about balances the other end with the rope and the filled bucket at its end."

82. There are similar passages in *Chuang Tzu* 16/6/23 and 74/26/22. This passage is also echoed in the *Shih Tzu* cited in TPYL 80 (p. 374). Yao (traditionally 2356–2257 B.C.) was a legendary ruler who appears throughout early Chinese literature as a paragon of sagely wisdom and moral virtue. Chieh (traditionally 1818–1763 B.C.), on the other hand, was the last ruler of the Hsia dynasty; his evil actions are regarded as having brought about the decline and fall of his empire (see note 66 above). Through a process of gradual inflation he has become known to Chinese tradition as a tyrant of boundless proportions.

83. Kao Yu interprets *shih* as meaning "opportunity."

84. I follow the LWT 9/10a text.

85. This natural propensity of "low ground" to attract is a popular Taoist metaphor. Compare, for example, *Lao Tzu* 39, 61, and an extended passage in *Lao Tzu* 66.

86. This passage in parentheses is repeated below in 9/7b. There are several reasons for suspecting that this first occurrence is interpolation. First, it breaks a rhymed passage which would otherwise be continuous. Second, the *Wen Tzu* B/12b echo is structured closer to the 9/7b passage. Finally, the context here is not really appropriate to the passage. It describes the ruler. The context of the 9/7b occurrence, however, is more consistent inasmuch as the discussion turns to the relationship between ruler and minister.

87. See similar and perhaps clearer passages in *Lü-shih ch'un-ch'iu* 17/8b and *Hsün Tzu* 48/12/94.

88. This is an adaptation of *Lao Tzu* 47.

89. An abridged version of this passage is found in *Ch'ün-shu chih-yao* 41/5a.

90. I follow Yang Shu-ta, p. 59, in his emendation of this phrase.

91. I follow the LWT text 9/10b. I also insert the character *erh* to make this parallel with the rest of the passage.

92. This entire passage would seem to be an adaptation of *Lao Tzu* 66.

93. There is a similar passage in *Huang-ti ssu-ching,* p. 34, and *Huai Nan Tzu* 1/10b.

94. I follow Wang Nien-sun (LWT 9/10b–11a) in his reading of this passage.

95. For an abridged version of this passage see *Wen Tzu* B/30b and *Ch'ün-shu chih-yao* 41/5b.

96. Passages with a similar purport can be found in *Kuan Tzu* 3:52-3, *Chuang Tzu* 34/13/18, and *Lü-shih ch'un-ch'iu* 3/10a.

97. An abridged version of this passage appears in *Wen Tzu* B/12b.

98. In the first occurrence of this passage (9/7a) the text has *yi* for *chih*. The character *chih* was a taboo of Emperor Huan of the Han (r. 147–167).

99. For King Wen see note 45 above.

100. For King Wu see note 60 above.

101. See similar passages in *Hsün Tzu* 25/8/121 and *Shuo yüan* 17/20a.

102. I translate the expression 1000 *chün* as "eight tons." According to Swann, p. 364, 30 catties *(chin)* = 1 *chün* = 16 pounds 2.2 ounces. Therefore, 1000 *chün* = 16,137.5 pounds which is approximately eight tons.

103. Wu Huo is a fabled strongman of antiquity who appears in classical texts as the paragon of physical strength. See *Mencius* 47/6B/2, *Hsün Tzu* 37/10/124, *Lü-shih ch'un-ch'iu* 1/8a. According to the account in the *Historical Records (Shih-chi),* p. 209, he was in the employ of King Wu of Ch'in (r. 310–307 B.C.) who, because of a love for sport, made such strongmen his high ministers.

104. I follow Yang Shu-ta, p. 60, and Yü Ta-ch'eng, pp. 277–278, in emending this passage. This emendation, based on an earlier passage in 9/7b, is only tentative, however.

105. The primary source for information on Yü is the first chapters of the *Book of Documents (Shu-ching).* He succeeded Shun to become the founder of the Hsia. He is remembered for his long and bitter struggle to drain the empire after the great flood. In the process of ridding the empire of the floodwaters, Yü divided the world into nine provinces, established a course for the nine rivers and led them to the sea, rid the world of venomous reptiles that infested its marshes, and succeeded in a series of incredible engineering feats. There is another reference to the redirection of the Yangtze in *Huai Nan Tzu* 1/6b.

106. Chi refers to Hou Chi, minister of agriculture under Yao and Shun. He was deified under the Hsia and worshiped as patron god of harvests, although he took a secondary position in relation to Shen Nung. When T'ang, founder of the Shang, degraded Shen Nung's son because of the seven-year drought, Hou Chi rose to prominence. He continued as god of agriculture through the Chou dynasty.

107. Compare the similar passage in *Lü-shih ch'un-ch'iu* 14/10a.

108. I follow Wang Nien-sun's emendation.

109. Tsao Fu, a charioteer, drove the famous horses of Mu Wang on the journey to the west. Throughout early literature, Tsao Fu appears as the byword for superlative charioting.

110. This passage is echoed in *Ch'ün-shu chih-yao* 41/5b.

111. At the suggestion of Yü Ta-ch'eng, p. 278, I emend the text on the basis of the same phrase in 9/5b.

112. I follow Wang Nien-sun, LWT 9/12a, in emending this phrase.

113. There are similar passages in *Chuang Tzu* 29/12/17 and below in *The Art of Rulership* 9/11b.

114. Equal in the sense of serving a unique purpose.

115. This passage appears in an abridged form in *Wen Tzu* B/12b; see also *Lao Tzu* 27.

116. I follow LWT 9/12b; I also follow Wang Nien-sun, LWT 9/12b, in his emendation.

117. This is an important theme in Confucian texts—in particular, the *Hsün Tzu*. See, for example, 44/12/2.

118. In ancient Chinese political theory, insight into human character is regarded as perhaps the most important skill of the ruler.

119. With respect to this "inking line," Hommel, pp. 250–251, remarks: "The carpenter's line marker . . . is a compact little instrument made of bamboo, a handle, roulette and string fastener. The square little wooden block . . . holds a pointed iron pin and to this pin the hempen string is fastened. The string passes through the inkwell, which is filled with silk-waste saturated with black ink, and thence to the drum or roulette around which it is wound. To mark lines the block with its iron point is pressed into the lumber worked upon, and the line is run out from the roulette through the inkwell and stretched taut over the place to be marked. Then the string is picked up with thumb and forefinger and let go, when it flies back into its former position, leaving a black line along its path."

120. Cf. *Kuan Tzu* 3:2-9.

121. I follow Wang Nien-sun, LWT 9/13a.

122. For this reference to King Ling of Ch'u, see *Yen Tzu ch'un-ch'iu* 7/13b; *Mo Tzu* 23/15/22; *Han Fei Tzu* 28:15; *Chan-kuo ts'e* 14/180/12b; *Kuan Tzu* 3:2-11; *Shih Tzu* A/13a; *Hsün Tzu* 45/12/31; *Yin Wen Tzu* 6a-b. The *Hsün Tzu* and *Yin Wen Tzu* have King Chuang of Ch'u.

123. For this reference to King Kou Chien of Yüeh, see *Yin Wen Tzu* 6b; *Yen Tzu ch'un-ch'iu* 7/13b; *Shih Tzu* A/13a; *Mo Tzu* 23/15/23 and 27/16/74; *Han Fei Tzu* 28:14.

124. I have emended this phrase.

125. For Yao see note 82; and for Chieh see note 66. There are similar passages in *Ch'ün-shu chih-yao* 37/7b (attributed to Shen Tao); *Han Fei Tzu* 297:5 and 155:7; *Hsün Tzu* 68/18/72.

126. Cf. *Ch'ün-shu chih-yao* 37/7b and *Han Fei Tzu* 297:8.

127. *Shang-shu* 47:0476. This passage also occurs in *Ta Tai li-chi* 3/5b and *Huai Nan Tzu* 10/7b.

128. There is a similar passage in *Ch'ün-shu chih-yao* 36/25b (attributed to Shen Tzu—see Creel, *Shen Pu-hai,* pp. 343–344). The passage in parentheses is probably an interpolation.

129. This system of *ts'an wu* is defined in some detail in the following *Huai Nan Tzu* 20/4b-5a passage:

In antiquity, the Five Rulers and the Three Kings in administering their governments and spreading their teachings used the *ts'an wu* as a matter of necessity. What does *ts'an wu* mean? Looking up, they took their signs from the heavens; looking down, they took their standards from the earth; and in the center, they took their laws from man. Thereupon, establishing the court of the Ming T'ang and carrying out its edicts, they thereby harmonized the *yin* and *yang* vapors. And coordinating the divisions of the four seasons, they thereby escaped the calamities of sickness and disease. Looking down and observing the topography of the land, they set up a system of weights and measures. Determining what would be appropriate to the lay of the land, the waterways, the fertility of the soil and the relief, they established occupations and produced goods, thereby staving off the adversities of hunger and cold. At the center scrutinizing human virtue, they set up social norms and music. Implementing the Way of benevolence and rightness, they thereby gave proper order to human relations and eliminated the disasters of violence and disorder. Then, purifying and arranging the natures of metal, wood, water, fire, and earth, they thus established the intimacy between father and child and instituted the family. Differentiating the mutually dependent norms of the pure and muddy notes, the five-note scale and the six *yang* notes of the twelve-note scale, they thus established the righteous duty between ruler and minister and instituted the state. Examining the four seasons and their *chi* through *meng* order, they thus established the social rules governing senior and junior and instituted the bureaucracy. This is called *ts'an*. They established the righteous duty between ruler and minister, the intimacy between father and child, the distinction between husband and wife, the precedence of senior over junior, and the intercourse between friends. These are called the *wu*.

130. Following Yang Shu-ta, p. 60.

131. This is a fragment. This entire passage is corrupt and any translation can only be tentative.

132. There is a similar passage in *Kuan Tzu* 3:56-2.

133. I follow the LWT 9/14a text.

134. See a similar passage in *Hsün Tzu* 49/12/107.

135. Following Wang Nien-sun, LWT 9/14a.

136. Following Wang Nien-sun, LWT 9/14b.

137. These are two of the eight famous steeds of Chou Mu Wang. Throughout early Chinese literature, they are representative of the finest and fastest horses.

138. This passage seems to be based on *Han Fei Tzu* 236:11.

139. Cf. *Han Fei Tzu* 73:13 and 70:15.

140. See *Tso chuan,* Ting 13.

141. *Han Fei Tzu* 75:11 has an abbreviated version of this Yü Jang story. This story is also found in *Policies of the Warring States (Chan-kuo ts'e)* 18/216/5a and in Yü Jang's *Historical Records (Shih-chi)* 86 biography, p. 2519.

142. Chou Hsin, last ruler of the Shang dynasty, was overthrown at Mu Yeh by King Wu (see note 60) in 1122 B.C. Like Chieh (see note 66) before him, the name of Chou is notorious in the annals of Chinese history for unbridled extravagance and cruelty. Together with his wicked consort, he outraged humanity and repaid honest remonstrators with a slow and painful end.

143. Cf. *Han Fei Tzu* 267:7 and *Shuo Yüan* 6/1a. I follow the LWT reconstruction of this passage.

144. For an abridged version of this section, see *Wen Tzu* B/21b.

145. For Yao see note 82 above.

146. Cf. *Han Fei Tzu* 340:2 and *Huai Nan Tzu* 7/7a. There is also a fragment in *Han-shih wai-chuan* 8/8b.

147. The primary source for Shun, like Yao, is the early chapters of the *Book of Documents (Shu-ching)*. Through his own virtue he was able to transform and civilize the world. Together with Yao, he stands in early literature as history's exemplary ruler—unsurpassed in virtue and statesmanship.

148. I follow the *Wen Tzu* B/21b and LWT texts.

149. This section appears in abridged form as a block in *Ch'ün-shu chih-yao* 41/5b-6b. The first portion also occurs in *Wen Tzu* B/21b.

150. See *Policies of the Warring States (Chan-kuo ts'e)* 3/42/5a. This expression also occurs in *Chia t'ai-fu hsin-shu* 1/16b and *Record of Rites (Li-chi)* 29/1a.

151. See similar passages in *Chuang Tzu* 29/12/17 and *The Art of Rulership* 9/8a.

152. For a detailed description of this herb, its various names and species, and its therapeutic properties, see *Pen-ts'ao kang-mu* 17, pp. 46–50. The herb is known as *Aconitum chinense*. The genus *Aconitum* covers about three hundred species of flowery perennial herbs which are more commonly known as monkshood, friar's cap, and wolfsbane. The roots of all these species contain aconitine (aconite), a toxic extract commonly used by the ancient Chinese for preparing arrow poisons. Medicinally, aconite was used externally as a local anesthesia and internally to treat hypertension, heart disease, and severe fever. There is still no known antidote for this poison.

153. Cf. *Lao Tzu* 27.

154. Cf. *Huang-ti ssu-ching,* p. 21.

155. This is a tentative reconstruction of the text.

156. I follow Wang Nien-sun, LWT 9/17b, and the *Ch'ün-shu chih-yao* 41/6b.

157. An abridged version of this section is contained as a block in *Wen Tzu* B/21b–22a. The last part of this section is also contained in the *Ch'ün-shu chih-yao* 41/4a–b.

158. Cf. *Shen (Tao) Tzu* 8a; *Han Fei Tzu* 305:16; and *Teng Hsi Tzu* 11a.

159. I follow Wang Nien-sun, LWT 9/18a.

160. See *Analects* 29/14/31 for this use of *ni.*

161. Cf. *Hsün Tzu* 1/1/8; *Shuo yüan* 16/5a; and *Ta Tai li-chi* 7/6b.

162. I follow Wang Nien-sun, LWT 9/18b.

163. An abridged version of this passage is found in *Ch'ün-shu chih-yao* 41/4a–b.

164. I follow Liu Wen-tien 9/18b–19a and the *Ch'ün-shu chih-yao* 41/4a–b.

165. I follow LWT 9/18b.

166. This section is contained almost in its entirety in two blocks in *Wen Tzu* B/30a–b and B/30a.

167. Cf. *Han Fei Tzu* 277:7.

168. Cf. *Han Fei Tzu* 265:16 and *Teng Hsi Tzu* 10b.

169. Cf. *Han-shih wai-chuan* 6/2a.

170. I follow Yü Yüeh, LWT 9/19b–20a, in rearranging the original order of the text; see also *Huai Nan Tzu* 3/11b.

171. Cf. *Huai Nan Tzu* 10/1b. This use of *shih* is found in *Lü-shih ch'un-ch'in* in which the Kao Yu commentary equates it with *chieh,* "right measure".

172. Cf. *Shen (Tao) Tzu* 11b–12a.

173. Cf. *Mo Tzu* 77/45/3 and *Yen Tzu ch'un-ch'iu* 3/20b. See also *Huai Nan Tzu* 10/3b.

174. Cf. *Yen Tzu ch'un-ch'iu* 3/18b.

175. This is a tentative reconstruction of the text.

176. See *Analects* 25/13/6.

177. This section is contained almost in its entirety as a block in *Wen Tzu* B/28b–29a.

178. For Tsao Fu see note 109 above.

179. Cf. *Lieh Tzu* 5/8a–b.

180. Cf. *Chuang Tzu* 50/19/59. This is repeated in *Lü-shih ch'un-ch'iu* 19/13a.

181. Wang Liang is often coupled with Tsao Fu as the foremost charioteers of antiquity.

182. For Yao see note 82; for Shun see note 147.

183. Kuan Chung (d. 645 B.C.) became prime minister under King Huan of Ch'i and administered the government so successfully that he became known to Chinese history as the model statesman. Under his name was gathered a varied collection of essays and commentaries on political and economic matters, probably in the late fourth century and early third century B.C., at Ch'i's Chi-hsia academy.

Yen Tzu (d. 493 B.C.), also a minister of Ch'i, has become known for his ascetic habits. Like Kuan Chung, a collection of writings was gathered under his name and called the *Yen Tzu ch'un-ch'iu*. The two main themes of this almost Mohist text are frugality and the promotion of worthy men. Perhaps our most reliable source for information on both Yen Tzu and Kuan Chung is the *Tso chuan*.

184. Robber Chih, a contemporary of Confucius and one of the archvillains of early Chinese literature, terrorized the countryside in search of booty and women. The twenty-ninth chapter of the *Chuang Tzu* portrays Robber Chih as a ruthless and yet not altogether unattractive man who gives the pious and obsequious Confucius a sound verbal lashing for the hypocrisy of his teachings. In Confucian texts, on the other hand, he is grouped together with the wicked emperors Chieh and Chou. See *Hsün Tzu* 3/1/45 and 89/23/54.

Chuang Ch'iao was a relative and a general of King Wei of Ch'u (r. 339–329 B.C.). His story is to be found in *History of the Han (Han-shu)* 95, p. 3838. He was sent out on an expedition by his king but, having his return cut off, he set himself up as king over a barbarian territory and adopted their ways.

185. Cf. *Shih Tzu* A/8b.

186. Cf. *Han Fei Tzu* 355:10.

187. I emend the text here. Another instance of this same corruption can be detected in a comparison between 14/9b and 7/10b. This expression occurs also in *Record of Rites (Li-chi)* 12/11.

188. See note 137 above.

189. The Kao Yu commentary identifies Tseng-huo as a man of Lu who was noted for his inability to drive a chariot. The encyclopedia *TPYL* 746, p. 3313, has Wu-huo. There are many occurrences in *Han Fei Tzu,* however, where *tseng-huo*—"slaves and servants"—are described driving horses. See, for example, 122: 5, 236:14, 272:6, 300:15, 301:4, 352:3, and 354:4.

190. I follow Wang Nien-sun, LWT 9/21b.

191. I interpret this phrase as expressing the notion of equal utility central to the notions *ke-te-ch'i-yi* and *yung chung*. This mode of expression is consistent with *Hsün Tzu* 12/4/77 (also 51/13/48): "Irregular and yet even, bent and yet in line, different and yet equal. . . ."

192. Reading *yü* for *yü*. As is apparent from Karlgren's reconstructions, these two characters would have been close in pronunciation during Western Han.

193. Cf. *Hsün Tzu* 9/4/23, 31/9/126, 38/11/26, and 39/11/35.

194. This passage is included as a block in *Wen Tzu* B/23b–24a.

195. Cf. *Lü-shih ch'un-ch'iu* 17/15a.

196. I follow Wang Nien-sun, LWT 9/22a.

197. Cf. *Lü-shih ch'un-ch'iu* 17/7a–b.

198. Cf. *Lü-shih ch'un-ch'iu* 17/13b.

199. I follow Wang Nien-sun, LWT 9/22a. Cf. *Teng Hsi Tzu* 9b.

200. I follow Wang Nien-sun, LWT 9/22a, and *Wen Tzu* B/23b.

201. I follow Yü Ta-ch'eng, pp. 289–290, and *Wen Tzu* B/23b.

202. Cf. *Lü-shih ch'un-ch'iu* 17/6b.

203. The LWT text has *tzu-jan* for *tzu-hsin*.
204. This is an allusion to *Chuang Tzu* 2/1/26.
205. This is an allusion to *Lao Tzu* 74.
206. I follow *Wen Tzu* B/23b here.
207. Po Lo was a famous horse trader and trainer renowned for his judgment of horses. He appears in *Chuang Tzu* 22/9/6 and 16; *Lü-shih ch'un-ch'iu* 24/3a; *Huai Nan Tzu* 2/6a and 11/9a–b.
208. For Wang Liang see note 181 above.
209. Cf. *Lü-shih ch'un-ch'iu* 25/6b.
210. I follow Wang Nien-sun, LWT 9/22b, and *Wen Tzu* B/24a.
211. These three examples are also found in *Huai Nan Tzu* 7/12a–b. There is a similar passage in *Han Fei Tzu* 28:15 which is echoed in *Huai Nan Tzu* 9/8b–9a above. For the Duke Huan of Ch'i story, see *Kuan Tzu* 2:40-8; *Han Fei Tzu* 51:15, 28:15, 266:8. For the ruler of Yü story, see *Tso chuan* 89/Hsi 2/3. For the King of the Hu story, see *Han Fei Tzu* 50:1.
212. This passage echoes *Lao Tzu* 54.
213. Cf. *Lü-shih ch'un-ch'iu* 17/4b.
214. Wang Nien-sun, LWT 9/23a, and Yang Shu-ta, p. 63, offer emendations, but neither suggestion improves the grammar.
215. Cf. *Lü-shih ch'un-ch'iu* 17/13b and also the *Wen Tzu* B/24a version.
216. This section is contained in abridged form as a block in *Wen Tzu* B/30b–31a.
217. Tzu Lu was one of Confucius' closest disciples. He first served in Lu and then later in Wei. In *Historical Records (Shih-chi),* p. 2191, he was noted for his courage. In 480 B.C. there was a revolt in Wei, and Tzu Lu died as a result of his loyalty to his overlord; for an account see *Historical Records,* p. 2193, and *Tso chuan* 491/Ai 15/2.
218. Kuan Chung was minister to Duke Huan of Ch'i; Yen Tzu was minister to Duke Ching of Ch'i. See note 183.
219. Emending the text by inserting *ho*.
220. The 45-character passage which ends here may be an interpolation.
221. Following Wang Nien-sun, LWT 9/24a.
222. Cf. *Shuo yüan* 16/2a.
223. The six arts are rites, music, archery, calligraphy, charioting, and mathematics.
224. The number of Confucius' disciples is mentioned in *Historical Records (Shih-chi)* 47 and 67, pp. 1938 and 2185; *K'ung Tzu chia-yü* 9/1a; *Lü-shih ch'un-ch'iu* 14/18b; *Ta Tai li-chi* 6/2b-3a; *Huai Nan Tzu* 21/7a; *Mencius* 12/2A/3; *Han Fei Tzu* 342:14.
225. I follow LWT 9/24b.
226. The king was trimming his sleeves and threw down the piece he had just removed. See *Lü-shih ch'un-ch'iu* 20/16b-17a for a thorough account.
227. For the circumstances leading up to this event, see *Tso chuan* 168/Wen 14/2. For a full account, see *Lü-shih ch'un-ch'iu* 20/16b-17a and *Historical Records (Shih-chi)* 40, p. 1702.
228. There is no reference to this penchant of King Wen of Ch'u in the *Historical Records (Shih-chi)* 40 account of his reign, but there is mention of the strange dress of King Wu-ling of Chao in *Historical Records* 43, p. 1810.
229. Since the text is obviously corrupt at this point, translation can only be tentative.
230. According to the Kao Yu gloss, this Pei-kung Tzu is the Pei-kung Yu who

in *Mencius* 10/2A/2 devotes himself to the cultivation of courage and boldness. Kao Yu identifies Ssu-ma K'uai K'uei as a *ssu-ma* under King Hsüan of Chou (r. 827-782 B.C.) and who thus took *ssu-ma* as his surname. With the decline of the House of Chou, the descendants of Po Hsiu-fu traveled to other states. Ssu-ma K'uai K'uei was a well-known swordsman of Chao.

231. Cf. *Lü-shih ch'un-ch'iu* 1/8a. For Wu Huo see note 103 above. According to Kao Yu, Chieh Fan like Wu Huo was a man reputed to have incredible physical strength.

232. Cf. *I-Chou-shu* 4/9a.

233. Cf. *Lü-shih ch'un-ch'iu* 25/11b.

234. For the story of Chou Hsin cutting the heart out of Prince Pi Kan, see *Historical Records (Shih-chi)* 3, p. 108. This passage would seem to be based on *Shang-shu* 210643. Watching men wading through a stream in the cold of the morning, Chou Hsin noticed that some of them could endure the cold better than others. To determine the reason for this endurance, he had several legs broken open to investigate. See commentary on *SPTK Shang-shu* 6/5a.

235. Large portions of this section are found in *Chia t'ai-fu hsin-shu* B/3a-4b; *Wen Tzu* B/24b-25a, 24a-b; *Ch'ün-shu chih-yao* 41/6b-7a and 7b-8a.

236. Cf. *Chia t'ai-fu hsin-shu* B/3b.

237. Instruments used for dancing.

238. I follow Wang Nien-sun, LWT 9/26b.

239. I follow Lau, "Tu *Huai Nan Hung Lieh* chiao chi," p. 156.

240. The raison d'être for music is "joy"—and "joy" and "music" are written with the same character.

241. Cf. *Chia t'ai-fu hsin-shu* B/56b and *Record of Rites (Li-chi)* 5/29.

242. Cf. *Chia t'ai-fu hsin-shu* A/57a; *Record of Rites (Li-chi)* 5/29. For a related passage see *History of the Han (Han-shu)*, p. 1123.

243. Cf. *Mencius* 19/3A/3.

244. Cf. *Kuan Tzu* 1:9-10 and *Chia t'ai-fu hsin-shu* B/43a.

245. Cf. *I-Chou-shu* 4/8a-b.

246. Cf. *I-Chou-shu* 4/8b and *Record of Rites (Li-chi)* 5/28.

247. Meaning when the heavy rains come.

248. I follow LWT 9/28b.

249. Cf. *Shang-shu ta-chuan* B/1b-2a and *Shuo yüan* 18/2b-3a.

250. The character *kuan* may be a corruption of *tao* here, although there seems to be a pun between "organs" and "officials" that is similar to "joy" and "music" (note 240 above).

251. Cf. *Lü-shih ch'un-ch'iu* 13/5b. This brief passage discussing good and evil seems very much out of context here and may well be an interpolation. There are twenty-seven characters in this passage—enough for one of the bamboo strips *(chien)* on which the text was originally written that might have become separated. Both Section 16 and the section which follows on from this passage are highly structured, and it is unlikely that they would contain this loose strand. While the *Ch'ün-shu chih-yao* 41/8a echo does contain the passage in question, *Wen Tzu* B/24a-b does not.

252. This section is contained almost in its entirety in *Wen Tzu* B/3b-4a. It is also contained in part in *Ch'ün-shu chih-yao* 41/8a-9a.

253. Cf. *Lü-shih ch'un-ch'iu* 20/12a-b; *Chia t'ai-fu hsin-shu* A/81b-82a; and *Kuo-yü* 158. *Ta Tai li-chi* 3/3a is almost identical with *Chia t'ai-fu hsin-shu* A/81b-82a cited above.

254. For Yao, see note 82; for Shun, see note 147; for T'ang, see note 48; for Wu, see note 60.

255. Cf. *Lü-shih ch'un-ch'iu* 24/5a and *Teng Hsi Tzu* 8b–9a.

256. I follow Lau, "Tu *Huai Nan Hung Lieh* chiao chi," p. 156.

257. Cf. *Hsün Tzu* 67/18/65.

258. This statement is from *Shih-ching* 59/236/3. It is also cited in *Record of Rites (Li-chi)* 32/10 and *Tso chuan* 422/Chao 26/4.

259. I follow Wang Nien-sun, LWT 9/30a.

260. Tradition records a series of actions undertaken by King Wu on assuming the throne. This stock list is repeated in the following texts: *Historical Records (Shih-chi)* 3, p. 108; *Shang-shu ta-chuan* 3/3b; *Lü-shih ch'un-ch'iu* 15/2b–3a; *I-Chou-shu* 4/3a–b; *Han shih wai-chuan* 3/8a; *Huai Nan Tzu* 12/17a, 20/13a.
For the account of Shang Jung, see *Han-shih wai-chuan* 2/11a–b. Pi Kan was a loyal minister of Chou Hsin who incurred his wrath by honest admonition. Chou Hsin had his heart cut out to see if sages really have seven orifices in this organ. Chi Tzu, also a minister of Chou Hsin, escaped execution by feigning madness. On his release by the victorious King Wu, Chi Tzu refused to serve the usurper. King Wu abolished the coffers and granaries which Chou Hsin had set up to show the people that he had not conquered the empire for his own gain.

261. There is a similar passage in *Mencius* 55/7B/6.

262. For King Wen, see note 45; for Yao, note 82; for Chieh, note 66; for Shun, note 147; for Chou Hsin, note 142.

263. For the Ming T'ang see note 18.

264. The expression *lüeh-chih* here is odd. Compare *Hsün Tzu* 100/27/95; *Mencius* 31/4B/20; *Record of Rites (Li-chi)* 12/52; *Chuang Tzu* 58/22/32.

265. Emperor Ch'eng (r. 1103–1068 B.C.) was the son of King Wu and came to the throne while still a boy. His uncle, the Duke of Chou, acted as regent until Ch'eng came of age. He spent his reign carrying out the projects planned by his father. See *Shih-chi* 4 (p. 132). Emperor K'ang (r. 1067–1042 B.C.) was the son of Ch'eng and, like his father, reigned with the assistance of an uncle, Duke Chao. He also carried on the work of his grandfather, King Wu. See *Historical Records (Shih-chi)* 4, p. 134.

266. The text from this paragraph on might well be a later accretion.

267. Ch'ang Hung is a rather cloudy figure in early Chinese literature. From the *Kuo-yü* 2778 and *Tso chuan* 470/Ai 3/1, we learn that he was a minister of Chou who sought to restore the wall around Ch'eng Chou. As a result of a dispute between the Liu clan of Chou and the Fan clan of Chin, Ch'ang Hung was put to death by the people of Chou in 492 B.C. In the *Chuang Tzu* 73/26/2 and 24/10/10, he is associated with worthy ministers like Kuan Hung-feng, Pi Kan, and Wu Tzu-hsü, all suffering unjust punishment. Three years after his death, his blood is said to have turned to jade. In the *Huai Nan Tzu* 13/12a–b, he was in charge of the calendar for the House of Chou. Even though he was wholly conversant with the vapors of the heavens and earth, the movement of the sun and moon, the climatic changes, and the calculations of the calendar, he was drawn and quartered by chariots. The *Huai Nan Tzu* 16/7a offers a similar observation.

268. Meng Pen was a native of Ch'i renowned for his physical prowess. Commentators record his feats—tearing horns from the head of an ox and slaying two water dragons (*Shih Tzu* B/2b). He is frequently associated with men like Wu Huo, *Historical Records (Shih-chi)* 70, p. 2293, and Hsia Yü, *Historical Records* 101, p. 2739, as a paragon of strength.

269. Cf. *Huai Nan Tzu* 12/3b; *Lü-shih ch'un-ch'iu* 15/4b; and *Lieh Tzu* 8/4a. It is interesting to note how this feat of holding up a portcullis was transferred from a man who came to be regarded as Confucius' father. From the introduction to Lau's *The Analects,* p. 9: "In the *Tso chuan* under the tenth year of Duke Hsiang, it is recorded that one Shu He of Tsou held up the portcullis with his bare hands while his comrades made their getaway. The *Shih-chi,* however, gives his name as Shu Liang He and added the information that he was Confucius' father." Since the feat of holding up the portcullis is attributed to Confucius as early as the *Lü-shih ch'un-ch'iu* 15/4b, this would indicate that Shu He had been regarded as the father of Confucius during the late Warring States period.

270. Cf. *Analects* 16/9/6.

271. The expression "uncrowned king" appears as early as the *Chuang Tzu* 33/13/9 to describe a man with the Way but no rank. In Han times a theory arose that Confucius in the *Ch'un Ch'iu* formulated the Way of the "uncrowned king." See Wu K'ang, p. 175, n. 7, for a discussion of Tung Chung-shu's support for this theory. This epithet is used for Confucius in *Shuo yüan* 5/2a and *Lunheng* 13/17a and 27/14b.

272. See *Analects* 16/9/5 and 21/11/21.

273. Comparable expressions occur throughout the *Sun Tzu* text.

274. Cf. *Hsün Tzu* 42/11/110.

275. Yang Shu-ta, p. 66, points out that Chang Yi was never drawn and quartered, and he suggests that this might be a mistake for Su Ch'in. Wang Shu-min in his *Huai Nan Tzu chiao-cheng,* p. 53, gives more conclusive evidence that Chang Yi is in fact an error for Shang Yang. Chang Yi, having been slandered in Ch'in, left and became chancellor of Wei. After holding this post for one year, he died. (See *Shih-chi* 70, pp. 2279 ff., especially p. 2304.) There are no biographical data to suggest that he was drawn and quartered. In the textual references to Shang Yang, on the other hand, it states that he suffered "dismemberment," the same expression used in this chapter; see *Historical Records (Shih-chi)* 68, pp. 2279 ff., especially p. 2237. See *Huai Nan Tzu* 10/12a and 18/5a as well as *Han-shih waichuan* 1/10b for references to Shang Yang being drawn and quartered. He is frequently coupled, as here, with Wu Ch'i.

Wu Ch'i (d. 381 B.C.) was a native of Wei who served the states of Lu, Wei, and Ch'u successively. He is known for his skill in military affairs and for his severity in enforcing his administrative reforms. Ultimately he suffered a violent death in being torn limb from limb by a conspiracy of people who had suffered under him.

276. I follow Wang Nien-sun, LWT 9/31b.

277. Kao Yu interprets the "six" as referring to Confucius, Mo Tzu, Chang Hung, Meng Pen, Wu Ch'i, and Chang Yi.

278. There are several examples in the early literary tradition which portray such an attitude, and this passage may be an allusion to one of them. There is the well-known story of Chi Kao, for instance, a disciple of Confucius who served as a magistrate in Wei. One day he ordered that a criminal have his feet cut off. Later this same man assisted Chi Kao in making an escape. On questioning him, the man replied that his punishment was just and, moreover, he saw that Chi Kao took on a pale and resigned expression when passing sentence. Confucius' comment on the affair is cited in *K'ung Tzu chia-yü* 2/3a–4a. A second version appears in *Shuo yüan* 14/15a–16a. There is a third version in *Han Fei Tzu* 218:10; Confucius' comment follows later in 220:1. For a similar example, see *Huai Nan Tzu* 18/21a, which describes the humane reluctance of Tzu Fa.

279. I follow Yü Ta-ch'eng, p. 301, emendation.
280. Interpret this passage on the basis of three passages from the *Analects*: 8/5/12, 22/12/2, and 32/15/24.
281. I emend this phrase on the basis of LWT 9/32a.
282. Since this phrase is obviously corrupt, my translation is only speculation.
283. Cf. *Han Fei Tzu* 347:5 and *Shen (Tao) Tzu* 17a.
284. I follow the LWT 9/32b text.
285. I follow Yü Yüeh, LWT 9/32b.
286. I follow the LWT 9/33a text.
287. Cf. *Mo Tzu* 31/19/5.
288. This statement appears to be based on *Analects* 31/15/18; see also *Analects* 6/4/2.
289. Cf. *Analects* 36/17/7 and 15/8/10.
290. I follow Wang Nien-sun, LWT 9/33b.
291. Cf. *Analects* 14/8/2.
292. I follow LWT 9/34a.
293. Cf. *Mencius* 28/4a/13 and *Record of Rites (Li-chi)* 31/18.

Bibliography

Classical works are listed alphabetically according to title; modern works are listed according to author.

Acta Archaeologica Sinica (K'ao-ku hsüeh-pao). Peking: K'o-hsüeh ch'u-pan-she.

Ames, Roger T. "Is Political Taoism Anarchism?" *Journal of Chinese Philosophy* 10(2)(1983).

Analects (Lun-yü). Harvard-Yenching Institute Sinological Index Series, Supp. 16. Peking: Harvard-Yenching, 1940.

Bodde, D. *China's First Unifier*. Leiden: E. J. Brill, 1938.

Bodde, D. and Morris, C. *Law in Imperial China*. Cambridge, Mass.: Harvard University Press, 1967.

The Book of Documents (Shu-ching). *Concordance to the Shang-shu*. Peking: Harvard-Yenching, 1936.

The Book of Lord Shang (Shang-chün shu). SPTK.

The Book of Odes (Shih-ching). Harvard-Yenching Institute Sinological Index Series, Supp. 9. Peking: Harvard-Yenching, 1934.

Chan, W. T. *The Way of Lao Tzu*. New York: Bobbs-Merrill Co., 1963.

⸻. *A Source Book in Chinese Philosophy*. Princeton: Princeton University Press, 1963.

Chang Hsin-ch'eng. *Wei-shu t'ung-k'ao*. Shanghai: Commercial Press, 1939 (rev. 1959).

Ch'en Ch'i-t'ien. *Chung-kuo fa-chia kai-lun*. Shanghai: Chung-hua shu-chü, 1936.

⸻. *Han Fei Tzu chiao-shih*. Shanghai: Chung-hua shu-chü, 1940.

Ch'en Ku-ying. *Lao Tzu chin-chu chin-i*. Taipei: Commercial Press, 1970.

Ch'en Meng-chia. *Shang-shu t'ung-lun*. Shanghai: Commercial Press, 1970.

Ch'en Ta-ch'i. *K'ung Tzu hsüeh-shuo*. Taipei: Cheng-chung shu-chü, 1964.

Ch'i Ssu-ho. "Hsi-Chou shih-tai chih cheng-chih ssu-hsiang." *Yenching she-hui k'o-hsüeh* 1(1948).

Chia t'ai-fu hsin shu. SPTK.

Chiang Hsia-an. *Hsien-Ch'in ching-chi k'ao*. Shanghai: Commercial Press, 1929.

Chiang Shang-hsien. *Hsün Tzu ssu-hsiang t'i-hsi.* Taipei: Lien-ho ch'u-pan chung-hsin, 1966.
Ch'ien Mu. *Hsien-Ch'in chu-tzu hsi-nien.* Hong Kong: Hsiang-kang ta-hsüeh ch'u-pan-she, 1956.
Ching Chih-jen. *Han Fei Tzu cheng-chih ssu-hsiang.* Taipei: Kuo-li cheng-chih ta-hsüeh cheng-chih yen-chiu-so, 1967.
Chu Shih-ch'e. *Shang-chün shu chieh-ku ting-pen.* Hong Kong: Chung-hua shu-chü, 1974 (orig. 1948).
Ch'u-tz'u. SPTK.
Ch'ü, T. T. *Law and Society in Traditional China.* Paris and The Hague: Mouton, 1961.
Chuang Tzu. Harvard-Yenching Institute Sinological Index Series, Supp. 20. Peking: Harvard-Yenching, 1947.
Ch'un-ch'iu. Harvard-Yenching Institute Sinological Index Series, Supp. 11. Peking: Harvard-Yenching, 1937.
Ch'un-ch'iu fan-lu. SPTK.
Ch'ün-shu chih-yao. SPTK.
Chung-yung. See *Ssu-shu chang-chü chi-chu.*
Cook, F. H. *Hua-yen Buddhism.* University Park: Pennsylvania State University, 1977.
Creel, H. G. *What Is Taoism?* Chicago: University of Chicago Press, 1970.
_____. *The Origins of Statecraft in China.* Chicago: University of Chicago Press, 1970.
_____. *Shen Pu-hai: A Chinese Political Philosopher of the Fourth Century* B.C. Chicago: University of Chicago Press, 1974.
Cultural Relics (Wen-wu). Peking: Wen-wu ch'u-pan-she.
Duyvendak, J. J. L. *The Book of Lord Shang.* London: Arthur Probsthain, 1928.
_____. "The Philosophy of Wu Wei." *Asiatische Studien* 3–4(1947): 81–102.
Fung Yu-lan. *A History of Chinese Philosophy.* Translated D. Bodde. 2 vols. Princeton: Princeton University Press, 1953.
Giles, L. *Sun Tzu on the Art of War.* London: Luzac and Co., 1910.
Graham, A. C. "How Much of *Chuang Tzu* Did Chuang Tzu Write?" *Journal of the American Academy of Religion Thematic Issue* 47(Three S)(September 1979):459–501.
Granet, M. *La Pensee Chinoise.* L'Evolution de l'Humanité series, vol. 25. Paris: Albin Michel, 1934.
Great Learning (Ta-hsüeh). See *Ssu-shu chang-chü chi-chu.*
Griffith, S. B. *Sun Tzu: The Art of War.* Oxford: Oxford University Press, 1963.
Guerin, D. *Anarchism.* New York: Monthly Review Press, 1970.
Han Fei Tzu. A Concordance to the Han-fei Tzu. Compiled by Wallace Johnson. San Francisco: Chinese Materials Center, Inc., 1975.
Han-shih wai-chuan. SPTK.
Historical Records (Shih-chi). Peking: Chung-hua shu-chü, 1959.
History of the Han (Han-shu). Peking: Chung-hua shu-chü, 1962.
Hommel, R. *China at Work.* New York: John Day Co., 1937.
Hsiao Kung-ch'üan. *Chung-kuo cheng-chih ssu-hsiang-shih.* 2 vols. Shanghai: Commercial Press, 1946–1948.
_____. *A History of Chinese Political Thought.* Translated by F. Mote. Vol. 1. Princeton: Princeton University Press, 1979.

Hsieh Yün-fei. *Han Fei Tzu hsi-lun.* Taipei: Ta-lin shu-tien, 1973.
Hsü Fu-kuan. *Liang-Han ssu-hsiang shih.* 3 vols. Hong Kong: Hsiang-kang chung-wen ta-hsüeh, 1975.
Hsü Kuang-ch'i. *Nung-cheng ch'üan-shu.* 3 vols. Peking: Chung-hua shu-chu, 1956.
Hsün Tzu. Harvard-Yenching Institute Sinological Index Series, Supp. 22. Peking: Harvard-Yenching, 1950.
Hu Shih. *Huai Nan Wang shu.* Shanghai: Commercial Press, 1934.
_____. *Chung-kuo ku-tai che-hsüeh shih.* Taipei: Commercial Press, 1968.
Huai Nan Tzu. SPTK.
Huang-ti ssu-ching. Transcribed in *Acta Archaeologica Sinica (K'ao-ku hsüeh-pao)* 1(1975):7–38.
I-ching. Harvard-Yenching Institute Sinological Index Series, Supp. 10. Peking: Harvard-Yenching, 1935.
I-Chou-shu. SPTK.
Kanaya Osamu. *The World of Lao Tzu and Chuang Tzu (Rō-sō teki sekai).* Tokyo: Heiraku-ji Shoten, 1959.
_____. *Researches into Ch'in and Han Thought (Shin-kan shisō-shi kenkyū).* Tokyo: Gakujutsuha Kyōkai, 1960.
Kao Heng. *Shang-chün shu chu-i.* Peking: Chung-hua shu-chü, 1974.
_____. *Lao Tzu cheng-ku.* Peking: Chung-hua, 1956.
Karlgren, B. "Legends and Cults in Ancient China." *BMFEA* 18(1946):199–365.
_____. (Trans.) "The Book of Documents." *BMFEA* 22(1950):1–81.
_____. (Trans.) *The Book of Odes.* Stockholm: Museum of Far Eastern Antiquities, 1950.
_____. *Grammata Serica Recensa.* Stockholm: Museum of Far Eastern Antiquities, 1950.
Kramer, S. N. *Mythologies of the Ancient World.* New York: Doubleday, 1961.
Kuan Tzu. A Concordance to the Kuan Tzu. Compiled by Wallace Johnson. Taipei: Ch'eng-wen ch'u-pan-she, 1970.
K'ung Tzu chia-yü. SPTK.
Kuo Hua-jo. *Shih-i chia chu Sun Tzu.* Peking: Chung-hua shu-chü, 1962.
Kuo Mo-jo. *Mo-jo wen-chi.* 5 vols. Peking: Jen-min wen-hsüeh ch'u-pan-she, 1957.
Kuo-yü. A Concordance to the Kuo-yü. Compiled by Wolfgang Bauer. Taipei: Ch'eng-wen ch'u-pan-she, 1973.
Kusuyama Haruki. *Enanji.* Tokyo: Meitoku Shuppan-sha, 1971.
Lao Chieh Lao. Compiled by Ts'ai T'ing-kan. (n.p., 1922).
Lau, D. C. *Lao Tzu: Tao Te Ching.* Middlesex: Penguin, 1963.
_____. "Some Notes on the *Sun Tzu.*" *BSOAS* 28(1965):319–335.
_____. "*Tu Huai Nan Hung Lieh* chiao chi." *United College Journal* 6(1967–1968):139–188.
_____. *Mencius.* Middlesex: Penguin, 1970.
_____. *The Analects.* Middlesex: Penguin, 1979.
_____. Review of H. G. Creel's *What Is Taoism and Other Studies in Chinese Cultural History. Asia Major* n.s. 18(1973):121–123.
Liang Ch'i-ch'ao. *Hsien-Ch'in cheng-chih ssu-hsiang shih.* Nanking: Ch'eng-hsien hsüeh-she, 1922.
Liang Ch'i-hsiung. *Hsün Tzu chien-shih.* Peking: Ku-chi ch'u-pan-she, 1956.
_____. *Han Tzu chien-chieh.* 2 vols. Peking: Chung-hua shu-chü, 1960.

Lieh Tzu. SPTK.

Liu Wen-tien. *Huai Nan Hung Lieh chi-chieh.* Shanghai: Commercial Press, 1933.

Lo Ch'ang-p'ei and Chou Tsu-mo. *Han-Wei-Nan-pei-ch'ao yün-pu yen-pien yen-chiu.* Peking: K'o-hsüeh ch'u-pan-she, 1958.

Lo Ken-tse. *Chu-tzu k'ao so.* Peking: Jen-min ch'u-pan-she, 1958.

Loewe, M. Review of H. G. Creel's *Shen Pu-hai. BSOAS* 39(1976):198–200.

Lü-shih ch'un-ch'iu. SPTK.

Lun-heng. SPTK.

Mencius (Meng Tzu). Harvard-Yenching Institute Sinological Index Series, Supp. 17. Peking: Harvard-Yenching, 1941.

Miyamoto Masaru. "Enanji shujutsu-kun no sieji-shisō to sono riron kōzō." *Chūgoku tetsugaku* 4(1966):1–43.

Mo Tzu. Harvard-Yenching Institute Sinological Index Series, Supp. 21. Peking: Harvard-Yenching, 1948.

Morgan, E. *Tao: The Great Luminant.* London: Kegan Paul, 1935.

Morohashi Tetsuji. *Dai Kan-Wa jiten.* Tokyo: Taishūkan shoten, 1957–1960.

Munro, D. *The Concept of Man in Early China.* Stanford: Stanford University Press, 1969.

Needham, J. *Science and Civilisation in China.* 5 vols. Cambridge: Cambridge University Press, 1954–

Novak, D. "The Place of Anarchism in the History of Political Thought." *Review of Politics* 20(1958):307–320.

Pen-ts'ao kang-mu. 2 vols. Shanghai: Commercial Press, 1955.

Policies of the Warring States (Chan-kuo ts'e). Index No. 10. Peking: Centre d'Études Sinologiques de Pekin, 1948.

Record of Rites (Li-chi). Harvard-Yenching Institute Sinological Index Series, Supp. 27. Peking: Harvard-Yenching, 1937.

Rickett, W. A. (Trans.) *Kuan Tzu.* Hong Kong: Hong Kong University Press, 1965.

Roth, H. D. "The Textual History of the *Huai Nan Tzu.*" Ph.D. dissertation, University of Toronto, 1980.

Rubin, V. A. *Individual and State in Ancient China.* New York: Columbia University Press, 1976.

Shang-shu. Concordance to the Shang-shu. Peking: Harvard-Yenching, 1936.

Shang-shu ta-chuan. SPTK.

Shen Tzu. SPTK.

Shih Tzu. SPPY.

Shuo yüan. Harvard-Yenching Institute Sinological Index Series, Supp. 1. Peking: Harvard-Yenching, 1931.

Soothill, W. E. *The Hall of Light.* London: Latterworth, 1951.

Sou-shen chi. Shanghai: Commercial Press, 1957.

Ssu-shu chang-chü chi-chu. Chu Hsi commentary. Shanghai: Commercial Press, 1935.

Sun I-jang. *Ming-yüan.* Ch'ing ed. (n.)

Sun Pin Art of Warfare (Sun Pin ping-fa). Transcribed in *Cultural Relics (Wen-wu)* 1(1975):1–11.

Sun Tzu. SPTK.

Sun Tzu Art of Warfare (Sun Tzu ping-fa). Fragments transcribed in *Cultural Relics (Wen-wu)* 12(1974):11–24.

Swann, N. L. *Food and Money in Ancient China*. Princeton: Princeton University Press, 1950.

Ta Tai li-chi. *SPTK*.

T'ai-p'ing yü-lan. 4 vols. Peking: Chung-hua shu-chü, 1960.

Takeuchi Yoshio. *Chūgoku shisō shi.*Tokyo: Iwanami Shoten, 1973 (orig. 1936).

T'ao Hung-ch'ing. *Tu chu-tzu cha-chi*. Peking: Chung-hua shu-chü, 1959.

Teng Hsi Tzu. *SPTK*.

Thompson, P. M. *The Shen Tzu Fragments*. Oxford: Oxford University Press, 1979.

Togawa Yoshio et al. *Enanji*. Tokyo: Heibonsha, 1974.

Ts'ao Ch'ien. *Han Fei fa-chih lun*. Shanghai: Chung-hua shu-chü, 1948.

Tseng-pu shih-lei-fu t'ung-pien. Shanghai: Sao-yeh shan-fang, 1930.

Tso chuan. Included in the Harvard-Yenching Institute Sinological Index Series, Supp. 11: *Ch'un-ch'iu*.

Tu Kuo-hsiang. *Hsien-Ch'in chu-tzu jo-kan yen-chiu*. Peking: San-lien shu-tien, 1955.

Wallacker, B. *The Huai-nan-tzu, Book Eleven: Behavior, Culture and the Cosmos*. American Oriental Society Monograph Series, 48. New Haven: American Oriental Society, 1962.

Wang Nien-sun. See Liu Wen-tien.

Wang Shu-min. "*Huai Nan Tzu* chiao-cheng'." *Wen-shih-che hsüeh-pao* 5(1953): 15–90; 6(1954):1–66; 7(1956):9–22.

———. "*Huai Nan Tzu* yü *Chuang Tzu*." *Tsing-hua hsüeh-pao*, n.s., II(1)(May 1960):69–82.

Ward, C. "The Organization of Anarchy." In *Patterns of Anarchy*, edited by L. Krimerman and L. Perry. New York: Anchor Books, 1966.

Watson, B. *Early Chinese Literature*. New York: Columbia University Press, 1962.

Watson, B. (Trans.) *Mo Tzu: Basic Writings*. New York: Columbia University Press, 1963.

Wei Cheng-t'ung. *Hsün Tzu yü ku-tai che-hsüeh*. Taipei: Commercial Press, 1966.

Welch, H. *The Parting of the Way: Lao Tzu and the Taoist Movement*. Boston: Beacon Press, 1957.

Wen I-to, Kuo Mo-ho, and Hsü Wei-yü. *Kuan Tzu chi-chiao*. Peking: K'o-hsüeh ch'u-pan-she, 1956.

Wen Tzu. *SPPY*.

Wu K'ang (Kang Woo). *Les trois theories politique du Tch'ouen ts'ieou*. Paris, 1932.

Wu Yüeh ch'un-ch'iu. *SPTK*.

Yang Hung-lieh. *Chung-kuo fa-lü ssu-hsiang shih*. Shanghai: Commercial Press, 1937.

Yang Shu-ta. *Huai Nan Tzu cheng-wen*. Peking: Chung-kuo k'o-hsüeh-yüan ch'u pan, 1953.

Yen Tzu ch'un-ch'iu. *SPTK*.

Yi-lin. *SPTK*.

Yin Wen Tzu. *SPTK*.

Yü Ta-ch'eng. *Huai Nan Tzu chiao-shih*. Offprint of thesis submitted to Taiwan Normal University, Taipei, 1969.

Glossary and Character List

This list of characters contains all romanizations included in the book with the exception of names and titles found in the Bibliography. Characters for textual emendations are also included.

cha 詐 deception
Chan-kuo ts'e 戰國策
ch'ang shih chi tz'u 嘗識及此
ch'ang shih fan tz'u 嘗試反此
chao yao 招搖 seventh star of the Big Dipper
ch'ao 巢
chen chih 真知 true knowledge
chen jen 真人 realizing person
ch'en 辰
cheng 政 government
cheng 正 to make upright, correct
cheng 鄭 the state of Cheng
cheng chang che 鄭長者 the elder of Cheng
Cheng Hsüan 鄭玄
cheng shih 正勢 regular deployments
ch'eng 誠 sincerity
ch'eng-hsin 誠心 sincerity of mind
ch'eng shen 成身 completion of one's character
ch'eng shih yin shih 乘時因勢 taking advantage of the right time and responding to prevailing circumstances
chi-li chung chih 積力眾智
ch'i shih 気勢 morale advantage
ch'i-shih 奇勢 irregular deployments
Ch'i-su 齊俗
ch'i tzu 谿子 the *ch'i tzu* crossbow
ch'i-yüan-ma 騎顯馬

ch'i-yüan-ma 騎原馬

Chia I 賈誼

ch'iang 強　might

chiao 焦

chiao hua 教化　instructing and transforming

chieh 節

Chieh-pi 解蔽

Chieh-yung 節用

chien 諫　to admonish

ch'ien 鈐　weighing up

chih 知　knowledge

chih 智　intelligence

chih 志　will

chih ch'eng 至誠　highest sincerity

chih ching 至精　essential vapors

chih jen 至人　consummate person

chih te chih shih 至德之世　age of superlative virtue

Chin-shu 晉書

ch'in ch'in 親親　treating relatives with familial affection

Ch'in ts'e 秦策

Ching-chi chih 經籍志

ch'ing ch'i chung che 輕其重者

Chiu-hsing 九刑

chu 助

Chu Hsi 朱熹

Chu hsing 竹刑

Chu-tao 主道

ch'u hsia/hou 處下, 處後　dwelling below or last

Ch'u-chen 俶真

Chuang-K'uei-chi pen 莊逵吉本

Ch'ü-ch'ieh 胠篋

ch'üan 權　weighing up

ch'üan shih 權勢　authority and purchase

chüeh-liang 絶梁

chün 君　ruler

chün tzu 君子　consummate person

Chün-tao 君道

ch'ün 群　to gather

chung 重　weightiness

chung-chih chung-li 衆智衆力

chung jen 衆人

Chung-li ssu-tzu pen 中立四子本

chung shih 衆適

Chung-yung 中庸

ch'ung 沖　vacuity

Glossary **265**

erh 而
erh ping 二柄 handles of reward and punishment
Fa-chia 法家 Legalists
Fa-ching 法經
fa ku 法古 "imitating the ancients"
fa kuan 法官 judicial ministers
Fan-lun 氾論
Fei shih-erh tzu 非十二子
fen 分 status and privilege
fen shih pu erh 分勢不二 where purchase matches status
Feng Yu-lan 馮友蘭
hai 害 harm, injury
Han-shu 漢書
ho 和 a reed flute
ho 合
ho 何
Ho-shang Kung 河上公
hsi 喜
hsi nu 喜怒
hsi pu hsien yü yin 喜不羨於音
hsi-yen 希言 seldom issuing commands
hsia 下
hsiao 孝 filial piety
hsiao jen 小人 inferior, morally stunted person
hsiao-k'ang 小康 Lesser Prosperity
hsiao-yao-yu 逍遙遊 free and easy wandering
Hsien-hsüeh 顯學
hsin 心 heart-and-mind
Hsin-shu 新書
Hsin-shu shang 心術上
Hsin-tu 心度
hsing 性 process of particular nature
hsing 形 shape, disposition
hsing 刑 penal code, punishment
Hsing-fa chih 刑法志
hsing-ming 形名 name and form, accountability
hsing-shih 形勢 the shape of things, prevailing conditions
Hsing shih chieh 形勢解
Hsing-shu 刑書
hsing te 刑德
hsiu 修
Hsiu-wu 修務
hsü-ching 虛靜 state of vacuity and tranquillity
hsü-wu wu-hsien 虛無無見 vacuity and showing nothing
hsüeh 學 learning or study

hsün . 循
Hsün Tzu 荀子
hua min 化民 transforming the people
Huai Nan nei erh-shih-yi p'ien 淮南內二十一篇
jen 仁 benevolence
jen 人 human being
jen cheng 仁政 benevolent government
Jen-chien-shih 人間世
jen chün 人君 ruler
jen she chih shih 人設之勢 political purchase initiated by a person
jen sheng 人生 people
jih 日
jou-jo 柔弱 soft and weak
ju-shen 如神 godlike
kao 告
Kao Yu 高誘
K'ao-ku hsüeh-pao 考古學報
ke te ch'i yi 各得其宜 each element achieving what is appropriate to it
ku 故
ku che 古者
k'ua ch'in 夸矜
kuan 寬 mildness
kuan 官
kuei kuei 貴貴 honoring the noble
kung 貢
kung tao 公道 public welfare
kuo shih 國勢 regional conditions
Kuo-yü 國語
Lan-ming 覽冥
li 禮 rites, social norms
li 利 personal profit
li 力 strength
Li-chi 禮記
li min 利民 benefiting the people
Li-yün 禮運
ling 舲 the *ling* craft of Yüeh (a small boat)
Liu An 劉安
lo 樂 pleasure
Lü-t'u 綠圖
lüeh-chih 略智
Ma-t'i 馬蹄
Mao I-kuei pen 茅一桂本
meng 猛 severity
min hua 民化 the people transforming
ming 命 destiny

ming 明
Ming-fa 明法
Ming-fa-chieh 明法解
mou 謀　plan or strategy
Nan-mien 南面
Nan-shih 難勢
nei-p'ien 內篇
nei-shu 內書
ni 擬
ni 逆
nu hsi 怒喜
Pei-Sung hsiao-tzu pen 北宋小字本
pen 本
pen-ch'in 本矜
Pen-ching 本經
pien 變　variability or maneuverability
Ping-lüeh 兵略
pu 不
pu-cheng 不争　not contending
pu yen chih chiao 不言之教　unspoken teaching
pu-yu 不有　not appropriating
p'u 樸　unworked wood (natural genuineness)
san ts'ai 三才　three powers or spheres
shan 善　good, goodness
Shan-hsing 繕性
Shang-chün shu 商君書
shen hua 神化　godlike transformation
Shen-shih 慎勢
sheng 生　to grow
sheng 上　above
sheng jen 聖人　sagely person
shih 適
shih 勢　political purchase, strategic advantage
shih 世　age
shih 時
Shih-chi 史記
Shih-ching 詩經
shih li 勢利　purchase and personal advantage
shih ming 勢名　purchase and rank
shih pu te wei fei 使不得為非　making certain the people have no chance to do wrong
shih wei 勢位　purchase and position
shu 術　techniques of rulership
Shu-ching 書經
ssu 思　to think

ssu-hsia　肆夏
Ssu-pu pei-yao　四部備要
Ssu-pu ts'ung-k'an　四部叢刊
Sui-shu　隋書
Sun Pin ping-fa　孫臏兵法
szu　私
szu li　私利　private interests
ta　達
Ta-cheng　大政
Ta-hsüeh　大學
ta-t'ung　大同　Great Unity
T'ai-tsu　泰族
Tan-shu　丹書
T'ang Chün-i　唐君毅
T'ang-hsing　湯刑
tao　道　the Tao
Tao-tsang pen　道藏本
Tao-yüan　道原
t'ao-t'u　騊駼
te　德　virtue
te hua　德化　transformation through virtue
t'eng　騰　a kind of snake
ti-shih　地勢　terrain advantage
t'ien　天　Heaven (nature)
t'ien chih tao　天之道
T'ien-hsia　天下
t'ien hsia chih ch'eng　天下至誠
t'ien jen hsiang ying　天人相應　mutual influence of human being and nature
T'ien-lun　天論
t'ien ming　天命　Heaven's mandate
t'ien shih　天勢　natural conditions
t'ien-ti　天地　heaven-earth
ting　鼎　ceremonial tripod
Ting-fa　定法
Ting-fen　定分
t'ing　艇　the *t'ing* craft of Shu (a small boat for rivers and lakes)
to pu chia rih chih ku　多不暇日之故
ts'ai-ch'i　采齊
Tsai-yu　在宥
ts'an wu　參伍　matrix of relationships
tsang-huo　臧獲
ts'e　冊
Tso chuan　左传
tso wang　坐忘　"sitting and forgetting"
ts'u　辭

tsung hsien shih neng 尊賢使能 exalting persons of superior qualities and
    employing the able

tuan ho pu wan 袒褐不完

Tung Chung-shu 董仲舒

tzu-hsiu 自脩

tzu-jan 自然 spontaneous natural arising

tzu-jan chih shih 自然之勢 inevitable natural cricumstances

tz'u 慈 parental compassion

wang 王 king

wang 往 to flock to

wang 忘 to forget

Wang P'u (Liu Chi) pen 王溥 (劉績) 本

wei 威 awe

wei 位 position

wei shih 未始 never

wei shih 威勢 majesty, authority

wei wu-wei 為無為

Wen wu 文物

wu hao 烏號 the *wu hao* bow

wu hsien 無見 showing nothing

wu hsing 五行 the five processes

wu-hsing 無行 nondeployment

wu sang wo 吾喪我 "I have left my ego-self behind"

wu-shih 無事 nonintervention

Wu Ti 武帝 Emperor Wu (of the Han)

Wu-tu 五蠹

wu-wei 無為

wu-wei erh ch'eng 無為而成 complete without acting

Yang-ch'üan 揚權

Yao-lüeh 要略

yen 厭

Yen Shih-ku 顏師古

yi 義 rightness

yi 易

yi 疑

yi 意

Yi-chou 益州

Yi-ping 議兵

Yi-wen chih 芸文志

Yin-ch'üeh-shan 銀雀山

yin-shih 因勢

Ying ti-wang 應帝王

yu 幼

yu shih che 有始者

yu-wei 有為 unnatural activity, interfering activity

yü　踰
yü　于
Yü-hsing　禹刑
yüan　袁
Yüan　顯
Yüan-tao　原道
yüeh　樂　music
yung chung　用衆　utilizing the people
yung jen　用人　effective use of personnel
Yung min　用民
yung shih　用氏　effective use of personnel

Index

HAWAII Production Notes

This book was designed by Roger Eggers. Composition and paging were done on the Quadex Composing System and typesetting on the Compugraphic Unisetter by the design and production staff of University of Hawaii Press.

The text typeface is Compugraphic Times Roman and the display typeface is Compugraphic Palatino.

Offset presswork and binding were done by Vail-Ballou Press, Inc. Text paper is Glatfelter Writers RR Offset, basis 50.